The Pulitzer Prizes

Portrait of Joseph Pulitzer I, by John Singer Sargent

THE
PULITZER
PRIZES

*A History of the Awards in Books, Drama,
Music, and Journalism, Based on the
Private Files over Six Decades*

JOHN HOHENBERG

Columbia University Press
New York and London

Library of Congress Cataloging in Publication Data

Hohenberg, John.
   The Pulitzer Prizes; a history of the awards in
books, drama, music, and journalism, based on the
private files over six decades.

   Bibliography
   1. Pulitzer prizes—History.   2. Columbia University.
Graduate School of Journalism.   I. Title.
AS911.P8H83   001.4′4   74-8282
ISBN 0-231-03771-6
ISBN 0-231-03887-9 (pbk.)

Other Books by John Hohenberg

The Pulitzer Prize Story
The Professional Journalist
Foreign Correspondence: The Great Reporters and Their Times
The New Front Page
*Between Two Worlds: Policy, Press, and Public Opinion in Asian-American
   Relations*
The News Media: A Journalist Looks at His Profession
Free Press/Free People: The Best Cause
New Era in the Pacific: An Adventure in Public Diplomacy

Copyright © 1974 John Hohenberg
Printed in the United States of America
10 9 8 7 6 5 4 3 2

For the
Winners of the Pulitzer Prizes

Contents

The Pulitzer Prizes

An Introduction: Prizes and Consequences

On the fiftieth anniversary of the Pulitzer Prizes, Archibald Mac-Leish observed to a brilliant company of prize winners, judges, and members of the Pulitzer directorate that it was time to pause,

> Draw rein, draw breath,
> Cast a cold eye
> On life, on death . . .

and take stock of the consequences.

The poet, a winner of three Pulitzer awards himself, graciously invoked literary hyperbole to describe the role of Columbia University in the proceedings as "restful, unambiguous, and unembarrassed." Then with an all-embracing gesture, he turned to his fellow laureates, saying:

"Whereas we, ladies and gentlemen—we who address you and a large proportion of you whom we address—*are* the consequences. We are Mr. Pulitzer's dream made flesh. . . ." [1]

It was a moment that Joseph Pulitzer would have appreciated, a moment that brought a reflective smile to his grandson, Joseph Pulitzer Jr., who was on the dais as the chairman of the Advisory Board on the Pulitzer Prizes.

There have been other consequences:

Professor Arthur Meier Schlesinger Jr., a Pulitzer Prize winner at the age of 28, was assured by an older laureate, Henry F. Pringle, that it was the "best label" anyone could have. Edward Albee, the dramatist, took an entirely opposite tack when he viewed his own award as a "declining honor" because it had not gone to his greatest play, *Who's Afraid of Virginia Woolf?* And Shirley Ann Grau, the novelist, being far more concerned about her ailing six-month-old son than her writing, snapped at a telephone caller who congratulated her for winning a Pulitzer, "Don't be silly." Then she asked herself, "Could it really be true?" It was. A far more practical reaction came from the diplomat, George F. Kennan, who promptly invested his prize money in a fine Swedish guitar—"for classical music," he took pains to explain.

In a remote village in Turkey, where Alfred Friendly of the Washington *Post* was vacationing, the townspeople wove him a wreath of native laurel and crowned him with it when they learned he had been honored. And in a steaming hotel room in Monrovia, Liberia, an Associated Press stringer greeted a visiting correspondent, Lynn Heinzerling, with a congratulatory cable and a toast in warm champagne. John Toland's Japanese wife, anxiously summoned to the telephone in Tokyo, was overwhelmed when the literary editor of Mainichi Shimbun exclaimed, *"Omedeto gozaimasu,"* the most formal kind of congratulations, and confirmed that her husband had won a Pulitzer Prize. Professor David Brion Davis, besieged for an interview in Hyderabad, India, wasn't quite certain what it was he had won because the information was meager and vague, having been filtered from the BBC through an improbable network of his Indian students. But he granted the interview anyway.

For Jean Stafford, the news of her prize wasn't real until she heard Walter Cronkite say it out loud, as she put it, on CBS News. Joseph P. Lash never had a chance to express doubts because his thoughtful editor, Evan Thomas, broke the news to him at home and brought him a bottle of champagne to help him celebrate. Professor Ernest Samuels' dean at Northwestern did even better, telephoning the prize winner to say, "Ernest, just throw away that letter I wrote you about next year's salary." His prospective pay increase, the dean announced, had been tripled. But for one of the most illustrious prize winners of all, Senator John Fitzgerald Kennedy, the award touched off a running battle with Drew Pearson to prove the authenticity of *Profiles In Courage.* It was weeks before the President of the United States-to-be forced a retraction from the columnist.

The mingled sense of jubilation and unbelief came to the most erudite and sophisticated of scholars when they were confronted with the prize news. Professor David Herbert Donald was at Princeton when a hoarse voice exclaimed over the telephone:

"Congratulations! You've just won the Pulitzer Prize!"

"Who's this?" he asked.

"Why, it's Blanche Knopf."

The scholar was incredulous. "You must be kidding."

"Well," she said sharply, "If you don't believe me, I'll hang up and you can call Alfred."

It was the beginning of one of the finest champagne parties ever thrown at Princeton.

For Roland Kenneth Towery, a country editor in Cuero, Texas, the news came by telephone while he was on camera before CBS-TV—an unexampled performance of amazement, dawning realization, triumph, and pure delight. For Otis Chandler of the Los Angeles *Times*, visiting the newest property of the Times-Mirror Company, *Newsday*, Pulitzer Day was a succession of surprises. First, he was interrupted during a ceremonial speech to the staff with the announcement that *Newsday* had just won the public service gold medal. He had no sooner finished with his congratulations than another message came in to say that *Newsday*'s cartoonist, Tom Darcy, had also won a prize. "It was," a *Newsday* editor said drily, "good orientation for Chandler." Paul Conrad, the Los Angeles *Times*'s cartoonist, received a different kind of orientation. He heard of a little girl on his block asking what a "pullet" was; told it was a chicken, she burst out in bewilderment, "Well, you know, that surprise Mr. Conrad won."

In Chicago, a neighborhood baker was so inspired by the Chicago *Tribune*'s picture of its prize-winning reporter, George Bliss, and the other eleven members of his family that the group photograph was faithfully reproduced on the icing of a tremendous cake and presented with a flourish at the Bliss home. And in Portland, Ore., Wallace Turner of the *Oregonian* was solemnly informed by an editor of the New York *Times* after winning a prize: "It will be pure gold some day." Peter B. Kann was awakened at 5 A.M. in Hong Kong by a telephone call from his jubilant *Wall Street Journal* editor in New York, told the good news, and could find nothing to celebrate with but a stale cigar, which he proceeded to light and smoke in bed.

A. M. Rosenthal of the New York *Times* had his moment of satisfaction in Geneva when his sister telephoned to tell him of his prize. But next day, when an American tourist approached with congratulations while Rosenthal was having a luncheon celebration with Daniel Schorr of CBS, the signals were slightly mixed. The tourist said, looking straight at Schorr, "It was a great show, and I have always wanted to meet you." But there was no expression of doubt from the father of Miriam Ottenberg of the Washington *Evening Star* when he learned of his daughter's good fortune. He shouted to her mother across the lobby of a hotel in the Middle East: "Pulitzer!"

To Arthur Miller, the prize didn't mean as much. "Like most good luck," he wrote, "the Pulitzer Prize usually comes to those who don't need it." Bernard Malamud's reaction was even more sour. He liked his National Book Award better. But for Archibald MacLeish, who picked up the old Paris *Herald* one morning on the Rue Jacob and saw himself plastered on Page 1 as a Pulitzer Prize winner, the thrill never wore off. And Virgil Thomson always remembered his Pulitzer because it was swiftly followed by a letter of congratulation from President Truman. For Lauren Soth, whose editorial first brought a Russian agricultural mission to Iowa, the Pulitzer award meant recognition of a breach in the cold war front. It also brought him a miserable letter: "You dirty Communist. Why don't you go to Russia?" But for John Strohmeyer, who fought for the rights of Spanish-speaking residents of Bethlehem, Pa., the prize touched off a string of honors—a testimonial dinner, a triumphant trip to Mexico, a $2,000 check from his publisher, and a silverhaired matron's loving tribute of a rose a day for twelve days.

Herman Wouk was so excited when he learned of his award that he phoned his wife at her hairdresser's to announce: "We've won the Pulitzer Prize!" For Max Frankel, who had just put the life of a correspondent behind him to become the Sunday editor of the New York *Times*, the magic moment came at a meeting of the *Times*'s top editors and managers at Hamilton, N.Y. Arthur Ochs Sulzberger, the publisher, interrupted a solemn budgetary discussion to announce that Frankel's China coverage had won him the Pulitzer. Another publisher, John Hay Whitney of the New York *Herald Tribune*, got on the trans-Atlantic telephone when the prizes were announced and summoned a young Paris correspondent to speak to him. Sanche de Gramont remembered wondering, as he picked up the phone, "What have I done now?" Whitney shouted, "You've won the Pulitzer Prize!"

John S. Knight of the Knight Newspapers summed it all up at the age of 73, when he won his Pulitzer along with the team of Will and Ariel

Durant, who were 82 and 70 respectively. Worrying about a *Wall Street Journal* editorial that suggested his next column might lack pungency and the Durants' next book could be a bomb, Knight wrote: "Could I maintain this quality of writing in the future? Or would I begin to write for other editors, rather than for readers? My view today is that I did manage to overcome the 'writing block' but others can judge that much better than I." [2]

This book, too, is a part of the consequences of Joseph Pulitzer's benefaction. It is the outgrowth of a discussion before the Advisory Board on the Pulitzer Prizes of the sixtieth anniversary of the awards in 1976 and the consideration of an appropriate way to memorialize the occasion. For most members of the Board, the fiftieth anniversary dinner at the Hotel Plaza in New York was still so fresh in their memories, and so glamorous an event, that it seemed folly to attempt to top it. Yet, nearly everybody wanted to do something. Finally, James Reston suggested, "Wouldn't it be worth while having the whole story of the Pulitzer Prizes told in all its aspects?"

The members of the Board agreed. As the Board's secretary and administrator of the Pulitzer Prizes for twenty years, I was asked to look into the project. It quickly became evident to both Joseph Pulitzer Jr. and to me that we did not want an "authorized history," a book that would seek merely to glorify the awards. All the consequences, both pleasant and unpleasant, gratifying and embarrassing, would have to be included. As Chairman Pulitzer put it to me: "If this is an accurate and truthful and interesting contribution to the cultural history of the country, then I'm for it and I think you should do it."

On that basis, I began a search for the long-missing reports and other private records of the prizes prior to 1954, when I became the administrator of the awards. Naturally, I had my own reports and records plus my diaries and voluminous correspondence, so I had no concern about the completeness of the story for the past two decades. But for the preceding four decades, I had only the oral recollections of my predecessor, Dean Carl W. Ackerman, and the newspaper records of the era. It was satisfying, but not particularly helpful, for me to recall that I had known all the leading figures in the establishment and development of the awards except the first Joseph Pulitzer. Without the records, I could do little.

While the search went on, I proceeded with a mail poll of the Advisory Board for final agreement on my undertaking the book and for a grant of unrestricted access to the records when they were found. The result was most heartening. President William James McGill of Columbia University, the sole Columbia member of the Board, generously gave me all the university approval I needed and a lot of encouragement as well. So did all the other Board members.

By the most fortunate of coincidences, not more than a week later, my treasured assistant in the Pulitzer Prize Office at Columbia, Mrs. Rose Valenstein, told me that the whole file of old jury reports, letters, protests, and the like had been found in a long unused portion of the Pulitzer archives. It did not take me long to determine that this was, indeed, the missing material—the first jury reports recommending Eugene O'Neill, Thornton Wilder, and John Steinbeck, the file that recorded the battles over Sinclair Lewis from *Main Street* through *Arrowsmith*, the denial of a prize to Ernest Hemingway's *For Whom the Bell Tolls*, and many another literary and journalistic cause celebre. I decided to do the book. And I asked Columbia University Press, the most disinterested of book publishers, to assume the task of publication. I considered myself fortunate that the Press agreed to handle what I believed to be the most important work I had ever undertaken. While I could not contemplate a five-volume work, such as was produced by the anonymous authors of the admirable history of *The Times* of London, I did accept as a model their almost painfully conscientious attitude of honesty and objectivity in dealing with their materials. I have left out nothing that matters.[3]

What is recorded here should give no cause for concern for the future of the Pulitzer Prizes; surely, in their sixth decade, they are strong enough and healthy enough to withstand close scrutiny. Nor is there any thought in this self-revelation of submitting, even by indirection, a form of defense for past deeds and misdeeds or even a plea for understanding. Rather, by setting forth the story of the Pulitzer Prizes in depth and recording both the achievements and the mistakes of the past, I would hope that the Pulitzer directorates yet to come will have something of substance on which to base their practices and policies of the future, and that professionals and public alike will know more about the awards. For in dealing with the Pulitzer Prizes, as with all other such rewards, there is something to be said for Santayana's familiar plea for a knowledge of the past.

With that, I conclude this introduction to the pageant of the Pulitzer Prizes. My debts for this work are very heavy; elsewhere in this volume, I have acknowledged them. Here, then, is the Pulitzer accounting, derived in large part from the private papers dealing with the prizes in books, drama, music, and journalism over six decades and from the letters of Pulitzer Prize winners. It is, as MacLeish said, "Mr. Pulitzer's dream made flesh."

JOHN HOHENBERG

Aquebogue, Long Island,
New York
March 1, 1974

1
The Grand Scheme
1902–1916

1
The Germ of an Idea

Joseph Pulitzer was restless and dissatisfied. For some years, he had thought of making a special contribution for the lasting benefit of his profession of journalism—a "grand scheme," as he called it. He had seemed mightily taken, too, with the notion of associating himself with a major American university. But somehow, for all his fine intentions, nothing had come of his vague plans.

Now, in the summer of 1902, he meditated on the future at his lovely estate, Chatwold, in Bar Harbor, Me., with its comforting granite "Tower of Silence." He was then 55 years old, intensely nervous and almost blind—a remarkable invalid who for fifteen years had roved the world in search of peace of mind and yet managed to control his newspapers, the New York *World* and the St. Louis *Post-Dispatch*. If he really meant to take some extraordinary action, for whatever reason, he realized that it would have to be soon. And so—irascible, demanding, intolerant of any standard short of excellence—he determined to move.

During the previous year, as he was well aware, the first prizes of worldwide significance had been bestowed on six distinguished Europeans through the munificence of the Swedish inventor of dynamite, Alfred B. Nobel, who had died in 1896. However, prizes were not then uppermost in Pulitzer's mind. He had learned privately that his rival, the younger James Gordon Bennett, was talking with associates about founding a school of journalism by placing the New York *Herald* in trust for it as a permanent source of income.[1] As matters turned out, Bennett never did anything to set up a school but he may very well have inadvertently stimulated Pulitzer to do so.

In any event, the times were propitious for large-scale philanthropy. The world was at peace. The nation, after acquiring a Pacific empire during the Spanish-American War, was basking in the glow of its expanding prestige and power. Although the belligerent Theodore Roosevelt was in the White House, he appeared to be content to flex his muscles against the trusts and the "malefactors of great wealth" at the outset of a period of domestic reform. As for the masters of industry, they were paying reluctant attention to a recent pronouncement by Andrew Carnegie, holding that rich men are in effect the "trustees" of their wealth and should administer it for the public's benefit.[2]

This kind of thinking very much suited Pulitzer. In his favorite resting spot at Chatwold, a small balcony overlooking a picturesque brook behind the "Tower of Silence," he could spend tranquil hours working out his ideas. Whether Nobel or Carnegie or Bennett finally influenced him, no one will ever be able to say because he gave his associates no clue and left none in his papers. But one day late in August of that year, he dictated what he called a confidential "rough memorandum" about a gift that would be "quite large, enough for any sensible purpose." He began as follows:

"Here is the germ of an idea which requires careful formulation to become useful, effective and legally binding.

"It is dictated roughly without having been previously discussed with anybody. . . ."[3]

There followed, in a rambling and diffuse style, the hazy and incomplete outline of a plan for a journalism school at Columbia University, which would be under the control of an advisory board consisting of the heads of from nine to thirteen newspapers in the New York area. The basis of his attraction to Columbia was, of course, that it was in New York; in 1893, he already had contributed $100,000 to the same institution for scholarships and an additional $3,000 for a journalism lectureship that never became a reality.[4]

"My idea," he explained, "is to recognize that journalism is, or ought to be, one of the great and intellectual professions; to encourage, elevate, and educate in a practical way the present and, still more, future members of that profession, exactly as if it were the profession of law or medicine."

On that particular day, because Pulitzer emphasized his anxiety "to do something for the profession," his first mention of the prospect of a series of annual prizes inevitably was directed very largely toward journalism. The paragraph about the awards, seemingly tucked into the dictated document toward the end as if it had been an after thought, stated his desires in this manner:

"Incidentally, I strongly wish the College to pay from the large income I am providing, a sum of _____ in annual prizes to particular journalists or writers for various accomplishments, achievements, and forms of excellence. For instance, they might offer an annual prize of one thousand dollars for the best editorial, another of double that sum for the best descriptive account of some event, or for some act of public service rendered by an individual, or by a newspaper. Above all, there should be a prize for the greatest accuracy and reliability."

The blank space for the sum of the prizes was filled in at the bottom of the document with the notation: "At least Twenty Thousand Dollars in prizes." It showed that Pulitzer was a good guesser in 1902; a little more than seven decades later, there were 17 annual Pulitzer Prizes of $1,000 each plus a gold medal worth approximately $500 for the 18th award, based on meritorious public service by an American newspaper.

Once President Nicholas Murray Butler of Columbia University was exposed to that "germ of an idea," he never got over it.

2
"To The Prizes I Am Much Attached"

Almost from the beginning, the Pulitzer Prizes began to develop a life of their own even though the donor had insisted on making them secondary to his precious school. Nor did Butler appear to worry very much about them. What Pulitzer offered was to set aside $500,000 of his proposed benefaction of $2 million for prizes "for the encouragement of public service, public morals, American literature, and the advancement of education." However, he would not permit the university to offer the prizes until it could prove that his journalism school had been in successful operation for at least three years. But it was also clear to him, as it was to Butler, that whoever controlled the school at the outset would also control the prizes.

With so passionate and didactic a benefactor as Pulitzer, it was inevitable that difficulties would arise in the execution of any scheme, no matter how perfect. He was not an easy man to deal with; nor, for that matter, was Nicholas Murray Butler, or "Nicholas Miraculous," as President Theodore Roosevelt called him. Both were determined, high-minded autocrats who deeply adhered to the moralistic, mid-Victorian society that gave the nation its character and motivation at the turn of the century. Both took pride in their power. Both were intent on preserving and broadening the establishments each had built with such painstaking care—Butler's university and Pulitzer's newspapers. Each was a representative leader of American thought, but there the resemblance stopped.

Pulitzer, lean and bearded, had the look of an eagle—bold, fierce, unafraid. He had left his native Hungary—he had been born in the town of Mako in 1847—to seek his fortune in the United States, had fought in the Union armies during the Civil War, turned to newspaper work in St. Louis, and made himself one of the mightiest journalists in the land. He was no pillar of the establishment, even though he had brought the Statue of Liberty from France and raised the money to place her in New York harbor. He had battled against presidents, governors, and mayors alike, torn into the plunderers of Tammany Hall and the richer and equally pitiless corporations, and had invariably taken the side of the poor and the weak. His principal fault was that he had permitted his newspapers to be drawn into the desperate circulation battle with William Randolph Hearst's journals and the excesses that followed in the war with Spain. But that, fortunately, was behind Pulitzer now and he would never go back to it.[5]

Butler, round and bald and moustached, was a bulldog of determination, a scholar of formidable academic proportions, and an administrator who had the ability to take over almost anything and make it work. At the time he began dealing seriously with Pulitzer in 1902, he had just become the president of Columbia University at the age of 40, in itself a stunning achievement during that less than progressive era in American education. He was fifteen years younger than the newspaper publisher, having been born in 1862 in Elizabeth, N.J. Whereas Pulitzer was self-taught, Butler was all Columbia—holder of a B.A. in 1882 and a Ph.D. in 1884. After a brief philosophical *wanderjahr* in Europe, he returned to Morningside Heights and became successively a teaching assistant, tutor, professor of philosophy, president of newly founded Teachers College, dean of the Columbia Faculty of Philosophy, and one of the prime movers in expanding Columbia College into Columbia University. As a politician, he was one of the intimates of President Theodore Roosevelt and had the temerity to rebuke him now and then. As a statesman, he was able to confound the impetuous Kaiser Wilhelm II; for, when the ruler of a martial Germany asked who was responsible for American fiscal policy, the president of Columbia University replied curtly: "God." [6]

Politically, Butler and Pulitzer did not fit together any more than they did on any other level. The educator was faithful to the principles of orthodox Republicanism and viewed the deviations of his friend in the White House with alarm. The journalist, while not formally associating himself with any party, had always been sympathetic to the progressive elements in the Democratic Party. How these two were able to get along at all, in view of the diversity of their beliefs and backgrounds, was something of a small miracle. In fact, many of the complications of the system of administering and awarding the Pulitzer Prizes stem in some measure from the conflicting pressures exerted by these unique and forceful men.

It should not be imagined that either Pulitzer or Butler entered into their first agreement without the strongest doubts and reservations. Even while Pulitzer's initial proposals were in their formative stage, between the summer of 1902 and the spring of 1903, there were signs of trouble for all concerned. Dr. George W. Hosmer, physician, journalist, and Pulitzer's chief secretary, had been assigned by the publisher to produce the first draft of a proposal for his gift to Columbia. Pulitzer gave the completed document to his biographer and one of his closest associates, Don C. Seitz, while they were traveling by train from New York to South Carolina in the winter of 1903. Just as Seitz finished reading it, Pulitzer felt his way down the corridor into his friend's stateroom and exclaimed accusingly:

"You don't think much of it."

"I do not," Seitz said.

"Well," he asked, "what shall I do? I want to do something."

Seitz replied: "Endow the *World*. Make it foolproof." [7]

That wasn't sufficient for Pulitzer. He thought he was doing enough for the *World*. Now, he wanted something on a grander scale. Obviously, he wasn't sure of exactly what it should be, how it should work, where it should be located, who should control it. Hosmer's initial document had been sent to President Charles William Eliot of Harvard as well as to President Butler on the chance that the Columbia negotiations might fall through. When Eliot was both tardy and lukewarm in his response, Pulitzer pushed resolutely ahead toward an understanding with Columbia. But, unhappily, the negotiations over the first agreement marked the beginning, and not the end, of the major differences between Butler and Pulitzer.

While numerous issues developed to delay the opening of the school and the awarding of the prizes, the heart of the crisis was the creation, the character, the personnel, and the powers of what was then called the Advisory Board of the School of Journalism (since 1950, the Advisory Board on the Pulitzer Prizes). Just why Pulitzer insisted on designating it as advisory in nature when in reality he wanted it to have complete power remains a puzzle to this day. Necessarily, the semantic confusion that was created at the outset contributed to some extent to the repeated clashes of temperament between Butler and Pulitzer.

At one point, the university Trustees' Committee on Education actually cut out the clause that created the Advisory Board, explaining that "such a new and permanent Board was of very doubtful expediency." Pulitzer reluctantly agreed to set a five-year limit on the board's existence; later, however, when Butler wrote that there was no real need to define its functions, Pulitzer angrily fired back a letter in Hosmer's name saying: [8]

"The long-continued relation of the Advisory Board and the concession to it of a well-defined authority in the formation of the plan are conditions *sine qua non*, but that body has been defined away till it has become merely a name. . . . No one can be surprised, I think, if a man inclined to do so much to give effect to a grand scheme, to put on foot on a good working basis, an institution designed to be of great value to the American people should feel disappointed and chagrined to find himself stayed and prevented at every point by objections that are illiberal, if not trivial and frivolous."

Butler backed down. Pulitzer appeared to do so, but actually he did not. He was firmly convinced that his Advisory Board should have primary control over the school and the prizes. On such points as the cost of the proposed new Journalism Building at Columbia and the basic requirements for admission to the school, he eventually let Butler have his way. As for the Advisory Board, he had Hosmer write as follows to Butler:

"He [Pulitzer] yields substantially his original demand that the Advisory Board should have greater authority than is given in this draft; but he requires that as its power is thus minimized the terms of its relation to the school shall be longer, say not less than 20 years."

Soon afterward, the first agreement was concluded; although it bore Pulitzer's birth date of April 10, 1903, a concession to the publisher's faith in the properties of the number 10, it was actually signed on July 20. The initial struggle had gone on four months, but not even Pulitzer's payment of the first $200,000 of his pledged $2 million resolved the crisis that had mounted over the Advisory Board. Before long, in advance of the public announcement of the "grand scheme," he and Butler were skirmishing again over the personnel and character of the Advisory Board.

It might have been expected that Butler, the scholar, would have wanted a committee of overseers that was broadly representative of the entire range of American arts and letters. Actually, because he and Pulitzer were thinking far more of who should control the school rather than who should dominate the prizes, the issue did not even arise until after the signing of the initial agreement. Both had submitted tentatively slates of prominent editors and publishers plus Secretary of State John Hay who, quite surprisingly, had been approached by a Pulitzer emissary and promptly agreed to serve.[9]

Columbia assumed that Pulitzer at last had been satisfied. However, Columbia was wrong. The publisher, turning from his concern over Butler's devious ways of undercutting the Advisory Board, now began worrying about the public reception of his "grand scheme." Probably because he wanted to bolster the image of his Advisory Board more than anything else, he began brooding in Europe over the lack of a broader representation of the nation's cultural leadership among its members.

By midsummer, he had come to a decision. The all-journalist board would not do. Andrew Dickson White, the president of Cornell University, and Charles William Eliot, the president of Harvard, must be included. Accordingly, he cabled his ultimatum to Butler, who was properly appalled. He could not for one moment permit Harvard and Cornell to be peering over Columbia's shoulder and helping run Columbia's business.

Somewhat more diplomatically, but not much, Butler wrote for Pulitzer's information: "Mr. Andrew D. White is a personal friend of mine and I esteem him highly but I do not care to have him upon the Advisory Board. He is completely identified, academically, with Yale and Cornell and bears no relations to journalism that would justify his appointment. There are also reasons, lying in the past, why he would not be persona grata to some of our trustees."

That took care of President White. As for President Eliot, he withdrew promptly with the aloofness of a Harvard man.

Pulitzer was distressed. To his associates, he cabled:

WOULD GIVE ANYTHING TO HAVE ELIOT ACCEPT. WORTH 20 EDITORS.

He reserved his heaviest blow, however, for Butler's refusal to consider membership on the Advisory Board for non-Columbia officials, cabling:

UNDERSTAND JEALOUSY. TELEGRAPH BUTLER MY INSISTENCE. UNALTERABLE. FINAL.[10]

Thus, when the announcement of the agreement was made public and published on Monday, August 17, 1903, Columbia omitted the names of all members of the Advisory Board while Pulitzer's New York *World* published a list of prominent journalists, plus Presidents White and Eliot. The entire emphasis was on the creation of a School of Journalism, which was optimistically slated to open in the following year, and the Pulitzer Prizes in effect were ignored.

On the day of the announcement, which was greeted with interest and even enthusiasm in the nation's press, Butler wrote to Pulitzer that he now hoped the work of educational organization and building construction could proceed without serious interrruption. Once again, however, he was disappointed. For in late September, Pulitzer wrote to him from Karlsbad to raise once again, in a most virulent form, the need for broadening both the powers and the membership of the Advisory Board. He asked Butler to take the issue once again before the Trustees of Columbia University in these terms:

"Naturally I am deeply interested in the character of the Advisory Board. Neither you nor the faculty at large can possess the specific professional knowledge necessary to its duties. . . . I wish to be sure that it is placed in the hands of men of high capacity, men who are the most competent to be found; and I wish to be sure also that you will use your great power in the spirit of the trust, not ignoring their advice, nor treating them as merely subsidiary and ornamental. . . . And I must suggest that until the Advisory Board is constituted and ready to advise, I should deem it very ill advised on your part to commit yourself to any plans concerning the contemplated building."

There was nothing for Butler to do but agree that the entire project would be suspended until the Advisory Board was named. And since Pulitzer made no formal nomination of his choice of members, the "grand scheme" had to be held in abeyance. George L. Rives, chairman of the university's Trustees, who occasionally had acted as a lawyer for Pulitzer, tried hard to get the publisher to move. But all he received for his pains was a letter from Pulitzer's retreat in Jekyll Island, Georgia, dated February 28, 1904, that put everything off for years.

It is true that Pulitzer gave Rives assurance that the remainder of the $2 million gift would still be available to Columbia, that negotiations could again be resumed one day under different circumstances, and that he wanted certain changes made in the original agreement. But beyond that, he gave notice that his "grand scheme" could not be put into execution until after his death. In this course, he paralleled the design of Alfred B. Nobel, whose prizes began five years after his death. However, Pulitzer had far different reasons, for he wrote to Rives:

"You can scarcely conceive the worry I have had over the effort to satisfy myself about the character and the very limited powers of the Advisory Board and the difficulty remains. . . . The worry mentioned, the state of my health, the knowledge of my temperament and the unfortunate difference with Dr. Butler . . . compel me, although with great reluctance and unwillingness, to adhere to the conclusions . . . to postpone the execution of the plan till after my death in order to save myself vexation and disappointment."

There was a postscript to the Rives-Pulitzer correspondence that showed that if the journalism school was a dead issue, for the time being, the prizes were not. As Pulitzer wrote to Rives: "To the plan of the prizes I am much attached and believe that in the future it will be of the greatest possible benefit and renown to the university, possibly greater than the school itself." [11]

In view of all the effort Pulitzer and Butler devoted to the creation of the Advisory Board and the definition of its powers, it is ironic to observe after the passage of more than seventy years that the Board's principal concern, after its first five years, has nearly always been the Pulitzer Prizes and not the School of Journalism.

3
The Will

Pulitzer evidently realized, with the passage of time, that professional educators would have more to say about the development of his school over the long run than he would. Nevertheless, he made no fuss over the revised agreements of March 19 and April 12, 1904, which both he and Butler approved, and he paid over the remainder of his first $1 million gift to the university. But in his will of April 16, 1904, he tied the Pulitzer Prizes so closely to the Advisory Board that it became the dominant agency of control. In effect, then, Butler had the school but Pulitzer maintained his grip on the awards bearing his name, both prizes and scholarships.

Pulitzer's will was his most powerful weapon in his long and difficult negotiations with Columbia. While there was little in it that essentially changed the arrangements for the journalism school, it set forth in precise detail the system through which the Pulitzer Prizes were to be awarded. Nor was this an empty legalistic exercise. Legal authorities since have held that wherever the Pulitzer will and the agreements with Columbia may be in conflict, the specifications in the will shall prevail.

Whatever Butler and the Columbia trustees may have intended to do about the Advisory Board after Pulitzer's death, the will made it perfectly clear that any attempt to diminish its powers would result in forfeiture of the gift in whole or in part. For the publisher specified that, if Columbia could not agree on a plan for the prizes, both the journalism school and the prizes would be offered to Harvard.

The Advisory Board, Pulitzer set forth in his will, "shall be continued in existence without limitation of time, and I direct that the selection of the persons who shall receive the said prizes or scholarships shall be under its control so long as it continues in existence." He also gave the Board "power in its discretion to suspend or to change any subject or subjects; substituting, however, others in their places, if in the judgment of the Board such suspension, changes or substitutions, shall be conducive to the public good or rendered advisable by public necessities, or by reason of change of time." And, he went on, if all prize nominees fell below the "standard of excellence fixed by the Board" in any subject in any given year, then the Board could withhold an award or awards.

Pulitzer made the Board the custodian of its own powers. For, as he specified in his will, the Board must finally approve any agreement made between Columbia and his executors about the prizes, if none were reached during his lifetime. These were stiff provisions, for they assigned no particular role to the university except as the seat of the prizes and, by implication, the agency through which the awards were to be announced. The Trustees of Columbia University were not specifically mentioned; as for the proposed Faculty of Journalism, its only suggested role was to assist the Board in "reading manuscripts," if the Board required it.

In the will, there were four journalism prizes, four for letters and drama, one for education, and five traveling scholarships, for a total of $16,500. While the terms of the journalism awards were professionally phrased, those for the arts bore the unmistakable imprint of the thinking of Pulitzer's era—a high-flown sense of morality, a sturdy reliance on the values of a Puritan society, a sense of uplift, and self-sacrifice. Butler accepted such terminology without question, as did nearly all others with whom he and Pulitzer dealt in creating the prize system. It was bound to make for difficulties in the future, when a changing American society looked at these somewhat less than eternal values in a different light.

Here were Pulitzer's specifications for his proposed prizes in the arts:

> Annually, for the American novel published during the year which shall best present the whole atmosphere of American life, and the highest standard of American manners and manhood, One thousand dollars ($1,000).
> Annually, for the original American play, performed in New York, which shall best represent the educational value and power of the stage in raising the standard of good morals, good taste, and good manners, One thousand dollars ($1,000).
> Annually, for the best book of the year upon the history of the United States, Two thousand dollars ($2,000).
> Annually, for the best American biography teaching patriotic

and unselfish services to the people, illustrated by an eminent example, excluding, as too obvious, the names of George Washington and Abraham Lincoln, One thousand dollars ($1,000).

Of these, only the history award remains in substantially the same form today, "the best" having been replaced by "a distinguished." It was discovered very early in the risky business of prize-giving that an award for "the best" of anything invariably created an unnecessary amount of argument and the Pulitzer authorities dropped the term.

As for the journalism prizes, three of them remain in the Plan of Award, and their themes, while somewhat changed and expanded, still resound with the original Pulitzer rhetoric:

> Annually, for the most disinterested and meritorious public service rendered by any American newspaper during the preceding year, a gold medal costing Five hundred dollars ($500).
>
> Annually, for the best editorial article written during the year, the test of excellence being clearness of style, moral purpose, sound reasoning, and power to influence public opinion in the right direction, Five hundred dollars ($500).
>
> Annually, for the best example of a reporter's work during the year; the test being strict accuracy, terseness, the accomplishment of some public good commanding public attention and respect, One thousand dollars ($1,000).

The fourth journalism prize, also for $1,000, was for the "best history" of services rendered to the public by the American press in the preceding year, but it soon was dropped for lack of competitors and lack of interest. It was awarded only once. As for the education prize of $1,000, it was for the "best and most suggestive paper" on the development and improvement of the Columbia School of Journalism, but no competitors ever appeared and it quickly vanished. The Pulitzer traveling scholarships, three for graduates of the journalism school and one each for students in music and art, were more enduring.

With the completion of the will, Pulitzer's own contribution to his prizes concluded. He did a great deal more for the cause of journalism education and dealt sporadically with Butler on details affecting the deed of gift for the journalism school. He even expressed interest in Talcott Williams, editor of the Philadelphia *Press*, as a prospective director for the school. But, throughout his remaining years, he held to his determination that his "grand scheme" must outlive him.

The end came unexpectedly on October 29, 1911, while he was aboard his yacht, *Liberty*, in the harbor of Charleston, S.C. He had been suffering from indigestion but appeared to have gotten over it that morning. A secretary was reading to him from the *Life of Louis XI*. As was the old man's custom, when he felt drowsy, he murmured, "Leise, ganz leise, ganz leise"—"Softly, quite softly." [12] These were his last words.

4

The Board Takes Over

President Butler and four members of the Advisory Board of the School of Journalism carried out a pleasant chore on the afternoon of May 24, 1915. They inspected the school, which had begun operations in Columbia's Hamilton Hall in the fall of 1912, and toured the new Journalism Building, which had been completed the following year. They then filed into the formal, shadowed Trustees' Room across the Columbia campus and proceeded to certify that all the conditions laid down in Joseph Pulitzer's will for the awarding of the Pulitzer Prizes had been met. [13]

Those who participated in this altogether satisfying exercise constituted a minority of the Board, but there was a Pulitzer among them—Ralph Pulitzer, then 35, the donor's oldest son and the publisher of the New York *World*. The other members who accompanied him were his associate on the *World*, John Langdon Heaton, Charles Ransom Miller of the New York *Times*, and Samuel Calvin Wells of the Philadelphia *Press*. Talcott Williams, the director of the school, and John W. Cunliffe, the associate director, were present by invitation.

The job of the Board members, as President Butler laid it out for them, was to determine if the School of Journalism had been in successful operation for three years, as required by the Pulitzer will, so that the university could proceed to organize the first award of the Pulitzer Prizes and incidentally collect the second and final million dollars from the Pulitzer estate. With another and younger Pulitzer facing him, and as chairman of the Advisory Board at that, Butler took no chances. He adhered strictly to the legal forms. Out of his years of struggle with the donor, he had learned that there was safety only in absolute precision. And this, too, had its effect on the Pulitzer Prizes in their formative period.

The manner in which the three-year operation of the School of Journalism was certified as a success would have delighted the heart of the strictest of lawyers. A minute, prepared by the university, specified that the Advisory Board had approved the school's proposed program of studies on January 15 and February 19, 1912, the selection of a director and associate director on February 19, 1912, the organization of the school on May 6, 1912, and its opening on September 25, 1912. Thereafter, at meetings on October 28, 1913, and May 24, 1915, the Board had inspected the organization and work of the school and at various other times individual members of the Board had conducted further checks. Therefore, it was now concluded, the school had been and now was in successful operation—a cheerful summation that was borne out by the competent faculty and enthusiastic student body that was at work in the new building.

With the adoption of that resolution, the Board got down to the main business of drafting a working plan for the Pulitzer Prizes. Here, too, Butler was well prepared. He presented a Plan of Award, drafted primarily by the then secretary of the university, Dr. Frank Diehl Fackenthal, which for the first time set forth the relationship between the Advisory Board and the Trustees of Columbia University, defined the limited powers of the Trustees in making the awards, and suggested the jury system without which the Pulitzer Prizes could not have functioned as their donor intended.

The Plan of Award began: "The award of prizes and traveling scholarships will be publicly made and announced at the annual Commencement in each year by the Trustees of Columbia University on the recommendation of the Advisory Board of the School of Journalism." [14]

This was and remains the basic requirement. Butler, the Board, and the Trustees thoroughly understood that this meant the Trustees could grant a prize only if they had a recommendation before them from the Board and they had no right to change such a recommendation. However, with some of the Trustees squirming because of a public belief that they were little more than rubber stamps, it was not many years before university lawyers were arguing that, if the Trustees had the right to award the prizes, they also had the power to withhold them. Nothing like this, however, appears in the Butler-Fackenthal draft of the Plan of Award.

The draft limited candidates for the journalism award to candidates from American daily or weekly newspapers who were proposed or endorsed by a member of the Advisory Board, but did not similarly circumscribe the nominations for letters or drama. To Butler, this raised the specter of a journalistic veto by a Board member over the nomination of a competitor and he made sure that anybody who wanted to submit an exhibit could do so by applying to an impartial member of the Board. Eventually, when it appeared that there was very real difficulty in obtaining nominations for Pulitzer Prizes in any category, all artificial limitations were removed.

Another of Butler's concerns was his fear that the use of the masculine pronoun throughout the Plan of Award might legally bar women from consideration. He took this always awkward literary form as seriously as any latter-day women's lib supporter and actually polled the entire Board to be certain that women as well as men would be eligible for the awards.

There was no mention of the jury system in the Plan of Award, primarily because the members of the Advisory Board apparently weren't sure to what extent the Butler-Fackenthal proposal would curb their own powers. What the Columbia administrators wanted, in effect, was the authority to ask the American Academy of Arts and Letters to appoint juries to consider recommendations for books and drama and to leave the journalism prizes to the Faculty of Journalism, which also would appoint juries. Moreover, because neither Butler nor Fackenthal relished the prospect of unlimited nominations at that particular juncture, they wanted to let the juries themselves propose the nominees.

In the light of subsequent developments, what actually happened was that the Academy of Arts and Letters did agree to nominate candidates for book and drama juries who were acceptable to Columbia (that is, Butler) and the Faculty of Journalism was told to form juries, find suitable nominees, and submit recommendations. But the Advisory Board took no formal notice of the jury system at the outset and even insisted on this provision in the Plan of Award:

"Nothing in this plan relating to the preliminary selection or nomination of candidates for the several prizes and traveling scholarships shall be deemed to limit in any way the authority and control of the Advisory Board who may, at their discretion, modify any of the provisions relating to the preliminary selection or nomination of candidates."

This was the first signal that the Board would regard all jury reports as advisory, that the Board would insist on its right to overrule juries and impose its own judgment on the contenders, and that the Board would, if necessary, select its own prize winners. It was, of course, not quite what Butler had intended. For in the Butler-Fackenthal draft, there was more than a hint that Columbia hoped the Advisory Board would do the nominating and leave the judging to the American Academy of Arts and Letters and the Faculty of Journalism. It didn't turn out that way.

Otherwise, the Plan of Award contained no surprises. It included all the prizes proposed in the Pulitzer will. It discreetly changed the status of President Butler from ex-officio to full membership in the Advisory Board and provided that the Board's members would consist of twelve other persons as well. All that remained of Pulitzer's insistence on membership for scholars like Charles William Eliot and Andrew Dickson White was a provision that the Board had the authority to "add to its numbers by the appointment of persons of distinction who are not journalists or editors." [15]

When the Board adjourned at 5:40 P.M. on May 24, 1915, the course to be followed by the Pulitzer Prizes in its formative years was set for all practical purposes. Its members did not meet the following year, there being no business to warrant a formal session. It was perfectly evident even then that the Board was content to leave the business of running the school to Butler and Talcott Williams, the director. In order to keep the Board fully posted, Butler circulated a letter to all members with notification that the first deadline for all nominations and exhibits would be February 1, 1917, and that the first Pulitzer Prizes would be announced at the Columbia Commencement in June 1917.[16] Thus, Pulitzer's dream materialized six years after his death and thus the Pulitzer Prizes, a frail craft of many masters, was launched directly into the tempest of World War I.

5
The Administration

In the somewhat tattered record books of the Advisory Board, there is a resolution of gratitude and a proposal for the text of a ceremonial scroll that reads as follows:

> To Dr. Frank Diehl Fackenthal, greetings and felicitations.
> You have been associated with the historical development of the Pulitzer Prizes from the beginning.

You were the author of the report which bridged the years between experiment and fulfillment of Joseph Pulitzer's dreams.

You participated in the formulation of all basic policies and procedures.

You initiated the jury system, communicated with, advised, and
at times even consoled juries.

As secretary, provost, and acting president of the university, you
were the personal tie between the Advisory Board and the
Trustees.

To you, on this occasion, the members of the Advisory Board
award the Pulitzer Prize of our friendship in perpetuity.[17]

The scroll did not exaggerate the extent of Fackenthal's services in
creating a strong and durable administrative framework for the Pulitzer
Prizes. The records of the Advisory Baord and of the university itself are
replete with evidence of Fackenthal's resourcefulness, tact, shrewdness,
and excellent judgment in resolving the many difficulties that cropped up
to confound those who tried faithfully to carry out the precepts laid
down in Pulitzer's will and the Plan of Award. Nobody formally appointed him to do the unrewarding chores of administration; in fact, it
was almost a decade before the Advisory Board got around to naming a
permanent executive secretary.

Since the Board generally met only once a year, however, somebody
had to keep things running in the interim—to get in the nominations and
exhibits, catalogue them, distribute them to the juries, persuade eminent
people to serve as jurors, coax them into making their reports within a
reasonable time, lay the whole business before the Advisory Board, and
then prepare for the formal announcement of the prizes and the inevitable arguments thereafter. This was Fackenthal's job, an unlooked for addition to his regular responsibilities as secretary of the university. He
generally depended on the Journalism Faculty to help judge the journalism exhibits, but he himself handled the always sensitive matters affecting books and drama.

Like Butler, with whom he worked so closely for a lifetime, Fackenthal was all Columbia. But unlike Butler, he was small, thin, modest,
unassuming, and almost always had a smile and a kind word for anybody who entered his office. He had been born in Hellertown, Pa., in
1883 and graduated from Columbia College in 1906, making such an impression on faculty and staff that he was immediately appointed chief
clerk of the university. After four years in that office, he was promoted

to secretary of the university—a post akin to chief of staff in President Butler's somewhat military table of organization. Although his responsibilities continually increased—he was university provost from 1937 to 1945 and acting president between 1945 and 1948—he never lost touch with the Pulitzer Prizes.

Fackenthal quietly organized the various administrative divisions and offices into a functioning whole to service the Pulitzer Prizes. His liaison with the Trustees was a veteran university official, Miss Vera R. Southard, whose spidery handwriting is so much in evidence in the Pulitzer papers. For finances, he depended for many years on the advice of the university's financial expert, W. Emerson Gentzler. For publicity in the early years, there was the taciturn veteran of the New York *Herald*, James T. (Judge) Grady, director of the university news office, and later the much-admired Robert C. Harron and his competent successor, John Hastings. Whenever necessary, and it often was, the efficient secretarial staffs of the president's and secretary's offices could be mobilized for double duty but, as was characteristic of Fackenthal, it was all done with a minimum of fuss. The director of this academic orchestra was seldom seen waving his baton.

While Butler and Fackenthal concentrated on the letters and drama prizes and their respective juries, they tacitly left the supervision of the journalism awards to the old pro who had become the first director of the journalism school, Talcott Williams. He had been the first choice of the Advisory Board (and very likely of Butler as well) and maintained the best of relations with both. Fackenthal, too, liked him and got on well with him.

Williams was 67 years old when the first prizes were awarded, having been born July 20, 1849, in a village near Beirut in what is now Lebanon. Following his graduation from Amherst in 1873, he had spent his life in newspaper work. During his long career as editor of the Philadelphia *Press*, where he had first come to Joseph Pulitzer's attention, he had collected honorary degrees from the University of Pennsylvania and half a dozen other universities. He was a rare bird in the newsroom—a journalistic academic. There were few like him.

However, Williams was far from an impressive figure. He was a small, stringy wisp of a man with a white, soup-strainer moustache, given to wearing a black skull cap and discussing odd subjects such as the importance of dancing in a reporter's life. Once, after a talk with a student on some such matter, he abruptly changed the subject, saying, "Young man, save your money," and scurried off.

From the outset, Williams promoted the Pulitzer Prizes and might have taken to drum-beating if it had not been for Columbia's deliberate policy of restraint. It was Fackenthal, more than anyone else, who enforced the view that the university should be reserved in publicizing the awards, commenting on them, and answering critics. He believed that Columbia should administer the prizes and award them annually through its Trustees, but should not undertake to discuss, debate, or defend them. That, he held, was a proper public policy and evidently he persuaded both Butler and Williams to agree with him.

At first, the muted publicity was a distinct handicap in making the Pulitzer Prizes familiar to the nation at large. But it has long since ceased to have any substantial effect on the public's reception of the awards.

2
Prizes for a Brave New World 1917–1923

1
The Beginning

Without festivities or fanfare, four dignified, elderly gentlemen came to the Columbia campus on the morning of May 24, 1917, to vote for the first Pulitzer Prizes. As they skirted old South Field and trudged slowly up the long concrete file of steps to Stanford White's beautiful Low Library building, they must have been painfully aware that the muse of history was occupied with more important business. They attracted no attention. Nor was there any prospect that there would be much interest in their decisions. The unpleasant truth was that the American people in general and this university in particular were ready for almost anything except the Pulitzer Prizes that tumultuous spring.

On April 2, President Woodrow Wilson, exercising a now almost forgotten Constitutional duty, had gone before the Congress to ask for a declaration of war against Germany—the upshot of the German campaign of unrestricted submarine warfare and rising American pressure for intervention on the side of the Allies. The stirring, idealistic rhetoric of his war speech was in tune with the intellectual climate of the time, an appeal to his fellow countrymen in terms of morality and justice and an almost holy feeling of patriotism:

"The right is more precious than peace, and we shall fight for the things which we have always carried nearest our hearts—for democracy . . . and make the world itself at last free."

Four days later, by an overwhelming vote in the Congress, the nation had gone to war. It became overnight a star-spangled adventure to make the world safe for democracy, but democracy suffered at home. All over the land, people went on a wild and unreasoning emotional binge. Everything German aroused passionate hatred. Villages called Berlin or Cologne overnight changed their names to Liberty or Freedom. Bach, Beethoven, and Brahms were verboten in concert halls. Goethe's books were removed from library shelves. The hamburger became a liberty sausage, the frankfurter a hot dog. Even little boys with German-sounding names had to defend themselves from infuriated schoolmates who called them Huns.

At Columbia, the infection took hold with unexpected virulence. Professor Charles A. Beard, one of the greatest of progressive historians, had to defend himself before a Trustees' Committee in 1916 on a charge of having supported a speaker who shouted "To hell with the flag" at a public meeting. While he was cleared, he was warned to caution all members of the Faculty of Political Science against teachings "likely to inculcate disrespect for American institutions." He soon left Columbia. But President Butler, with America's entry into the war, proclaimed a moratorium on academic freedom in which he threatened all faculty members who "are not with whole heart and mind and strength committed to fight with us to make the world safe for democracy." There were two casualties—Professor James McKeen Cattell and Assistant Professor Henry Wadsworth Longfellow Dana, who were dismissed by the Trustees for activities that "tended to promote disloyalty." [1]

The war fever hit Joseph Pulitzer's school particularly hard. With the declaration of war, classes were suspended, students plunged into research for a series of Columbia war information projects. There was even a special Washington news bureau, set up by Professor Walter B. Pitkin, with M. Lincoln Schuster, Lenoir Chambers, and George A. Hough Jr. as student correspondents.[2] The atmosphere, for a few weeks, was supercharged and it took all summer to wear off. Except for those who enlisted, the students resumed classes in the fall.

Under such circumstances, very little detachment was possible in studying the various jury reports recommending Pulitzer Prizes to the Advisory Board. It is significant that only four of the Board's members met with President Butler that morning of May 24 in the Trustees Room to make the first binding recommendations to the Trustees. They were Solomon B. Griffin of the Springfield *Republican*, John L. Heaton of the New York *World*, Charles R. Miller of the New York *Times*, and Samuel C. Wells of the Philadelphia *Press*.

It was not a majority but nobody challenged Butler, who appeared determined not to put off any longer the inauguration of the Pulitzer Prizes. The minutes of the meeting noted that those absent were George S. Johns of the St. Louis *Post-Dispatch*, Victor F. Lawson of the Chicago *Daily News*, Melville E. Stone of the *Associated Press*, and Charles H. Taylor of the Boston *Globe*. Those absent and excused were Edward P. Mitchell of the New York *Sun* and Ralph Pulitzer of the New York *World*.

Stone, Miller, Mitchell, Heaton, Johns, Lawson, Taylor, and Wells had been members of the first Board that met on January 15, 1912. The others at the 1912 session had been Whitelaw Reid of the New York *Tribune*, chairman; St. Clair McKelway of the Brooklyn *Eagle*, vice chairman; and Samuel Bowles of the Springfield *Republican*. Because of age, indisposition, or unwillingness to attend meetings, changes in the Board's membership were frequent in the early years. The terms of service of each member, then as now, was four years but members then could be re-elected indefinitely, the Board being the principal authority for choosing its membership. While the Trustees were required to ratify each choice, the Board was accustomed to ratification of its selections in the first fifty-seven years.[3]

There was a great deal of reluctance on the part of most jurors to submit recommendations to the Board for the first awards in 1917; those who did, with few exceptions, proposed prizes that amply reflected the patriotic tenor of the times. Butler, who reported to the Board on behalf of the juries in letters and drama, evidently shared the ambivalent feelings of the judges for he suggested no changes and the Board went along with him. On the president's initiative, Chancellor William M. Sloane of the American Academy of Arts and Letters had recruited the first juries in the non-journalism categories. In asking a number of eminent literary figures to serve, Sloane had told them that the university would submit nominations, but each jury could also make proposals on its own initiative.[4]

That didn't make it any easier for the first judges. The correspondence between the chairmen and the chancellor, whose role in subsequent years was assumed by Fackenthal, indicated that there were few important works to be judged in any of the categories, that the jurors had too little time for their work, and that the phrasing of the terms of the awards severely limited their choices. They passed the first fiction and drama awards for 1917. Nor did they find an American historian worthy of a prize that year; instead, they recommended *With Americans of Past and Present Days*, by Jean Jules Jusserand, French ambassador to the United States, who had helped swing American sentiment toward the Allies. As for the biography prize, it also had a symbolic martial touch, for it went to *Julia Ward Howe*, a book about the lyricist of the "Battle Hymn of the Republic," by her daughters, Laura E. Richards and Maude Howe Elliott, assisted by Florence Howe Hall.

Unlike the literary juries, which included such national figures as Professor William Lyon Phelps of Yale, Hamlin Garland, and Professor Barrett Wendell of Harvard, the journalism juries assembled from the journalism school's teaching staff were little known outside their own field. But Williams, with one eye on the Advisory Board, assigned himself to each jury he appointed in order to remove all doubt of professional competence and personally reported on their findings.

Like their colleagues in books and drama, the journalists were heavily influenced by the martial spirit and their Eastern backgrounds. It is not surprising, therefore, that their first reports to the Board nominated a New York newspaper, the *Tribune*, for a spirited anti-German editorial on the anniversary of the sinking of the *Lusitania*, and a New York reporter, Herbert Bayard Swope of the *World*, for his series of dispatches, "Inside the German Empire." These were the only prizes in journalism proposed for work done in 1916, since the teaching staff made no suggestions for a public service prize and had no entries for the two other awards.

The Advisory Board, concluding that first rather desultory session on the prizes, quietly voted the recommendations of all the juries, approved paying the cost of administering the prizes out of the Pulitzer Prize Fund, authorized payment of $50 to each juror who was not a member of the Columbia faculty, and adjourned after a session of less than two hours. The university Trustees, just as matter-of-factly, accepted the recommendations and voted for the first prizes, which were awarded at Commencement, June 6, 1917. Except for the Pulitzer newspapers and a few others, little public notice resulted.[5]

That was, to a considerable extent, the pattern for the two following war years, which were represented by the awards of 1918 and 1919. With the exception of biography, prizes in each category from 1917 to 1919 were passed at least once and the one for the best paper on improving the School of Journalism was abandoned altogether. Thus, out of a possible 27 awards, 15 were made and 12 were withheld. The drama prize was passed over twice and fiction, history, public service, reporting, and editorial writing once each.

On May 20, 1919, in a show of concern, the Advisory Board discussed the problem of non-prize-giving juries and adopted the following statement of policy:

"While the Advisory Board is glad to sustain the juries in maintaining severe standards of excellence for these prizes, at the same time the Board calls the attention of juries to the fact that the usefulness of the prizes themselves depend upon their being awarded, and the Board would be glad to have them awarded whenever, in the opinion of the jury, there was sufficient merit in the candidate to justify an award."

Fortunately, the Pulitzer Prizes did not appear to suffer from these internal difficulties during the World War I era and the comparative lack of attention that was given to the annual announcement of the awards. In a way, the noncontroversial early years actually stimulated growth. Outside the garish spotlight of public cynosure, and relatively free of critical inspection, the system for determining the awards was molded into a reasonably efficient operation.

Butler had to abandon some of his pet notions and adapt others to the spirit of the times. The first to go was the idea that the Advisory Board and the American Academy of Arts and Letters between them could control the nominations and the designation of jurors for the letters and drama prizes. It just wasn't possible. Nor could the Board and the teaching staff of the journalism school do the nominating and judging for the journalism awards. Inevitably, there would be conflicts of interest. Moreover, as the prizes became better known, nominations slowly increased from a variety of sources and they could scarcely be ignored. The jury structure, accordingly, had to be broadened.[6]

As for the Advisory Board, after two years of minimal attendance during World War I, it became more responsive to its task and usually drew a majority of its membership to its annual meetings. At almost every session in this formative period, there were personnel changes that increased its strength. Among these was the election to membership in 1920 of the donor's youngest son and namesake, Joseph Pulitzer of the St. Louis *Post-Dispatch*, and the Board's repeated choice, beginning in 1923, of the oldest son, Ralph Pulitzer of the New York *World*, as its chairman for its annual meetings.[7]

The swift changes in American society immediately after World War I presented the Pulitzer Prize system with its first real test of public acceptance as a national award of consequence. For many of the ideals and standards that had seemed so immutable to both Butler and Pulitzer, and which were imbedded in the Plan of Award, came under severe attack.

With the coming of a shattering national revulsion to the American wartime experience, the public mood of exaltation and adventure was transformed with dramatic suddenness into a dour and suspicious cynicism. Gone was the soaring idealism, the feeling of glory, and the vibrant patriotism that Woodrow Wilson had aroused in those who believed in America's sense of mission in the world. A different and far more volatile America was being shaped out of Wilson's tragic failure to swing the Senate behind the Versailles Treaty and the League of Nations, the election of Warren Gamaliel Harding to the presidency on a platform calling for a return to normalcy, and the American retreat into isolation, dollar-chasing, and a reckless search for novelty.

The forces of reaction and progress clashed at almost every level of American life. Fear of an aroused labor movement, coupled with ignorance and even panic over the triumph of Communism in Russia, led to what seemed like a political inquisition presided over by Attorney General A. Mitchell Palmer in 1920 and later continued by his successor, Harry M. Daugherty. The genii of hate, let out of their bottle by the war, could not be put back again so quickly. The "Red menace" stalked the land. And with it came race riots, lynchings, and the rise of the Ku Klux Klan as a political power.

Economically, after a brief postwar depression, a frenzy of virtually uncontrolled speculation swept the New York Stock Exchange and its affiliates. Paper millionaires were the talk of the land and the envy of the unthinking. Even worse, people who had no business in the stock market tossed their savings into irresponsible ventures on the theory that prices would almost always go up and hardly ever down. It was an era when everybody was somebody else's financial adviser, from banker to boot-black, and the accumulation of easy money seemed to be a worthy goal. Furthermore, with the advent of prohibition and gang warfare over con-trol of illegal liquor in 1920, easy virtue became socially acceptable.

The impact of such frenetic changes on a culture that owed much of its strength and character to John Calvin was not long in making itself felt. New ideas, new fashions, a more realistic attitude toward sex and a far more ambitious and vibrant literature burst upon a people that had been nurtured for years on few authors more revolutionary than William Dean Howells. The world of Joseph Pulitzer, who had been dead only about a decade, existed now only in the history books and the fading imagination of an older generation. It remained to be seen whether his prizes could change with the times.[8]

2
Warriors and Peacemakers

Ralph McGill once observed that much of the work of the editorial giants of the past has little relevance today and asked plaintively, "Why did they say these were great editors?" This was his own explanation:

"They spoke and wrote in the context of their times. And, they had something to say. They caused people to say fervently, 'Amen,' or to shout an angry 'No.' They reached people. They participated in the lives of the people of their years." [9]

Certainly, this was true of Henry Watterson, the fabulous "Marse Henry" of the Louisville *Courier-Journal*. He was the last of the fiercely and devotedly personal journalists of a bygone era. During his 81 years, he was far more the bold warrior than the peacemaker—an 80-pound cavalryman in the Civil War and one of the most determined supporters of American intervention in World War I. Through sheer force of char-acter and journalistic skill, he lifted what had begun as a small regional newspaper into a distinctive publication that was nationally known and admired.

Despite "Marse Henry's" appearance in his prime—a portly figure with a distinct military bearing, thick snow-white hair, gray walrus moustache, and tiny goatee—he was no prototype of the mint julep colonel from a decaying Southern plantation. He went out of his way to deny that he ever had been a colonel, real or fancied; that he smoked, or that he drank anything stronger than wine or beer. But the legend, peculiar to Kentucky, persisted anyway.

Watterson was born into the newspaper business in Washington, D.C. in 1840, the son of a Tennessee editor and congressman. At 16, he put out his first paper. At 19, he covered John Brown's raid on Harpers Ferry. At 21, he met Abraham Lincoln and managed to get an advance on the first inaugural address. After the Civil War, he became the editor of the Louisville *Courier*, which he merged in 1868 with the Louisville *Journal*, and attained national fame for both his newspaper and himself with his savage attacks on the Ku Klux Klan.

It was like him, upon the outbreak of World War I, to refuse to follow President Wilson's plea to the nation to be "neutral in thought." Three days after the German hordes began smashing through Belgium, "Marse Henry" wrote: "Bravo Belgium, and bravo all who fight for national liberty and life. . . . The word of the modern world is, Down with Tyranny, autocracy and brute force." Less than a month later, on September 3, he coined a slogan that echoed through the nation: "To Hell with the Hohenzollerns and the Hapsburgs!"

There was never anything halfhearted about "Marse Henry." In the presidential campaign of 1916, he unfairly attacked the Republican nominee, Charles Evans Hughes, as "the Kaiser's candidate" and hailed Wilson's narrow re-election as a "vindication of Democracy." As far as Watterson was concerned, the United States was at war from the moment Germany resumed unrestricted submarine attacks on American shipping.

In an editorial entitled "Vae Victis" on April 7, 1917, the day after Congress had declared war, "Marse Henry" pulled out all the stops:

"First of all on bended knee, we should pray God to forgive us. Then erect as men, Christian men, soldierly men, to the flag and the fray— wherever they lead us . . . no peace with the Kaiser—no parley with Autocracy, Absolutism and the divine right of Kings—to Hell with the Hapsburg and the Hohenzollern!"

There was more of this three days later in an even more bellicose editorial, "War Has Its Compensations."

To a disillusioned and war-weary nation only three years later, such sentiments were repugnant and even Watterson had his regrets, but at the time the editorials were published he set the war hawks wild with delight. At the Columbia School of Journalism, when the teaching staff met with Director Williams on April 19, 1918, to recommend the Pulitzer Prizes in Journalism, Watterson's two war editorials won a unanimous vote. These articles, the jury declared, were "directed toward arousing the American people to their international duty and toward convincing a section of the country by tradition hostile to universal military service of the wisdom and necessity of its establishment." The Advisory Board heartily concurred.

When the wire services flashed the news to Louisville, the 77-year-old editor was delighted. To the assembled editorial writers, he said proudly, "The gander-legged boys in the city editor's room will find out that the old man is a promising journalist." It was his last achievement as a working newspaperman. That summer, he and a majority of the *Courier-Journal*'s share-holders sold their interest to Robert Worth Bingham, a former mayor of Louisville and a prominent lawyer who had been familiar with the paper's operations.

As editor-emeritus, Watterson celebrated victory and the downfall of the hated Kaiser. But soon, like the veritable weather vane of public opinion that he was, he swung about into opposition to Wilson, the League of Nations, and further American participation in European affairs. The *Courier-Journal*, which had come out for the League, printed his isolationist editorials for a time, but eventually had to ask him to retire, which he did in 1919. Almost to the end of his life in 1921, he was active, eager, provocative. In one of his last letters, he wrote to a youthful colleague in Washington, Arthur Krock, to ask for a visit: "There's lots to talk about and still a bit of sugar in the bottom of the glass." [10]

The commencement of 1918 at Columbia, during which Watterson's Pulitzer Prize was announced, fairly bristled with patriotic fervor. Talcott Williams appeared with two service stars on the hood of his academic gown in memory of two of his school's graduates who had been killed in action. The first and so far the only student winners of a Pulitzer Prize, Henry Beetle Hough and Minna Lewinson of the School of Journalism, won that year with a paper on the history of the wartime services of the American press. Hough, who had enlisted and been assigned to the Office of Naval Intelligence in Washington, was present in his white sailor's uniform; years later, his share of the prize went to pay for depression era paper bills on his weekly *Vineyard Gazette* in Martha's Vineyard. Miss Lewinson became the first woman reporter on the *Wall Street Journal*.

There was only one more commencement for Williams. After supervising the journalism judging for 1919, he retired as director of the school and was replaced by the scholarly British journalist and teacher, Dr. John W. Cunliffe, who was then 54 years old. While the Advisory Board agreed to accept Cunliffe upon Butler's insistence, he never was given the same broad privileges and trust accorded his predecessor and usually had to communicate with the Board by letter instead of being present at its meetings by invitation. That made a major difference in the manner in which the journalism prizes were judged and administered. Before long, a few of the teaching staff's choices were being overruled and its advice at times was being ignored.

Cunliffe, a genial and sophisticated gentleman of the old school, never let the Board's treatment of him affect his work. He had come to Columbia from a post in Canada to be Williams' associate in 1912 and was a familiar figure on the campus. Often, he padded around the corridors of the Journalism Building, smoking his pipe, in black velvet jacket and carpet slippers. To avoid being interrupted during his lectures on contemporary American and English literature and drama, which he delivered with eloquence and good humor, he would lock the big glass doors of the second-floor newsroom at 9 A.M., to the visible discomfiture of latecomers.

All in all, this slender, white-bearded scholar with the twinkling blue eyes was scarcely what Pulitzer would have envisioned as a leader in the judging of American journalism for Pulitzer Prizes, but he maintained his role with a certain amount of elegance despite his troubles with the Advisory Board. To assist him, he had several wise and respected veteran newspapermen who served on his teaching staff—Charles P. Cooper of the New York *Times*, Roscoe Conkling Ensign Brown of the New York *Tribune*, and Allen Sinclair Will of the Baltimore *Sun*. They carried on the Williams tradition.

Under Cunliffe, in consequence, the policies of the journalism juries continued along the lines that had been formulated by Williams. Thus, the awards for wartime journalism and the coverage and comment on the consequences of war became one of the most enduring themes in the history of the Pulitzer Prizes in Journalism. The award to Watterson was symbolic. For during the initial period of the prizes, 1917–1923, wartime and war-related journalism won eight out of seventeen prizes that were bestowed, while six others were passed entirely. All types of newspaper work were recognized, both during and immediately after the end of World War I, with a strong feeling of patriotic sentiment running through everything.

The New York *Times* was rewarded with the public service gold medal in 1918 for its publication of war reports and documents during the previous year. In 1919, the Milwaukee *Journal* received the gold medal for its "courageous campaign for Americanism" in a community where there were many Americans of German ancestry. In addition to Herbert Bayard Swope's 1917 prize for reporting from wartime Germany, others went to his colleague on the New York *World*, Louis Seibold, for an exclusive interview with President Wilson, and to Kirke L. Simpson of the Associated Press for his report on the burial of the Unknown Soldier. Honors for the Unknown Soldier figured, too, in the editorial writing prizes, one going to Frank M. O'Brien of the New York *Herald* for a patriotic piece on that theme. The only anonymous editorialist on the list was the New York *Tribune*'s first prize winner while the most vociferous was "Marse Henry."

There was enormous professional interest in Seibold's work because the exclusive presidential interview was such a rarity at the time. It was well understood, of course, that the *World*'s reporter had been favored because the paper had fought hard for the League of Nations; basically, the interview, published on June 18, 1920, conveyed Wilson's warning to the Democratic National Convention not to sidestep a pledge for the League. Nevertheless, the propaganda content of the interview did not detract from Seibold's prize. For his was a historic first in journalism.

Of all the early journalism prizes, the one that evoked the greatest national acclaim was Simpson's piece on the night wire of the AP for November 11, 1921, that began:

"Under the wide and starry skies of his own homeland America's unknown dead from France sleeps tonight, a soldier home from the wars. Alone, he lies in the narrow cell of stone that guards his body; but his soul has entered into the spirit that is America. . . ."

The story was unsigned, for it was against wire service policy then to identify writers. But the response was of such a stunning nature that the AP gave Kirke Larue Simpson his first byline. His Pulitzer Prize was the first to be won by anybody from the wire services.[11]

Even in an era dominated by war and the consequences of a cynical peace settlement, the earliest Pulitzer Prizes also developed a strong interest in the championing of civil liberties. The crusading spirit, nurtured by Joseph Pulitzer, is stamped upon seven of the prizes awarded from 1917 to 1923. The themes are familiar in any list of awards today, but some were refreshing novelties when the Pulitzer Prizes were established—investigations of the Ku Klux Klan, medieval prison conditions, "get-rich-quick" schemes, and the appalling backgrounds of race riots.

Despite the limited number of nominations that came before the journalism school juries and the Advisory Board during the first seven years, there was evidence in abundance to show that newspapers devoted to public service existed in all parts of the land even though their numbers were relatively small. It was no surprise, however, that the New York *World* set the example with a resolute attack on wrongdoing and that the mainspring of its campaigns was an aggressive and domineering journalist who already had won one Pulitzer Prize, Herbert Bayard Swope. In his prime, he was a red-headed battering ram of a man, six feet tall and weighing 200 pounds, with a hoarse voice that could rise to a magnificent bellow of impatience or anger. To his contemporary, Stanley Walker, he was a "snorting Caesar in a company of Caspar Milquetoasts."

Swope was 27 when he came to New York to join the *World*, having been born and educated in St. Louis and begun his career on the *Post-Dispatch*. Within three years, he broke the biggest crime story in town—the murder of Gambler Herman Rosenthal outside the Hotel Metropole on July 14, 1912—by pinning responsibility on Police Lieutenant Charles Becker and four hired assassins. He developed the evidence that helped District Attorney Charles S. Whitman send them to the electric chair. Later, Whitman was elected governor of New York State.

As for Swope, he became city editor of the *World* but not for long. Soon, he was on his way to Germany for his prize-winning series. And after the war, at the Versailles peace conference, he published the first draft of the League of Nations Covenant (with an assist from President Wilson). Once, just to show it could be done, he donned formal diplomatic attire, hired a long black limousine and unceremoniously crashed the solemn councils of the peace makers at Versailles.

All this was preparation for the *World*'s major crusades after Swope became executive editor in 1920. He exposed the Ku Klux Klan by publishing original documents that had been taken from its files and other secret materials. For that feat, the *World* won the Pulitzer Prize in public service in 1922. During the next year, by following the *World*'s lead, the Memphis *Commercial Appeal* also won the public service gold medal for an expose of the Klan. What these two prizes did was to recognize and stimulate the investigative function of the press in reporting on the threat to civil liberties that the Klan represented. Numerous other awards flowed from those first gold medals for attacks on the Klan.

As the *World* won still more honors for its crusades under Swope's leadership, there was an almost inevitable rise in criticism of "Pulitzer Prizes for Pulitzer Papers." Columbia and the Advisory Board, which included representation from the *World*'s principal rivals, made no response in public. Privately, however, Joseph Pulitzer moved to disqualify papers and people who had already won a prize, but the Board wouldn't hear of it. Evidently, the feeling was the same then as it is today—that if the prizes were sound, they could withstand criticism.

But there was at least one member of the *World*'s high command who refused to permit himself to be nominated and wouldn't even let himself be considered for membership on the Advisory Board. He was Walter Lippmann, whom Swope had hired in 1923 from the *New Republic* to be editor of the *World*'s editorial page. At least three times while he was on the *World*, Lippmann disqualified himself from consideration for a prize. And even while he was on the New York *Herald Tribune* thereafter, he asked Ralph Pulitzer not to nominate him. When Lippmann finally did win a Pulitzer special citation and a Pulitzer Prize, the Pulitzer papers and Pulitzer family had no dominant role in the process.

Such sensitivity was too much for Swope. He was an innovator and he believed in accepting credit where credit was due, but he did not maneuver for a Pulitzer Prize, much as he respected and treasured the awards that came to him. He never really thought of himself as a liberal, and actually was quite conservative in his political beliefs. With him, it was the story that counted. He went out of his way to publish a tale of inhuman punishment and murder in Florida's prison camps, smashing the peonage system and winning another public service gold medal for the *World* in

1924. He caused the *World* to cover so many lynchings that the paper acquired a reputation for being pro-Negro at a time when such an attitude was unpopular with advertisers.

In the field of labor relations, he encouraged the type of labor reporting that won a Pulitzer reporting prize for John J. Leary Jr. in 1920 for his coverage of the national coal strike of the previous year. Instead of tiptoeing around the coal fields, taking management handouts, Leary boldly exposed the activities of a collegebred gunman and management hireling who had terrorized the coal fields until he was beaten to the draw by a miner in the United Mine Workers headquarters. This was strong stuff, but Swope wasn't afraid of having the *World* called pro-union any more than he feared the pro-Negro label.

Basically, these innovations helped the *World* in what was soon to develop into a fight for its own life. In broadening the field of reporting and lifting the standards of journalism, Swope also gave greater depth and enlarged responsibilities to his profession.[12]

Under the rolling reaction of the Harding era of "normalcy" and the hate and fear it stimulated, the buoyant good sense of hardheaded newspapermen frequently kept dangerous situations under control. One of the outstanding instances of this kind of journalism occurred in Omaha at the height of a race riot there. Harvey E. Newbranch, in the Evening *World-Herald*, attacked mob rule and mob violence in such brave terms in a piece published September 30, 1919, that he was credited with having shamed the instigators and halted the fighting.

That kind of journalistic intervention had its impact in other areas of American life. When Harold A. Littledale of the New York *Evening Post* visited the underground dungeons of the New Jersey State Prison at Trenton, he was sickened by the medieval torture that still was being practiced there in the winter of 1917. He wrote a furious indictment that brought almost immediate reform action from the new governor, Walter E. Edge. The series won Littledale the Pulitzer Prize for reporting in 1918.

In a much less familiar and far more difficult area of reportage, the financial community, the Boston *Post* distinguished itself by exposing the "get-rich-quick" swindles of Charles Ponzi, leading to his arrest and punishment. The feat so impressed Robert L. O'Brien of the rival Boston *Herald* that he nominated the *Post* for the public service gold medal in a letter to the Advisory Board, of which he was a member. It was,

O'Brien wrote, "a piece of newspaper enterprise of the first importance in the interest of public service." His plea for his competitor swung the 1921 gold medal for public service to the Boston *Post*.[13]

While there were other campaigns of consequence in the era, the journalists quickly learned that those of the most immediate importance were the ones in which they themselves became the central issue and freedom of the press was at stake. There have been many such conflicts in American history, from the time of John Peter Zenger to the Pentagon Papers; without doubt, there will be many more. One of the most unusual cropped up in Kansas in the summer of 1922 during a railway shopmen's strike and involved one of the least belligerent and best-loved of American journalists—William Allen White of the Emporia *Gazette*.

Bill White need not have intervened in the strike. He was well established as a leading Republican. His newspaper, which he had purchased in 1895 at the age of 27, was widely known and respected. He was the confidant of presidents and a close friend of the then governor of Kansas, Henry J. Allen, who was trying to crush the strike. However, when the governor issued an order forbidding the posting of placards in support of the strike, White intervened. He placed a placard in his own shop window and defied the governor to arrest him.

White's defiance became national news. If labor was enthusiastic, many of the middle-class readers of the *Gazette* were not. He received numerous protests and, in response to one of them, wrote his classic editorial, "To An Anxious Friend," which he published on Page 1 on July 27, 1922. He opened with the theme: "You say that freedom of utterance is not for time of stress and I reply with the sad truth that only in time of stress is freedom of utterance in danger." And he closed with this assurance:

"So, dear friend, put fear out of your heart. This nation will survive, this state will prosper, the orderly business of life will go forward if only men can speak in whatever way given them to utter what their hearts hold—by voice, by posted card, by letter, or by press. Reason has never failed men. Only force and repression have made wrecks in this world."

The governor's suit against White was dismissed. The strike was settled. And, by recommendation of a jury and the Advisory Board, William Allen White was awarded the Pulitzer Prize for Editorial Writing in 1923.[14]

There were prizes that had more public appeal, such as the first award for editorial cartooning in 1922 that went to Rollin Kirby of the New York *World*. There were prizes that went to more sophisticated work, such as the reporting award to Alva Johnston of the New York *Times* for his coverage of atomic research in the 1922 proceedings of the American Association for the Advancement of Science. But none in the Pulitzer list was given for a more fundamental principle in American life than the one that went to White's editorial in defense of the right to post a placard in the United States.

3
The Emergence of Eugene O'Neill

The American theater was stagnant at the time the first Pulitzer Prizes in Drama were awarded. While there was a lot of excitement on Broadway, particularly about the *Ziegfeld Follies* and George M. Cohan's brassy musical shows, much of the standard fare was both trivial and banal. In the hinterlands, there were a few struggling stock companies and occasional road shows. What it all added up to, in the words of one distinguished critic, was distressingly little, for "the standards of prudery and decorum were high." [15]

The first Drama Jury, consisting of Hamlin Garland, Richard Burton, and Augustus Thomas as chairman, saw such plays as *Good Gracious Annabelle* by Clare Kummer and *The Thirteenth Chair* by Bayard Veiller. Thomas, a homespun dramatist who was to complete 57 plays in his lifetime, wrote to the Board: "Considering the conditions of the Pulitzer award for drama, its aims and requirements, your committee is not agreed upon a recommendation." The dour verdict won the concurrence of Garland, the crusty mid-Westerner whose *Son of the Middle Border* became a near classic, and Burton, the head of the University of Minnesota's English Department.

In 1918, the same jury weakened and recommended a slender but agreeable comedy, *Why Marry?* by Jesse Lynch Williams, which the New York *Evening Sun* termed Shavian in style and the New York *Evening World* called "the best American comedy in years." There had been no major work in an indifferent season and 1919 was no better. With Hamlin Garland succeeding Augustus Thomas as chairman and Clayton

Hamilton joining Richard Burton to complete the jury, the verdict once again was to pass the award. *Lightnin'*, with Frank Bacon as the star and co-author with Winchell Smith, was on its way that year to a total of 1,291 performances, but comedies about lovable drunks weren't up to the high-minded specifications of the award as it then stood.

The one act of the Drama Jury in the first three years that has withstood the test of time was to make the theatrical season, and not the calendar year, the period of judgment for the Pulitzer Prize. Considered as a whole, the years of World War I were difficult for serious dramatists—more so in many ways than for other writers—and the unimpressive Pulitzer verdicts of the first three years reflected the vapid character of the American theater.[16]

In the Spring of 1920, the Drama Jury was divided. Hamlin Garland, the chairman, did not care for *Beyond the Horizon*, the first play of a strange young newcomer, Eugene O'Neill, to be produced on Broadway. Garland thought it lacked the quality that a prize play should have. The two other jurors, Richard Burton and Walter Pritchard Eaton, were just as determined that O'Neill should have the prize because they thought they had detected the mark of genius in his work.

As the struggle developed, O'Neill remained blissfully ignorant; at the time, as he later confessed, he had never even heard of the Pulitzer Prize. He was then 31 years old—a moody, shy, dark-haired, dark-eyed denizen of New York's Bohemia, Greenwich Village, with a driving ambition to write for the theater and an unquenchable thirst for alcohol. He was attractive in a gloomy way; even in repose, his handsome, moustached face was tinged with sadness.

O'Neill had been born October 16, 1888, in New York's theatrical district at the Barrett House on 43d Street just off Broadway, the son of an actor, James O'Neill. He had been a seaman, an actor, a reporter on the New London (Conn.) *Telegraph* and, in 1916–1917, had had his first one-act plays produced at the Wharf Theater, Provincetown, Mass., and the Provincetown Playhouse in Greenwich Village. These one-acters, *Bound East for Cardiff* and companion works, were the forerunners of *Beyond the Horizon*, which had been optioned to a Broadway producer.

It was an accident that brought O'Neill to Broadway. Richard Bennett, a popular actor of the era, was playing in Elmer Rice's *For The Defense* toward the end of 1919 when he glanced through the script of *Beyond the Horizon* while he was in the office of the producer, John D.

Williams, who held the option. Bennett talked Williams into presenting the play at the Morosco Theater at special matinees when there was no performance of *For The Defense*. It wasn't a very satisfactory way to launch a playwright's career, but O'Neill had to be content with it. The opening was on February 3, 1920 at 2:15 P.M., which was unusual in itself, but the major critics all were present.

There was nothing sweet or attractive about *Beyond the Horizon*, not a single scene to enchant or bemuse an audience. It was harshly realistic, uncompromising in its fidelity to the cruelties of life. Most forbidding of all, it was a tragedy, put before the footlights on Broadway by an American dramatist. And yet, there was a rough kind of tension to this story of two brothers who loved the same girl and mismanaged their lives—one a poetic dreamer who mistakenly tried to run a farm and married the girl, the other a practical farmer who wasted his life at sea. It gripped the first Broadway audience, which included O'Neill's father and his mother who had only lately broken herself of drug addiction. But the dramatist thought after the opening performance that he had failed.

Much to O'Neill's surprise, most of the critics were enthusiastic and all were respectful. The leaders, Alexander Woollcott in the New York *Times* and Heywood Broun in the New York *Tribune*, were complimentary. To Woollcott, the play was "an absorbing, significant, and memorable tragedy," which had made the theatrical season "immeasurably richer and more substantial." Broun wrote that it was "a significant and interesting play by a young author who does not as yet know all the tricks." Others were less restrained. In the New York *Telegram*, Robert Gilbert Welsh termed the play "a masterpiece" while Charles Darnton in the New York Evening *World* hailed "the advent of an American realist who promises to go far."

The O'Neill drama began drawing such crowds that Williams closed the Elmer Rice play and concentrated on Richard Bennett's starring role in *Beyond the Horizon*, which ran for 111 performances and shifted theaters several times. But if recognition came to the dramatist on Broadway with evident ease, it was quite another story two months later as the Pulitzer Prize Drama Jury deliberated.

The first indication that something was amiss on Morningside Heights came in a letter in mid-April from Hamlin Garland to the Columbia University secretary, Frank D. Fackenthal:

"Did you see MacKaye's *Washington?* I did not get back from the

South in time but my wife saw it and thought it admirable. *Beyond the Horizon* is a powerful piece of work but I am not sure of the man's motive. It seemed to me ruthless for the sake of ruthlessness. I did not feel just the quality a prize play should have. If the Committee can agree on MacKaye's *Washington* I will vote for it for I have read the play and I know how high the work is. I shall see the other men soon."

Garland, however, couldn't get the votes for Percy MacKaye's ballad play, *Washington*, starring Walter Hampden, which was neither a critical nor a popular success. Still, despite his own reputation as a realist, the sage of Middle America couldn't accept O'Neill's realistic treatment of a sensitive human theme without gagging. Soon he wrote again to Fackenthal, conceding that *Beyond the Horizon* was the "only outstanding play" but complaining that it could not be called "ennobling." He continued:

"If you have not seen *Beyond the Horizon* it would be a safe thing to see as there is much discussion of it. Most of even the good plays like *Clarence* and *Shavings* are just pleasant entertainments. MacKaye's *Washington* is the only one that has dignity and beauty of appeal, and that alas I was unable to see."

One of the things that bothered Garland was the specification for the Drama Prize: "For the original American play, performed in New York, which shall best represent the educational value and power of the stage in raising the standard of good morals, good taste, and good manners." But beyond that, his correspondence only thinly conceals his active dislike of O'Neill as a dramatist, a prejudice he shared with the original Drama Jury chairman, Augustus Thomas, who served in 1917 and 1918.

Garland tried to win support from Clayton Hamilton, who had been drama critic for the *Forum*, *Bookman*, and *Vogue* and had produced and written plays with A. E. Thomas. But Hamilton responded: "Burton has left for the west on a long lecture tour; but I saw him twice before he went away. He believes unfalteringly that *Beyond the Horizon* by Eugene G. O'Neill is the best American play of the season and probably the best American play that ever has been written, and in this opinion I concur."

Seemingly, that was enough for Garland, for on April 26 he wrote to Fackenthal:

"With Burton, Hamilton, Montrose Moses and most of the critics agreed on O'Neill's *Beyond the Horizon*, I am ready to add my vote. The play is powerful and American and significant. I've no doubt Eaton will be enthusiastically for it. As soon as I hear from him, I shall write a formal note."

Eaton, who had been drama critic for the New York *Sun* and the New York *Tribune* and was an eminent authority on the American stage, soon dispatched his enthusiastic approval of the O'Neill play, which caused Garland to send his report to Fackenthal on April 30 as follows:

"The enclosed letter from Mr. Eaton concludes the poll of the committee. Up to the present moment, *Beyond the Horizon* by Eugene O'Neill has no competitor as 'the outstanding play of the season.' It is not an 'uplifting' play in the terms of the Pulitzer bequest but it is highly significant and I will join the other members in commending it for the prize although I am still in doubt about the author's motive. It certainly is not a mere 'show' and could not have been compared with any commercial success in mind. It is well written and presents some of the literary characteristics which have made the short stories of Mary Wilkins Freeman so honorably representative of village New England."

It was apparent, in pointing out that the O'Neill play had no competitor "up to the present moment," that Garland was still hoping for something else to come along. He gave O'Neill another dig in a note of May 6 enclosing a strong letter from Burton for *Beyond the Horizon*, observing, "I wish his play did not go quite so far in its depressing delineation of a decaying family." Finally, five days later, in a letter to President Butler, he announced that he had tried in vain to swing the jury into a consideration of another new play, *Abraham Lincoln*, by the British dramatist, John Drinkwater. He wrote:

> The Committee was deeply disturbed by my test query as to whether they would be willing to give the prize to Drinkwater, provided the terms of the bequest permitted it. The Committee said that such an award would be a rebuff of American authorship and act in a way directly opposite to the intention of the donor of the Endowment. The Committee is almost a unit in favor of *Beyond the Horizon*, Eugene O'Neill's play. Dr. Burton and Walter Eaton are very emphatic on the choice, and they are supported by Clayton Hamilton and Montrose Moses, two of our best informed men. So far as my own judgment is concerned, I cannot bring myself to vote for a prize to a mere entertainment such as most of the successful plays are, and yet I cannot regard O'Neill's play as "noble"

or "uplifting" which are I believe the expressed terms of the
bequest. Nevertheless as it is the outstanding play of the season
thus far, I will join in the award.

Butler himself probably raised the issue of the Drinkwater play before
the Advisory Board. Whether he did it to save face for Garland or
whether he himself had some reason for not wishing to give full honors
to O'Neill's play could not be determined either from the minutes of the
Advisory Board meeting of May 20, 1920, or his own voluminous correspondence in the Pulitzer Prize papers. But even though the Board
agreed with the Drama Jury and recommended *Beyond the Horizon* for the
prize, it approved the following statement for issuance at the time of the
announcement:

"The Advisory Board recorded their high appreciation of *Abraham Lincoln*, by John Drinkwater, and regretted that by reason of its foreign
authorship, this play was not eligible for consideration in connection
with the award."

Without further ado, the university Trustees voted to give O'Neill his
first Pulitzer Prize and announced it on June 3. His reaction, as he later
recalled, was ambivalent:

"In 1920 I had honestly never heard of the Pulitzer Prize, or if I had,
hadn't listened. So when a wire reached me . . . saying I had won it,
my reaction was a disdainful raspberry—'Oh, a damned medal! And one
of those presentation ceremonies! I won't accept it! (I have never been
fond of medals or ceremonies.)

"Then a wire from my agent arrived which spoke of a thousand dollars
and no medal and no ceremony. Well, I practically went delirious! I was
broke or nearly. A thousand dollars was sure a thousand dollars! It was
the most astoundingly pleasant surprise I've ever had in my life, I
think."

To a friend, he was somewhat more complimentary about the aes-
thetic value of the prize but he was far from overawed. "Can you imagine me at the point where Columbia University actually confers one of
its biggest blue ribbons on me?" he asked. "And the funniest part of it is
that I never knew that such a prize existed until I received a wire . . .
saying I had won it."

In his formal response to Columbia following his notification, he was
polite and proper:

It is with a deep feeling of gratitude that I wish to thank the
University for awarding the Pulitzer Prize to my play, *Beyond the
Horizon*. I can only say that this honor is an added stimulus to me
to keep my future work on a high plane of artistic integrity in harmony with the fine purpose for which the prize was founded and
the admirable standard of worth it demands.

All my gratitude!

He signed with a flourish, including his middle initial, G. For Glad-
stone, which he soon dropped. It was the beginning of a long and profitable relationship between O'Neill and the university, for he was to win
two more Pulitzer Prizes in his lifetime and one posthumously for his
bitter and tragic evocation of his family's life, *Long Day's Journey into
Night*. The Nobel Prize came to him in 1936, eight years after his third
Pulitzer Prize, making him the first American dramatist to be honored
with such international recognition.

Whatever the effect of the Pulitzer Prize may have been on O'Neill's
career, the internal fight that was waged over his first award had important consequences for the Advisory Board and the jury system and probably for Columbia as well. For the jury, in ignoring what Garland called
the "noble" and "uplifting" terminology that Joseph Pulitzer had drafted
for the drama prize, pointed to the direction in which future awards
would have to go if they were to reflect truthfully the growth of the
American theater.

Not all juries, however, were to demonstrate this kind of independence by making merit the basic condition for the award, rather than the
moral uplift that had been characteristic of older generations. Years were
to elapse before the terminology of the Plan of Award realistically described all the prizes that were bestowed annually by Columbia. Nor
would it be possible in all circumstances to maintain privacy over the differences between the conservatives, basing themselves on a rigidly Cal-
vinistic outlook on life and literature, and the progressives, with their insistence on realism and fidelity to the spirit of a new era. Some of the
infighting was bound to break into the open.

The only semblance of critical comment on the battle over O'Neill
was made some time after the award by Eaton who wrote, while preserving the confidentiality of his status as a juror:

Prizes of this sort do not always have great significance; they
may, for instance, merely mean that all the other plays were pretty

poor. However, it is well remembered that all the other plays were
not pretty poor during the year of the contest and *Beyond the Horizon* was not victor without competition.

That the judges, though, could have hesitated long over their
decision is difficult to imagine, for Mr. O'Neill's drama possesses
so conspicuously one merit over all competitors, the merit of a
tense, driving, emotional sincerity, imparting to the spectator—
when he withdraws a little from the spell of the tragedy—the sense
that the dramatist has been imaginatively at the mercy of his people; not manipulating them so much as being manipulated by
them.

As early as 1918, Paul Elmer More of the Biography Jury had reported to Columbia that he and his colleagues did not want to be bound
strictly by the terminology of the Plan of Award. They did not interpret
the phrase, "American biography," in such a manner as to exclude a
book about the foreign-born John James Audubon, for example; moreover, they believed that the requirement for "teaching patriotic and unselfish services to the people" should be interpreted liberally. The Drama
Jury of 1920, in its award to O'Neill, took a much firmer stand, set what
amounted to its own terms, and was upheld (despite the nod to Drinkwater's *Lincoln*) by the Advisory Board.[17]

There was another argument within the Drama Jury in 1921, but it
wasn't very serious. The principal plays under consideration were a
domestic comedy by Frank Craven, *The First Year*, and Zona Gale's
dramatization of her novel, *Miss Lulu Bett*, a realistic comedy about small
town prejudice and feminine emancipation. Seemingly, the Gale play
was barred by the Plan of Award's insistence on an "original" American
play, being an adaptation, but the jury ignored the requirement for the
first time.

Miss Gale, a Wisconsin-born short story writer and novelist, was then
47 years old. She had begun her career as a newspaperwoman and had
worked briefly on the New York *World*. Her collection of short stories,
Friendship Village, an idealization of small town life, had brought her to
public attention but her far more realistic novel, *Miss Lulu Bett*, had made
her reputation. Professor William Lyon Phelps, a member of the Fiction
Jury of 1920, had even tried to persuade the Advisory Board to bestow
the fiction award for that year upon Miss Gale. The Board, however,
regretfully pointed out that only novels published in 1919 could be con-

sidered, whereas the Gale novel had been published in 1920. There was
no award for 1920.

Miss Gale was a prodigious worker. In eight days, she turned out the
stage version of her novel, a successful play that opened December 27,
1920, at the Belmont Theater and ran for 176 performances. The critics
didn't exactly turn handsprings; furthermore, when Miss Gale within a
week provided a new third act and a happy ending, the outlook for an artistic triumph did not seem to be enhanced. As perceptive a critic as
Robert Benchley in *Life* called the play "great because of its pitiless fidelity to everyday people and everyday life," although he added with a
twist of the critical knife that "it takes an artist to be dull on purpose."

The jury that included Hamlin Garland as chairman, Professor
Phelps, and Richard Burton had its troubles. At first, Garland and Bur-
ton were inclined to give the prize to Craven's *The First Year*, but, as
Garland wrote later, "Phelps will not listen to it." For a time Phelps and
Burton even thought of voting for a play that was not among the season's
successes, *Nemesis*, and Garland would have reluctantly joined them
rather than miss another award. Then came the swing to *Miss Lulu Bett*.
Garland wrote to Fackenthal:

"Feeling that it would be a handsome thing to give the prize to a
woman, Burton will join Phelps and me in giving the award to *Lulu Bett*.

"*Lulu Bett* is not a great play, but it is original and interesting, and
Miss Gale is a woman to whom such an honor can go with justice. I
know her intimately and I know her work in fiction as well as in the
drama. As the award has not gone to a woman before perhaps it would
be a graceful concession to give her this year's prize. I leave the matter in
the hands of your Advisory Committee." [18]

The Advisory Board had no objection and Miss Gale won the prize.

Eugene O'Neill once again became an active contender for the Pulitzer
Prize in 1922 with a more conventional play, *Anna Christie*, which did
not please the critics as much as his earlier work because of what seemed
to be an unconvincing happy ending. While the reviews were favorable
on the whole, the notion that a prostitute could be reclaimed from a
squalid life in a sordid waterfront saloon and sent into the arms of a
stalwart sailor at the final curtain did not ring true. But O'Neill argued
in reply that the happy ending was an illusion, that "dat ole davil,
sea"—his symbol for fate—would in the end overwhelm Anna, her

lover, and her tugboat captain father. It was much the same type of response that George Bernard Shaw made when his critics reproached him for letting Eliza make up to Professor Higgins at the end of *Pygmalion*.

O'Neill had come a long way in the two years since his first Pulitzer Prize for *Beyond the Horizon*. His tour de force, *The Emperor Jones*, had made a deep impression and even his lesser plays—including *Diff'rent*, *Gold*, *The Straw*, and an outright failure, *The First Man*—had been interesting. The dramatist now was far beyond the ecstasy of having received $1,000 with the Pulitzer Prize; but, while his financial situation had improved, his drinking habits had not. He had become a familiar figure in the prohibition era bars of lower Manhattan, some of which he was to make famous in plays of a later era. He had even acquired his own bootlegger, a sign of prestige in the swinging New York of his middle years. His father had died and his mother was dying; his first marriage was showing signs of strain. But with the frenzied single-mindedness of the supreme artist, he let nothing interfere with his work. He produced. He worried about the staging of his plays. He jousted with the critics. And with the opening of *Anna Christie* on November 2, 1921, at the Vanderbilt Theater, where it ran for 177 performances, he should have been pleased with his progress. But he wasn't.

The New York Evening *Post*'s J. Ranken Towse was typical of the critics who made O'Neill furious. Towse had written that the play was "a remarkable work for a young man but something that falls a good way short of a masterpiece," principally because of the use of "the most violent expedients to bring about a happy ending." The *World*'s critic, too, thought the story had been "tampered with." Even Alexander Woollcott in the *Times*, an O'Neill supporter from the beginning, believed the play less than the dramatist's best although he called it a "rich and salty play that grips the attention with the rise of the first curtain and holds it fiercely to the end."

O'Neill fired back: ". . . . To those who think I deliberately distorted my last act because a 'happy ending' would be calculated to make the play more of a popular success, I have only this to say: The sad truth is that you have precedents enough and to spare in the history of our drama for such a suspicion. But, on the other hand, you have every reason not to believe it of me."

There was worse to come. On March 4, 1922, *The First Man* opened at the Neighborhood Playhouse with the critics all against it. Five days later, at the Provincetown Playhouse, *The Hairy Ape* opened with the rough, gravel-voiced Louis Wolheim playing the part of "Yank," who became frantic because he "didn't belong"—in O'Neill's mind the prototype of Everyman. That same night his mother's body arrived by train from California, where she had died, which was distracting enough. But when the critics seemed to O'Neill to have misunderstood his message, he was downright angry and kept explaining to all who would read or listen that this was not a tract, but an expressionistic play.

There was another who misconstrued O'Neill's intentions—the Police Commissioner of New York City. For the department, in its wisdom, sent charges to the Chief Magistrate that *The Hairy Ape* is "obscene, indecent, and impure" and threatened to close it down. But when the city's editorial pages reacted in furious protest, the police backed down. However, at Columbia University, George C. D. Odell, a professor of English, gravely accused O'Neill of debasing the stage and stimulating the use of profanity in the American theater.

It was at just about this juncture that the Pulitzer Prize Drama Jury began its annual deliberations. In 1922, it consisted of Hamlin Garland and Jesse Lynch Williams, who had won the first drama prize awarded, with Professor Phelps as chairman. It was to be expected that Garland would be repelled by the scene, the concept, and the principal character of *Anna Christie* and he was; in fact, the stern old Midwesterner didn't even see the play. In two crisp, succinct paragraphs, Phelps gave the jury's verdict:

"Mr. Jesse Lynch Williams and I vote for *Anna Christie* by Eugene O'Neill. In our opinion this deserves the prize for the best play of the year, and we have no second choice; in fact we are quite strongly of the opinion that the prize should not be given to any other play.

"Mr. Hamlin Garland has not seen *Anna Christie* but feels sure that he would not like it and will not vote for it. He has no other play to suggest and in his opinion the prize should not be given at all; he thinks that it would be better for the interests of the drama that no prize should be given this year. Mr. Williams and I feel, on the contrary, first, that it is exceedingly important that the prize should be given, and second, that it should be given to *Anna Christie*."

Even after Garland saw *Anna Christie*, his opinion was unchanged. He wrote to Professor Brander Matthews at Columbia that it would be "absurd" to give a prize to O'Neill for a play that was not as good as *Beyond the Horizon*. Worse still, the sage believed the Pulitzer Prizes would be "cheapened" if an award were given "to plays not entirely worthy of it."

Garland lost the decision, however. Phelps's championship of O'Neill was upheld by both the Advisory Board and the Trustees. In addition, the enthusiastic Yale professor besought Columbia to try to do something more to publicize the drama prize.

Phelps's wish was to be fulfilled, although not precisely in the manner in which he intended. Irate juries and even angrier critics would see to that. But when the prize for *Anna Christie* was announced on May 21, 1922—O'Neill's second in the first five years of the awards—it received nothing but applause and a gratifying amount of publicity. O'Neill remarked playfully to a friend:

"Yes, I seem to be becoming the Prize Pup of Playwriting—the Hot Dog of the Drama. When the Police Department isn't pinning the Obscenity Medal on my Hairy Ape chest, why, then it's Columbia adorning the brazen bosom of Anna with the Cross of Purity. I begin to feel that there is either something all wrong with me or something all right. . . . 'It's a mad world, my masters! ' "

That same day he wrote to Columbia:

"I wish to express my deep appreciation of the honor of being awarded the Pulitzer Prize for the second time. This encourages me immensely; for to me it means that in the eyes of others competent to judge justly my own opinion of my work is sustained—that I have 'hewed to the line' set by *Beyond the Horizon* and not strayed therefrom or fallen by the wayside."

There is a footnote to these first two prizes. Evidently pleased that Columbia and the Pulitzer Board and Drama Jury had vindicated his own good opinion of *Anna Christie*, O'Neill sent the manuscript of *The Straw*, a play over which he had labored with little result and critical indifference, to the university. There was no particular reason for him to do so; nor, for that matter, was there anything the university could do about it. Fackenthal returned it to him in the summer of 1922 with a note that the manuscript of *Anna Christie* was being permanently preserved in the Pulitzer Prize collection at Columbia.

This was the manner in which O'Neill emerged as the founder of the modern American drama, the most powerful and influential dramatist in American theatrical history. As George Jean Nathan once observed,

"Alone and single-handed, [he] waded through the dismal swamplands of American drama, bleak, squashy, and oozing sticky goo, and alone and single-handed bore out of them the water lily that no American had found before him." And Brooks Atkinson wrote: "O'Neill . . . transformed the backward American drama into a form of literature and art." These are judgments that four Pulitzer Prizes sustained.[19]

4
The Novel: Whole or Wholesome?

A 39-year-old professor of English at the University of Illinois, serving for the first time on a Pulitzer Prize Fiction Jury, became deeply concerned in 1920 over the problem of choosing a novel of merit that would conform to the terms of the Plan of Award. He was Stuart Pratt Sherman, an Iowa-born graduate of Williams who had earned his Ph.D. at Harvard and was soon to become editor of the New York *Herald Tribune*'s literary section. He had thought of recommending Joseph Hergesheimer's *Java Head* for the prize until he re-read the terms of the Plan of Award: "For the American novel published during the year which shall best present the wholesome atmosphere of American life, and the highest standard of American manners and manhood."

In a letter to Judge Robert Grant, a Boston jurist and sometime novelist who was the Fiction Jury's chairman that year, Sherman agreed that the Hergesheimer novel "doesn't at all obviously conform" to the conditions of the award but protested:

"If the jury sticks to the letter of these conditions, will it not make itself a laughing stock to the younger generation? . . . We ought not to crown a licentious work, but I don't believe we should hold off till a novel appears fit for a Sunday School library."

Sherman's argument for a loose interpretation of the rules was rejected. Judge Grant wrote to President Butler that the jury, with Professor William Lyon Phelps of Yale as the third member, had agreed that there should be no award for a novel published in 1919.

Had Professor Sherman examined the text of Pulitzer's own specifications for the novel prize in the will of April 16, 1904, he would have found that what the publisher wanted was a prize novel that would represent "the *whole* atmosphere of American life" (italics added). At the

Advisory Board's meeting of May 24, 1915, it approved the Plan of Award for the Pulitzer Prizes in substantially the same form as the wording of Pulitzer's will. But on June 10, 1915, when President Butler presented the Plan of Award to the university's Trustees and the executors of the Pulitzer estate, he included in it amendments that he called "slight" and "insubstantial." Apparently, he had made them himself. The only one that affected the specifications for the prizes was the change in the fiction award from "whole" to "wholesome"—which was carefully indicated with the added four letters being printed in italics. It was, as the discerning critic John K. Hutchens said long afterward, the difference between Theodore Dreiser and Booth Tarkington.

Evidently, the Pulitzer executors must have had their doubts. They asked Butler to refer this change, with the rest, to the Advisory Board for its approval. The president, never one to leave anything to chance, wrote individually to the Board members on June 22, 1915, enclosing a revised, printed Plan of Award dated June 10, 1915, and asking them to agree to it. They did, without argument.

What prompted Butler's historic afterthought remains a mystery. But after the requirement for "wholesome" fiction went into the Plan of Award, it remained there from the beginning in 1917 until the year after the public brawl over Sinclair Lewis' refusal to accept a Pulitzer Prize for *Arrowsmith* in 1926. In 1927, without comment or explanation, the "wholesome" phraseology was quietly dropped and Pulitzer's original stress on the "whole atmosphere of American life" was restored.

The only reference to the change in the Pulitzer Prize papers that has come to light, after diligent search, is a memo from Fackenthal to Butler on February 6, 1931, saying:

"We have almost from the first been in difficulties with the Pulitzer Novel Prize. In some way, we got into our documents a definition of the Prize which indicated that the award should go to 'the American novel . . . which shall best present the *wholesome* atmosphere of American life and the highest standard of American manners and manhood.' The 'wholesome' was a typographical error, but even so it is difficult in this day to reconcile some of the awards with the definition, even in its correct form."

There is no record of a reply by Butler. Evidently, if Fackenthal chose to define the change as a typographical error, the president was willing to let it go at that. It could be argued in his defense that Pulitzer's emphasis on "the highest standard of American manners and manhood" would have handcuffed juries almost as much as the change from "whole" to "wholesome." But in any event, a truly conscientious juror like Professor Sherman would have had a better argument in the early days of the prizes for awards to novels that were made of sterner stuff.[20]

It was foreordained that the first Fiction Jury would have its troubles finding a respectable prize winner that was also "wholesome" in the Butlerian sense. To complicate the problem, only five books published in 1916 were submitted to the jury for 1917, which consisted of Judge Grant, Professor Phelps, and William Morton Payne, former literary editor of the Chicago *Daily News*. It was, to be sure, not a vintage year for the American novel which, with a few brilliant exceptions, was almost as encrusted with the Victorian prejudices of the age as was the theater. However, the judges might have considered a struggling young novelist, Sherwood Anderson, for his first novel, *Windy McPherson's Son*. Or they could have rewarded two writers of greater eminence, William Dean Howells for his *The Leatherwood God* or Ellen Glasgow for her *Life and Gabriella*. These novels, however, were not considered sufficiently distinctive for the prize and the jury passed the award.

The same jury came up with a winner the following year, recommending the first Pulitzer Prize in Fiction for *His Family* by Ernest Poole. The book had not made anything like the impression of Poole's earlier and more successful work, *The Harbor*, which was similar in spirit to the Edward Bellamy–Jack London type of sentimental Socialism. So, while *His Family* carried off the award, there wasn't much of a stir about it.

Messrs. Grant, Phelps, and Payne struggled with their problem again in 1919, but twice notified Fackenthal that they had not been able to decide on a winner. However, on the day after the Advisory Board had again passed the novel award, Fackenthal received a note from Professor Phelps proposing Booth Tarkington's *The Magnificent Ambersons*. Judge Grant was willing to go along, rather than not award a prize.

As soon as Butler learned of the suggestion, he fired off telegrams to each member of the Advisory Board and drew unanimous approval for *The Magnificent Ambersons*. It was, accordingly, enshrined as the fiction

winner for 1919 at Columbia's commencement.[21] But in 1920 once
again, despite Professor Sherman's fight for *Java Head*, the award was
passed. *Java Head* hadn't been "wholesome" enough.

The issue posed by Sherman finally broke into the open with the
publication of Sinclair Lewis' *Main Street*, the most controversial book of
1920, which attacked the *mores* of Middle America and tore apart the
hitherto sacred values of the people of its small towns. By a coincidence,
one of Lewis' earliest literary heroes, the crusty Hamlin Garland, was
the chairman in 1921 of both the Fiction and Drama Juries. As a virtual
beginner, Lewis had once written an admiring note to the sage and in
1917 had been enthusiastic in praising *Son of the Middle Border*. "Nowhere
else," he assured Garland in a letter, "may be found a more convincing
picture of the Middle Border as it was in the making."

Garland was 60 years old when he was the chairman of the Fiction
Jury that considered *Main Street* and the other novels of 1920. Lewis was
35. Their beginnings had been similar. Garland, born near West Salem,
Wis., had had a difficult youth in Iowa and the Dakotas before going to
Boston to begin his career as a writer. Lewis, born in Sauk Center,
Minn., had been more fortunate—a graduate of Yale, but he, too, had
begun in Iowa as a small-town newspaperman and battled his way to
success in the East.

There, however, the similarity between the two men ended; Garland
had been a realist, but he wasn't at all taken with Lewis' iconoclastic
brand of realism. For what Lewis wrote now angered and sickened the
older man. He was so outraged when he read *Main Street* that he asked
Henry Seidel Canby, editor of the New York *Evening Post*'s *Literary
Review*, to denounce writers who, like Lewis, were "belittling the descendants of the old frontier."

Canby refused. Lewis, despite his awkward style and his tendency to
sketch cartoons rather than full-scale characters, had touched something
vital in America and people had responded by rushing to buy his works.
The old values were toppling in the postwar world. And Lewis, by giving them a lusty shove, had become internationally famous as an American satirist.

Garland, however, still kept his guard up against Lewis and the other
infidels. In general, the sage found American literature surrendering to
the libertines. In particular, he held *Main Street* to be "vicious and venge-

ful" and accused Lewis of "taking it out on the small Middle Western town." As late as March 1921 he was writing, "All the novels I have read recently are lacking in style, workmanship. I cannot vote a prize to any of them." And on May 22, in the Drama Jury's report, he added: "Personally, I do not feel deep enthusiasm for any of the plays and novels of the year. Not one has in it the element of greatness. Not one really stands out in a commanding position."

Yet, Garland joined in the Fiction Jury's vote for *Main Street*, according to his colleagues, Stuart Pratt Sherman and Professor Robert Morss Lovett of the University of Chicago, a former editor of *The Dial*. If the sage submitted a minority report or spoke privately to President Butler, as Lewis himself always suspected, there is no indication of it in the records. The Fiction report to the Board, at its meeting on May 24, 1921, was for *Main Street*.

As the minutes of the session dryly recorded, there was "considerable discussion" of *Main Street*. It takes very little imagination, even without a specific report, to conjecture that President Butler was concerned over the question of whether the Lewis novel matched the "wholesome" specification for the fiction award. And it must have been equally apparent to the Board's membership that Butler shared Garland's essentially conservative views of the work that was being judged. In any event, the Board unanimously overturned the jury's proposal of *Main Street* and decided by a split vote to give the prize to Edith Wharton's *The Age of Innocence*, which also had been favorably mentioned in the report.

Professors Sherman and Lovett publicly protested in *The New Republic*, of which the latter was a staff member, when the reversal became known. There is no record that Garland ever said or did anything to support his fellow jurors, however. He maintained a discreet silence.

Lovett, in his letter to the editor headed, "The Pulitzer Prize," paid his respects to Mrs. Wharton as the *grande dame* of American letters, saying that "no one will regret" the award to *The Age of Innocence*. But, he went on, the public had a right to know that the Wharton award was made in the face of a jury recommendation for *Main Street*. Neither Lovett nor Sherman threatened publicly to resign from a jury to which they had not yet been reappointed, an awkward action to which some protestors later resorted. They merely wanted the record to show what actually had happened.

Despite the row, Sherman was asked to be chairman of the Fiction

Jury in the following year. Naturally enough, he asked for assurance that a unanimous verdict of the jury would not be vetoed "by an unexplained action" of the Advisory Board. The ever-diplomatic Fackenthal gave him the assurance and sent with it an explanation that convinced him the Advisory Board "had not been at fault." With that rather enigmatic observation, the authorities on Morningside apparently hoped that the affair would be closed.

It wasn't.

Mrs. Wharton, after reacting initially with pleasure over her Pulitzer Prize, which she called a "Virtue Prize," was appalled when she learned of the circumstances under which she had been honored. In a minor work called *Hudson River Bracketed*, which she later wrote, she ridiculed a "Pulsifer Prize" that was taken away from her hero. She was pleased, however, when Sinclair Lewis gallantly dedicated *Babbitt* to her.[22]

In retrospect, *The Age of Innocence* has outlasted the vogue of *Main Street*. Mrs. Wharton's book is still recognized as a classic, while Lewis' is sadly dated in an era when the Gopher Prairies of America are bound by television to New York, Chicago, Los Angeles, and Washington, D.C. Curiously, both novels reflected accurately in their day the decline of a particular part of American society—the know-nothing small towners that Lewis portrayed and the snobbish aristocrats of old New York whom Mrs. Wharton knew so well.[23] True, *The Age of Innocence* has proved to be the better book but that was not the point the judges made. And because the point was ignored, the arguments over the prizes increased.

It is difficult, more than a half-century later, to document President Butler's position in the controversy. But if the Advisory Board was not primarily responsible for the reversal of the Fiction Jury, as Fackenthal assured Sherman, then obviously it was the strong-minded Butler who insisted on barring *Main Street* from a Pulitzer Prize. He took very seriously his role as an overseer of what he considered to be the best in American literature. On a later occasion, he was to bar another of the nation's outstanding novelists from a Pulitzer Prize by threatening to overrule the Advisory Board itself.

Whatever the future was to bring, peace was restored to Morningside in 1922. The Fiction Jury—Professor Sherman, chairman; Professor Jefferson B. Fletcher of Columbia; and the Rev. Samuel M. Crothers, a

Unitarian clergyman—successfully proposed Booth Tarkington's *Alice Adams* for the Fiction award that year. With Fletcher as chairman and Dr. Crothers and Professor Bliss Perry of Harvard as members, the 1923 Fiction Jury rejected Sinclair Lewis' *Babbitt*, a lampoon of American business. Instead, they voted "without enthusiasm," as Professor Fletcher wrote, to give the prize for 1923 to another major American novelist, Willa Cather, for *One of Ours*. He added: "We are of the opinion that Miss Cather's novel, imperfect as we think it in many respects, is yet the most worth while of any in the field."

This time, Lewis said that he didn't "care a hang." [24]

5

History: The Aristocrats

In a moment of pedagogical grandeur, Henry Adams once informed his publisher that history is "the most aristocratic of all literary pursuits." With magnificent disdain for the lower literary orders, among which his less fortunate colleagues labored to earn their living, he proclaimed that if the writing of history ever became profitable, "the luxury of its social distinction would vanish."

Adams accurately reflected the nature of the conservative historical scholarship of his time, which so critically influenced the beginnings of the Pulitzer Prizes in both history and biography. The older generation of American historians, the distinguished amateurs, had been accustomed to write about their country in the romantic, uplifting tradition of George Bancroft and Francis Parkman; and, although dazzled by the style and scholarship of John Lothrop Motley and William Hickling Prescott, few others had tried to write significantly about lands other than their own.

Mostly, they had been content with the heroic American imagery of their elders. Indeed, for those like Bancroft who were determined on deeper research, they found the expense to be a considerable burden. Thus the historian, in Adams' words, had to be "rich as well as educated" if he intended to amount to much. [25]

Not many had been formally trained to write history, but some had entered academe and helped to create the professional historians of later years who often broke with tradition. From the triangle of learning formed by Boston, New York, and Baltimore, in which Princeton and New Haven were included, the professional emerged slowly, even haltingly, and aspired to become more national and flexible in character. The swift growth of the American university system may have stimulated the development of the professional, but it was years before he was able to overcome criticism of his tendency toward empty pedantry and dreary prose. An eminent amateur, Theodore Roosevelt, once wrote contemptuously of the "painstaking little pedants" whose conceit had made them "distinctly noxious" and concluded: "They solemnly believed that if there were enough of them, and that if they only collected enough facts of all kinds and sorts, there would cease to be any need hereafter for greater writers, great thinkers." [26]

The professional historian, nevertheless, had established himself as a force in academe by the time the first Pulitzer History Prize was awarded, but control of the honor at first rested mainly with those who espoused the genteel tradition. There were two reasons for this. First, Nicholas Murray Butler was scarcely the type of educator who would have accepted at once the progressive, revisionist historians. He had had trouble enough with Charles A. Beard, the most formidable of the breed. Equally as important as Butler's conservatism was the discouraging reality, of which Frank D. Fackenthal complained, that few American historians were members of the American Academy of Arts and Letters, from which the early jurors were drawn. Even when members of the affiliated National Institute of Arts and Letters were included, the pool still was too small to make much difference.

It fell, therefore, to Professor Barrett Wendell of Harvard to set the pattern for the first awards in history as the jury chairman from 1917 through 1920. Wendell was Boston-born, Harvard-educated, and a lifelong teacher of history at Harvard, the first to conduct a class in American literary history at Harvard and the author, in 1900, of *A Literary History of America*. He was also the teacher of a whole generation of professional historians, among them his successor as a major American literary historian, Vernon Louis Parrington.

Wendell's associates on the History Juries in the early years were men who were very much to his liking. From 1917 through 1920, they included: Worthington C. Ford, editor of the Massachusetts Historical Society, 1917–1920; John H. Finley, editor-to-be of the New York *Times*,

1917–1918; and Henry Dwight Sedgwick, a Harvard law graduate turned historian, 1919–1920. In 1921, the biographer-historian, William Roscoe Thayer, editor of the *Harvard Graduates' Magazine* for twenty-three years, was the chairman for one year. He was succeeded by Ford, who had continued as a jury member in 1921 and who served as chairman in 1922–1923. Ford's associates were John Bach McMaster, who had turned from engineering to become a professor of history at the University of Pennsylvania, 1921–1922–1923, and a Columbia history professor, Charles Downer Hazen, 1922–1923.

The cult of the gentleman amateur dominated the Pulitzer Prize selections of this group, beginning with Ambassador Jusserand's *With Americans of Past and Present Days* in 1917. They blandly overlooked the underlying theme of Pulitzer's will that Americans should be honored, since it was not specifically stated in the terms of the history award. But in 1918, they singled out James Ford Rhodes's *A History of the Civil War*, a truly distinguished work, and passed in 1919 when they could find nothing to match it. Their other recommendations were Justin Harvey Smith's *The War With Mexico* for 1920, Rear Admiral William Sowden Sims's *The Victory at Sea* (in collaboration with Burton J. Hendrick) for 1921, James Truslow Adams' *The Founding of New England* for 1922, and Charles Warren's *The Supreme Court in United States History* for 1923.

No one on the Advisory Board raised a question about any of these works, for they were considered eminently satisfactory selections at the time. Some, in fact, still have the respect of professional historians of various persuasions and at least one, the Rhodes work, is still recommended reading for students of American history.

It is remarkable that Rhodes, Smith, Adams, Warren, and Hendrick, Admiral Sims's collaborator, all were self-made historians who came into the profession from a variety of other endeavors.

Rhodes, who made a fortune in the coal and iron business in Cleveland, turned to the writing of history in 1891 when he moved to Cambridge, Mass. His seven-volume *History of the United States from the Compromise of 1850* established his reputation so that, at the time he won the first Pulitzer History Prize, he was widely and favorably known.

Warren, born in Boston and a Harvard graduate, became a historian after a quarter-century as a highly successful lawyer. His prize-winning work was published when he was 54 years old and for many years was a basic text on the work of the high court.

Smith, born in New Hampshire, spent part of his adult life as a book publisher, first with Scribner's and later as a member of the firm of Ginn & Co., and began writing history upon his retirement in 1898. His Pulitzer Prize work was his first great honor, but he won others as a history professor at Dartmouth, among them the first Loubat Prize in 1923.

Hendrick, who was to win two Pulitzer Prizes in Biography on his own, was born in New Haven, a Yale graduate, a one-time reporter on the New York *Evening Post* and a writer for *McClure's* magazine. He was the Theodore H. White of his time.

Of all these self-made historians, it was James Truslow Adams who emerged as the most successful popularizer of historical writing. To be sure, when he began publishing his work after World War I, he was a part of an American cultural revolution that had attacked sentimentalism and conventional notions in both fiction and drama. A huge new reading audience was being created—one that embraced F. Scott Fitzgerald and Theodore Dreiser; Sinclair Lewis, Ernest Hemingway, and John Dos Passos. It followed that someone who was willing to take a fresh look at American history would be welcomed.

Adams' venture into history, however, was far from deliberate. He was a Brooklyn-born descendant of the Adamses of Virginia, unrelated to the more celebrated branch of the family in Massachusetts, and was educated at Brooklyn Poly and Yale for a career in Wall Street. After serving in military intelligence as a captain in World War I, he found himself unable to go back to the money marts; instead, he planned a massive history of New England in the form of a trilogy.

His approach, at the outset, was conventional. The old German-influenced school of American historian, which had conceived of the town as the basis of American political organization, no longer appeared to be sound to younger historians. Many of them took the approach of the imperialists, who were willing to consider that British policy had a much more dominant influence on the formation of American colonial government than the colonialists themselves. Adams began with the imperial view in his New England history, but it didn't last long. Instead, he ventured into an extensive study of the rise of a sturdy frontier democratic spirit despite the inhibiting force of the leaders of the Puritan theocracy in New England.

Thus, the first volume of the New England trilogy, *The Founding of*

New England, published in 1921, became in effect an attack on the Puritan spirit that was enormously popular in the free-living era after World War I. It was widely read, extravagantly praised, and accepted as a scholarly work worthy of the Pulitzer Prize in History for 1922. From such beginnings, Adams mounted in popular favor with his two succeeding volumes on New England and, in 1931, he became the No. 1 best-selling nonfiction author in the land with his *The Epic of America.* Like H. G. Wells's *Outline of History* and Hendrik Willem Van Loon's *The Story of Mankind,* the *Epic* was a spectacular and well-deserved success.

If James Truslow Adams was unable to maintain his high standing of the 1920s, his decline is understandable. Few popularizers of history are able to extend their vogue even in their own lifetime; moreover, few historians today would be satisfied with Adams' views of the Puritan spirit and its influence.[27] The urge to "debunk" is not enough to sustain a historian for his entire career. Yet, there is reason for Adams to be remembered with gratitude; in a sense, he opened the way for the historical best-seller and a larger public appreciation of such writers as James Harvey Robinson and Van Wyck Brooks, Carl Sandburg and Arnold Toynbee. That was justification, in the earliest years of the Pulitzer Prizes, for Joseph Pulitzer's faith in an award for history.

The vogue for biography in the United States, at the time the Pulitzer Prizes were inaugurated, was even greater than the urge to find different approaches to American history. The American public fairly reveled in highly personal books about the great and the near-great and rewarded the irreverent authors with both wealth and heady praise. At one point, Professor Henry Steele Commager of Columbia, an outstanding scholar, commented bitterly that the biography craze had become "so extreme that history as such has all but disappeared."[28] It wasn't quite that bad, of course. But Commager did have a point when he complained of the excessive effort by otherwise well-intentioned scholars and journalists to feed the public appetite with overwrought biographical sensations.

If the Pulitzer Prizes in Biography avoided this pitfall from 1917 through 1923, their formative period, it was attributable in part to the watchfulness of the Biography Juries. But more important, perhaps, was the very high standard set by two of the early award-winning works, the posthumous prize in 1919 for *The Education of Henry Adams* and the 1920 prize for Albert J. Beveridge's four-volume *The Life of John Marshall.* Both have maintained their standing as major biographical works over the years; without doubt, each will continue to be read with appreciation and respect for years to come. They tower over the other awards for the early period—the Julia Ward Howe biography for 1917; *Benjamin Franklin, Self-Revealed,* by ex-Senator William Cabell Bruce of Maryland, for 1918; *The Americanization of Edward Bok,* by the magazine editor, Edward Bok, for 1921; Hamlin Garland's *A Daughter of the Middle Border,* for 1922; and Burton J. Hendrick's *The Life and Letters of Walter H. Page,* for 1923.

Like the fiction jurors, those in biography were gravely handicapped in their choice of prize-winning works by the conditions in the Plan of Award. There was no question here of any substitution of words, as in the case of fiction, that changed the sense of the award. The biography prize conformed exactly to the specifications laid down in the Pulitzer will—"For the best American biography teaching patriotic and unselfish services to the people, illustrated by eminent example, excluding, as too obvious, the names of George Washington and Abraham Lincoln." It was, in fact, thirty years before the prohibition against biographies of Washington and Lincoln was removed; meanwhile, in 1940, Carl Sandburg's monumental biography of Abraham Lincoln was recognized with a history prize. And it was almost a half-century before events forced a change in the idealistic wording of the Plan of Award for biography.

Professor Paul Elmer More of Princeton, who was biography chairman from 1917 through 1920, may have interpreted the specifications liberally, but neither he nor his successor, Maurice Francis Egan, a Philadelphia teacher, diplomat, and author, could get away from the very real limitation on their range of choice. If there were complaints other than More's in the early years, they were muted.

The jurors, like those in history, came to biography from a wide range of activities. Those who served with More were Professor Edward Channing of Harvard, a distinguished professional historian, 1917 through 1920; Ripley Hitchcock, former New York *Tribune* art critic and a director of Harper & Bros., 1917–1918; and Meredith Nicholson, the novelist, 1919–1920. Egan, who had negotiated the treaty with Denmark under which the Virgin Islands became American possessions, was chairman from 1921 through 1923. In 1921, he worked with Nicholson and Hobart C. Chatfield-Taylor, a Chicago journalist and author; in 1922 and 1923, with William Roscoe Thayer and William Allen White.

Although historians liked to think of biography as their particular province, none of the winners in the formative years of the Pulitzer Prizes was a professional historian. Laura E. Richards, co-author of the biography of her mother, Julia Ward Howe, was a writer of children's books. Messrs. Bruce and Beveridge were former United States Senators. Bok was the editor of the *Ladies' Home Journal*, Garland an author and critic, and Hendrick a journalist. Henry Adams, the most remarkable of all, never considered himself a professional historian and he had no intention, when he began his *Education*, of writing a mere autobiography. He once called the book "an incomplete experience which I shall never finish." Had he known his book would be cited as an example of "patriotic and unselfish services to the people," he would have been embarrassed. But he never lived to receive his Pulitzer Prize.

By birth, education, appearance, and temperament, Henry Adams was an aristocrat and made no apologies for it. He was born in Boston in 1838, the great grandson of President John Adams, the grandson of President John Quincy Adams, and the son of Charles Francis Adams, minister to the Court of St. James's. He was graduated from Harvard in 1858, taught history there for seven years and thought himself a failure at it, edited the *North American Review*, and gradually turned his attention to the writing of history. His nine-volume *History of the United States During the Administrations of Jefferson and Madison*, (1889–1891), became a classic.

His most famous and enduring work, *The Education of Henry Adams*, originated as a part of a lengthy inquiry he had determined to make in order to test his theories about the interaction of science and history. What he did was to study two periods, the first between 1050 and 1250, which he incorporated in his *Mont Saint-Michel and Chartres*, privately printed in 1904, and the second dealing with his own era, which became the *Education*, privately printed in 1906. He distributed 100 copies of the *Education* to his friends and put it aside.

But the book world wasn't willing to let so profound and universal a work slide into neglect. When *Mont Saint-Michel and Chartres* was eventually published to wide critical acclaim, the pressure on Adams mounted to offer the *Education* to the public at large. Finally, on his 77th birthday in 1915, he agreed to permit his friend, Henry Cabot Lodge, the new president of the Massachusetts Historical Society, to supervise posthumous publication of the *Education*. And Ferris Greenslet of Houghton,

Mifflin & Co., the most persistent of publishers' agents, won the contract with this prediction from the author: "You will lose money on it. That will be your punishment."

Adams was wrong. When the *Education* was published six months after his death in Washington, D.C., in 1918, it sold 12,000 copies in three months. The award of the Pulitzer Prize for Biography in 1919 added to its fame. And more than fifty years later, when the *Education* was still being read with respect, the Adams Fund of the Massachusetts Historical Society had well over $50,000 in unexpended royalties.

To Adams' Pulitzer Prize-winning biographer, Professor Ernest Samuels, he was a "pilgrim of power"—"a student hungry for results." Yet throughout his life he thought of himself as a failure in many of his endeavors and he appeared, throughout his *Education*, to be profoundly sorry for himself. To Professor Samuels, this was precisely the reason for the success of the book in appealing to a large and varied public. It was a "triumph of art," he wrote, for Adams to depict himself as a "man of average naïveté for his class, a man of ordinary attainment. . . . In the imagined discovery of his own ignorance and littleness lay the beginning of moral victory." [29]

Adams himself never realized such a moral victory in his lifetime. He once told the philosopher, George Santayana, "I once tried to teach history there [at Harvard] but it can't be done. It really isn't possible to teach anything." In the end, he asked for very little—a quiet old age, "a little sunny and a little sad." [30]

6
Two Poets from Maine

Toward the end of the record of the Advisory Board's meeting on May 24, 1921, at Columbia, there is a dry notation: "It was suggested that a prize ought to be given for verse." Without delay, the Board established an annual award of $1,000 "for the best volume of verse published during the year by an American author."

The motivation for the new prize came from the Poetry Society of America, which had been organized in 1917. It had given an award in 1918 to Sara Teasdale for her *Love Songs* and, in the following year, had bestowed similar recognition on Margaret Widdemer for her *Old Road to*

Paradise and on Carl Sandburg for his *Corn Huskers.* President Butler thought well of the Poetry Society. Being active in the American Academy of Arts and Letters, which he was to head from 1928 to 1941, it was only natural that he would want to do something to stimulate interest in American poets.

Joseph Pulitzer had had little interest in American poetry. While he had quoted Shakespeare and Goethe extensively, and while he had been passionately interested in music and art, he had omitted any mention of poetry from his will. In consequence, there was no poetry prize in the original Plan of Award. Nor was there any particular concern among the newspaper members of the Advisory Board over the omission. Although Walt Whitman had once been editor of the Brooklyn *Eagle* and William Cullen Bryant had served for many years as editor of the New York *Evening Post,* poetry attracted relatively few American journalists.

How, then, could a Board with so little affinity for poetry preside over the annual award of a prize for American poets? The answer was, of course, to set up a knowledgeable jury that would be given a wide latitude of choice and provide it with a strong chairman. Butler did not have to look very far for his chairman. Dean Wilbur Lucius Cross of the Yale Graduate School, "Uncle Toby" to his students, a professor of English at Yale since 1902 and the editor of the *Yale Review,* was both ready and willing to serve. He did so well, in fact, that he remained as chairman of the Pulitzer Prize Jury in Poetry for twenty-five years, including the eight years that he was governor of Connecticut from 1931 to 1939. For the first four years of the poetry prize, from 1922 to 1925, his associates on the jury were Professor Richard Burton, who had previously been a drama juror, and Ferris Greenslet, the Houghton Mifflin editor who had corralled *The Education of Henry Adams* for publication.

There were twenty-eight competitors for the first prize in 1922, among them Edwin Arlington Robinson's *Collected Poems,* Amy Lowell's *Legends,* Edna St. Vincent Millay's *A Few Figs from Thistles* and *Second April,* Ezra Pound's *Poems 1918–1921,* and Conrad Aiken's *Punch: The Immortal Liar.* The jury narrowed the choice to the work of Robinson, Miss Lowell, and Miss Millay and on February 13, 1922, pitted Robinson against Miss Millay. Dean Cross then wrote to Fackenthal: "With the reluctant consent of one member, the Committee recommends that the award be made to *Collected Poems,* by Edwin Arlington Robinson."

Edna St. Vincent Millay won the prize for 1923, even though her work was not submitted in the competition, as Dean Cross duly noted in his report of March 26, 1923. He and his associates, however, availed themselves of the privilege of putting into competition her eight sonnets, published in *American Poetry, 1922,* as well as the two brief volumes they had previously considered in 1921 even though they were technically ineligible. This was the prize package which Dean Cross described as follows in his letter to Fackenthal: "The poems of Miss Millay, for which we recommended the award, are rather slight and few in number, but they do represent, so far as the Committee can discover, the best verse published in 1922." [31]

With the approval of the Advisory Board and the Columbia Trustees, the poems of Robinson and Miss Millay therefore set a standard of sorts for the Pulitzer Prize in Poetry during its earliest years. Except for the coincidence that both poets had been born in Maine and done some of their best work in New York City, they were a study in contrast. Robinson, whose work has been neglected for years, was 53 when he won the prize, his first major recognition. Miss Millay, who had soared to fame at 20 with her first poem, *Renascence,* received her Pulitzer when she was 31. Robinson was a loner, deeply compassionate over the failures and the losers in a mechanistic society, an unhappy man who sat by himself in embarrassment at Mabel Dodge Luhan's lively soirées in Greenwich Village. Miss Millay was a small, fragile beauty with a vivid crown of lovely reddish hair, a "goddess," Floyd Dell called her, who became the golden girl of Greenwich Village and a symbol of the jazz age. Her poetry mirrored the romantic glory and the self-pity of a youthful generation that thought of itself as "lost."

Robinson caught his self-image in the concluding lines of his "Miniver Cheevy," who wept that he was ever born and kept on drinking. [32]

Miss Millay's self-image was in her most famous quatrain, included in one of her Pulitzer Prize-winning works, *A Few Figs from Thistles,* and quoted so often that it was almost her epitaph. Truly, as she wrote, she burned the candle at both ends, and rejoiced in its lovely light. [33]

When the Pulitzer Prize came to Robinson, with its aura of success, he was too old and set in his ways to change his style of life. He refused to be lionized. Nor did he permit any intrusion on his habitual solitude. He had come up the hard way, fearing life and yearning at times for death, showing little faith in his fellow men and even less in women. What he wrote limned the despair of the idealist, the lonely disciple of Ralph Waldo Emerson—the guardian of "the perilous gates of Truth."

Like Henry Adams, Robinson always thought of himself as a failure. But unlike Adams, the poet of despair was born in poverty and struggled all his life, until fame finally came to him too late, for enough money to keep body and soul together. He was the "child of scorn," as he called Miniver Cheevy, born December 22, 1869, in Head Tide, Me., and reared in nearby Gardiner, named Edwin when a man pulled a slip out of a hat, with Arlington added for good measure because the slip-holder came from Arlington, Mass. He was a dropout from Harvard, which he attended for two years. His first privately printed verse, when he was 27 years old, attracted so little attention that he left for New York City to find work, labored in the subway, and often didn't have enough to eat. When he was 35 years old, he had a stroke of luck like one of his literary heroes, Nathaniel Hawthorne, and entered the Customs Service through appointment by President Theodore Roosevelt. Five years later, still struggling to write poetry, he resigned and became a member of the MacDowell Colony in Peterborough, N.H. It was not until he was 47, however, that one of his works, *The Man Against the Sky*, found a wider public and it was six more years before his Pulitzer brought him the acclaim he had always sought, but could not now endure. There were two more Pulitzers yet to come for his longer and more ambitious poems, the last of which, *Tristram*, was to bring him the 1928 prize and more money than he had ever hoped to earn. But, like Cheevy, it didn't make him content with his self-image. And, like Cheevy, he kept on drinking.[34]

The Pulitzer meant a great deal more to Edna St. Vincent Millay. In a burst of enthusiasm when she won the prize, she called it "my thousand bucks which I ain't going to bust for god or hero—going to start a bank account with it." A few weeks later, shortly after her marriage to Eugen Boissevain at Croton-on-Hudson on July 18, 1923, she had to undergo major surgery at a New York hospital and told a friend, "Well, if I die now, I shall be immortal."

If Robinson was the poet of despair and death, Miss Millay's poetry was vibrant with the challenge and defiance of rebellious youth. She had been born February 22, 1892, in Rockland, Me., and given the name of

St. Vincent, patron saint of the sick, as testimony to the fortunate recovery of a cherished uncle at St. Vincent's Hospital. As a child, when her parents were divorced, she lived with relatives in Rockport, Me., and later with her mother in nearby Camden. From the time she was five, she wrote poetry; as a teen-ager, she was published in *St. Nicholas* magazine and at 14 won a gold medal for her work. When she entered a poetry contest at 20 with her first long poem, *Renascence*, it finished fourth but when it was published in a book, *The Lyric Year*, it was hailed as the work of a brilliant young genius. As one critic said, she was the only poet who became famous by *not* winning a prize.

She was soon to make up for it. Friends raised money and sent her to Vassar. The Poetry Society of America gave her a party on her graduation in 1917. And when she joined the Provincetown Players in New York, Greenwich Village took her to its heart. She and her sisters were treated in those joyous years as if they had been visiting royalty. And in a sense they were until after her marriage to Boissevain, a prosperous businessman who built a home for her in the Berkshires and took her from the Village, where she had spent the merriest part of her life.

An admirer, Elizabeth Atkins, wrote in 1936 that Miss Millay was "our most popular and representative poet." Such adulation made her wonder two years later why she had received only one Pulitzer Prize while others, Edwin Arlington Robinson and Robert Frost, had been honored several times. She complained to a friend, Arthur Davison Ficke, that she felt she had been discriminated against because she had been jailed in Boston for demonstrating against the execution of the radicals, Nicola Sacco and Bartolomeo Vanzetti. Robinson and Frost, however, had been more to the liking of the Pulitzer judges, she believed, because of what she called their "blameless lives . . . both sexual and political."

Her judgment was less than generous. A critic, Hyatt H. Waggoner, observed that if she had been able "to think about the matter calmly and self-critically," she might have come up with another explanation: "She probably had never written so well again as she had in the poem which first brought her fame, *Renascence*."

Her candle with its lovely light guttered out slowly in disillusion, as did the mad era in America of which she was so representative.[35]

3
Changing Times,
Changing Awards
1924–1933

1
Journalism: The Public Interest

Oliver Kirby Bovard, managing editor of the St. Louis *Post-Dispatch*, was a stern and righteous man. He pursued the news and sometimes even created it, using his staff with the relentless authority of a general in combat. When he learned on July 29, 1922, that U.S. Marines were clearing unauthorized claimants from the great government oil reservation at Teapot Dome in Wyoming, he assigned his best investigative reporter, Paul Y. Anderson, with instructions to follow the story wherever it led.

Anderson was a digger, one of the most determined and devoted in the profession. He had been a copy boy on the Knoxville *Journal* and a reporter for the same paper at the age of 17. When he came to the *Post-Dispatch* seven years later in 1917, he was long on experience and courage even if he was short on formal education. On his first assignment, the East St. Louis race riots of 1917, he developed evidence that helped send twenty of its leaders to prison. And a year later, when he covered the lynching of a German miner in Collinsville, Ill., he persuaded the mob's chieftain to confess before a coroner's jury.

The Teapot Dome scandal was a much tougher job. In response to reports that Secretary of the Interior Albert B. Fall had granted secret oil leases to companies dominated by Harry F. Sinclair and Edward F. Doheny, millionaire oil promoters, President Warren Gamaliel Harding had rushed to the defense of his crony, saying: "If Albert Fall isn't an honest man, I'm not fit to be President of the United States." The Senate already had begun an investigation at the time of Anderson's assignment, forcing him to make common cause with the leading spirit of the Senate Committee on Public Lands, Thomas J. Walsh, Democratic Senator from Montana.

Soon, Harding was wailing to William Allen White: "My God, this is a hell of a job! I have no trouble with my enemies. But my damn friends, my God-damn friends, White, they're the ones that keep me walking the floor nights!"

Fall resigned on March 3, 1923, at the end of his second year in office, but nobody at the time was able to prove he had done anything wrong in leasing government lands at Teapot Dome to Sinclair and at Elk Hills, Calif., to Doheny. When the former secretary said farewell to President Harding to go to Russia in mid-June with Sinclair in search of more oil leases, the President still thought enough of him to remark cheerfully: "I hope you make some money." They never saw each other again. On August 2, 1923, Harding died in San Francisco upon his return from a trip to Alaska.

Senator Walsh continued to work on the Teapot Dome case, but for a long time Anderson was the only reporter who covered him and the committee's efforts. But even as late as October 23, 1923, when Fall finally was obliged to testify in the Senate's inquiry, he challenged Walsh to produce evidence of wrongdoing. Because the Montana Senator failed to do so, the hearing was put off for a month during which his telephone was tapped, his mail ransacked, his office searched, and his daughter threatened with harm unless the investigation ended.

Walsh remained on the job. Finally, during January 1924 the break came that electrified the Congress and brought the press swarming into the committee room. Doheny admitted at a public hearing that he had loaned Fall $100,000 and others alleged that the former secretary also had received large sums in Liberty Bonds from Sinclair. Now, grim and silent under attack, Fall took the Fifth Amendment while Sinclair challenged the jurisdiction of the Senate and was promptly indicted for contempt.

President Calvin Coolidge, who had come into the White House upon Harding's death, was hard put to re-establish the credibility of the administration he had inherited. First, he appointed two special prosecutors for the Teapot Dome case, Owen J. Roberts and Atlee Pomerene. Next, he forced the resignation of Secretary of the Navy Edwin Denby, who had turned the oil reserves over to Fall's exclusive jurisdiction. Then, Harding's Attorney General, Harry M. Daugherty, who had been involved in numerous other charges of wrongdoing, also had to leave office under fire.

Thus, despite the Democratic outcry over Teapot Dome that was led by the party's presidential nominee in 1924, John W. Davis, President Coolidge was swept into office by a public that already was entranced by the glitter of a booming stock market and easy times. The stain of oil splattered on the White House didn't seem to matter. Nor did grafting in high places seem very exciting to a people titillated by almost daily wars among the gangsters created by prohibition, who fought each other to the death for control of the illicit liquor racket.

After Coolidge's election, almost everybody who had anything to do with the Teapot Dome inquiry was ready to quit. Everybody, except Anderson and Bovard. What they had accomplished in the first stage of the Teapot Dome inquiry was to maintain broad and complete coverage of the case in the *Post-Dispatch*, one of the few newspapers to do so. For this, they had won Walsh's gratitude but there is no evidence that any profound change in public sentiment resulted, even in the *Post-Dispatch's* own circulation area. America, in the midst of its monumental postwar binge of false prosperity, was heedless of almost everything else.

Anderson, backed by Bovard, kept plugging away. At length, during the government's successful action in 1927 to void the Elk Hills and Teapot Dome oil leases before the United States Supreme Court, there was another break in the case. It was brought out that Fall had received $233,500 in Liberty Bonds from a defunct dummy corporation in Canada, the Continental Trading Co., Ltd., which had mysteriously invested more than $3 million in Liberty Bonds. Sinclair had been one of the organizers of the company, but the government was unable at the time to prove a connection that would have involved him in the payment to Fall.

Anderson, spurred by Bovard, tried to get the Justice Department to move, but failed. The reporter then wrote a celebrated article, "Who Got The Bonds?" which the *Post-Dispatch* published on November 12, 1927. It was his contention that Continental's funds had been used to corrupt American government officials and this time he got action. The Senate approved a resolution proposed by Senator George W. Norris of Nebraska under which its Committee on Public Lands reopened the Teapot Dome case.

In January of 1928 Walsh was able at last to establish the connection between Fall and Sinclair through testimony from Fall's son-in-law, Mahlon G. Everhart. The witness had to admit that he took Liberty Bonds from Sinclair and gave them to Fall, but argued the payment was for a one-third interest in Fall's New Mexico ranch. Walsh called it bribery.

Through other witnesses, it was also established that the dummy Canadian corporation had bought and sold oil for the benefit of its organizers, among them some of the most influential figures in the oil industry, with Sinclair alone receiving $757,000. Of this total, testimony showed, more than $200,000 had gone to the Republican National Committee in gifts and loans. The scandal, which Anderson's persistence helped uncover, should have rocked the White House and the Republican Party, but it didn't turn out that way. Despite the best efforts of the Democratic presidential nominee in 1928, Governor Alfred E. Smith of New York, the Republicans elected Herbert Hoover with ease. Their campaign cry of two chickens in every pot, two cars in every garage, had been more alluring to a dollar-chasing public than the cleansing of political pollution in Washington.

With Hoover in the White House in 1929, the Pulitzer Prize for Reporting was awarded to Paul Y. Anderson for his "highly effective work in revealing the disposition of Liberty Bonds in connection with naval oil leases." Anderson was also credited with having framed some of the questions that confounded witnesses in the inquiry and to have helped the government to collect $2 million in back income taxes from various oil promoters in the case. Both the Advisory Board and the university Trustees confirmed the award, the first in which a reporter had dared to oppose the power of the White House.

That same year, Fall at last was found guilty in District of Columbia Supreme Court of accepting a bribe from Doheny and sentenced to a year in jail and a $100,000 fine. Sinclair and Doheny, strangely enough, were acquitted as alleged bribers, but the former went to jail that year anyway for seven and a half months for contempt of the Senate. At the end of October, the financial crash toppled the era of easy money and easy virtue. For a fat, indolent, and heedless America, the party was over.[1]

Not all the crusading journalists of that era were as fortunate as Anderson. Don R. Mellett, editor of the Canton (Ohio) *Daily News*, was shot and killed July 16, 1926, because he had campaigned against police-supported bootlegging, vice, and gambling in Canton.

Within two hours, his paper was on the street with the news of the tragedy and an editorial pledge: "The thoughtful must now know that what Mr. Mellett charged was true. His passing does not mean the end of the battle. The *Daily News* will carry on." And it did, under the leadership of former Governor James M. Cox of Ohio, the owner of the group of which it then was a part. Three ex-convicts and a captain of detectives in the Canton Police Department were arrested, tried, and convicted in connection with the crime. Canton's police chief, S. A. Lengel, also was convicted at his first trial but, upon being granted a retrial, he was acquitted when a key witness refused to testify against him.

The Canton *Daily News* was awarded the 1927 gold medal of the Pulitzer Prize for Public Service "for its brave, patriotic and effective fight for ending the vicious state of affairs brought about by collusion between city authorities and the criminal element, a fight which had a tragic result in the assassination of the editor of the paper, Don R. Mellett."

The battle against the Ku Klux Klan, begun with such fanfare by the New York *World* and the Memphis *Commercial Appeal*, also received continuous encouragement from the Pulitzer Prize juries and Advisory Board. Public service gold medals were awarded to the Columbus (Ga.) *Enquirer Sun* and the Indianapolis *Times* in 1926 and 1928 respectively for their successful attack on the political influence of the Klan. And two editorial writing prizes went to Grover Cleveland Hall, editor of the Montgomery (Ala.) *Advertiser*, and Louis Isaac Jaffe, editor of the Norfolk *Virginian-Pilot*, in 1928 and 1929 respectively for their campaigns against lynching.

The campaigns against graft in local and regional government, which had been of such manifest importance to Joseph Pulitzer during his lifetime, were even more numerous and widespread. Public service gold medals for such crusading went to the New York *Evening World* in 1929, the Atlanta *Constitution* in 1931, the Indianapolis *News* in 1932, and the New York *World-Telegram* in 1933. And John T. Rogers of the St. Louis *Post-Dispatch* won a reporting prize in 1927 for digging up the evidence of improper conduct that led to the impeachment, and later the resignation, of a Federal judge in Illinois.

Despite the essentially conservative character of the Advisory Board and most of the journalism jurors of the period, the strong Pulitzer tradition of support for causes involving civil liberties continued to grow. Not every prize, however, was bestowed for a victory. One of the worthiest of all was for a lost cause.

To the generation that is coming of age today, Nicola Sacco and Bartolomeo Vanzetti are names out of a dusty corner of the history of the Twenties. But to the generation that came of age at the time, they were—to many—symbols of colossal injustice. One could not be neutral about Sacco and Vanzetti, the Italian-born radicals, in the tense, anti-Communist atmosphere of the era, any more than one could be neutral thirty years later about Senator Joseph R. McCarthy Jr., the anti-Communist crusader from Wisconsin. In both instances, they were the product of their times.

From the day Sacco and Vanzetti were indicted in connection with the payroll murder of a shoe factory paymaster and guard on April 15, 1920, at Braintree, Mass., they insisted on their innocence. But in a highly prejudicial atmosphere, a jury before Judge Webster Thayer convicted them in 1921 and for six years thereafter a worldwide conflict of opinion raged unchecked.

It was not popular to plead for justice for Sacco, the shoemaker, and Vanzetti, the fishmonger, anywhere in the United States, but it was least popular of all in Boston. Yet, the Boston *Herald* did not permit itself to be dissuaded from a cool summing up of the weakness of the Sacco-Vanzetti prosecution in an editorial written by F. Lauriston Bullard and published on October 26, 1926. While the *Herald* disclaimed sympathy for the defendants' "half-baked views," it reversed its original position which upheld their conviction. The editorial concluded:

"We hope the Supreme Judicial Court will grant a new trial on the basis of new evidence not yet examined in open court. We hope, in case our supreme branch finds itself unable legally to authorize a new trial, that our governor will call to his aid a commission of distinguished men of the highest intelligence and character to make an independent investigation in his behalf, and that the governor himself at first hand will participate in that examination if, as a last resort, it should be undertaken."

There was no new trial. Instead, the commission suggested by the *Herald* was appointed by Governor Alvan T. Fuller with President A. Lawrence Lowell of Harvard as chairman. The *Herald* was voted the 1927 Pulitzer Prize for editorial writing that spring, with the jury praising its "great courage to reverse itself when it had reason to believe it was mistaken."

The *Herald*'s plea came too late. Judge Thayer sentenced Sacco and Vanzetti to death but deferred execution pending receipt of the commission's report. President Lowell's group upheld the judge. Governor Fuller thereupon refused to intervene. And on August 23, 1927, at Charlestown Prison, Sacco and Vanzetti were put to death in the electric chair, still proclaiming their innocence. One superb editorial could not prevail against the deep-seated prejudices of both the governors and the governed in this tragedy of political passion.

It fell, therefore, to the reporters rather than the editorial writers to hold up to public view the distorted image of the age. They did not do it consciously as moralists who deliberately participated in the news they were trying to cover. What they could do, and what they often did do in Pulitzer Prize-winning feats, was to follow the news wherever it led them with a fierce and uncompromising honesty that, more often than not, helped them to uncover the truth.

This was the way James W. Mulroy and Alvin H. Goldstein worked on May 22, 1924, when they were assigned by the Chicago *Daily News* to cover the kidnaping of 14-year-old Bobby Franks. They were very young—Mulroy was 22 and Goldstein 21—but they made up in energy what they lacked in experience. When a boy's naked body was found jammed into a railroad culvert, Mulroy and Goldstein were the first to identify it as that of the kidnap victim. They also talked the boy's family out of paying a ransom. From then on, they worked day and night, chasing down leads and annoying the more experienced reporters.

Soon, they picked up an acquaintance at the University of Chicago, Richard Loeb, who drove them around and seemed inordinately interested in the case. Once, he even remarked jocularly that if he had ever thought of killing anybody, it would have been "just such a cocky little —— as Bobby Franks." Through Loeb, Mulroy and Goldstein met another student, Nathan Leopold. When it turned out that the ransom note had been written on an Underwood typewriter, the two cubs recalled that Leopold had such a typewriter, obtained samples of the classroom work he had done on it, and found that his typing tallied with the characteristics of the ransom note. It was enough to clinch the case, force Leopold's confession implicating Loeb, and reveal to a shocked world that they had killed a little boy just for the thrill of it. Subsequently, they were tried and convicted in a sensational trial in which their skilled, old-fashioned lawyer, Clarence Darrow, saved them from the electric chair.

Mulroy and Goldstein won the Pulitzer Prize for Reporting in 1925 in the best traditions of the legendary Hildy Johnson and *The Front Page*. Together, they triumphed over a tough Chicago newspaper crowd that gloried in the work of Ben Hecht, Charles MacArthur, Carl Sandburg, and Bob Casey. It was a feat that set the two youngsters apart from the pack for the remainder of their long and useful lives as newspapermen, Goldstein with the St. Louis *Post-Dispatch* and Mulroy with the Chicago *Sun*.[2]

Another 21-year-old reporter, William Burke Miller of the Louisville *Courier-Journal*, became a national hero as well as a Pulitzer Prize winner by trying for eighteen days to save the life of Floyd Collins, a mountain youth, who had been trapped on January 29, 1925, in Sand Cave, Ky. While on a solitary venture of exploration, Collins had been pinned sixty feet below the surface of the cavern when a huge boulder fell atop his left foot in a narrow passage. He lay on his side and couldn't move.

"Skeets" Miller, who weighed only 120 pounds and was only five feet two inches tall, risked his life many times to wriggle through the narrow tunnel to the spot where Collins lay. In the words of the Pulitzer Reporting Jury for 1926, "He carried food and stimulants to Collins. He worked with fierce energy in an effort to release him. As long as it was possible for any one to get to Collins, Miller made these journeys. He went three times in one day."

Collins has long been forgotten, but in the 18 days of his agony he dominated the front pages of the nation—a symbol of human torment, a remorseless reminder of the inevitability of man's fate. When he died on February 18, 1925, his cave became his tomb. Miller's pieces for the *Courier-Journal*, vivid in their descriptive detail and painfully accurate in reporting Collins' declining energy and hope, remain in the Pulitzer Prize files as a memento of a strange and wonderful time.[3]

The daring and enterprise of more experienced reporters were also rewarded with Pulitzer Prizes as the high living of the Twenties ended in economic disaster and the Great Depression fastened its withering grip upon the land. Awards went to Russell Owen of the New York *Times* in 1930 for his radio reports of the Byrd Antarctic Expedition, to A. B. MacDonald of the Kansas City *Star* in 1931 for solving what had been called "the perfect crime" in Texas, and to Francis A. Jamieson of the Associated Press in 1933 for his coverage of the kidnaping and murder of the infant son of Charles A. and Anne Morrow Lindbergh.

If these dramatic stories transfixed the attention of a very large public at home, they did not deter newspaper people from the far less glamorous but even more important task of trying to make sense out of the confusing and menacing turn of national and international events. In Correspondence, a new category created in 1929, and in Editorials and Cartoons, the nation's press tried to illuminate the problems of the Depression and the parlous state of a world in which Hitler, Mussolini, and the Japanese militarists were massing their armed forces against their terrified neighbors.

The ravages of the Depression was the subject of Charles G. Ross's Pulitzer Prize-winning article in the Correspondence category in 1932: "The Country's Plight: What Can Be Done About It?" And in 1933, when the banks closed and factories fell idle and Franklin Delano Roosevelt tried to rally the country from the White House, E. P. Chase cried out editorially in a small paper, the Atlantic (Iowa) *News Telegraph*, "Where Is Our Money?" It was a question so universally asked that he was given the Pulitzer Prize for Editorial Writing the following year. Another prize-winning small-town editor, Charles S. Ryckman of the Fremont (Neb.) *Tribune*, did not fare so well in 1930 when he attacked his neighbors in general for their selfish attitudes and in particular assailed the liberal-minded Senator George W. Norris. Although he received the editorial writing award for 1931, both he and his peers were criticized for what was widely construed as a smear against Norris.

Perhaps the best-remembered and most poignant piece of Depression era journalism, however, was neither an editorial nor an interpretive dispatch but a cartoon—John T. McCutcheon's 1931 drawing in the Chicago *Tribune* entitled, "A Wise Economist Asks a Question." The famous confrontation between a thrifty squirrel and a thrifty citizen who had saved his money, but lost it through no fault of his own, won the Cartoon Prize for 1932, the pit of the Depression.

The economic issue also preoccupied the first two winners of the Correspondence award, Paul Scott Mowrer of the Chicago *Daily News* in 1929 for coverage of the German reparations question and Leland Stowe of the New York *Herald Tribune* in 1930 for his dispatches on the founding of the international bank. For 1931 and 1932, the focus of the Correspondence juries shifted to the Soviet Union, a subject that had long attracted the nation's cartoonists. In the former year, H. R. Knickerbocker of the New York *Evening Post* won for his series, "The Red Trade Menace," and in the latter the award went to the New York *Times*'s Russian specialist, Walter Duranty, for his description of the Soviets' current Five Year Plan.

In 1933, the bells began tolling the alarm all over Europe. Adolf Hitler had become the master of Germany.

Many a generous and intelligent American had deluded himself during the 1920s into believing with Woodrow Wilson that World War I had indeed been the war to end all wars. True, Rollin Kirby of the New York *World* had made fun of a League of Nations peace compact in the 1925 prize-winning cartoon that showed three hobo-like outcasts—the United States, Soviet Union, and Mexico—reading the news in disbelief. But far more idealistic cartoons won subsequently, including two anti-war drawings in the Brooklyn *Eagle*—Nelson Harding's "Toppling the Idol" in 1927 and Charles R. Macauley's "Paying for a Dead Horse" in 1930. It was in 1933, finally, that the threat of a new war was recognized in the annals of the Pulitzer Prizes with a cartoon award to Harold M. Talburt of the Washington *Daily News* for his savage indictment of Japan, "The Light of Asia." That year, too, an international drama was played out in the august government buildings in Berlin—an unequal test of strength between Hitler's Nazi regime and a spunky American correspondent, Edgar Ansel Mowrer of the Chicago *Daily News,* the younger brother of Paul Scott Mowrer.

Edgar Mowrer had come to Europe in 1914 to study at the Sorbonne, having graduated the previous year from the University of Michigan, but almost at once found himself caught up in World War I as a correspondent for the Chicago *Daily News.* He learned to know the Germans in Belgium at Louvain, and in France at the Marne. And after the war he learned to know the meaning of Fascism at first hand as he watched Mussolini take over Italy in a bloodless coup. With such prescient Europeans as Marcel William Fodor of the Manchester *Guardian,* Mowrer realized early on the menace that Hitler represented to Germany and covered his rise to power. Had the wiry and determined young American been a mere recording stenographer of a reporter, so objective that he could not look the news in the face, he would have done nothing. But as it became clear that President Paul von Hindenburg would give way to Hitler and his Nazis in 1932, Mowrer arrived at a firm and conscious decision. It was time, he determined, to awaken the American people to the danger of Hitlerism in Germany.

With deadly accuracy, from then on, he reported every move Hitler made in his jack-booted march to power in Germany. He also wrote a book, published late in 1932 and based in part on his dispatches, *Germany Puts the Clock Back,* in which he warned that a Hitlerite Germany would mean another world war. On January 30, 1933, his worst fears were realized when Hitler took over as Chancellor.

The Pulitzer Prize Correspondence Jury had no difficulty on March 14, 1933, in singling out Mowrer for the 1933 award. Herbert Brucker, the chairman who then was the associate dean of the journalism school, wrote the report in which the correspondent was praised for his daily coverage of the news and his accurate interpretation of the course of events. It had become customary for the American Society of Newspaper Editors to put a representative on each jury and the ASNE member who worked with Brucker that year, Sevellon Brown of the Providence (R.I.) *Journal-Bulletin,* heartily concurred as did the third juror, Carl C. Dickey, a faculty member.

It so happened that the prize was announced in the middle of a monumental row because the Nazi propaganda minister, Paul Joseph Goebbels, had taken exception to Mowrer's election as president of the Foreign Press Association in Berlin. "That made me a target for every sort of Nazi pressure and discrimination," Mowrer wrote. The issue came to a head when Goebbels said he would have no further relations with the Foreign Press Association as long as Mowrer remained its president. Whereupon the correspondent offered his resignation at just about the time he won the Pulitzer Prize. But when the association's members met, they voted almost unanimously to reject the resignation. "I think it is fair to say," he commented dryly, "that without the Prize my resignation would have been accepted. Had it been, I believe the Nazi government would have expelled me immediately from Germany." [4]

It was the first time that the Pulitzer Prizes had been made an issue in foreign affairs, but it would not be the last.

There was so much emphasis on the developing role of public service journalism in this dark and difficult era that there was little room for much else among the Pulitzer Prizes in Journalism. There were no awards for sports writing until 1935. With few exceptions, American newspapers did little at the time for art, music, sculpture, and literature. Even the craft of writing received little encouragement, with only one award being given in that period for mastery of the English language— the prize to the Detroit Free *Press* in 1932 for its account of an American Legion parade. And in science, there was but one award from 1924 to 1933—to Magner White of the *San Diego Sun* for describing an eclipse of the sun.

With the exception of the addition of awards for Correspondence and Cartooning, the Pulitzer Prizes in Journalism remained substantially the same as those Joseph Pulitzer had first envisioned. Administratively, the Advisory Board in 1925 created the post of executive secretary, a move intended to stimulate interest in the journalism awards. The first two occupants, Jerome Landfield from 1925 to 1929 and R. A. Parker in 1930–31, did comparatively little to carry out the Board's wishes. But in 1933, after Carl W. Ackerman had been dean of the journalism school for two years, he also was elected secretary of the Advisory Board, took control of the journalism awards, and retained it for more than twenty years.

Thus, between 1924 and 1933, the Pulitzer Prizes in Journalism became an intrinsic part of the profession in the United States. If they were not perfect, they were at least respected. Their permanence was not questioned. By reason of their widespread support, they were secure. However, Joseph Pulitzer's New York *World*, to which he had devoted so much of his life, died on February 27, 1931, being merged with Scripps-Howard's New York *Telegram*. His youngest son, the second Joseph Pulitzer, kept the family's tradition of public service alive on the St. Louis *Post-Dispatch*.

2
The Embattled Novelists

Sinclair Lewis, who loved a good fight, had been planning his revenge on the Pulitzer Prizes ever since his failure to win an award with *Main Street*. He had to wait awhile.

A jury consisting of Professor Jefferson B. Fletcher of Columbia as chairman, with the Rev. Dr. Samuel M. Crothers and Professor Bliss Perry of Harvard as members, settled on Margaret Wilson's *The Able McLaughlins* for the 1924 Fiction Prize. There wasn't much cheering. Another jury wrangled in 1925 over Joseph Hergesheimer's *Balisand*, Edna Ferber's *So Big*, and Lawrence Stallings' *Plumes*. William Allen White wanted *So Big*, Professor O. W. Firkins of the University of Minnesota was for *Balisand*, and Fletcher had trouble making up his mind. Before the Advisory Board, White carried the day for *So Big*. He confessed to a "devilish lust for propaganda" and therefore favored Miss Ferber's appeal for a better creative spirit in America.

There was a new Fiction Jury in 1926, the year that Lewis' *Arrowsmith* was an obvious contender. Richard Burton of the University of Minnesota, who had served in Drama and Poetry, became the Fiction chairman and Robert Morss Lovett and Edwin Lefevre, a popular writer, served with him. To nobody's surprise, they concluded unanimously that *Arrowsmith* deserved the prize and so informed Fackenthal privately on March 17, 1926. On March 30, Alfred Harcourt of Harcourt, Brace & Co., Lewis' publisher, wrote to him in Kansas City that he would win the Pulitzer Prize, upon which Lewis fired back a warning that he intended to refuse the award because of what he called the *"Main Street* burglary."

The Advisory Board recommended *Arrowsmith* for the prize on April 22 and Fackenthal wrote Lewis about it in confidence the following day because final action by the Trustees would not be taken until May 3. It gave Lewis all the time he needed to compose his letter of refusal, which he proceeded to do in consultation with Harcourt. Once the prize was announced, the letter was made public.

While Lewis argued that all prizes are dangerous, he attacked the Pulitzer Prize for Fiction as "peculiarly objectionable" because its terms had been consistently misrepresented. He held that what the award actually stood for was not literary merit, but "obedience to whatever code of Good Form may chance to be popular at the moment." And, he went on, since the prize now tended to become a "sanctified tradition," the administrators in time might become "a supreme court, a college of cardinals, so rooted and so sacred that to challenge them will be to commit blasphemy." This was what he denounced. "Only by regularly refusing the Pulitzer Prize can novelists keep such power from being permanently set up over them," he wrote.

In the age of ballyhoo, this was a master stroke. It echoed like thunder in the nation's headlines. The literati rallied to Lewis' side, headed by the Columbia author and critic, Professor Carl Van Doren, with H. L. Mencken leading the editorial cheering section in the Baltimore *Evening Sun*. However, the press in general criticized Lewis for his thirst for publicity and questioned the sincerity of his motives.

There was a post-mortem at Columbia. Fackenthal wrote to Lewis on May 7, mildly protesting that his publishers should not have nominated *Arrowsmith* if they had known of his attitude. To this, Lewis replied with a straight face on May 14: "Indeed, my publishers did not have the slightest notion of my attitude toward the Pulitzer Prize. Otherwise they would not, of course, have nominated *Arrowsmith* for the prize."

The $1,000 check, which Lewis had returned, was put back in the Pulitzer Prize Fund. The last word was President Butler's, when he was asked what disposition was to be made of the 1926 Fiction Prize in the Pulitzer records. "The award stands," he said. And so it has.[5]

Instead of glorifying the poor but devoted scientist, Martin Arrowsmith, the Fiction Jury might have ducked the issue entirely and recommended either F. Scott Fitzgerald's more enduring *The Great Gatsby* or Theodore Dreiser's plodding *An American Tragedy*. But Lewis' literary standing was so great at the time that he towered over everybody else. In any event, neither Fitzgerald nor Dreiser wrote "wholesome" works within the meaning of the term as President Butler understood it.

Long afterward, Professor Lovett reflected his own doubts as a juror over Lewis' actions, writing: "We were flattered at the attribution of power to alter the current of literature and realized more than ever our responsibility to exercise it wisely. We were happily surprised, however, when Mr. Lewis withdrew his objection [to prizegiving] a year or two later by accepting the Nobel Prize." [6]

For the next three years, the Fiction Jury remained determinedly academic, with Professor Burton as chairman and Professors Lovett and Fletcher as members. President Butler and the Advisory Board quietly returned to the original wording of the Fiction award, as Joseph Pulitzer had set it down in his will. The insistence on "wholesome" fiction, in theory at least, was dropped in favor of Pulitzer's specification for an American novel that best presented the "whole atmosphere" of American life and the "highest standard of American manners and manhood."

Hopefully, in this new dispensation, the jurors turned to one of the younger and uncontroversial American novelists, Louis Bromfield, and recommended his third novel *Early Autumn* for the 1927 award. However, this dour tale of the downfall of a New England dynasty did not set off any critical skyrockets when the prize was announced.

The jury's choice for 1928 was happier—a 31-year-old prep school teacher, Thornton Niven Wilder of Lawrenceville, who had written an appealing tale of old Peru, *The Bridge of San Luis Rey*. It had nothing to do with American life or American manners and manhood, but the Advisory Board quickly accepted it. The critics already had hailed a major new talent, with Edmund Wilson praising Wilder's "felicity of style."

Wilder was to become a multiple Pulitzer Prize winner. Like Eugene O'Neill, his first award came to him when he was still young enough to appreciate it. From Madison, Wis., his birthplace, he had come to Lawrenceville in 1921 by a circuitous route that included China, Yale (AB, 1920), and Princeton (AM, 1925). He had published one previous novel, *The Cabala*, which had had a respectful reception in 1925.

Fackenthal sent Wilder a confidential notification in early April 1928 that the *Bridge* had won the Pulitzer Prize and he promptly lost the letter. In mingled happiness and dismay, he wrote to Columbia of his "pride and happiness at the reception of this honor" and explained: "I am a preparatory school teacher and in the confusion of examination week and in the sheer pleasure of the news I must have bestowed the letter away so carefully that I cannot find it."

Fackenthal replied reassuringly after the Board had acted on April 24 and, following the formal decision of the Trustees on May 7, sent the young writer his $1,000 check. This time, Wilder didn't lose it. Except for six years at the University of Chicago and a year at Harvard thereafter, he devoted himself entirely to his writing. His was a fortunate choice among the early winners of the Fiction Prize.[7]

One result of the Fiction Jury's successful recommendation of a story about Peru was still another change in the much-amended wording of the terms of the award. The insistence on the "highest standard of American manners and manhood" was dropped. Instead, in a general revision of the Plan of Award that took effect for the 1929 prize season, the requirement in fiction called for a prize "for the American novel published during the year, preferably one which shall best present the whole atmosphere of American life." With so much leeway, the academic jurors went swinging into a heady new adventure by picking a literary unknown, Dr. John Rathbone Oliver of Johns Hopkins University, for his novel, *Victim and Victor*, the story of an unfrocked Episcopal priest and his yearning for the spiritual comfort of the church from which he had been expelled. The selection was unanimous.

Professor Burton wrote on March 13: "The committee's choice is made on the ground that this novel is of fine quality as a piece of literary work, deals with important elements in the native life, and has most unusual spiritual elevation and significance. It is a sound piece of literature and a noble interpretation of human character. For these reasons it stands out from the rank and file of current fiction, although the year brought forth a few admirable stories, and it may interest you to know that *Scarlet Sister Mary*, by Julia Peterkin, came close in our estimation to winning the prize."

After having written Fackenthal about the jury's verdict, Professor Burton became so enthused that he discussed *Victim and Victor* during a lecture in Minneapolis before the Advisory Board had acted. It was, he said, "a book not just for a year but for many years." Despite the supposed secrecy that shrouded the Pulitzer Prize proceedings, Burton's role in the awards became known and an avalanche of nation-wide publicity engulfed the unfortunate Dr. Oliver at Johns Hopkins. Although Burton denied that he had let out the secret, his colleague, Professor Lovett, concluded years later that the chairman had let the news slip "as a *bonne bouche* in one of his popular lectures." It is difficult to determine whether President Butler and the Advisory Board were annoyed by the premature publicity or the theme of the book itself. In any event, in advance of the Board meeting on April 25, Fackenthal asked Professor Burton to amplify his jury's report. Burton obliged by writing on April 18 that he would have chosen Julia Peterkin's *Scarlet Sister Mary* had not *Victim and Victor* appeared. In a discouraging postscript, Burton asked to be relieved as a Ficton juror "in view of the undesirable publicity concerning the award this time and the fact that I am always open to misrepresentation in connection with my lecture work."

When the Advisory Board met a week later, with President Butler absent due to illness, the members soon became involved in debate over the merits of Dr. Oliver's story of the unfrocked Episcopal priest as compared with Mrs. Peterkin's tale of a black woman with seven illegitimate children and her redemption from a life of sin. For a group that had stood for more than a decade for novels that represented the "highest standard of American manners and manhood," it was quite a change. What the membership eventually decided to do was to read both books, then vote by mail ballot. On the showdown, *Scarlet Sister Mary* won and the Trustees approved the award to Mrs. Peterkin.

Except for the jurors who were reversed, the only person who appeared to be upset by the proceedings was Dr. Oliver. Two weeks later, he wrote a three-page letter of protest to Dr. Fackenthal. As a physician, he explained, he was not dependent on his writing for a living and he did not challenge the award to Mrs. Peterkin's book. But, he went on, he had been mightily embarrassed by the premature publicity and hoped the announcement would be better managed in the future. He concluded:

"I would not, of course, suggest that the Pulitzer Committee should wall themselves into one of the buildings of the University and set guards at the doors; but I do feel sure that it would save a great deal of trouble if it were definitely understood that the only source of information about the Pulitzer awards was the Central Committee itself and that this Central Committee had such a high sense of its duties that it would not permit any premature news of its activities to reach the outside world."

Fackenthal apologized to Dr. Oliver and offered a routine defense of the Advisory Board's procedures, including a defense of Burton. But in a memorandum for President Butler, attached to the proposed Pulitzer Juries in Letters for 1930, the diligent secretary observed: "Burton's difficulty is that he lectures on current literature and in expressing his opinions of books is quite likely indirectly to indicate his choice for the Pulitzer Prize."

The upshot of the debate inside the Columbia administration was the beginning of a determined effort, which took shape over the next four decades, to keep the lid on all public information about the prizes until the university Trustees took final action. It was a difficult decision for a university to make, and it proved even more difficult to enforce, but the embarrassment to Dr. Oliver was not something that anybody wanted to happen again.[8]

With the agreement of President Butler, the Fiction Jury was reorganized after the debacle over *Victim and Victor*. Although it was a risky business to put a Columbia man in charge of a prize that the university administered, Professor Fletcher was asked to be chairman and accepted. Those who served with him were Professor Lovett and Albert Bigelow Paine, Mark Twain's literary executor, his authorized biographer, and the author of several novels. It was a combination that remained together through the 1937 awards.

Almost at once, the reconstituted jury was split over the merits of Thomas Wolfe's first great novel, *Look Homeward, Angel,* and Oliver LaFarge's tale of a tragic American Indian love affair, *Laughing Boy,* the front runners for the 1930 prize. Paine's first choice was Wolfe's book and he pressed it with vigor, writing: "That, humanly considered, as a vital picture, is the bigger achievement, the work of a genius, slightly demented, as a genius is likely to be." Professor Fletcher was for *Laughing Boy,* which seemed to him to present a "poignant situation, in which living and appealing characters move against a picturesque and historically interesting background." Professor Lovett's first choice was another book entirely, *It's a Great War,* by Mary Lee.

While Paine and Lovett eventually agreed to join Fletcher in voting for *Laughing Boy,* their reservations were such that the chairman wrote to the Advisory Board: "The members of the committee are not quite in accord, but have individually expressed their willingness to compound their differences by voting for *Laughing Boy* by Oliver LaFarge. At the same time, especially since the Trustees have reserved the ultimate decision to themselves, it seems advisable to let each member of the committee speak for himself."

President Butler was absent once again when the Advisory Board met on April 24, 1930, being out of the country, but the eight newspaper members found no difficulty in agreeing on *Laughing Boy,* a choice the university Trustees accepted. It was not a popular selection. Nor was there any letup in the critical barrage against the Fiction Prize.

Fackenthal wrote to Butler, just before the opening of the judging for the 1931 prize, to suggest still another change in the terms of the award for fiction. Reviewing the patchwork that already had been done and the old argument over whether the novel should be "wholesome," he concluded: "The [Fiction] jury feels that in its present form the definition makes the Prize almost useless and what they would like would be a redefinition that would place the Novel Prize on the same basis as the Poetry Prize—that is, 'For the best novel published during the year by an American author.' " [9]

While the Advisory Board pondered the latest suggestion, the jurors without argument recommended Margaret Ayer Barnes's *Years of Grace* as the 1931 Fiction Prize winner that best presented the "whole atmosphere of American life." It was selected over Elizabeth Madox Roberts' *The Great Meadow* and Dorothy Canfield's *The Deepening Stream* because of "its vivid and interesting presentation of the changing in character and *mores* throughout three generations of an American family." The Advisory Board accepted the Barnes book, and also agreed to the jury's latest suggested change in the terms of the award. On May 4, the university's Trustees adopted the Board's recommendations without change, but there were not many critical cheers for the fiction choice.

There was no doubt that President Butler was mightily annoyed. He was too much the realist to believe that the mere juggling of words in the Plan of Award would solve any problems. He went to the heart of the matter in a memorandum to Fackenthal:

"I have been wondering whether, in view of the sharp criticism of the Pulitzer literary awards in recent years, particularly this year, we ought not to make some alterations in our juries. The jury on the novel is the one which is most vigorously attacked, and perhaps it would make less disturbance if we should go through the list and suggest a variety of alterations. You might be considering this during the next few weeks."

Evidently, Butler thought better of the literary jury list upon reflection for no change was made in the 1931 lineup, from fiction through poetry, for four more years.

The Fiction Jury came up with a more popular recommendation for the following year, Pearl S. Buck's best-selling novel about Chinese life, *The Good Earth*. It was chosen, the jury reported, for "its epic sweep, its distinct and moving characterization, its sustained story interest, its simple and yet richly colored style." The principal contenders were Willa Cather's novel about seventeenth century Quebec, *Shadows on the Rock*, and R. E. Spencer's *The Lady Who Came to Stay*. While the jury noted that Miss Cather already had received a Pulitzer Prize, it added: "This fact, however, was not determining." With the concurrence of the Advisory Board, over which President Butler presided that year, *The Good Earth* won the fiction award for 1932. For the time being, the critical uproar subsided into a continuing grumble. To a bewildered people mired in a terrible economic breakdown, the story of the hardships of Chinese peasants somehow was most appealing. Mrs. Buck's book, therefore, was popularly accepted as "the best novel published during that year by an American author," regardless of somewhat muted critical objections.

There was little argument over the 1933 selection, *The Store*, T. S. Stribling's novel about race relations in the South. In an unusual action coincident with the announcement of the Pulitzer Prizes that year, Columbia made public the jury's recommendation: "*The Store* was selected chiefly because of its sustained interest, and because of the convincing and comprehensive picture it presents of life in an inland Southern community during the middle eighties of the last century." As it turned out, the plug was not really necessary. Although Stribling is little read today, he was respected in his time as a novelist who attempted to grapple with the realities of life in the South.[10]

There is nothing in the record of the years from 1924 to 1933 that shows the works of Ernest Hemingway or William Faulkner were considered by any of those who served on the Pulitzer Prize Fiction Juries. Yet, Hemingway's *The Sun Also Rises* was published in 1926 and his *A Farewell to Arms* in 1929 while no fewer than five of Faulkner's novels appeared during that period—*Soldier's Pay* in 1926; *The Sound and the Fury*, 1929; *As I Lay Dying*, 1930; *Sanctuary*, 1931; and *Light in August*, 1932.

It is easier to explain the neglect of Faulkner in that era than the failure to recognize Hemingway. For outside a small circle of discerning critics and readers, Faulkner's novels for the most part did not receive the attention they deserved upon publication in the United States. Instead, his true stature as a novelist was first recognized in Europe and only belatedly in his own country.

Hemingway, however, attained a deserved success with *The Sun Also Rises* and was considered a major novelist with the appearance of his antiwar novel, *A Farewell to Arms*. True, he was not a "wholesome" novelist, any more than Faulkner was, but the Pulitzer juries of the late Twenties and early Thirties abandoned that most troublesome and artificial qualification. President Butler's personal antipathy toward Hemingway's works became known to members of the Advisory Board only in the early Forties; if he ever confided his feelings to Professor Fletcher or any other fiction jurors, it never became a matter for comment. The only conclusion that can be reached on the basis of the record is that the conservative fiction jurors of the time were unable to recognize the literary merit of Hemingway and Faulkner in their earlier years. Neither received an award until long after they needed it.

The case of F. Scott Fitzgerald, who never received a Pulitzer Prize and apparently never was even considered, is somewhat different. Professor Carlos Baker of Princeton, who has experienced the uncertainties of judging literature as a member of Pulitzer Prize juries, has pointed out that just as Sinclair Lewis' reputation was over-inflated in his lifetime, the work of Fitzgerald was decidedly undervalued until after his death. Professor Baker wrote: "It wasn't until the middle 1950s, at a rough guess, when the young began to rediscover the alleged glamor of the Jazz Age, that he [Fitzgerald] was suddenly elevated to his present—in my view highly over-inflated—position. It has amounted in the last twenty years to a kind of enshrinement."

John Barkham, the critic who served for many years as a Pulitzer Prize juror and chairman, agreed that Lewis' reputation perished quickly and credited Edmund Wilson with leading in the posthumous rediscovery of Fitzgerald, his old Princeton classmate. Barkham added:

> Since then, Fitzgerald's reputation has steadily grown, chiefly as the major writer he is but partly, too, as a tragic, Byronic figure who died with ultimate fame almost within his grasp.
>
> Such, I suggest, were the conditions in which Pulitzer juries considered Lewis and Fitzgerald—Lewis basking in the glory of his satirical, if short-lived triumphs, Fitzgerald frittering away in scandalous behavior a talent which had shown itself all too briefly.[11]

Malcolm Cowley once wrote that literary reputations follow no more predictable charts than the stock market. Most Pulitzer Prize literary jurors over the years would agree with him, although few would contend that such uncertainty is a sufficient excuse for not recognizing and rewarding talent.

3

Drama: Winners and Losers

Professor Brander Matthews, who had taught dramatic literature at Co-
lumbia University for thirty-three years, wrote privately to President
Butler on April 22, 1924, to protest the Drama Jury's selection of George
Kelly's satirical comedy, *The Show-Off*, for a Pulitzer Prize. He had
learned about the jury report from the chairman, Professor William
Lyon Phelps of Yale, and now wanted to head it off before the Advisory
Board meeting. Instead, the outraged dean of the American theater
called for a prize for *Hell-Bent Fer Heaven*, a hillbilly drama set in the
Kentucky mountains, by a fellow member of the Columbia faculty,
Hatcher Hughes.

The Show-Off, Matthews wrote, was only a middling comedy, "a thing
of the moment, so up-to-date that it is certain soon to be out-of-date,"
while he praised the Hughes play as "a genuine contribution to American dramatic literature." He disclosed that Phelps had not even seen
Hell-Bent Fer Heaven at the time the jury's report was sent in and concluded: "As I understand it, the committee [jury] has power only to
make a recommendation, the actual award being made by the Advisory
Board. I sincerely hope that the Board will disregard the recommendation of the committee and that it will bestow the prize on *Hell-Bent Fer
Heaven*."

With that, Matthews rested his case. President Butler had the letter
read before the Advisory Board meeting of April 28, 1924, together with
the Drama Jury report dated April 3, 1924, which said merely that *The
Show-Off* was "an extremely good and original American play."

As the Advisory Board undoubtedly was informed, although it does
not show in the minutes, there had been an argument within the Drama
Jury about *The Show-Off*. Owen Johnson, the author of *Stover at Yale*, had
been for *The Show-Off* and Clayton Hamilton had been for *Hell-Bent Fer
Heaven*, with *The Show-Off* second. Evidently, Hamilton had been persuaded to shift to *The Show-Off*, whereupon Phelps had made the selection unanimous.

The Board knew there would be trouble if it reversed the jury. In the
previous year, there had been sharp criticism of the selection of Owen
Davis' *Icebound* over Elmer Rice's remarkable play about human beings

whose lives had been compressed into mere ciphers, *The Adding Machine*. Davis' reputation as the reformed king of melodrama, who had turned to serious drama after he was 40 years old, had been good enough to face down the critics. But this time, the Board knew it would have to account for the intervention of a Columbia professor for a faculty colleague through the president of the university. Nevertheless, it voted for *Hell-Bent Fer Heaven*.

The storm broke as soon as the prize was announced, with Owen Johnson hurling the journalistic thunderbolts for himself and Professor Phelps. The old Yale blue smote Columbia hip and thigh, saying: "The value of the Pulitzer award is greatly impaired by the overshadowing influence of Columbia University, especially when it is exercised to give the award to a member of its own teaching staff. Professor Phelps and I feel we were treated with gross discourtesy and we will never serve on a Pulitzer jury again."

Had it not been for Matthews's meddling, *Hell-Bent Fer Heaven* would have gone into the theatrical record as a play that had good-to-excellent reviews and ran for 122 performances on Broadway. Burns Mantle in the New York *Daily News*, for example, called it "darned good melodrama" while Alexander Woollcott in the New York *Sun* also praised it. As for *The Show-Off*, it was good theatre but no one has ever seriously contended that it is a classic. Had it not been beaten out by the Hughes play under puckish circumstances, it would be remembered at best as a lively minor comedy of the Twenties that was typical of its time.[12]

Owen Johnson never did serve on another Pulitzer jury, true to his word. But Professor Phelps relented and became the chairman of the Drama Jury from 1935 through 1942.

The explosion of creativity that changed the face of American literature in the 1920s made life difficult for the Pulitzer Drama Juries, as well as those in fiction and other literary categories. There was scarcely a year in which the drama jurors were not called on to choose between two or more theatrical works of considerable merit and originality. Moreover, the style of American drama was changing swiftly from song and dance confections and poor imitations of Scribe to realistic and outspoken efforts to reflect American life on the stage with honesty. The introduction of frank discussions of sexual problems, with the accompaniment of a modicum of profanity now and then, was titillating for audiences of the

Twenties, although the new theatrical freedom didn't approach the limits of the late Sixties and early Seventies. By today's standards, whatever pillow talk and cussing there were behind the footlights in the Twenties was relatively mild; in fact, one of the biggest sensations, a mere suggestion of sexual intercourse on the stage in Arthur Schnitzler's *Reigen*, was performed in such dim lighting that the audience could only use its imagination. And there was, then as now, no accounting for imagination in the mass mind.

The critics and the Pulitzer jurors, who were for the most part members of the critical fraternity, had only two choices: to adapt to the times or quit. Many tried to adapt, more or less successfully, depending on the point of view, but there was at least one major casualty, Hamlin Garland. When Fackenthal asked him to serve on the Drama Jury for 1925, in view of the vacancies created by the uproar over the selection of *Hell-Bent Fer Heaven*, he replied testily:

"I hardly know what to say in respect of your invitation to serve again on the Pulitzer Committee. I am all out of key with the pornographic drama of our day and I could not vote an award to any such play no matter what its technical excellence might be. I hate the entire over-sexed fiction and poetry of today. I regard it as a passing phase of the corruption of war experiences. Now if with this plain statement of my prejudices you still think I should serve, I will do so. . . ."

Fackenthal accepted the sage's position but asked him to overlook his prejudices, which was quite an order. So, with extreme reluctance, he became a member of a reconstituted Drama Jury with Jesse Lynch Williams, the first Pulitzer Prize winner in drama, as the chairman, and Clayton Hamilton, who alone had been for *Hell-Bent Fer Heaven* in 1924, as the third member. It didn't work. Toward the end of the judging season, Garland rebelled. On March 9, 1925, he wrote to Fackenthal:

> I have just had a conference with Clayton Hamilton, the first of our meetings. He had a letter from Jesse Williams in which he spoke of only two possibilities, *What Price Glory?* and *They Knew What They Wanted.* Mr. Hamilton is opposed to *Glory* and I am opposed to giving a medal to any of the plays I have seen.
>
> In view of the fact that an agreement is almost impossible in the case, I am writing to ask you to drop my name from the jury. I can not afford to have my name published as voting for plays that I hold in contempt. I have not yet seen the Howard play, but from

Hamilton's statement of the plot it does not "best represent the educational value and power of the stage in raising the standard of good morals, good taste, and good manners." I shall see the play but as I wrote you in an early letter I will not vote for any pornographic drama.

Fackenthal, as the conscientious administrator he was, tried to keep the Drama Jury from being disrupted just before a crucial vote. He pleaded with Garland to stay on and turn in a minority report, regardless of any decision that was reached by his colleagues. On March 8, Hamilton traveled from Buffalo to New York City and pleaded with Garland to see *They Knew What They Wanted*. The sage said he would, then changed his mind and on March 14 wrote peremptorily to Fackenthal: "Please drop my name from the jury."

And that was that. He was right, of course, in pointing out that the definition of the award, if honestly construed, did not fit the plays that were under consideration. Even so, President Butler and the Advisory Board could not bring themselves to change the terms for five years and even then the new wording proved to be more shadow than substance. In effect, therefore, what the jurors had to do if they were to reflect their honest judgment was to disregard the specifications of the Plan of Award and hope that the Advisory Board would understand.

It was on this basis, evidently, that Hamilton and Williams saw the season through and constituted themselves as a majority of the Drama Jury. While Williams had gone to California on January 10, he had seen all the plays in contention and left it to Hamilton to do the report. They remained in touch by mail and telegraph.

The reduced jury's task was not simple. The 1924–25 season had been fine. In addition to *What Price Glory?* and *They Knew What They Wanted*, the New York stage had featured O'Neill's *Desire Under the Elms* and John Howard Lawson's experimental drama, *Processional*. It was an exciting time for audiences, a perplexing one for the prize givers.

There was a spine-tingling thrill about *What Price Glory?*—the first collaboration of two New York *World* colleagues, Maxwell Anderson and Laurence Stallings. The crowds that stormed into the Plymouth Theater were prepared for a harsh but somehow romantic antiwar play and that was what they got. It was the story of a hard pressed and ill-trained American unit, pulled briefly out of the front lines during World War I, and the rivalry of a ferocious, broken-nosed captain and a tough but wily

sergeant for the favors of a French prostitute. Yet, instead of a denunciation of the futility of fighting that post-Vietnam audiences would have
understood, the play ended with the captain leading his men back into
combat and the sergeant, hobbling along after a self-inflicted wound,
yelling, "Hey, wait for baby!" They were still gallant patriots.

Louis Wolheim as Captain Flagg and William Boyd as Sergeant Quirt
became Broadway heroes. Their pungent dialogue about this "goddam
army," in which everybody was supposed to respond to orders "toot
goddam sweet," electrified a generation that had been brought up on less
outspoken theater. The favorite tale on the Broadway of the time had to
do with a sweet old lady who fussed about having lost something during
the first act and remarked to her husband, "I seem to have lost my goddam program."

Although it was an entirely different play, *They Knew What They
Wanted*, written by the able and talented Sidney Howard and produced
by the Theatre Guild, had just as great an attraction for audiences and
ran for 414 performances at the Garrick Theatre. It was, its author said,
"shamelessly, consciously, and even proudly derived" from the legend of
Tristram and Isolde and set in the vineyards of California's Napa Valley.
Here, a prosperous middle-aged farmer employs his handsome young
helper to help win the hand of a waitress, who promptly betrays her
benefactor and has a baby by the youth. Unlike the tragic ending of the
legend, however, the farmer in Howard's play forgives his erring bride,
concludes that it is better to accept life as it is, and decides to raise her
child as his own.

The reviewers were complimentary, even enthusiastic. Alexander
Woollcott thought the play a "true, living, salty comedy" and Heywood
Broun, then reviewing for the New York *World*, called it a "soul-rousing
play out of American life." Even the usually acid Percy Hammond wrote
in the New York *Herald Tribune* that Howard's play was "an excellent
tale, told with fine veracity."

Hamilton's verdict for the Drama Jury, in which Williams concurred,
was for *They Knew What They Wanted*. In a three and a half page single-
spaced typewritten report dated March 15, he called it "one of the best
plays ever written by an American author" and said that, with the exception of *What Price Glory?*, it stood "head and shoulders above all the other
American plays of the season." He gave only cursory attention to

O'Neill's *Desire Under the Elms*, calling it inferior to the dramatist's two previous prize-winning plays.

The Howard play, the report said, "treats a difficult and delicate theme with rare human insight and even rarer philosophical profundity." The jurors applauded the comparatively happy ending of what was inherently a tragic situation, calling it "as logical and sound as it is charitable and salutary." And, the report went on, "Although, as critics, we do not believe that it is the necessary business of the dramatist to teach moral lessons, we have been profoundly impressed by the inherent moral soundness of this serious and earnest play."

What Price Glory? was termed "the second outstanding American play of the season" and characterized as a "vivid piece of reporting." But, the report said, "We regard it as inferior to *They Knew What They Wanted* because it is comparatively deficient in those qualities which make for permanence. It is less broadly human in its outlook, less varied in its characterization, less architectonic in its structure, and more deliberately sensational in its dialogue. It treats a timely journalistic theme in a partisan and popular manner that is somewhat prejudiced in its point of view."

On April 22, the Advisory Board accepted the jury's recommendation and the university's Trustees later awarded the prize to *They Knew What They Wanted*. There was an argument, of course. It would have been a dull year if the Pulitzer Prize had not fomented a debate. After the passage of almost a half-century, the issue seems largely academic even though Howard, with his habitual gallantry, called *What Price Glory?* the "great American play" in an article for *Stage* magazine in February 1935.

There was one curious aftermath. Walter Pritchard Eaton, the former drama critic of the New York *Tribune* and the New York *Sun*, wrote in the *Theatre Annual* for 1944 that he had been a juror in the 1924–25 season and that the failure to award the prize to *What Price Glory?* had been a "boner." He ascribed it to "just plain esthetic dumbness." Eaton, the record shows, did serve as a Pulitzer Prize Drama Juror from 1926 through 1934 but there is no mention of him in Hamilton's 1925 report or in other readily available papers for that year. It is possible, naturally, that he might have been consulted but he had no share of the responsibility for the formal verdict.[13]

George Kelly won his Pulitzer Prize in 1926 for *Craig's Wife*, with

Eaton and Owen Davis on the jury under the chairmanship of the journalist-playwright, A. E. Thomas, author of such feathery comedies as *Come Out of the Kitchen* and *No More Ladies.** It was a play about a domineering woman who wrecked her marriage by alienating her husband from his friends. Except for Marc Connelly's fantasy, *The Wisdom Tooth*, Kelly's domestic tragedy had no rivals for the award.

There was a wealth of glittering, professional material in the Broadway show shops in the 1926–27 season. Sidney Howard had two good plays, *The Silver Cord* and *Ned McCobb's Daughter*. Maxwell Anderson did a light comedy, *Saturday's Children*. George Abbott and Philip Dunning wrote a rousing melodrama, *Broadway*, which was good theater. Two other plays of that genre, *Chicago* by Maurine Watkins and *The Barker* by Kenyon Nicholson, also attracted large audiences. George Kelly, too, was back with a new play, *Daisy Mayme*.

However, the Drama Jury, which that year consisted of Eaton, Hamilton, and A. E. Thomas as chairman, voted unanimously for a little-known, 32-year-old North Carolina teacher, Paul Green, for his tragedy of life among the blacks in the South, *In Abraham's Bosom*. It was the first play in Pulitzer annals that took serious account of the nation's greatest social problem.

In Abraham's Bosom had a modest run, 123 performances, mainly because of the prize. It was not a thriller; on the contrary, it tended to repel comfortable white audiences. Nor was it a well-made play; it sprawled, even repeated itself. But it did place the troubling relationships between blacks and whites on the Broadway stage and it did so with honesty and even fervor. The story dealt with a young black, determined to educate himself and improve the lot of his people, who is taunted and beaten by a white mob, driven to kill his half brother and finally lynched.

"The play does not sentimentalize over the tragic situation of the Negro," Hamilton wrote in the jury's report. "It is scrupulously fair to the white race. Yet it brings us face to face with one of the most serious social problems of this country and forces us to view this problem in the light of tragic pity.

"*In Abraham's Bosom* is not without its faults, most of which are merely technical; but the jurors feel that it is an admirable example of precisely

---

* Albert Ellsworth Thomas was 15 years younger than Augustus Thomas, and both wrote for the Broadway stage for years. They were not related.

the sort of composition which Mr. Pulitzer most desired to encourage when he established the Pulitzer Prize for Drama."

So it turned out that Paul Green, a stranger to the alluring qualities of Broadway and the very antithesis of the box-office type of playwright, won the Pulitzer Prize for 1927. The critics glowered for the most part because such favorites as Kelly, Anderson, and Howard had been passed over. But Eaton replied long afterward, in defense of *In Abraham's Bosom:* "Because this play came up out of the soil of the South, and with a passionate sincerity tried to say something important about the Negro problem, and because it seemed to us that the prize, if given to Green, might be a great encouragement to regional American drama, we recommended *In Abraham's Bosom.* We knew we would be criticized, but I still think we did right." Both the Advisory Board and the university Trustees agreed.

There was no argument over the Pulitzer Prize winner for the 1927–28 season, Eugene O'Neill's *Strange Interlude,* his third award. It was a prodigious play—nine acts that ran five hours at the Golden Theatre. As produced by the Theatre Guild, it obliged audiences to attend in the afternoon, take a break for dinner, and then return for the entire evening.

The story of Nina Leeds's relationships with her three men, encompassing a twenty-five-year period, was strong stuff for an American theater that had been moribund only a decade before. It broke new ground in the drama. Despite its weightiness and ponderous length, enthusiastic audiences kept it going for 432 performances but it never did win over all the critics. George Jean Nathan in the *American Mercury* was the most admiring, saying that O'Neill had written "the finest, the profoundest drama of his entire career." Brooks Atkinson in the New York *Times,* usually an O'Neill enthusiast, was reserved, and Alexander Woollcott, the New York *World*'s reviewer at the time, wrote such an antagonistic piece about *Strange Interlude* before its opening that he was barred by his editors from his usual first night critique.

For the Drama Jury, A. E. Thomas wrote: "This drama of the subconscious and of frustration is sound and thoughtful in its development; but it also has great intensity of feeling, moments of beauty, and above all it shows dramatically that the conscious emotions, which give us dignity in our own eyes as individuals, cannot be ignored. In spite of too great length, some pretentiousness, and the abnormality of the 'case' studied, *Strange Interlude* gets its fingers deeply tangled in the web of human life. It has depth and intellectual power above any and all of its rivals. It is, in your jury's opinion, the logical recipient of the Pulitzer Prize for 1927–28."

Compared with such standard Broadway fare as *The Royal Family*, *The Trial of Mary Dugan*, *Paris Bound* and *Coquette*, all of which were considered in the jury's report, there was no question about the superiority of *Strange Interlude* that season. The only play of consequence that was overlooked was DuBose Heyward's unpretentious dramatization, with his wife, Dorothy, of his 1925 novel, *Porgy*, an all-black play about life on Catfish Row.[14] But then, Edna Ferber's *Show Boat* also had been brushed aside, only to become one of the best loved pieces in the American musical theatre in 1927 by reason of Jerome Kern's beautiful score and the sensitive lyrics of Oscar Hammerstein II. *Porgy*'s time was yet to come.

Elmer Rice's time for his Pulitzer Prize was the 1928–29 season when he set down a faded New York brownstone house in the center of the Playhouse's stage, peopled it with gossipy neighbors and doomed lovers, and called it *Street Scene*. This was life as New Yorkers knew it—from love-making and frenzied jealousy to eviction and murder. It rang true— so much so that it registered 601 performances. And it made, for the time being, a major playwright out of Rice, who at 21 years of age had made a fortune with his melodrama, *On Trial*, and who had gone on to do his admired expressionistic drama, *The Adding Machine*. The same jury that had recommended *Strange Interlude* now proposed to give the 1929 prize either to *Street Scene*—or nothing. The reason for the studied alternative was that Chairman A. E. Thomas had heartily disliked *Street Scene* while Hamilton and Eaton had been just as fervently for it.

Street Scene might not have had much of a chance if the terms of the drama award had remained for the American play "which shall best represent the educational value and power of the stage in raising the standard of good morals, good taste, and good manners." It was scarcely a play that was written to illustrate these admirable qualities. However, in the 1929 revisions of the Plan of Award, the drama prize was to be given to the original American play "which shall best represent the educational value and power of the stage." There was no question that *Street Scene* was powerful stuff; as for educational value, however, that depended on who was to be educated and why.

Once again, Hamilton made the most telling arguments in the jury report. Writing in the third person, he put the case this way: "Mr. Hamilton's enthusiasm for *Street Scene* is positive and emphatic. He regards it not only as the outstanding American play of the current season, but as one of the foremost American plays of any season. He admires it not only for its striking originality and its extraordinary technical dexterity but even more for the author's accuracy of observation of local life, his rigid objectivity of mental attitude toward his materials, and his refusal to make concessions to the ordinary canons of theatrical taste which are supposed to attract money to the box office. Under these conditions, the fact that *Street Scene* is playing to capacity nine times a week, and that the seats are selling at a premium sixteen weeks in advance may be regarded as a veritable triumph."

Street Scene won the prize; except for A. E. Thomas, nearly everybody seemed pleased and certainly the audiences were. But such are the tricks that time plays with the worthiest dramas and such are the quirks of public taste that a rowdy melodrama of 1929, *The Front Page*, by Ben Hecht and Charles MacArthur, actually outlasted *Street Scene* in public favor. To audiences of the 1970s, *The Front Page* had a nostalgic appeal that no jury of 1929 could possibly have recognized, nostalgia having been in short supply in a world that was shortly to plunge into the abyss of economic chaos.

The winner for 1930 was even more of a certainty than *Street Scene*. It was Marc Connelly's classic, *The Green Pastures*, with Richard B. Harrison as "De Lawd" leading an all-black cast in a fanciful recreation of the tales of the Bible. True, the show owed its inspiration entirely to Roark Bradford's sketches, *Ol' Man Adam an' His Chillun*, so that it didn't really qualify as an original American play within the definition of the Plan of Award.

The jury tackled that issue head-on before writing its report. The second Joseph Pulitzer, son of the donor, was consulted by Eaton and Hamilton, as chairman, and a new member, Austin Strong, the author of a play called *Three Wise Fools*. Pulitzer asked, "Does it add something original, making the work a new and perhaps larger thing, as Shakespeare added to the stories he took?" The jurors said they thought it did. "Then give it the prize," Pulitzer said.

The jury wasted no time in echoing the play's entrance line: "Gangway! Gangway for de Lawd God Jehovah!" In one of the most effusive of all Pulitzer Prize reports, they wrote:

> One play—*The Green Pastures* by Marc Connelly—towers so far above the other American plays of the season and comes so near to

setting a new standard of excellence for the American drama of all time that the jurors desire, with unusual enthusiasm, to recommend it for the Pulitzer Prize. It is a work of astonishing originality and it is rich in those qualities which Mr. Pulitzer, in the opinion of the jurors, desired most to foster and encourage. It is simple, gentle, kindly, tender, humorous, compassionate, wise, beautiful, exalted, and exulting. It interprets the religion of thousands of Negroes in the deep South with the simple sincerity of the very best of the Medieval mystery plays. A delicate task has been accomplished with faultless taste; and the piece deserves to be cherished as a Divine Comedy of a living religion interpreted consistently in the terms of its believers.

On this occasion, the jurors state emphatically that they have no second choice.

There was a cheerful postscript from Eaton, who scribbled after his signature that he didn't "subscribe to quite all the adjectives used above but most heartily to the verdict."

The fortunes of the black American have undergone vigorous and sometimes violent change in the forty years since the Connelly-Bradford collaboration presented the sentimental image of a black community in the South that was peopled largely by simple, happy children of nature who believed with Hosea in a God of love. But this was the image that appealed so movingly in 1930 to white Americans, north and south, when *The Green Pastures* received the accolade of the Pulitzer Prize. It will always be an impressive part of the cultural history of the land.[15]

Maxwell Anderson was back with a much-admired verse play, *Elizabeth the Queen*, during the 1930–31 season and the brilliant Lynn Fontanne and Alfred Lunt made it a shimmering, memorable affair for the Theatre Guild. Anderson was then 43 and at the peak of his career as a dramatist. While he never achieved the great stature of Eugene O'Neill in the American theatre, he was nevertheless one of the playwrights who added luster to the Broadway stage. As a craftsman, his best work was flawless. He tackled great themes and brought them to life, often with a touch of infinite beauty, and was a favorite with the critics of the period.

Anderson came to the theater by chance rather than design. He was the son of a Baptist minister, a pacifist during World War I, and briefly a teacher before he took to newspaper work and eventually landed on the

New York *World*. Although his first play was a failure, he scored one of the finest successes of his career with the play he wrote with his *World* colleague, Laurence Stallings, *What Price Glory?* During the next four-teen years, his work on Broadway was consistently good, even brilliant on occasion. Few other playwrights of his time could point to a record of such proportions—one that included plays of the stature of *Elizabeth the Queen, Mary of Scotland, Winterset, Knickerbocker Holiday, Joan of Lorraine* and *Anne of the Thousand Days*.

The Pulitzer Prize Drama Jury for 1931, the same as the one that had picked *The Green Pastures* in the previous year, was well aware of Ander-son's reputation and of the wide critical approval he had won for *Eliza-beth the Queen*. In searching for the "original American play which shall best represent the educational value and power of the stage" that year, the jurors also considered such winners as Philip Barry's *Tomorrow and Tomorrow*, the hilarious *Once in a Lifetime* by George S. Kaufman and Moss Hart, and the sensitive and poetic *Green Grow the Lilacs*, by Lynn Riggs, which later became the basis for *Oklahoma!* There was, finally, a struggling play by Susan Glaspell, one of the founders of the Province-town Playhouse, called *Alison's House*. It had been suggested by the ca-reer of Emily Dickinson, an American poet who had died in 1886 and had been recognized as a major figure in American poetry after her death. And it had been produced by Eva LeGallienne's Civic Repertory Theatre in a rickety old building on 14th Street, far off Broadway, with Miss LeGallienne and the lustrous Josephine Hutchinson as the stars.

Although the Civic Repertory had received a certain amount of en-couragement, it had a hard time making ends meet. There were no foun-dations in that era to make princely gifts to support an experimental theatre and a show that opened off Broadway had two strikes against it before the curtain went up. To a regular Broadway critic, therefore, it appeared unbelievable to mention *Alison's House* in the same breath with *Elizabeth the Queen*. And yet, that year, *Alison's House* won the sympa-thetic attention of two out of the three members of the Drama Jury, Hamilton and Eaton. Strong, the third juror, wanted to pass the award.

The majority opinion, which Eaton wrote, did not bother to argue against *Elizabeth the Queen* because it lacked an American background, a specious reason at best. Instead, it plumped wholeheartedly for *Alison's House* because of "the fine sincerity of the dramatist, her choice of a theme which is fresh, taken out of American life, and worthy of serious attention, and her evident interest in what she had to say, quite apart from any considerations of temporal styles or box office appeal."

The Advisory Board recommended the Glaspell play without comment on April 14, 1931, and the Trustees ratified the decision on May 4. A cry of outrage went up from the New York drama critics almost at once, dwarfing all previous protests against the Pulitzer Prizes. Even the gentle Brooks Atkinson commented in the New York Times:

"Prize committees are always unpopular and under suspicion. But sometimes the drama committee for the Pulitzer Prize goes out of its way to make its glory hollow."

The war dance continued for a little longer than usual that year, but it eventually subsided. There was no response from Morningside Heights in accordance with Columbia's practice of administering and awarding the prizes and letting them speak for themselves. But years later, Eaton fired back a mild salvo at the jury's detractors:

"Again I have no apologies for this choice. *Alison's House* somewhat bored the critics in New York but it was acted for a long time by many theater groups throughout the country, and in a production I saw only three years ago [1941], it was still a moving and provocative play which deserved a recognition Broadway refused." [16]

Not a bit dismayed, President Butler and the Advisory Board sent the same jurors back to Broadway in the next season and were rewarded with a surprise selection, *Of Thee I Sing*, for the 1932 Pulitzer Prize. In a time of monstrous public discontent with the American establishment, this was a musical that made a sorely tried people laugh at themselves and their institutions. During the worst years of the great depression, in which *Of Thee I Sing* ran for 441 performances at the Music Box Theatre, that was a major accomplishment.

Once again, the jury could have played it safe by going to a conventional Pulitzer Prize candidate, such as O'Neill's five-hour *Mourning Becomes Electra* or Philip Barry's *The Animal Kingdom*. But the unanimous verdict went to *Of Thee I Sing*, the authors of the book, George S. Kaufman and Morrie Ryskind, and the lyricist, Ira Gershwin. It is a pity, as Richard Rodgers pointed out long afterward, that the jury did not have the imagination to push its innovative decision a step further by including the composer, George Gershwin, among those it honored. For after all, if there had been no Gershwin music, there would have been no play.

In its report, the jury tried to maintain the fiction that the book and lyrics could be separated from the music. "Not only is it coherent and well knit enough to class as a play, aside from the music," said the report, "but it is a biting and true satire on American politics and the public attitude toward them. The play is genuine and we feel the prize could not serve a better purpose than to recognize such work."

Much to the surprise of the jury, the award was well received when it was made public with the approval of the university Trustees and the Advisory Board. With the exception of Brooks Atkinson, the principal New York critics appeared to be happy over the unexpected turn of events. As Eaton put it, "The critics were either stunned or pleased—I can't say which—perhaps a little of both."

The winners solemnly debated over how to divide the $1,000 check and finally split it three ways: Ryskind, $333.33; Ira Gershwin, $333.33; and Kaufman, $333.34. Kaufman explained, "I got the extra penny because I was the eldest."

The same jury climaxed this period of development of the Pulitzer Prizes in 1933 by giving Maxwell Anderson his long deferred award for a play about a crusading Congressman, *Both Your Houses*. It ran for a moderate 120 performances under the aegis of the Theatre Guild. Anderson, the crusader for worthy causes, was less exciting than Anderson, the dramatic poet. For all his idealism and indignation over graft in government, he could not win the public's attention in the same manner as the light-hearted *Of Thee I Sing*.[17]

4
History's Progressives

While the day of the gentleman amateur was by no means over, the professional historians came into their own during the changing era of the late 1920s and the early 1930s. In a time of unequaled economic stress, when the faith of tens of millions of Americans in self-government was being tried as never before, new voices demanded attention in academe and new views of the American past had to be taken into account by those who were trying to shape the nation's future. Two of the most influential of these challenging professionals were the progressive historians, Vernon Louis Parrington and Frederick Jackson Turner. Both were introduced to mass audiences with the award of Pulitzer Prizes to them for their major works, Parrington's first two volumes of his trilogy, *Main Currents of American Thought* in 1928 and Turner's *The Significance of Sections in American History* in 1933. The jury that honored Parrington consisted of Worthington C. Ford, chairman; James Truslow Adams; and Professor Charles D. Hazen of Columbia, who worked together from 1925 through 1929. Those who selected Turner's major work were Professor Hazen, chairman; Burton J. Hendrick; and the historian and biographer, M. A. DeWolfe Howe, who served as a unit from 1931 through 1934. In both cases, the Advisory Board went along with strong jury recommendations and thereby underlined the rising influence of the progressives at the time.[18]

The less controversial professionals were well represented, too, in the prizes for that period. Among them were Charles Howard McIlwain's *The American Revolution—A Constitutional Interpretation*, in 1924; Frederic L. Paxson's *A History of the American Frontier*, in 1925; Edward Channing's *The History of the United States*, in 1926; Samuel Flagg Bemis' *Pinckney's Treaty*, in 1927; Fred Albert Shannon's highly critical, *The Organization and Administration of the Union Army, 1861–1865*, in 1929; Claude H. Van Tyne's *The War of Independence*, in 1930, a posthumous award, and Bernadotte E. Schmitt's *The Coming of the War: 1914*, in 1931. The sole representative of the amateur tradition in this list was the 1932 award to General John J. Pershing for *My Experiences in the World War*, which was mainly a compliment to the general's military reputation.

Despite the lack of controversy on the surface, the members of the History Juries did not find life to be entirely serene although their differences were not as highly publicized as those who served in fiction and drama. For example, the prize to the Van Tyne book, which was much kinder to the Loyalist cause than more conventional revolutionary histories, was voted by the Advisory Board despite a 2–1 jury report in favor of Claude Bowers' *The Tragic Era*. And in 1926, the Board turned down a 2–1 jury decision in favor of Bernard Fay's *L'Esprit Révolutionnaire en France et aux Etats-Unis*, ruling it ineligible because it was written in French, and awarded the prize to the jumbo-size Channing history, the sixth volume of which had been published that year.

There was no argument about Parrington's work which was hailed upon publication as a path-breaking inquiry into the American past and an intellectual history of stunning proportions. Worthington C. Ford, in writing his unanimous jury report, said: "The decision rests upon the following considerations: that the work is original in conception and in performance; it shows research and scholarship; and it throws fresh light upon many aspects of our history. It is penetrating and acute." [19]

Parrington was 57 years old when he won the Pulitzer Prize in 1928 and he died the following year, just after the completion of the third and concluding volume of his *Main Currents in American Thought.* While he lived to enjoy the recognition that came to him so late in life, and with such incredible swiftness, neither he nor his supporters could have foreseen the decline of a reputation that had been developed through so much effort. Many of his ideas and his interpretations, which seemed so fresh and so heartening to liberals in the 1920s and early 1930s, have long since been supplanted by far more modern research and scholarship.

But in his time, Parrington represented the best among the relatively few venturesome ones who specialized in American intellectual history. Howard Mumford Jones credited him with seeming for a time "almost to obliterate literary histories." Lionel Trilling wrote that Parrington had "an influence on our conception of American culture which is not equaled by that of any other writer of the last two decades." In 1950, when the decline in Parrington's reputation had set in, Henry Steele Commager still looked upon *Main Currents* as a "magnificent tract" and a "great study of American thought." Many American historians at the time still shared Commager's view; in a poll, they put Parrington's work first among all books in their field that were published between 1920 and 1950, with Turner's interpretation of the American frontier a close second. Both led substantially over the third great progressive historian of the era, Charles A. Beard, who with his wife, Mary, wrote the highly regarded *Rise of American Civilization.*

Among the younger historians, Richard Hofstadter's perception of Parrington's importance was fairly typical:

"Reading him for the first time in 1938, I found his volumes immensely rewarding. What other historian had written about American letters with such a wealth of democratic enthusiasm? What other writer had covered the whole span of American letters from 1620 to the end of the 19th century in a work which had so much of a personal stamp on it, and yet with so consistent an effort to put American writing into its social setting?" [20]

To the depression-bound American liberals of the 1930s, taken as a whole, Parrington's voice was that of a seer who viewed the American past in terms with which they sympathized—perhaps, even a prophet who foretold the coming of a new land cast in the kind of liberal image that was then fashionable. All kinds of things could be—and were—read into Parrington by his supporters. The realists and the naturalists among American writers seized upon him as their champion and their guide, for most of Parrington's judgments were political rather than literary and he dealt scarcely at all with the imponderables of esthetic thought. His heroes and villains were drawn in clear, stark terms; moreover, he turned away from the nuances of sociology to lay out his ideas along political lines that more or less coincided with the thinking of the admiring critics of the left.

Yet, while Parrington looked upon himself as a modern representative of the Populist-Progressive movement in history, he could scarcely have been considered a member of the avant garde. He was a maverick, true enough, and a loner more often than not. In a profession of congenital insiders, who shared each others' thoughts and prejudices to a remarkable degree, he was an outsider. He had been born in Aurora, Illinois, reared in Kansas, and educated at the College of Emporia, a small Presbyterian institution, and at Harvard, from which he was graduated in 1893. All that Harvard gave him was a set of violent prejudices and an inferiority complex that dogged him through his subsequent teaching career at the College of Emporia and the University of Oklahoma. It was only when he went to the University of Washington in 1908 that he finally began to shape his career and visualize his greatest work.

While *Main Currents* was valuable for its perceptions of many of the writers and thinkers who shaped American thought, its weaknesses soon became apparent to discerning critics and historians. For Parrington had adopted so conscious a bias against British influence on American thinking and the very real contribution of the Puritan heritage and Calvinist discipline that some of his most important judgments proved to be shaky. He saw the evolution of American thought as a result of the conflict of opposites, in the main, and he even dealt with his central characters in terms of contrasting influences. Finally, without sufficient evidence, he plumped for the theory that the early settlers in America were motivated primarily by the teachings of Martin Luther and the government they evolved owed more to Rousseau than to John Locke and other English philosophers.

Parrington was perfectly honest about his partisanship. As he explained in the introduction to *Main Currents*, he was "liberal rather than conservative, Jeffersonian rather than Federalistic, and very likely on my search I have found what I went forth to find, as others have discovered what they were seeking." Yet, it will not do to dismiss Parrington as some of the new critics have sought to do. His was a vital work for its time, despite all its faults, and his mind was given to original reflection even though his sometime admirer, Lionel Trilling, called it "too predictable to be consistently interesting."

Richard Hofstadter's verdict was perhaps more realistic:

"If we want to understand the presuppositions of the American Progressive mind and trace what has happened to it, we must again interest ourselves in a book which, as Alfred Kazin has put it, 'represents the most ambitious single effort of the Progressive mind to understand itself.' " [21]

The reputation of Frederick Jackson Turner evolved over a considerably longer period than Parrington's and it has, on the whole, proved to be more durable. Although he matured at Harvard, where he taught for fourteen years, he stemmed from the American heartland by birth and disposition. He was born at Portage, Wis., in 1861, received his B.A. from the University of Wisconsin in 1884, took his M.A. there four years later, and his Ph.D. from Johns Hopkins in 1890. Three years afterward—vigorous, enthusiastic, and strikingly handsome at the age of 31—he electrified the Chicago convention of the American Historical Association with a paper entitled, "The Significance of the Frontier in American History." It was, as Charles A. Beard pointed out later, "to have a more profound influence on thought about American history than any other essay or volume ever written on the subject." Eighty years later, Professor David Herbert Donald of Johns Hopkins, himself a Pulitzer Prize winner, still considered Turner to be a "towering" figure in his profession even though the general historical view of the importance of the American frontier had undergone revision.[22]

Regardless of the continual ebb and flow of ideas in his time, Turner stoutly championed the American frontier throughout his life as the great formative experience in American democracy and the underlying reason for the toughness of the American national character. It was the frontier, as he said in his 1893 address, that "promoted the formation of a composite nationality for the American people." And, he went on, "It was this nationalizing tendency of the West that transformed the democracy of Jefferson into the nationalizing republicanism of Monroe and the democracy of Jackson." But even more important, in his view, was the individualism that grew out of frontier life for, he said, "Frontier individualism has from the beginning promoted democracy." He concluded:

"What the Mediterranean Sea was to the Greeks, breaking the bond of custom, offering new experiences, calling out new institutions and activities, that, and more, the ever retreating frontier has been to the United States directly, and to the nations of Europe more remotely. And now, four centuries from the discovery of America, at the end of a hundred years of life under the Constitution, the frontier has gone, and with its going has closed the first period of American history." [23]

The surprising aspect of Turner's work, considering the vastness of his influence during his lifetime, is that there is so little of it. There are only four volumes in all, produced over a teaching career that spanned four decades. Two of these were published during his lifetime—*The Rise of the New West* in 1906 and the essays collected in *The Frontier in American History* in 1920. His Pulitzer Prize-winning work, the collection of essays entitled *The Significance of Sections in American History*, was issued shortly after his death in 1932 and won a posthumous award the following year. In 1935, his last book was published even though it wasn't completed: *The United States, 1830–1850: The Nation and Its Sections*.

Nevertheless, Turner is important because he was the first historian of consequence to dramatize the importance of the American frontier in the history of the country. In the latter stages of his career, in developing the concept of sectional influences on American history, he continued to insist on the impact of Western individualism and Western ideas as an underlying factor in American national development. If he didn't write very much—"I hate to write," he once told a student—he lectured with grace and skill and he taught with an infectious enthusiasm that made him sought after by students both at the University of Wisconsin and, later, at Harvard. Even at Huntington Library, where he ended his days in research, his associates were impressed with his warmth and his fervor when he discussed his ideas or came upon what he thought was a new discovery.

There seemed to be no limit to Turner's influence in his time. He encouraged a youthful Harvard-bred historian, Theodore Roosevelt, upon the publication of the first two volumes of *The Winning of the West* in 1889, writing in the *Dial* of the "vivid portraiture of the backwoodsman's advance." Woodrow Wilson, too, owed something to Turner, his friend and guide. For Wilson once wrote, "The 'West' is the great word of our history. The 'Westerner' has been the type and master of our American life. . . . The Westerner, in some day soon to come, will pass out of our life, as he so long ago passed out of the life of the Old World. Then a new epoch will open for us. Perhaps it has opened already. Slowly we shall grow old, compact our people, study the delicate adjustments of an intricate society, and ponder the niceties, as we have hitherto pondered the bulks and structural framework of government." Of Turner, Wilson said simply, "All I ever wrote on the subject came from him."

It was this sense of hopelessness in the future, of decline, that Turner had to combat in arguing over the years for his frontier ideal. For once the frontier had gone, once free land no longer existed, once the West became heavily populated and the tall towers of its cities resembled those of the East, what was there to sustain the argument of Western influence beyond a pleasant and engaging myth that was spread before the nation nightly on television in later years? Turner was conscious of the weakness of his position here and once argued in terms that President John Fitzgerald Kennedy would have approved:

"In place of old frontiers of wilderness, there are new frontiers of unwon fields of science, fruitful for the needs of the race; there are frontiers of better social domains yet unexplored." [24]

On March 17, 1933, after Turner's death, the Pulitzer Prize History Jury decided that his work should be honored and called to the attention of a larger public. The vote, however, was not unanimous. Professor Hazen, the chairman, and DeWolfe Howe were for Turner's path-breaking essays in *The Significance of Sections in American History*. The remaining juror, Burton J. Hendrick, favored his fellow journalist, Mark Sullivan, for *Our Times, 1909–1914*. Referring to Turner's essays, Hazen wrote:

> They treat important aspects of the evolution of American civilization in a thorough and fresh way, are based upon a wide reading of sources, and are clear and careful in their point of view. They are supported by bibliographical and scholarly material regarding the topics of investigation. They represent slow and thorough research and are destined to exercise a distinct influence upon the thought of attentive and reflecting Americans.
>
> We feel that they should be considered on their own merits, and

also as representative of the scholarly researches of one of the leading historians of America. They are briefly, carefully, justly and judicially presented by the author and merit high consideration. Two of the committee, therefore, recommend that this book, *The Significance of Sections in American History*, be given the Pulitzer Prize for 1933.[25]

There was no discussion in the Advisory Board. The prize was voted to Turner in what became, certainly, one of the major awards for history in Pulitzer annals. For the work that Turner began is likely to continue without limit in time. As Richard Hofstadter has said:

"The frontier idea, though dissected at one point and minimized at another, keeps popping up in new forms, posing new questions to its questioners, always prodding investigation into new areas. Turner once said that his aim had been not to produce disciples but to propagate inquiry. He did both; and the inquiry propagated among critics and friendly revisionists has now reached a volume that overmatches the work of his disciples. This mountain of Turner criticism is his most certain monument. Among all the historians of the United States it was Turner alone of whom we can now say with certainty that he opened a controversy that was large enough to command the attention of his peers for four generations." [26]

Not all the progressive historians were satisfied with the deterministic theories of Turner and Beard. As research opened the way for new ideas and new interpretations of their work, some of those who had followed them branched off into the less controversial art of biography. For it was, like intellectual history, a major part of the study of ideas and it had deep roots in American culture as Parrington already had demonstrated. Of the new biographers, the most prominent and by all odds the most industrious was Allan Nevins of Columbia, a book critic for the New York *World* who had with enormous effort turned himself into a professor of history. In his rejection of the impersonal approach to the American past, he also cast aside much of the intellectual baggage of Turnerism. The one thing he retained was Turner's tendency to idealize his heroes, notably the Westerner. The Pulitzer Prize that was awarded to the biography, *Grover Cleveland* in 1933, the first of two to be won by Nevins, testified to the measure of his success in attracting both a critical and a popular audience to his way of thinking.

To be sure, Nevins was not a professional historian to begin with. Nor was he alone in turning from journalism to biography by way of a general preparation in historical studies. It was a time when journalists were tramping unceremoniously into the once sheltered groves of academe, elbowing the gentlemen amateurs and discomfiting the established historical professionals.

Among Nevins' fellow journalists who won Pulitzer Prizes for biography in that changing period were Charles Edward Russell, a Chicago editor, for his *The American Orchestra and Theodore Thomas*, in 1928; Burton J. Hendrick, who topped his 1923 award for his Walter Hines Page biography with still another Page book in 1929, *The Training of an American: The Earlier Life and Letters of Walter H. Page;* Marquis James, a writer for the *American Legion Monthly*, for his Sam Houston biography, *The Raven*, in 1930; and Henry F. Pringle of the New York *World* for his *Theodore Roosevelt* in 1932.

Had it not been for the disqualification of biographies of Washington and Lincoln, that extraordinary Chicago poet-journalist, Carl Sandburg, would surely have won with his earliest work on Lincoln in 1927 over Emory Holloway's *Whitman*. Royal Cortissoz, art critic of the New York *Herald Tribune*, who was the Pulitzer biography chairman from 1925 through 1944, wrote in his 1927 report that he would have been "glad if we could have given the prize to Sandburg's book."

The gentlemen amateurs were still around, of course. A physicist, Professor Michael Idvorsky Pupin of Columbia, won in 1924 for his autobiography, *From Immigrant to Inventor*. A neurosurgeon, Dr. Harvey Cushing, received the 1926 award for his two-volume *The Life of Sir William Osler*. A lawyer, Henry James, who was the son of William James and a nephew of the novelist, Henry James, won in 1931 for his biography of the president of Harvard, *Charles W. Eliot*. And another Cambridge stalwart, M. A. DeWolfe Howe, received the 1925 award for his work about Harvard's literary historian, *Barrett Wendell and His Letters*.

Oddly enough, as the jury memberships for the period show, the encouragement to the journalists came primarily from academics who have never, as a group, been particularly struck with admiration for journalism. For serving with Cortissoz were such authoritative personalities as Professor George M. Harper of Princeton, 1928–1933; Van Wyck Brooks, 1928–1929; Professor Richard Burton, 1930–1932; M. A. De-Wolfe Howe, 1927 and 1932, after the award of his own prize; Professor

John Spencer Bassett of Smith, 1926; and Henry Dwight Sedgwick, 1924–1925. There were only two journalists other than Cortissoz on the juries in those years—William Allen White in 1924 and Woodrow Wilson's biographer, Ray Stannard Baker, in 1927. And there was one clergyman, the Rev. Dr. George A. Gordon of Boston in 1925. These were, in the main, conservatives—typical of the kind of Pulitzer jurors who served on the literary juries in the Butler regime.

Nevins' appeal, too, was essentially conservative with a strong overlay of conscious idealism. He had, by the time he became a Pulitzer laureate, put a considerable distance between himself and the Populist-Progressives from whom he drew his earliest inspiration. He was not ashamed to conjure up inspiring images and he, like Samuel Eliot Morison at Harvard, skillfully practiced the literary tradition in biography and turned aside with a shudder from dry-as-dust scholarship. On the eve of World War II, he was to cling to his faith in history as an inspirational force, saying:

"History is the sextant and compass of states which, tossed by wind and current, would be lost in confusion if they could not fix their position. . . . By giving peoples a sense of continuity in all their efforts, and by chronicling immortal worth, it confers upon them both a consciousness of their unity, and a feeling of the importance of human achievement." [27]

Nevins was born in 1890 in Camp Point, Ill., received his B.A. and M.A. from the University of Illinois in 1912 and 1913 respectively, and soon turned to newspaper work by day and the writing of history by night. While he was on the New York *World* in the 1920s, he published six historical works of substance. It was not done without strenuous effort; often, leaving the *World* Building on Park Row at four in the afternoon, he would race to the New York Public Library at 42nd Street and study until closing time.

He broke with daily journalism in 1931 after teaching history at Cornell for a year and at Columbia for three years on the lower levels of academe. In that year, his reputation and his progress were such that his Columbia colleagues accepted him as a full professor.

As an organizer and innovator, Nevins also left his mark on his profession. At an early age, he visualized a new kind of magazine that would popularize history for the masses, fought with the American Historical Association when it rejected the project, and finally saw it materialize with the publication of *American Heritage*. He, too, was the first to see the possibility of a unique form of historical research with the invention of the tape recorder and persuaded Columbia University to found the Oral History Project, which is today a large and successful undertaking with an impressive file of taped historical interviews from eminent Americans and others.

Frequently, Nevins had to fight for progress. Although he was a peaceful man, he never failed to shake off the restraining hands of his pedantic colleagues. Once he struck savagely against pedantry in the *Saturday Review of Literature* as follows:

"The pedant . . . has found the means in our university system and our learned societies to fasten himself with an Old Man of the Sea grip upon history. Though the touch of this school benumbs and paralyzes all interest in history, it is supported by university chairs, special foundations and funds, research fellowships, and learned bodies. It is against this entrenched pedantry that the war of true history will have to be most determined and implacable." [28]

Nevins' second Pulitzer Prize in Biography for his *Hamilton Fish* in 1937 did not make him less aggressive in pursuing his manifold aims. He embarked on his great Civil War history soon afterward. And in 1960, when he finally made his peace with the American Historical Association, he accepted its presidency with a vow to bring about greater unity in the profession. "We are all amateurs, we are all professionals," he said in his presidential address. When he died in 1971, he left Columbia $500,000 to endow historical researches.

The ebbing of the progressive tide in American history left behind it a high water mark of innovative scholarship, as noted in the Pulitzer Prize records, that may have been approached by new forces but never surpassed.

5
Poetry: From Frost to MacLeish

Harriet Monroe, the founder and editor of *Poetry*, a magazine of verse, attacked the poetry awards of what she called the "Pulitzer Prize System" in 1927. The immediate cause of her complaint was the 1927 prize to Leonora Speyer for *Fiddler's Farewell*, which she believed to be inferior to Sara Teasdale's *Dark of the Moon*. With ladylike primness, neverthe-less, Miss Monroe went on to compliment Mrs. Speyer as a poet of "fine quality" and praised her "extraordinary record," then got down to the main business of the indictment—the character and quality of the judges. It seems that they were not poets, which was the main trouble with them.

Miss Monroe's dissatisfaction, she wrote, was "not so much with the awards themselves as with the manner of choosing them." What she proposed was the decapitation, in a literary sense, of the 1927 Poetry Jury consisting of Dean Wilbur L. Cross and Ferris Greenslet, familiar figures from the opening era of the prizes, and a newcomer, Professor John Erskine of Columbia, who had among other things written three volumes of verse. Instead, she wanted a jury of working poets who alone, in her opinion, were qualified to judge poetry.[29]

Dean Cross, whose jury had weighed Miss Teasdale's volume in the 1927 report and rejected it because it was narrower in range than Mrs. Speyer's, wasted no time in taking up Miss Monroe's challenge. In 1928, the Poetry Jury consisted of Dean Cross, Professor Erskine, and Robert Frost, who had won the Pulitzer Prize in 1924 and was to become the only four-time poetry winner of the awards. If it wasn't an all-poet jury, poets were at least in the majority. Their verdict, which didn't satisfy Miss Monroe's quest for new faces and new talent, mainly from the midwest, was for Edwin Arlington Robinson's *Tristram*, his third Pu-litzer Prize in seven years. Nevertheless, she had known Frost since 1917 when he had come to Chicago at her invitation to lecture for $150, so nothing more was heard for the time being of her campaign to have poets alone judge poetry. In later years, however, it was a concept that won favor with the administrators of the Pulitzer Prizes.

Except for Miss Monroe's complaint, there was comparatively little criticism of the selections that were made by Dean (and later Governor) Cross and his associates during the 1920s and early 1930s. Beginning with Robert Frost's *New Hampshire* in 1924, it was a notable list and recognized many and diverse talents; Robinson in 1925 for *The Man Who Died Twice*; Amy Lowell in 1926 for *What's O'Clock*, a posthumous award; the Speyer and Robinson works in 1927 and 1928 respectively; Stephen Vincent Benet in 1929 for *John Brown's Body*; Conrad Aiken for *Selected Poems* in 1930; Frost again in 1931 for his *Collected Poems*; George Dillon in 1932 for *The Flowering Stone;* and Archibald MacLeish in 1933 for *Conquistador.*

It was quite a distance from the apolitical Frost, with his Emersonian heritage and his preoccupation with country life and the forces of nature, to the politicized MacLeish, who so resembled Thomas Stearns Eliot early in life but continued to change and grow with the most modern poets. In manners, methods, and outlook, they spanned the gap from the mid-Victorian age to the era of the atom and the exploration of the moon and outer space. In qualities of heart and mind, they differed as well, for it was an innate toughness of mind that enabled Frost to survive the cruel and constant testing of the literary life while MacLeish was sustained by his calculated urbanity and his readiness to meet the forces of change head on.

Between these two monuments to American poetry, marked by Frost's four Pulitzer Prizes and MacLeish's three (one for a poetic drama), there was room for representatives of the often conflicting trends in the field, from the enthusiasts of the Modernist poetic revolution of the 1920s to the forerunners of the modern poets. Over the years, this was the difference between Eliot and Robert Lowell, Ezra Pound and Theodore Roethke, William Carlos Williams and Robert Penn Warren. For the 1920s and early 1930s, in the Pulitzer Prize list, the differing schools were represented by the idol of the Imagists, Amy Lowell; the poet of ideas, the philosophic Conrad Aiken; and the grim figure of Edwin Arlington Robinson, who antedated the Modernists and whose work outlasted many of the products of their revolution.

It says something about the flexibility of the Pulitzer Poetry juries of the era that so panoramic a view of American poetry could be maintained. The mainstays of the judging were Cross, of course, and Professor Bliss Perry of Harvard, a poetry juror from 1929 through 1943. Those who served in addition to Frost and Erskine were Brian Hooker, 1930 through 1935; Ferris Greenslet, 1922 through 1927; Richard Burton, 1922–1925; Stuart P. Sherman, 1926; and Robert Morss Lovett, 1929.

Their judgments were unanimous except in 1925, when Cross and Burton were for John Crowe Ransom's *Chills and Fever, Poems,* although both considered Robinson's *The Man Who Died Twice* to be the best work of the thirty-five volumes submitted. They set Robinson's work aside, however, because he had won a Pulitzer three years previously. The trouble arose when the third juror, Burton, argued that Ransom's work was "a very mannered, freaky, morbid affair, representative of the introspective Freudian tendencies in our contemporary verse and literature." The 2–1 report in favor of Ransom was sent to the Advisory Board, where the decision was made to give the prize to Robinson instead.

The only other time the Advisory Board intervened in the affairs of the Poetry Jury during that period was in 1933, when the jury consisting of Cross, Perry, and Hooker reported it was "impressed" by Elinor Wylie's *Collected Poems*, but set the volume aside because the author "is no longer living." The jury's unanimous choice was MacLeish's long poem about the conquest of Mexico, *Conquistador*, of which Cross's report said:

"*Conquistador*, extremely modern in its technique, is rather oversophisticated. It is, however, in the opinion of the jury on the whole the best poem that has been submitted this year. I have read it several times and am greatly impressed by it. The other two members of the jury agree with me. Accordingly, we are unanimous in the recommendation that the prize be awarded to *Conquistador*."

Fackenthal, acting on behalf of the Advisory Board, inquired if the jury would have given the prize to Miss Wylie if she had been living. The answer was no, upon which the Board promptly voted the award to MacLeish's poem.[30]

What additional criticism there was of the 1924–1933 awards centered mainly on the failure of the Pulitzer Prizes to recognize the two expatriate poets, Thomas Stearns Eliot and Ezra Pound, and the tendency to keep most of the awards in New England. As to the former, there is no indication in the record that either Eliot or Pound was ever considered, leading to the conclusion that their work was believed by the jurors to be outside the scope of the Plan of Award. As for the criticism of excessive regionalism, which consisted mainly of charges of discrimination against Miss Monroe's Midwesterners and such Southern poets as John Crowe Ransom, Allen Tate, and Robert Penn Warren, it took some time before the problem could be handled. Warren eventually won two prizes, one for poetry and another for fiction. And the Midwesterners led by Carl Sandburg became more prominent among the later poetry winners.

Of all those represented in the long list of Pulitzer Prize winners for poetry, Robert Frost remains the giant of his time. With his death, it was natural to expect that his stature would diminish. The avant garde critics tried to belittle him as a mere "nature poet." The younger poets of the left thought him painfully square. However, his reputation has endured and the great volume of his work has become a part of the American heritage, richly evocative of the best that is in the land. And yet, there was a dark side to Frost, the agnostic, the contemplative thinker who could envision a world that would be destroyed by fire or ice. It was MacLeish who wrote of him that he had "looked as long and deeply into the darkness of the world as a man well can." Yet, essentially, Frost retained to the last in his poetry a toughened shield of optimism that sheltered his faith in what Emerson called "the good of evil born." [31]

How much he actually owed to the Pulitzer Prizes in establishing and maintaining his position as America's unofficial poet laureate would be difficult to determine. But certainly, his four awards broadened his readership and made him known to a mass public that might otherwise never have heard of him. The memory of his appearance on national television as a benevolent father figure at the inauguration in 1961 of President John Fitzgerald Kennedy, struggling in the cold January wind to hold the manuscript of his "The Gift Outright," is still shared sympathetically by the millions who saw him.

For all the honors that came to him, Frost's was not an easy life. It began in hardship and ended in the untimely deaths of some of those dearest to him, which might have destroyed a weaker and less dedicated man. He was born in 1875 in San Francisco but grew up in Lawrence, Mass., where the family moved when he was 10 years old after the death of his father. His mother, a school teacher like his father, encouraged him to go to college but he dropped out of Dartmouth and attended Harvard later for only two years, from 1897 to 1889. He had been married at the age of 20 to his high school sweetheart, Elinor Miriam White, whom he supported by taking a variety of jobs until they settled on a farm in Derry, N.H. in 1900. Eventually, in 1905, he became a teacher in the Pinkerton Academy at Derry, all the while writing poetry that lay unpublished, until in 1912 he sold the farm in discouragement and moved his family to England. That, finally, gave him his start.

For in England at last, he found friends who were impressed with his poetry and helped him arrange for the publication of his first two volumes, *A Boy's Will* in 1913 and the celebrated *North of Boston* in 1914. When *North of Boston* was published in the United States with such famous poems as "Mending Wall" and "After Apple Picking," its author was established and his future career was assured.

When Frost came home in 1915, he was a public figure of consequence and no longer a struggling unknown. During much of the time between 1916 and 1943, with the exception of short periods at Harvard and the University of Michigan, he taught English at Amherst and was also poet in residence there. It was the best and most fruitful period of his life. His prizes, after the first two in 1924, and 1931, came in 1937 for *A Further Range* and in 1943 for *A Witness Tree*. As the Pulitzer Prize reports in poetry make evident, he was also considered in almost every other year in which his work was published.

His Pulitzer awards did not, however, lead him into public life as some of his friends hoped. If anything, they only intensified his desire to remain a poet and to concentrate on his work. Once, when Louis Untermeyer wanted him to become an American propagandist during World War II and lend his prestige to the war effort against Nazi Germany, he replied that he wasn't interested in heaving his poetry at Hitler from Manhattan. To a friend in the Pacific during that war, he wrote: "Nobody's war effort counts much that doesn't get him into danger. . . . But even for the sake of risking my life on an equality with the soldiers I admire so much, I can hardly bring myself to do that. There is no use in being foolhardy." [32]

His patriotism was best expressed in "The Gift Outright," which he wrote in 1935 and first read publicly two days before the Japanese attack on Pearl Harbor—lines that were derived from his feeling about the Revolutionary War. [33]

Frost was sternly determined to the end of his life not to mix poetry and politics, however noble the motive and however dear the cause. And in this, too, he ran counter to many of those who were closest to him. For in a land where the image of the working poet generally coincided with that of a long-haired freak of the left, a kind of Maxwell Bodenheim on roller skates, Frost remained a stolid conservative. He was suspicious of big government, of the noble pretensions of the Welfare State, even of the usefulness of the New Deal although toward the end of his life he did see some good in Franklin Delano Roosevelt. Once, when his friends wanted him to run for the Harvard Board of Overseers, he complained:

"Politics will creep in on me in the most innocent of poems. I suppose we have to have politics if we are going to get the New Deal out of office. But I don't see why I can't leave such matters to others as I did for forty years of my voting life. What's come over me that I can't get over?" [34]

In Frost's work there is the endless pounding of the surf against the rocky headlands of time. He could not celebrate himself, as Walt Whitman did, or advertise himself with Whitman's "barbaric yawp." And yet, just as the Americans of Whitman's era learned to love his poetry and recite it with immense relish, their more sophisticated and better educated descendants liked to chant Frost's most familiar lines with him both in the lecture hall and classroom. If he had labored for two decades over his poetry before recognition came to him belatedly, something he had in common with another of America's finest poets, Emily Dickinson, he shielded carefully whatever hurt he may have felt. Nor was he bowled over by his prizes and other honors. It was his way to approach his most serious moments with a lightness of touch even on ceremonial occasions. When he heard himself likened to Sophocles by the critic, Lionel Trilling, he took it with a twinkle and a small reserved smile.

Poetry was Robert Frost's life and the making of a poem was of transcendent importance to him. He wrote in mid-career: "It begins in delight and ends in wisdom. The figure is the same as for love. . . . Its most precious quality will remain its having run itself and carried away the poet with it." The definition has been as enduring as its author. [35]

Archibald MacLeish, the practical poet of affairs, took a considerably different view of his work. He once quoted a poetic Chinese general who had the bad judgment to lose a battle and was executed in 303 A.D.:

We poets struggle with Non-being to force it to yield Being;
We knock upon silence for an answering music.
We enclose boundless space in a square foot of paper;
We pour out deluge from the inch space of the heart.

To MacLeish, this was indeed illustration of what poetry is all about, for he commented:

"The poet's labor is not to wait until the cry gathers of itself in his own throat. The poet's labor is to struggle with the meaninglessness and silence of the world until he can force it to mean: until he can make the silence answer and the non-Being *be*. It is a labor which undertakes to 'know' the world not by exegesis or demonstration of proofs but directly, as a man knows apple in the mouth." [36]

Whatever else may be said of MacLeish, he invariably demonstrated that he knew his world. Like Bob Dylan, he never needed a weatherman to tell him which way the wind was blowing. The aloofness of a Robert Frost, the breast-beating self-pity of a Walt Whitman, were not for him. He was one of the few poets who dared to plunge into the dust-choked arena of politics to do battle for his beliefs and for the people of his time. And, miraculously for a poet, that impractical visionary, he emerged from his testing with his artistic reputation somewhat battered but still all of a piece.

MacLeish, as a young man, was one of those rare and fortunate human beings who were able to give a good account of themselves in whatever they attempted. He was born in 1892 at Glencoe, Ill., graduated from Yale at 23 as a star athlete and the holder of a Phi Beta Kappa key, ranked among the highest at Harvard Law School, fought in World War I as a captain of artillery, and then embarked on what seemed like a safe and lucrative career as a lawyer in Boston. But having married meanwhile and inherited an income that made him independent, he took to writing poetry instead of legal briefs. And in 1923, the law having palled on him, he left Boston with his wife and two children and traveled for five years, scattering poems along the way as he went.

The name of Archibald MacLeish began to mean something to a small but discriminating public in the 1920s. It also turned up with surprising frequency in the staid reports of the Pulitzer Poetry Juries, as written by Dean Cross. In 1927, for example, the year of the Speyer-Teasdale argument, MacLeish's *Streets in the Moon* was the only other work mentioned in the report. Cross wrote: "Mr. Greenslet expressed admiration for the work of Archibald MacLeish, whose verse seemed to the other two members of the committee to be clever rather than really fine." Four years later, MacLeish was back in the running with *New Found Land* but finished behind Frost and Robinson with Cross commenting dryly: "MacLeish does not quite succeed in the extreme innovations he had attempted." When he won in 1933 with *Conquistador* the product of his *wander-jahren*, there was no doubt that he had mastered the art that he finally had chosen for his life's work.[37]

Almost forty years later, the glow of the first of MacLeish's Pulitzer

Prizes had not worn off. "I don't remember anything of interest about the second or the third," he wrote, "but my first Pulitzer Prize is *engraved*, as they say, on my memory. I was back in Paris staying at a little hotel in the Rue Jacob and somebody dropped the Paris edition of the *Herald Tribune* outside my door! There I was! On Page One! You can imagine what the rest of the day was like." [38]

It was MacLeish's particular virtue that, at the time of the Modernist revolution led by Eliot and Pound, he could be as disillusioned as his masters over the seeming dominance of science over the life of man. But quickly enough, as the Modernist movement went into a decline, he took rank with the most modern of the Modern poets and once again emphasized the importance of the individual. Yet, he could not contemplate the world—especially the darkening world of Hitler and Mussolini and the Japanese militarist—with unflagging optimism.

If Frost viewed the world's end as a choice between destruction by fire or ice, MacLeish thought of it as a "sudden blackness, the black pall/ Of nothing, nothing, nothing at all." His was not the kind of disposition, however, that would have permitted him to sit with folded hands and wait for the end. He was, for all his lyric spirit, a man who was conscious of the vastness of time and space as he looked upon the earth and he wanted to stir that kind of consciousness in his readers, too. His feeling is best expressed in two of his earlier poems, "You, Andrew Marvell," which evoked the spirit of an older poet, and "Einstein," a poetic interpretation of the great scientist's work.

But metaphysics and the mirage of words, which preoccupied MacLeish for so much of the 1920s, were not enough to keep him going when the Depression stifled the land. With the winning of his first Pulitzer Prize came the banking of the nation's industrial fires and the closing of the strongholds of finance, the breadlines and the apple sellers in Wall Street. Coincident with the inauguration of Franklin Delano Roosevelt, MacLeish's poetry took on a strong political cast as in his *Frescoes for Mr. Rockefeller's City*, in which he challenged those who had betrayed Thomas Jefferson's vision of a democratic society. He titled his 1936 volume of poetry *Public Speech*, which it was in effect, and soon he was calling his fellow artists to defend the cause of freedom. Those who would not join up, he said scornfully, were "The Irresponsibles."

The result was predictable. When MacLeish accepted appointment in 1939 as the librarian of the Library of Congress, without having had any library experience, there was a yelp of protest from those who deplored his activism but he paid little attention to it. If anything, he intensified his anti-Fascist activity. Before the attack on Pearl Harbor, he became the director of the Office of Facts and Figures, the forerunner of the Office of War Information, and in 1942–43 served as assistant director of OWI. When he concluded his work at the Library of Congress, he became an assistant secretary of state in 1944–45 and thereafter was active in the formation of the United Nations Educational, Scientific, and Cultural Organization. All the while he produced verse, verse plays, and prose for print and radio that underlined in many and imaginative ways his own part in the struggle for a free world.

His poetry did not suffer. After World War II, he won his second Pulitzer Prize for his *Collected Poems, 1917–1952*, which was awarded in 1953. Six years later, his reverent poetic play, *J.B.*, won the Pulitzer Prize for Drama. These awards testified to the poet's flexibility and adaptability to his times and his inner capacity for continual growth. It was no mere whim, when man first set foot on the moon, that Archibald MacLeish willingly worked against the pressure of an edition deadline and produced a poem in celebration of this occasion for Page 1 of the New York *Times*. His life had conditioned him for a demonstration of the ultimate in the work of a practical poet. No other artist in America could have reflected so dramatically the change in the world through his own works over four decades.[39]

4
The Laureates Face the
Storm 1934–1942

1
The Press During the New Deal

There was so much concern over the staggering economy at home and the threat of war abroad during the doleful 1930s that most Americans took their independent newspapers for granted. If anything, the vast majority who had supported President Franklin Delano Roosevelt were more critical than ever of the press because it had in such large measure fought Roosevelt in his glory years and opposed some of the worthiest reforms of the New Deal.

Consequently, when the ultraconservative Los Angeles *Times* was held in contempt of court in California for urging stiff sentences in labor dispute convictions late in the decade, there was little public protest. The press had been crying "wolf" for too long to be readily believed now. Moreover, the *Times* was by no means the influential national newspaper that it is today, being mainly a partisan Republican organ with strictly regional interests. And its opponent was the formidable Los Angeles Bar Association, which had taken the newspaper into court, arguing that its editorial demand for tough sentences against labor could influence a weak or spineless judge.

The ruling of the lower court against the *Times* opened a three-year legal battle that led to the United States Supreme Court and a notable decision involving freedom of the press. On December 8, 1941, the day after the attack on Pearl Harbor, the *Times* was cleared of contempt with Associate Justice Hugo L. Black writing the majority decision—the same Justice Black whose one-time membership in the Ku Klux Klan had been exposed by the Pittsburgh *Post Gazette* and brought its Raymond Sprigle the 1938 Pulitzer Prize for Reporting. Basically, the Supreme Court held that there can be no restriction upon freedom of speech or the press unless there is substantial proof of a "clear and present danger" to the conduct of government.[1]

As the nation was swept into the vortex of World War II, the Advisory Board on the Pulitzer Prizes unanimously approved the award of the 1942 public service gold medal to the Los Angeles *Times*. Even in the midst of a war for national survival, the Board at least was aware of the landmark nature of the *Times*'s defense of freedom of the press. For the time being, the issue was set aside because American newspapers as a whole had accepted a voluntary program of self-censorship during World War II out of concern for national security. Soon, it was forgotten in the press of business as usual.

It is one of the anomalies of journalism that, despite the depth and duration of the Depression in the United States, there are relatively few instances in the Pulitzer Prize records in which the press won recognition for its work on that specific assignment. Among the public service winners from 1934 to 1942, there was only the Bismarck (N.D.) *Tribune* in 1938 for its campaign, "Self Help in the Dust Bowl." And among the prize reporters there was only Thomas L. Stokes of Scripps-Howard Newspaper Alliance in 1939 for his exposé of political intimidation of employees of the Works Progress Administration.

By and large, most public service prizes were for campaigns against local and national corruption, vote frauds, and the like. They were scattered broadly across the country, including such papers as the Medford (Ore.) *Mail Tribune* in 1934, the Sacramento (Calif.) *Bee* in 1935, the Cedar Rapids (Iowa) *Gazette* in 1936, the St. Louis *Post-Dispatch* in 1937, the Miami (Fla.) *Daily News* in 1939, and the Waterbury (Conn.) *Republican-American* in 1940. The principal variant was a 1941 prize to the St. Louis *Post-Dispatch* for its campaign against the city's smoke nuisance, the first instance in the Pulitzer files in which the pollution menace was recognized.

The reporting prizes were more of a mixed bag, some rewarding individual enterprise and others recognizing work on the kinds of stories that were popular in the 1920s. Two members of the staff of the New York *World-Telegram*, S. Burton Heath and the columnist, Westbrook Pegler, won awards in 1940 and 1941 respectively for helping jail a grafting Federal judge and a labor racketeer. In 1936, Lauren D. (Deak) Lyman of the New York *Times* was rewarded for disclosing that the hero of the 1927 trans-Atlantic solo flight from New York to Paris, Charles A. Lindbergh, was leaving the United States with his family to live in England. In 1934, Royce Brier of the San Francisco *Chronicle* was recognized for covering the lynching of two kidnapers, and in the following year the reporting prize went to William H. Taylor of the New York *Herald Tribune* for covering the America's Cup yacht races.

The principal break with traditional news, in its familiar mold, was the decision to give the 1937 prize to six science writers who had covered their specialty at the Harvard University tercentenary. One of them, William L. Laurence of the New York *Times*, was to be heard from again in spectacular fashion as the first reporter of the atomic age. It was one of the instances in the annals of the Pulitzer Prizes when innovative prize-giving served as encouragement in the development of different kinds of news. The ideal, as it was envisioned at Columbia, was to have the prizes reflect the character of the times in which they were awarded and to look to the future. But too often, nostalgic juries settled for familiar and well-tried formulas of the news in the Depression era.

It was different in Washington. For in an age when the well-meaning government tipster was little known and there was no traffic in government documents, Arthur Krock established himself as the most formidable and influential reporter in the land. To his colleagues and rivals in the nation's capital, Krock was a veritable Mount Olympus wreathed in blue clouds of cigar smoke. To the public he was, in the words of a *Saturday Evening Post* article about him, a "typewriter statesman." To his editors, he was the only reporter who, when asked about his sources, could reply grandly that this was an entirely confidential matter—and get away with it. Nobody quite like him had ever held the title of The Correspondent of the New York *Times* in Washington, as the paper's chief of bureau was known. He set a standard that was uniquely his own.

Krock's was a deceptively mild gray personality in his Washington years. He was a bit on the portly side, quietly and conservatively dressed, and soft-spoken to the point of self-effacement at times. Yet, not even his friend and sometime colleague, Herbert Bayard Swope, could outroar him if he chose to shake the Establishment for good and sufficient reason. Unlike Swope, Krock had few highly publicized attributes, being noted chiefly for his flashing eyeglasses and his big cigar. He had the demeanor of a judge, the manners of a Kentucky gentleman (which he was), the quick mind of a consummate gambler, and the cast-iron gall of the expert reporter.

What Krock did, upon taking charge of the New York *Times* Washington bureau in 1932 at the age of 45, was to overturn the notion—typical of his time—that it was unseemly for a lordly Washington correspondent to scuffle for the news. He had always been a tough competitor. From modest beginnings—birth in 1887 in Glasgow, Ky., and schooling in Chicago—he became successively a reporter in Louisville at the age of 20, a Washington correspondent for the Louisville *Times* at 23, editor of the paper less than a decade later, and editorial writer for the New York *Times* at 40. Once he reached his peak in the nation's capital, he showed that he was innovative as well as aggressive. And since he began his operations in earnest in the historic 100 days of the New Deal in 1933, he had ample scope for his talents.

On April 18, when rumors were circulating of curtailment of American gold payments abroad, Krock telephoned one of his government sources and asked if scrip might soon be used. His source couldn't help him, but remarked:

"Don't you think it is fine what the President has decided to do about gold?"

Always the gambler, Krock guessed: "You mean the export embargo?"

"Right," said his source.

Krock boldly put the story up to Treasury Secretary William H. Woodin in such a way that he received prompt confirmation. The *Times* broke the story of the American embargo on gold on April 19 under Krock's byline on Page 1. Coincidently, a week later, he began writing his editorial news column on Washington affairs, a feature that continued for more than two decades.

Either in the news section or in his column, he pursued every major story with an awesome intensity and often developed news that no other reporter could get. When Cordell Hull amiably remarked that he'd soon need a larger Washington apartment, Krock suspected he would be Roosevelt's secretary of state, soon confirmed what was a mere guess, and broke the story in next day's *Times*. It was no wonder, by 1935, that he was unanimously recommended by a journalism school jury for the Pulitzer Prize in Correspondence, an honor that was promptly voted by the Advisory Board.

He could have rested on his laurels, but that wasn't his style. On February 28, 1937, after Roosevelt's magnificent 46–2 state re-election victory over Governor Alfred M. Landon of Kansas, Krock broke a story on Page 1 of the *Times* that began:

> WASHINGTON, Feb. 27—"When I retire to private life on Jan. 20, 1941," the President this week has been saying to his friends, "I do not want to leave this country in the condition Buchanan left it to Lincoln. If I cannot, in the brief time given to me to attack its deep and disturbing problems, I hope at least to have moved them well on the way to solution by my successor. It is absolutely essential that the solving process begin at home."

It was Krock's exclusive interview with F.D.R., the first since Louis Seibold's 1920 interview with Wilson for the New York *World*, and it brought the New York *Times*'s bureau chief his second Pulitzer Prize in three years. Two years later, he was made a member of the Advisory Board with unlooked-for consequences. For in 1950, once again, he landed a presidential exclusive, this time with Harry S Truman. However, the Board concluded that his work had been so outstanding that it could not recommend anybody else for the 1951 National Reporting award, so it was left vacant. That was perhaps the rarest of all Pulitzer Prize honors, for it has gone to no one else before or since.

Krock retired from the Board in 1954, and shortly afterward gave way to James Reston as chief of the *Times*'s Washington bureau. When he stopped writing his column, his last line was: "All right, Officer, I'll go quietly."

He didn't, of course. Years later, as an octogenarian, he was still making news with a best-selling memoir subtitled, *Sixty Years on the Firing Line*. And during the Watergate scandal in the 1970s, he wrote once again for the *Times*. While his influence inevitably declined with his retirement, his interest in the news remained as strong as ever.[2] He made Page 1 for the last time when he died April 11, 1974, and the *Times* gave him the ultimate accolade.

Krock's associate on the *Times*'s editorial page, Anne O'Hare McCormick, also was something special in the journalism of her time. When she won a Pulitzer Prize in 1937 for her foreign news reporting, she became the first woman journalist to receive such an award. It says something about the status of women on the newspapers of the era when the editors and publishers of the Advisory Board let twenty years elapse before honoring one of their own, although they had not hesitated from the outset to bestow prizes on women authors, poets, and dramatists.

Mrs. McCormick was one of the rare few who had sounded the alarm against a militant totalitarianism in Europe from the very beginning. With two of the other *Times* prize winners for Correspondence, Frederick T. Birchall in 1934 and Otto D. Tolischus in 1940, she had been untiring in her efforts to awaken a somnolent America to the danger presented by the Axis powers in Europe. As early as 1921, as a free-lance in Europe, she had seen with remarkable clarity that Benito Mussolini and his Fascist movement would become the masters of Italy. At the time she won her prize, Mussolini was swaggering over prostrate Ethiopia, the first victim of Fascist aggression in the Western world, and Adolf Hitler's re-armed Germany was threatening its European neighbors.

Like Krock, Mrs. McCormick was considerably more than a reporter although she had established her reputation in a difficult and highly competitive field primarily through her reportorial ability. A few months before she received the Pulitzer Prize, Arthur Hays Sulzberger, publisher of the *Times*, placed her on the newspaper's editorial board, the first woman to be so honored, and assigned her to write an editorial page column on foreign affairs. Her field, he said, was to be the freedoms and she was to guard them against encroachment from any source. She took him at his word.

From the time her column began on February 1, 1937, Mrs. McCormick was "must reading" both in Washington and the chanceries of world diplomacy. Herbert Bayard Swope once wrote to Clare Boothe Luce, upon her election to the House of Representatives, that she would have to read Mrs. McCormick regularly. The column, "Abroad," alternating with Krock's pieces from Washington, gave her a journalistic presence superior to that of any other woman of her time and all save a handful of her male colleagues.

No one ever doubted where she stood, before or after she was given her column and the liberty to go anywhere and write on almost anything she wished. She foresaw World War II just as surely as she predicted the rise of Mussolini and traced the evil growth of Hitler's grasp on Germany. Four years before the Nazi armies crashed into Poland and the dive-bombing Stukas roared over Danzig, she wrote:

"Nothing better or more stable can be established by more war, but in the long view it is equally certain that there must be war—not all the sanctions in the world can stop it—until there is a league not only to enforce but to create peace." [3]

It is difficult to compare Mrs. McCormick's work with that of the editorial writing laureates for the period, primarily because particular editorial points of view were seldom cited in the record, one exception being an award to the New York *Herald Tribune's* Geoffrey Parsons in which his patriotic purpose was praised in supporting the Roosevelt interventionist policies. Otherwise, the only editorial that was mentioned by name was Ronald G. Callvert's 1939 winner in the Portland *Oregonian*, "My Country 'Tis of Thee." Although Reuben Maury of the isolationist New York *Daily News* also won a prize, the citation merely referred blandly to the body of his work during the year, a usual formula for the editorial writing award. There was very little to show the depth of the split in the country over the war.

It was in the work of the editorial cartoonists, rather than the editorial writers, that the mood of the country was more sharply recorded. For in 1937, the year of Roosevelt's "Quarantine the Aggressor" speech in Chicago, the Pulitzer Prize was won by C. D. Bachelor of the New York *Daily News* for his stunning portrayal of a death's headed prostitute labeled "War" saying to a figure labeled "Any European Youth," "Come on in, I'll treat you right. I used to know your Daddy." But once Hitler struck, the isolationist mood gave way to scorn and righteous anger against the aggressors. In 1940, for example, Edmund Duffy of the Baltimore *Sun* won his third Pulitzer Prize with a cartoon of a savage Hitler holding out a bloodstained hand to Europe in a false gesture of peaceful intent. And in 1941, Jacob Burck of the Chicago *Times* was rewarded for his drawing of a little girl praying in a bombed-out ruin over the caption, "If I should die before I wake." Finally, in 1942, Herbert Lawrence

Block, the fabulous Herblock, received his first Pulitzer for a cartoon, "British Plane," drawn for the Newspaper Enterprise Association, which showed an apprehensive Nazi soldier looking skyward while French villagers smiled in satisfaction.[4]

On the basis of such evidence, it was clear enough that the Advisory Board, after an initial period of hesitation, had dropped all thought of neutrality with the approach of World War II, emulating its founding members in World War I. Before Pearl Harbor, the Board bestowed a group award on all American war correspondents in 1941, gave the New York *Times* a special award in the same year for its foreign report and honored four individual war correspondents. They were Wilfred C. Barber of the Chicago *Tribune*, who received a posthumous award in 1936 after his death of fever during the Ethiopian War; Louis P. Lochner of the Associated Press and Otto D. Tolischus of the New York *Times*, both based in Berlin, who were honored in 1939 and 1940 respectively; and Larry Allen of the Associated Press in 1942 after he was saved from a torpedoed British warship in the Mediterranean Sea. Upon making the Allen award, the Board split the Correspondence prize into two separate sections, national and international, and gave the national award to Louis Stark of the New York *Times* for his labor reporting. With the outpouring of photography from domestic sources and the combat zones, a new photography prize was also created in 1942. It went for the first time to a Detroit *News* photographer, Milton Brooks, for a picture of rioting strikers at the Ford plant. But for the next four years, war pictures were to be dominant in both the prizes and the news.

There was no question that American journalism had served the nation well in forecasting the shape of things to come in Europe. But there were relatively few foreign correspondents and even fewer editors who had expert knowledge of Asia. Except for the devotees of the yellow peril theory, the public was bored with Asian lands. Not even the assault of Japanese militarism in China seemed to make much difference. In the average American home, Asia was dreamily remote.

Carlos Pena Romulo, the editor of the Philippines *Herald* in Manila, was well aware of American indifference to what was going on in Asia when he undertook a far-reaching assignment for his paper in 1941. He was then 40 years old, a graduate of the University of the Philippines in 1918 and the holder of a Master's degree from Columbia in 1921, a member of the Philippine Independence Commission, and an officer in the Philippine Army Reserve. During his twenty thousand miles of travel that year to the main danger spots in Asia, he saw the rising Japanese threat at first hand. And in a series of articles, which were distributed in the United States by the King Features Syndicate, he warned that Japan would shortly unleash a new aggressive thrust in the Pacific, that the United States would be drawn into the war, that the white colonial powers would lose most if not all their colonies during the conflict, and that eventually the United States would defeat the Japanese.

A little more than a month after the publication of Romulo's final article, the Japanese attacked Pearl Harbor and the Philippines. Soon Manila fell and Romulo, now a colonel on the staff of General Douglas MacArthur, helped lead the desperate and losing defense of Bataan and Corregidor. Just before both were overwhelmed, the Filipino soldier-journalist flew with his chief to Australia—the last men off Corregidor. His prophecies thus far had been bitterly realized.

One day in the spring of 1942, when the American war effort was being reorganized, General MacArthur was in Melbourne and summoned Romulo, now a colonel in the American army, into his office. "Sit down, Carlos," he said.

Romulo was surprised. The regal MacArthur had never before permitted any aide to sit in his presence. Uneasily, the colonel perched on a chair until MacArthur suddenly said:

"Congratulations! You've just won the Pulitzer Prize!"

Noting the dazed colonel's look of utter disbelief, the general grandly showed him the dispatches from Washington and New York. It was a glorious moment for the courageous Filipino, the first Asian ever to win a Pulitzer award. Long afterward, even though he had received many other honors and was serving for the second time as his country's foreign minister, he recalled the incident and remarked: "I thought—and I still think—that winning the Pulitzer Prize marked the summit of my journalistic career, a career that I had abandoned to become a soldier, and later a diplomat. Receiving the prize was for me like being conferred the knighthood in England." [5]

In the 1934–1942 period, when the United States was being drawn steadily into the vortex of world affairs, the Advisory Board also recognized a foreign newspaper for the first time. A special bronze plaque was awarded in 1938 to the Edmonton (Alberta) *Journal* in Canada for its defense of freedom of the press. No other foreign publication has been so honored, for at the time of Romulo's mission he was an American citizen and his newspaper was an American publication. Foreign journalists, however, have won and will continue to win Pulitzer Prizes because eligibility is determined not by citizenship but by the publication of their work in the newspapers of the United States.

2
Fiction: The Mid-Victoria Cross

Malcolm Cowley, the *New Republic*'s literary critic, once called the Pulitzer Prizes the "Mid-Victoria Cross." [6] The name never stuck but the criticism it represented did, particularly as it applied to the fiction award. On May Day, 1934, when Fackenthal was preparing for the prize announcement, he was worried about this. The Advisory Board on April 26 had overruled both the Fiction and Drama Juries and he doubted if either of them would take it lying down. It was still a week until the university Trustees would meet to consider the situation, but they could only accept or reject the Board's recommendations and they had never seemed particularly anxious to start a fight. Not having much else to do at the moment, he wrote President Butler the following memorandum:

"I am pretty sure we are in for a storm over the Pulitzer Prizes. The basis of the criticism is going to be along the line of my conversation with Clayton Hamilton yesterday which I think you will remember and that is the fact that we ask some literary men to read, for instance, a hundred or more novels in order to render an opinion concerning them, only to have their opinions disregarded by men whose training is not in the literary field."

Butler was no help at all. He scrawled on the bottom of the memo: "I'm sorry, but there is no help for it. The Advisory Board is its own master." [7]

However, when the storm broke after the Trustees' decisions became public on May 7, it was Clayton Hamilton's Drama Jury that reacted violently over the sidetracking of its choice, Maxwell Anderson's *Mary of Scotland*, in favor of Sidney Kingsley's *Men In White*. The Fiction Jury, consisting of Professors Fletcher and Lovett and Albert Bigelow Paine, made no public protest over the prize award to their second choice,

Caroline Miller's *Lamb in His Bosom*, an episodic novel of rural life in Georgia during and after the Civil War. They had split, as their report indicated, with the majority favoring a historical novel by Helen C. White, *A Watch in the Night*, but their choice had been set aside.

While the argument over the Pulitzers was at its height on May 8, Butler suggested that a public announcement should be drafted, curbing the authority of the juries. What he wanted to do was to emphasize the final authority of the Advisory Board, which wasn't a new thought, but in so doing he advanced the novel thesis that juries should not make any recommendations at all. He believed they should be restricted to presenting a list of eligibles to the Advisory Board, with a statement of their reasons for each nominee's presence on the list.

Fackenthal reacted sorrowfully: "I anticipate a certain amount of difficulty next year in securing men to serve on the Pulitzer juries, at least, men of the type we have been having. As some of them have said to me, maybe with not too great seriousness, they are quite willing to read all the books in order to come to a judgment as to an award of the prize, but they hardly feel that they want to do the literary hack work of sorting out the material for an inexpert judgment by literary amateurs. Whether the attached statement would raise those questions at once in a helpful or disrupting way, I have no judgment."

A much milder statement was issued, although Butler's point of view echoed through the years at Columbia almost every time a major controversy erupted over the Pulitzer Prizes. Fackenthal had no trouble in persuading the Fiction Jury to continue, even though the majority may not have liked being so rudely reversed. The identity of the minority member who carried the day for Caroline Miller was not revealed.[8]

The Fiction Jury had its troubles in 1935, too, being unable to agree on anything, as Chairman Fletcher frankly reported, except that there was, in their opinion, "no outstanding novel." They sent a list of eight novels to the Advisory Board, but weren't even unanimous on which ones to include. Among them were W. W. Haines's *Slim*, the story of a young electrical worker in love with his job; Ruth Suckow's *The Folks*, which dealt with the fortunes of a middle class American family; Josephine Johnson's *Now in November*, a poetic first novel about a farm family in Middle America during the Depression; Albert Halper's *The Foundry*, a proletarian novel about industry and laboring men; and Stark Young's best-selling post-Civil War novel, *So Red the Rose*.

The Advisory Board chose Miss Johnson's novel but did not elaborate on the process by which it was selected. However, since Chairman Fletcher devoted more space to this work in his report and since his attitude toward it was more enthusiastic than the rest, it is obvious that he must have had some influence on the final choice. Moreover, it was not unknown for President Butler to consult jury chairmen when there were split verdicts, particularly when the chairmen were Columbia professors.[9]

Evidently the jury's difficulty in finding the "best" novel of the year and the somewhat less than epic character of the recent selections had its effect on the Advisory Board. Under Dean Ackerman's administration of the journalism prizes, the formula for these awards had been redrafted beginning in 1934 to avoid use of the term "best." They were given, instead, for "a distinguished example" of the work of a reporter or cartoonist, for "distinguished editorial writing," for "distinguished service" as a foreign or Washington correspondent, and for "the most disinterested and meritorious public service rendered by an American newspaper." Accordingly, the Ackerman formula was now applied to the prizes in Letters, which beginning in 1936 called for "a distinguished novel published during the year by an American author, preferably dealing with American life," for "a distinguished book of the year upon the history of the United States," a "distinguished American biography teaching patriotic and unselfish services to the people," and a "distinguished volume of verse . . . by an American author." In drama, the term "best" was also dropped, the revised formula being: "For the original American play, performed in New York, which shall represent in marked fashion the educational value and power of the stage, preferably dealing with American life." [10]

After having completed this write-through of the Plan of Award, the Advisory Board awaited fresh and striking results from the Fiction Jury—a recommendation that would divert if not exactly halt the annual salvos of critical shellfire. The Board had reason for hope, since 1935 had been a banner year for fiction. Among the 99 books submitted for the 1936 prize were Thomas Wolfe's *Of Time and the River*, Humphrey Cobb's *Paths of Glory*, John Steinbeck's *Tortilla Flat*, and Ellen Glasgow's *Vein of Iron*. Not one of these, however, was among the first seven books that were recommended in order by the Fiction Jury—a list that was headed by a satiric book about backwoods types in Oregon, H. L. Davis'

Honey in the Horn, which had won the Harper $10,000 fiction prize. The Board followed the jury's recommendation, fully realizing that criticism of the fiction award would continue. And it did. Changing the formula, as always, really changed nothing.

However, there was one news development for the 1936 fiction award, which was as puzzling as it was unexpected. Sinclair Lewis, who was described by the New York *Times* as a judge of the prize contest, praised *Honey in the Horn* as a book "full of raciness, of adventure, of color." He went on: "It is one of those uncommon books that really express a land and an age and, by expressing them, really create them." Yet, Lewis' name does not appear in the records, nor did he sign the fiction report for 1936, which listed Professors Fletcher and Lovett and Albert Bigelow Paine, the old standbys of the 1930s. Mark Schorer, Lewis' biographer, dismissed the whole business as Lewis' "kind of joke" and called his claim of jury membership "improbable." [11]

Returning to the fictional barricades in 1937, the year in which they were called on to choose between Margaret Mitchell's romantic bestseller, *Gone With The Wind*, and George Santayana's *The Last Puritan*, the jurors simply threw up their hands. They wrote to the Advisory Board in a report listing these two novels as equal choices:

"No comment on the first two novels seems called for. They have been too fully and widely discussed. Obviously, the jury recommends them, not as best sellers but as deservedly best sellers. Indeed, it feels a certain reluctance in recommending either book for a money prize or for publicity. It seems decidedly like carrying coals to Newcastle. Still, the Trustees may desire to reward the best novel of the year regardless."

There was, however, an asterisk after Santayana's name, and a polite cop-out: "Would Santayana be eligible? Does not appear ever to have been American citizen: now listed in British edition of *Who's Who* (see attached Vita)." While there were no further remarks about the two leaders, the jury put Walter D. Edmonds' colorful Revolutionary War romance, *Drums Along the Mohawk*, at the bottom of its recommended list of six books and said it had considered but discarded John Steinbeck's bitter and disenchanted proletarian novel about a labor organizer, *In Dubious Battle*.

The Advisory Board, like the American public, wasted no time in embracing Scarlett O'Hara and Rhett Butler, the endearing figures in the most popular and enduring of all Civil War romances. As usual, the critical buffeting of *Gone With The Wind* as a best-selling Pulitzer selection was strong and merciless but this time the hard-pressed Advisory Board was proved right. For with the passage of time, Margaret Mitchell's story became a part of American folklore—a novel that was read by millions of people inside and outside the country, a movie that was shown and reshown, and shown on television to a new generation, even a musical drama that originated in Japan with an all-Japanese cast singing a score by the American composer, Harold Rome. Whatever the critics may have thought of the book's sentiment and magnolia-scented romance, the public loved it and still does. *Gone With The Wind* was an eminently defensible choice.[12]

President Butler, however, reshuffled the fiction jury. For 1938, he retained the services of Professor Lovett, dropped Professor Fletcher as chairman but kept him on as a member, and tapped another Columbia English professor, Joseph Wood Krutch, a critic for *The Nation*, as chairman. The reconstituted jury came up with a unanimous vote for the novel of a proper Bostonian, John P. Marquand, about a proper Bostonian, *The Late George Apley*. It was a gentle satire which appealed to the jury as "remarkable." It appealed to the Advisory Board, too, and it mollified the critics for the time being. The same jury boldly proceeded to choose another best-seller with broad public appeal, Marjorie Kinnan Rawlings' *The Yearling*, for 1939—"an interesting and sensitive account of the coming of age of a poor boy in a remote part of Florida," its report said. This, too, won the Board's approval even though the critics grumbled.[13] They wanted something new, raw, and tough. And in 1940, with war flaming in Europe and an apprehensive America sitting weak and divided between its broad oceans, they got it.

John Steinbeck is scarcely considered today to be a revolutionary force in American literature. But in the 1930s, when labor organizers were appealing to the discontented in a suffering land and some of the more frightened captains of industry saw anarchy in every New Deal reform of consequence, the affluent conservatives viewed Steinbeck's proletarian novels with a certain degree of suspicion. Although his style was graceful and engaging and although he was not afraid to apply the leavening touch of humor to his grimmest situations, he did not have a very good press on the whole. The liberal critics liked him, it is true, but their largely conservative editors had distinct reservations. His progress, therefore, was not as swift and his talent was not as quickly recognized as it should have been.

At the outset of his career, Steinbeck seemed to be destined to turn himself into almost anything except a successful novelist. He was born in Salinas, Calif., in 1902, briefly attended Stanford and came to New York City by ship when he was 23 years old to try his fortune at almost anything. His first job, wheeling cement for the construction of the Madison Square Garden on Eighth Avenue, almost killed him although he was big and strong. With gratitude, he took a job on William Randolph Hearst's New York *American* as a reporter at $25 a week, but that didn't last long. After he was fired, he tried almost everything from peddling short stories to day laborer's work but he couldn't earn a living. In despair, he boarded a ship and worked his way back to San Francisco, writing in later years:

"The city had beaten the pants off me. Whatever it required to get ahead, I didn't have. I didn't leave the city in disgust—I left it with the respect plain unadulterated fear gives. And I went back to my little town, worked in the woods, wrote novels and stories and plays, and it was eleven years before I came back." [14]

Steinbeck's first three books, his introduction to American literature, were modestly received and attracted little public attention. But with *Tortilla Flat* in 1935, *In Dubious Battle* in 1936, and *Of Mice and Men* in 1937, he established himself as a writer of consequence. After the publication of *The Grapes of Wrath*, in 1939, he was recognized as an American writer of the first rank, for this powerful tale of the migration of the Dust Bowl Okies to California went to the heart of the nation. If it tore holes in the American dream, it did nothing more than tell the truth about what had happened to millions of Americans during the Depression. If it was tough and coarse and profane, that was because its people were tough and coarse and profane. Although, by the standards of the 1970s, its profanity and vulgarity were mild, indeed.

To the jury of Professors Krutch, Fletcher, and Lovett, *The Grapes of Wrath* was the book of the year and there was no argument about it. In his report, Krutch wrote: "We are unanimously agreed to recommend as our first choice *The Grapes of Wrath* by John Steinbeck. Despite the fact that it is marred by certain artistic blemishes, this novel has, we believe, excellences which make it the most powerful and significant of all the works submitted for our consideration."

When the report was distributed to the Advisory Board, two of the members were outraged. One of them, predictably enough, was Walter M. Harrison of the Oklahoma City *Daily Oklahoman* and the other was Robert Lincoln O'Brien of the Boston *Herald*. Both wrote letters to try to influence their colleagues against *The Grapes of Wrath* in advance of the Advisory Board meeting of May 3, 1940.

Harrison appeared to consider the book a slur on the people of his state, for he wrote:

> Nothing we can do will add or detract from the success of the publication. But the seal of the Pulitzer selection will write an approbation of smut in contemporary work that I am not quite willing to participate in. Such a decision would encourage more efforts in erotica by a host of authors writing for the market and promote a false sense of value with the immature reader which surely is neither enlightening nor constructive.
>
> While a segment of the migrants probably are of the moral and mental level of some of the Joads and their unfortunate neighbors, there is another unit, clean in their habits and minds, decent in their living and speaking. I do not know which is the larger class. This is a factual fault which should be considered. The errors of locale, the quarrel about the cause of the problem, the lack of a solution, are too trivial to carry weight.
>
> I do not wish to confine juvenile reading to the Elsie Dinsmore books, neither am I willing to help elevate cocktail hour wit and the filth of the jungle to the dignity of immortal literature.

O'Brien took it from there, questioning whether employers in California were as hard-hearted as *The Grapes of Wrath* made them out to be:

> I note the recommendation in reference to *The Grapes of Wrath*. I wonder if the jury has given any consideration to the question whether the main thesis of that book, which is that employers have allured the multitude into California into such numbers as to keep the wages depressed—is true? I read some articles in the New York *Times* several weeks ago in which the investigator reported quite emphatically that the charge is not true, that the LaFollette Civil Liberties Committee could not find anything of the sort, although it would have liked obviously to do so. I note that Mr. Hearst refers to the book in his column as *Grapes of Rot*.
>
> I wonder if we have no responsibility for the fundamental veri-

ties involved in a matter of this kind? I wonder if it is not the business of the juries to tell us how this work does square with the fundamental verities? If somebody wrote a corresponding book based upon the thesis of the innocence of Sacco and Vanzetti I would have opposed the award because I do not think they were innocent. Why is not the same issue involved here?

When the Board met, there was a new chairman, Joseph Pulitzer, for his brother, Ralph, who had held the post so often from the outset, had died in the intervening year. The two objectors were in attendance, as was President Butler and all save one member who had been excused, Stuart H. Perry of the Adrian (Mich.) *Telegram*. There is no record of the discussion of the fiction award, but it must have been lively. In the end, however, Messrs. Harrison and O'Brien were unable to stop Steinbeck any more than Hamlin Garland had been able in the earliest years of the prize to stop Eugene O'Neill. When the award was voted by the university Trustees and made public, it was received with universal approval. For, as Malcolm Cowley wrote in the *New Republic*, *The Grapes of Wrath* stands "very high in the category of great angry books like *Uncle Tom's Cabin* that have aroused a people to fight against intolerable wrongs."

The Pulitzer Prize served to confirm John Steinbeck's stature as a major American novelist. However, since he was 38 years old when he received the award and at the high point of his productive and distinguished career, it is doubtful that the award had any particular impact on his fortunes. In fact, even though he received the Nobel Prize for Literature in 1962, his best work had been done long before and *The Grapes of Wrath* marked his peak. It is not often that a prize dovetails so neatly with the finest work of an artist's career, but this was what made the 1940 fiction award to *The Grapes of Wrath* all the more notable.[15] Now, certainly, there was some reason to believe that the Pulitzer Prize for Fiction finally had been able to surmount the criticism that had plagued it from the outset. But unfortunately, in the following year, the Advisory Board itself became involved in a bitter argument with President Butler over the fiction award, the result of which was lamentable.

Mrs. Dorothy Canfield Fisher, the novelist, joined Professors Krutch and Fletcher on the Fiction Jury in 1941 for what seemed at first like a rather easy and uncontroversial year. The *Saturday Review*, which in

1937 had begun polling the nation's book reviewers on their Pulitzer Prize nominations, reported that Ernest Hemingway's jumbo-size novel about the Spanish Civil War, *For Whom The Bell Tolls,* had been the overwhelming choice of the critics for the Fiction award with Kenneth Roberts' Revolutionary War novel, *Oliver Wiswell,* as runner up. The Pulitzer jurors, however, didn't see it that way. They unanimously recommended two coequal fiction prizes for Conrad Richter's novel of American pioneer life, *The Trees,* and Walter Van Tilburg Clark's rousing Western, *The Ox-Bow Incident.* They put down the Hemingway and Roberts books, along with Richard Wright's black tragedy, *Native Son,* as secondary to their first choices. Of *For Whom The Bell Tolls,* Chairman Krutch wrote:

"This best seller is unquestionably vivid, picturesque, and interesting. It is, however, the opinion of the jury that its faults partly outweigh its merits—the faults being romantic sensationalism and a style so mannered and eccentric as to be frequently absurd."

The report ran into heavy weather almost as soon as the Advisory Board met on May 2 in the formal, dark-paneled Trustees' Room of Low Memorial Library, with the portraits of former presidents of Columbia gazing upon the proceedings. With Joseph Pulitzer presiding and President Butler in attendance, the newspaper members of the Board rose in revolt against the jury's choices and voted for the Hemingway book. Butler, who was horrified, urged them to reconsider and told them he had found the book both offensive and lascivious. However, as Arthur Krock recalled long afterward, neither he nor any other newspaper member of the Board had found anything offensive in the book. Rather, they concluded, in Krock's words, that "the novel's literary quality and the power of the story it told overshadowed every other entry and met the purpose of a Pulitzer award for fiction written by an American and published in the year 1940." In consequence, the Board's newspaper members defiantly reaffirmed their choice of *For Whom The Bell Tolls.*

Butler angrily moved to the doorway of the Trustees' Room and there announced that he would refuse to submit the Board's recommendation to the Trustees, whose approval then as now was necessary before any prize could be granted. Krock liked to tell years later of Butler's "Olympian mien as he uttered a few words of adverse comment on this particular prize recommendation: 'I hope you will reconsider before you ask the university to be associated with an award for a work of this nature.' "

The president's prestige was so great and his personality so awesome that no member of the Board at that time dared to stand against him. The cause of *For Whom The Bell Tolls* was lost. But the Board also turned down the jury's report as well, voting to give no prize in fiction for 1941. Curiously enough, those who participated in the proceedings chose not to make any public revelation of the abortive revolt, although they could have flooded the nation's press with the news on a few minutes' notice. It was not until Krock wrote a column about the incident in the New York *Times* twenty-one years later that it came to public attention.

President Butler's reaction was odd, too. When Fackenthal told him that the Fiction Jury's members felt they had been badly treated, he dashed off a memo on July 11 from Southampton, L.I.:

> "The Novel Jury seems to me so very good that I should certainly want to have them invited again. In what way were they badly treated? I have no recollection of anything having been done by the Advisory Board that was not perfectly conventional. They always discuss the Novel award more than any other, and this year, after desultory discussion of the two or three books which the jury put at the head of the list, someone suddenly moved that this year there be no award, and that motion was carried. There was in this, as I recall, no reflection whatever upon the Jury, but simply a difference of opinion as to the selection of one of the two or three books named to receive the prize. I think Professor Krutch was sent for by the Advisory Board, and answered their questions freely and in interesting fashion. If anything else happened of which I have no knowledge or recollection, I should like to know."

Fackenthal, who knew perfectly well what had happened, wrote back on July 12:

> "From the purely conventional point of view, I suppose the Novel Jury was not badly treated, but when you consider that they are all fairly busy people, are serving us without compensation, are specialists in their field, and this year went to great trouble to recommend a book of merit that had not been in all the headlines, then to have it turned down is a bitter disappointment.
>
> "Of course, the Advisory Board and the Trustees are under no compulsion to accept the jury recommendations, but I would on the whole think that a group like Krutch, Fletcher, and Mrs. Fisher, who spend from six to eight months reading books—and in

the case of the novel, a tremendous number—would find it difficult to have their recommendations disregarded by a group, many of whom have not read any of the books under discussion. One member of the Advisory Board went so far as to say to me that the book recommended seemed so inconsequential in size compared to the thousand-page novels, that he felt the award would not be appropriate. That, I take it, has nothing to do with the merit of a volume of fiction."

The upshot was that the two Columbia professors, Krutch and Fletcher, were back on the job next year but Mrs. Fisher was not. Her place was taken by a third Columbia professor, Gilbert Highet, the classical scholar.

Only the *New Yorker* and the *New Republic* published brief reports that the Hemingway book had been turned down for the Fiction award. "Other editors have considered the rumor untruthful or have telephoned the university and then not printed the story," Dean Ackerman wrote to President Butler. Butler's last words were: "Someone is trying to make mischief." [16]

President Butler's all-Columbia Fiction Jury had a brief and unhappy experience. In 1942, they recommended four novels in no particular order: *Windswept*, by Mary Ellen Chase; *The Great Big Doorstep*, by E. P. O'Donnell; *Storm*, by George Stewart; and *Green Centuries*, by Caroline Gordon. But their report added: "Had it not been for the fact that no prize was awarded last year, the jury would probably have recommended that none be given this year."

At least two members of the Advisory Board jumped into the breach with alternative suggestions. Joseph Pulitzer forwarded a letter from the novelist, W. E. Woodward, proposing that the prize be given to Upton Sinclair's *Dragon's Teeth*, and said that the Board might want to consider the recommendation. However, the Sinclair novel, having been published in 1942, was not eligible until the next year. A far more forceful, and even brilliant, presentation came from Julian LaRose Harris of the Chattanooga *Times* who urged recognition, however belated, for Ellen Glasgow for her novel, *In This Our Life*.

"I can think of no other writer of her ability, her realism and her graces who has gone entirely unrecognized for the Pulitzer award," Harris wrote to President Butler. "Can we afford longer to overlook her?

Viewed from the quality of this book alone, the award is deserved. When the whole of her accomplishment is viewed, that opinion becomes more than justified, it appears imperative. And this will be an award which will honor donor as well as recipient. To recognize Ellen Glasgow is not only to do justice where justice is due, but to convince lovers of American literature everywhere that the Advisory Board, itself, is discriminating as well as just."

The discriminating Advisory Board, still smarting over its rebuff the previous year, once again swept aside a jury report and recommended Ellen Glasgow's novel of Southern life for the Fiction Prize. It was, in fact, recognition of a distinguished career, as has occurred so often before and since, even though under the terms of the Plan of Award it had to be hitched to a particular book published during the year.[17]

The all-Columbia jury quietly accepted the rebuff and dissolved itself. For the following year, Butler and Fackenthal had to assemble an entirely new team, and with the nation at war and the public utterly disinterested in the annual jousting over American fiction, it wasn't easy. There was, in addition, no assurance now that the Advisory Board would accept with docility any novel that was handed to it by a Butler-appointed jury of experts. What the Hemingway and Glasgow cases meant was that the Butler era was approaching its end.

3
Drama: The Battle of Broadway

The skirmishes over the Pulitzer Prize in Fiction were relatively mild compared with the full-scale critical fray that developed over the Drama Prize in the 1930s. This was more than a mere academic rumpus. It became a matter of principle for all the participants, with the jurors insisting that their judgments should not be lightly disregarded and the Advisory Board maintaining its right to hand down the final verdict.

While there had been jury reversals before 1934, the Board's selection of Sidney Kingsley's *Men In White* over Maxwell Anderson's *Mary of Scotland* in that year became the signal for the opening of hostilities. *Men In White*, the first of a long series of hospital dramas, was a first play by a 27-year-old writer and the first real success of the struggling Group Theatre, whereas Anderson's play, produced by the Theatre Guild, was the work of a mature dramatist. Moreover, *Men In White* hadn't even been mentioned in the Pulitzer jury's report, which hurt more than anything else.

The jury of Clayton Hamilton, Walter Pritchard Eaton, and Austin Strong handed in its report in mid-March and heard nothing until Chairman Hamilton received a curt note, which also was sent to his colleagues, that the prize would go to *Men In White*. Hamilton at once demanded of President Butler the publication of a statement, at the same time as the prize announcement, that the jurors had voted unanimously for *Mary of Scotland*. None of the jurors questioned the right of the Board to reverse them, but they did not want to accept responsibility for a verdict they had not made. Consequently, when the prizes were announced and the jury's reversal was made known, the recriminations began.

Eaton said, "They don't want dramatic experts any more. They want office boys. No self-respecting, intelligent critic would serve on such a jury." Hamilton called the affair an "outrage." And A. E. Thomas, a former chairman of the Drama Jury, termed the Advisory Board incompetent to make judgments affecting the theater. With that, the critics took up their battle stations and the New York *Evening Post* even contributed an editorial denunciation of the Board for refusing to give the prize to an "honest and important drama."

Burns Mantle, the New York *Daily New*'s critic, was one of the few who said something in favor of the award. He wrote:

> By winning the prize, *Men In White* again reveals the Pulitzer Prize Committee as an interesting human body of men. They evidently vote their minds as playgoers and not as experts. And when their judgment is at variance with that of experts who are chosen to guide them, they speak up and say so. So long as the Pulitzer Prize represents the whole theater thus honestly, it will never stray far from the intent Joseph Pulitzer had in mind when he wrote his will, however frequently he may have disagreed with the committee's choice.[18]

President Butler's reaction was twofold. First, he publicly asked all juries to refrain from proposing henceforth a "definite recipient" for a prize, but to list instead their recommendations in order of preference. Next, he invited Messrs. Hamilton, Eaton, and Strong to serve again in the following year, subject to the new terms of reference. When all three refused, he promptly obtained the services of Professor William Lyon Phelps of Yale, who had quit in disgust at the end of the 1924 season and who now became the 1935 drama chairman. In the intervening years, Phelps had become celebrated as a didactic critic who once paid tribute to Robert Browning's ghost by leading a Yale cheer for him on the Yale library steps and who later delighted an English class by obtaining the services of Gene Tunney, the world's heavyweight boxing champion, as a guest lecturer on Shakespeare. Serving with Phelps were Professor John Erskine of Columbia, a comparatively recent biographer of Helen of Troy, and Stark Young, a critic of the New York *Times* and the *New Republic*. All were aware that they were in a difficult spot.

The 1935 theatrical season was brilliant. It sparkled with such plays as Lillian Hellman's *The Children's Hour*, Clifford Odets' *Awake and Sing!*, Robert E. Sherwood's *The Petrified Forest, Merrily We Roll Along*, by George S. Kaufman and Moss Hart, and Maxwell Anderson's *Valley Forge*. A seeming also-ran was Zoë Akins' *The Old Maid*, a dramatization of Edith Wharton's short novel of the same name, which did not impress the critics even though it featured two top-ranking actresses, Judith Anderson and Helen Menken.

Yet, when the jury report came in, dated March 14 and signed by all three members, it unanimously listed these four plays in the order of preference: 1. *The Old Maid;* 2. *Personal Appearance;* 3. *Merrily We Roll Along;* 4. *Valley Forge.*

Soon rumors were flying along Broadway that the odds-on favorite for the prize, *The Children's Hour*, had aroused Professor Phelps's ire because of its preoccupation with Lesbianism, that he had walked out on the performance, and that it was unlikely to win a Pulitzer Prize. While the drama chairman was mystified over the source of the rumors, and at his identification with the Pulitzer Prizes, he did nothing to counteract them. He also did not explain the jury's choices in his still-secret report, but on March 20 he informed Fackenthal that he and his colleagues were "in absolute harmony." Four days later, the New York *Times* ran a Pulitzer Prize form chart with *The Children's Hour* leading at 9–5 and *The Old Maid* last at 40–1. Fackenthal sent a *Times* clip to Butler with the notation that the jury's choice was "a 40–1 shot." If the president was concerned, he said nothing. He had backed long shots before.

Within a month, Phelps was heard from again when he wrote to Fackenthal: "I go to Europe Friday night. When the annual Pulitzer row breaks loose, if any one should say I had never seen *The Children's Hour*, I *did* go and see it."

The tip that the jury was against *The Children's Hour* came from the knowing Burns Mantle in the New York *Daily News* on April 21 when he publicly identified the jurors, hinted that President Butler was against Miss Hellman's play on moral grounds and predicted that Professor Phelps would swing the jury around to *The Old Maid*. Thus, when the Advisory Board met on May 3 and voted for Miss Akins' play and the university Trustees gave it the prize three days later, the critics had plenty of time for their annual foray.

Clayton Hamilton, still angry over his reversal of the previous year, led off with a blistering NBC network attack, saying, "The prize jury has labored and brought forth a mouse." Brooks Atkinson called the selection "commonplace" in the New York *Times*. And Percy Hammond in the New York *Herald Tribune* wrote: "I believe *The Children's Hour* to be the best play of the year. Yet, had I been an occupant of the Pulitzer bench, I would have known better than to vote for it."

Fackenthal wrote to Phelps, in response to criticism that *The Old Maid* was not an original play, with word that *The Children's Hour* was based on *The Great Drumsheugh Case*, as described by William Roughead. The point, however, wasn't valid because the prize already had gone to *The Green Pastures*, certainly not an original play.

The debate lingered on into the fall, with Clayton Hamilton writing long letters to Columbia demanding a check on the powers of the Advisory Board. Fackenthal, however, pointed out to him that the Board had authority under the Pulitzer will to do as it wished. The last word came from Phelps, billed as "America's Most Interesting Commentator" by his syndicate, in a column in which he wrote:

"For my part, I am very glad that every year the award of the Pulitzer Prize stirs up so much argument and controversy; the sharper, the better. Surely it is a good thing for the American public to become excited over a question of art."

On the strength of its Pulitzer Prize and the resultant publicity, *The Old Maid* ran for 305 performances at the Empire Theatre, not bad for a 40–1 shot.[19] However, the controversy had one unlooked-for result—the creation of the New York Drama Critics Circle as a rival to the Pulitzer Prize Drama Jury. The critics promised to do a lot better.

The inspiration for the organization of the Drama Critics Circle came from a clever and talented press agent, Helen Deutsch, who happened at the time to be promoting the cause of Maxwell Anderson's *Winterset*. After the uproar over the Pulitzer Prize for *The Old Maid* had subsided, Miss Deutsch gently corralled the critics, persuaded them to form the Critics Cricle and, as their unpaid secretary, witnessed the adoption of the Circle's constitution on October 22, 1935. It marked the birth of the Drama Critics Prize for the best new play by an American playwright. Later, awards were added for the best new foreign play and the best new musical production.

The first consequences of the formation of the rival group was a bill of divorcement, temporary as it turned out, between the seventeen founding fathers of the Critics Circle and the Pulitzer Prize Drama Jury. With Stark Young electing to go with his fellow critics and John Erskine bowing out at Columbia to become president of the Juilliard School of Music, President Butler had to go with a two-member Drama Jury for 1936. Professor Phelps was the chairman and the other member was Mary Maguire Colum, an Irish-American critic and the wife of the poet, Padraic Colum.

In any event, Miss Deutsch's faith in the critics was justified. After five ballots in April, 1936, the first award of the Critics Circle went to Maxwell Anderson's *Winterset*, the vote being 14–3. Emulating Clayton Hamilton's attack on the Pulizer Prizes the previous year, Percy Hammond of the New York *Herald Tribune* marred a broadcast of the presentation ceremonies by declaring *Winterset* was "spinach and I say to hell with it." And years later Brooks Atkinson called it "third rate Shakespeare." All it proved to the critics was that the lives of prize givers are fraught with difficulty, which was not a surprise on Morningside Heights.[20]

Coincident with the founding of the Critics Circle, President Butler in 1935 put a proposal through the Advisory Board under which the Pulitzer Prize would be given only once to a particular dramatist. Almost the first thing Professor Phelps and Mrs. Colum did when they accepted jury service was to persuade Butler and the Board to reverse themselves, which they did in 1936. It was just as well. Had the rule been permitted to stand, Robert E. Sherwood would have refused the Pulitzer Prize that was voted to him for *Idiot's Delight* upon the recommendation of the

Drama Jury and the Board. "Any self-respecting dramatist would have done the same," he said in making public his acceptance of the honor.

That was the first of four Pulitzer prizes for Sherwood, three in drama and one for biography. If the critics passed up his sugar-coated antiwar comedy in their anxiety to honor Anderson, it was understandable. But both organizations, as things turned out, overlooked that year one of the greatest contributions to the American theater, George Gershwin's *Porgy and Bess*, his classic musical achievement.

Professor Phelps, in his report, compared Sherwood to Molière. Whatever future critics may think of this assessment, there is no doubt that this grave and thoughtful six-foot-seven-inch playwright was talented in many fields and had a forceful impact on the life of his era. He was born in 1896 in New Rochelle, N.Y., and came to the Broadway theater by way of Harvard, the Canadian army during World War I, and the editorship of *Life* magazine in the pre-Luce years. His first two plays, *The Road to Rome* in 1926 and *The Queen's Husband* in 1928, won him a respectful audience. His anti-dictatorship comedy, *Reunion in Vienna*, in which Alfred Lunt and Lynn Fontanne starred for the Theatre Guild, brought him to the top in 1931 and *The Petrified Forest* in 1935 kept him there. The Pulitzer Prize for *Idiot's Delight* served to confirm his status.

There was more to Sherwood than droll, sophisticated comedy, as became evident in *Abe Lincoln in Illinois*, which won him his second Pulitzer Prize in 1939 on the eve of World War II. Two years later, with his emphatic defense of the democratic ideal in *There Shall Be No Night*, his third Pulitzer Prize came to him. From then on, he devoted all his energies to government service for the duration of the war both as a propagandist and close associate of President Roosevelt. What emerged from that experience was no play but a monumental biography, *Roosevelt and Hopkins*, which was awarded the Pulitzer Biography Prize for 1949.[21]

Sherwood, like Thornton Wilder, never did win a Critics' award.

Farce was not recognized in the Pulitzer Prize awards until the 1937 prize went to *You Can't Take It With You*, by George S. Kaufman and Moss Hart. Kaufman already had had a hand in one worthy Pulitzer innovation, the recognition of musical plays with the award to *Of Thee I Sing* in 1932. But it wasn't quite as easy for the busy Broadway play doctor, the finest theatrical craftsman of his era, to carry off his second award five years later.

Professor Phelps, Mrs. Colum, and Professor Arthur Hobson Quinn of the University of Pennsylvania, the jurors, submitted three separate reports for 1937. Professor Quinn wanted Maxwell Anderson's *High Tor*, Professor Phelps was for *You Can't Take It With You*, and Mrs. Colum didn't like anything. The report's key paragraph read:

"Mr. Phelps thinks *You Can't Take It With You* is the best play of the season because it is first-rate theater and keeps the audience in a continuous excitement and delight; secondly, because it is wholly original in plot, dialogue and treatment; third, because the philosophy, as expressed by the chief character, contains valuable ideas."

This last was an undoubted reference to the refusal of Grandpa Vanderhof, the sage of the zany Sycamore family in the play, to pay income taxes because he didn't believe in them. There is no way of knowing whether this playful hint influenced Grandpa Vanderhof's covert sympathizers on the Advisory Board, but at any rate *You Can't Take It With You* won the prize. The award had the virtue of recognizing Kaufman's peculiar comic genius and battering down the bars against still another valued form of American theatrical activity.

Kaufman had little enough to begin with—born in Pittsburgh to a family in modest circumstances, meagerly educated, and thrust by accident into the newspaper business at an early age, first in Washington and later in New York. He made himself known by becoming a regular contributor to "The Conning Tower" in the New York *World*, conducted by the renowned F.P.A. (Franklin Pierce Adams), eventually became the drama editor of the New York *Times* and was welcomed as a member of the Algonquin Round Table, a collection of literary personalities who lunched at the Hotel Algonquin in New York.

Kaufman wrote only one play on his own, *The Butter and Egg Man* in 1925, but his collaborations made theatrical history. The favorites among those with whom he worked were Marc Connelly, Edna Ferber, Morrie Ryskind, and Moss Hart. With Edna Ferber, Kaufman wrote *Dinner at Eight*. With Moss Hart, in addition to their Pulitzer Prize winner, he turned out the Hollywood satire, *Once In A Lifetime*, and the slightly disguised comedy about Alexander Woollcott, *The Man Who Came To Dinner*.

Woollcott didn't appear to mind, for he called Kaufman "the first wit of his time." An even greater tribute came from Brooks Atkinson, who wrote: "When he started his particular kind of comedy, the theater was very musty and mawkish and artificial, and being the honest kind of person he was, I think he could not stand this kind of sentimentality. When he came into the theater, it became very stimulating because he destroyed nonsense." [22]

It was not a bad epitaph.

A strange and beautiful play, Thornton Wilder's *Our Town*, opened on February 4, 1938, at Henry Miller's Theatre on Broadway after failing in Boston. It nearly failed in New York, too, despite a favorable review from Brooks Atkinson in the New York *Times*.

The play was not very exciting. It was set in a place called Grover's Corners, N.H., from 1901 to 1913. For scenery, there were only a couple of ladders, some chairs, and two arched trellises. There wasn't even a curtain. A kindly old man identified only as the Stage Manager, the leading player, gave the theme in his opening speech: "This is the way we were in the provinces north of New York at the beginning of the 20th century. This is the way we were: in our growing up and in our marrying and in our dying." Then came, little by little, the universal story of life on earth, with the final act played out in the cemetery.

To the relatively few who came to the theater in the early days of that Broadway run, the impact of *Our Town* was tremendous. But the Broadway critics as a group gave up on the Wilder play. They voted their prize to John Steinbeck's dramatic adaptation of his *Of Mice and Men*, a good show. On March 15, however, the Pulitzer Drama Jury of Professor Phelps, Mrs. Colum, and Schuyler Watts "unanimously and enthusiastically" recommended *Our Town* for the Pulitzer Prize and refused to name a second choice because "no other play is quite in the same class."

When the ever-cautious Fackenthal asked for an additional report, evidently because he felt the Advisory Board might need some convincing before going out on another limb, this was what the jurors fired back:

"The play seems to us the most original, the most beautiful and the most impressive of the season. . . . The structure of the play is original, the dialogue is written by a master of English, and there is a dignity and nobility about the whole play and its performance worthy of the highest praise."

The Advisory Board recommended *Our Town* for the Pulitzer Drama Prize on April 29 and the university Trustees ratified the selection on

May 2. Suddenly, after a three-month struggle, Wilder's play caught on. For with the award of the Pulitzer Prize, audiences began to respond to *Our Town*'s universal appeal and its eloquent declaration of faith in the human spirit. It ran for 336 performances on Broadway; even more important, it has been performed ever since in almost every part of the world where there is freedom to speak and to think and to pray.[23]

From the superior awards to *Our Town* in 1938 and *Abe Lincoln in Illinois* in 1939, the Pulitzer Drama Jury descended in 1940 to less satisfactory theatrical fare. The jury of Mrs. Colum and Messrs. Phelps and Schuyler Watts agreed that the season had been "the poorest in years," but rather than pass the award they decided to recommend *The Time of Your Life* by William Saroyan. In doing so, they passed up *Life With Father* by Russel Crouse and Howard Lindsay, which ultimately ran for 3,224 performances on Broadway. Apparently, the jury rejected *Father* because it was based on Clarence Day's *New Yorker* short stories.

The Time of Your Life was a formless "saloon play" about the inherent goodness of mankind which, the jury said, "contains more promise for the future than any other play of the past season." Saroyan, a picturesque Californian who had tried his hand at many occupations and boasted that he had written his winning play in six days, rejected the $1,000 prize immediately after the announcement because he said it would compromise his art to accept it. To this, Fackenthal replied merely that the award was an "accomplished fact" and "a part of the permanent record." The check, when it was returned, went back into the Pulitzer Fund. The play won the Critics award, as well, but without fireworks.[24]

W. Somerset Maugham, the British novelist and playwright, joined Mrs. Colum and Professor Phelps on the Pulitzer Drama Jury for the war year of 1942, but they found nothing that pleased them. All the leading plays had war themes—Lillian Hellman's *The Watch on the Rhine*, John Steinbeck's *The Moon Is Down*, and the Kaufman-Ferber collaboration, *The Land Is Bright*. Phelps reported for his colleagues and himself on April 12 that the jury was "positively and unanimously agreed" on passing the award. To this, Maugham added his own estimate:

"It is with great regret that I have to state my opinion that no play has been produced during the last year that deserves the honour that it is in the power of Columbia University to confer. If, as I understand, the purpose of the Pulitzer Prize is to reward definite achievement, I cannot but think that to confer the prize on a poor play because it is the least poor of a poor lot would be to lessen its value. It would be no encouragement to the art of the drama." [25]

It is impossible to say whether the 1942 decision to withhold the award for drama had anything to do with the unpleasant reaction to the selection of Saroyan's play in 1940, another below average season. However, the Critics Circle, too, saw nothing that season which it cared to honor. In any event, the country was far too preoccupied with more important matters to worry about the slump in playwriting.

From then on, with the annual announcements of the decisions of the Pulitzer Prize organization and the Critics Circle, the battle of Broadway became little more than a holding action. There were flareups, of course; a prize that creates no excitement is seldom held in high regard. John Anderson of the New York *Journal-American*, who was not regarded as a critic of the first rank, blasted the Pulitzer Prizes in 1943 upon assuming the presidency of the Critics Circle. And Maxwell Anderson, the recipient of two Critics' awards for *Winterset* in 1936 and *High Tor* in 1937, was so upset by poor reviews for his *Truckline Cafe* in 1946 that he bought an ad in the New York *Times* to denounce the critics as the "Jukes Family of Journalism." It was at least one insult he had not yet applied to the Pulitzer organization.

After reviewing the record, Brooks Atkinson of the New York *Times* concluded with magisterial severity: "The average taste of the Critics Circle is no more discerning than the average taste of the Pulitzer judges. Neither the Circle nor the Pulitzer Prizes can be intimidated by genius; both of them have on occasion preferred commonplace plays to classics."

Walter Pritchard Eaton, despite his displeasure with President Butler and the Advisory Board, was a bit more generous when he made his own review in 1944: "On the whole and in recent years, matched award for award with the Critics Circle choices, the Pulitzer Prize has not been unworthily administered. When one considers that the French Academy did not admit Moliere till he had been dead a century, one might even say that the Pulitzer Prize has been awarded with distinction." [26]

There were to be more arguments, including jury reversals and jury resignations from non-existent appointments. But the intensity of the battle of Broadway, as it was waged in the 1930s, would not be duplicated in the three decades that followed.

4
History: The Professionals Take Over

The Advisory Board recommended Herbert Agar's *The People's Choice* for the Pulitzer Prize in History for 1934, setting aside a 2–1 jury verdict for Mark Sullivan's *Over Here, 1914–1918*, the fifth volume in the veteran political writer's *History of Our Times*. There wasn't a peep from the jurors—Burton J. Hendrick, M. A. DeWolfe Howe, and Professor Charles Downer Hazen, chairman. And the Board's minutes noted only that President Butler had persuaded the membership to reduce the history award from $2,000 to $1,000.

When the prize was announced, however, the roof fell in. Lewis Gannett in the New York *Herald Tribune* blasted Agar's essays on the presidency as an appeal "for American Fascism." His paper wondered darkly if there was "some unnamed power behind the Pulitzer throne." And the New York *Evening Post* called for the discontinuance of the prizes.

There had never been such an outburst over the history prize. Actually, whatever the demerits of the book, Agar himself was no Fascist. He was the Louisville *Courier-Journal*'s London correspondent, later became its editor, spent World War II working for the government and thereafter became a founding father of Freedom House.

The controversy had one major effect. It discouraged the Board from further intervention in the field of history, very largely leaving the judgments to the professionals who were the dominant factor in the juries. Actually, even to their critical contemporaries, the work that had been done by the jurors from 1917 through 1935 appeared to have been good. Malcolm Cowley of the *New Republic*, who seldom had anything pleasant to say about any of the Pulitzer awards, conceded in 1935 that the Pulitzer history prizes "have been consistently better than the others, even though there have been occasional lapses like the choice of General Pershing in 1932 and of Herbert Agar in 1934." [27]

With the exception of Carl Sandburg's *Abraham Lincoln: The War Years* in 1940 and Margaret Leech's *Reveille in Washington* in 1942, professional historians dominated the history award from 1935 through 1942. Two of the outstanding works were *The Colonial Period of American History*, the 1935 winner, in which Professor Charles McLean Andrews of Yale climaxed his massive life's work as a colonial historian, and the 1936 selection, Andrew C. McLaughlin's impressive *Constitutional History of the United States*. By all odds the most popular of the winners for the era was *The Flowering of New England* by the editor and literary critic, Van Wyck Brooks, who could scarely be called an amateur historian. The other professional winners were Paul Herman Buck of Harvard in 1938 with *The Road to Reunion, 1865–1900; A History of American Magazines*, by Dean Frank Luther Mott of the University of Missouri School of Journalism in 1940; and a leading historian of immigration to the United States, Marcus Lee Hansen, in 1941 for *The Atlantic Migration, 1607–1860*.

The juries for the decade, 1935–1945, were professional historians except for Hendrick, who continued to serve until 1937 with Professor Hazen as chairman and Guy Stanton Ford as the third member. Ford, the former secretary of the American Historical Association who became the president of the University of Minnesota, then took over as chairman of the History Jury with Professor Arthur Meier Schlesinger Sr. of Harvard and President James Phinney Baxter III of Williams as his associates. They served until the end of World War II.

Of all those who won the Pulitzer Prize in History between 1933 and 1942, Carl Sandburg seemed at the outset of his glamorous career to be the least likely to succeed. He never pretended to be a scholar in a profession that made a fetish of scholarship. He was a newspaperman turned poet, a poet turned historian, a historian turned wandering troubadour, a man to whom people instinctively gave their trust and affection wherever he went. His love of Abraham Lincoln dominated his life to an even greater extent than his poetry, and in both he won the highest recognition in the power of his countrymen to bestow.

Sandburg was no child of fortune. He was born in Lincoln country at Galesburg, Ill., in 1878, the son of a Swedish-born blacksmith, and received whatever schooling he bothered with in what was later to become Knox College—"Old Siwash." Formal education, however, bored him and he dropped out. His first job was as a day laborer. Later, during the Spanish-American War, he took up soldiering briefly. At length, he drifted into newspaperwork in Chicago. It was the era of the fabulous ones of print—Ben Hecht and Charles MacArthur, Bob Casey, and the legendary Hildy Johnson who was lionized in *The Front Page*.

At first Sandburg was far out of their orbit. He worked for a Scripps paper, *The Day Book*, that suspended publication in 1917. Later, he caught on with Hearst's Chicago *Evening American*, writing editorials at a princely $100 a week, but quit before a month was up. "I didn't belong," he said simply. Next, Ben Hecht in 1917 wrote a note to Henry Justin Smith, managing editor of the Chicago *Daily News*, his boss, saying, "There's a good reporter you ought to hire. His name's Sandburg, and he's not only a good reporter but he writes superb poetry." Smith hired Sandburg at once—the beginning of a long and pleasant association. The poet covered the labor beat, Chicago's Black Belt and the city's race riots of 1919. Immediately afterward, he became the paper's film critic, which gave him enough leisure time to work on the first two volumes of his massive biography, *Abraham Lincoln: The Prairie Years*. After they were published in 1926, they brought him so much money that he was able eventually to quit his daily newspaper chores.

From then on, Sandburg earned his living as a wandering poet, reading his works and strumming on his guitar, and all the while doing research for the climactic four volumes of his life's work on Lincoln. In 1939, thirteen years after the publication of the first two volumes, he won nationwide acclaim for his *Abraham Lincoln: The War Years*. By reason of the continued prohibition of Washington and Lincoln as subjects for the Pulitzer Prize in Biography, it took the professionals of the History Jury to do him justice.

Messrs. Ford, Baxter, and Schlesinger wrote in the climax to a long and unanimous report:

"We have lived again, as even Lincoln's contemporaries could not and did not, through four crisis years in the history of the nation. If Sandburg did that to us and for us while we were struggling to keep our critical faculties alert, we felt obliged to lift our eyes from our garner of errors of omission and commission and pronounce the whole mass, both in substance and form, an achievement worthy of the reward to which we recommend it."

There was no dissent of consequence from that award, one of the historical monuments in the Pulitzer Prizes.

The presidents of the University of Minnesota and Williams College and the Harvard professor were just as scrupulous in their judgment of another newcomer to the field of history—Margaret Leech, whose *Reveille in Washington* was published in 1941 and became a candidate for the Pulitzer Prize in 1942. She had been a writer since her graduation from Vassar in 1915, had collaborated with Heywood Broun on a biography of Anthony Comstock, and was the widow of Ralph Pulitzer. He re-creation of life in Washington during the Civil War in *Reveille in Washington* was, as the jury pointed out, her first historical work. The report went on:

"We were agreed, however, that in this volume she has given a complete and satisfying picture, well based on sound historical work, of the capital of the nation during four most critical years. We felt that the topic was important, the coverage as nearly definitive as anyone could justifiably expect and that to an extraordinary degree she organized diverse materials to make a picture that is vivid and exceptionally interesting."

The jury's judgment of Miss Leech as a historian, which brought her the Pulitzer Prize in History for 1942, was confirmed eighteen years later when two different jurors, Dean Roy Franklin Nichols of the University of Pennsylvania and Provost John A. Krout of Columbia, successfully recommended her for the 1960 award for *In the Days of McKinley*.

The one time that Messrs. Ford, Baxter, and Schlesinger disagreed was over the 1938 award to Paul Herman Buck of Harvard. Ford was in the minority in favoring *A History of Chicago*, by Bessie Pierce, and referred in his lengthy opinion to his colleagues as present or past associates of Professor Buck at Harvard. They protested, upon which Ford reassured them in a warm "My Dear Jim and Arthur" letter:

"I think if you will look at it carefully you will see that I was really deferring to your judgment about quality in the book that I was not convinced of. . . . I should be quite unhappy if either one of you thought that I was doing more than point out my own disqualifications in both cases."

The correspondence was distributed to the Advisory Board. The prize was voted to the Buck book without further comment and the incident was closed, but it did show that the professionals could be quite as hard on each other as they were with the candidates for the prize. They could be generous, too, as witness Professor Hazen's report for the 1935 History Jury in urging a prize for Professor Charles McLean Andrews of Yale for *The Colonial Period of American History:*

"This volume is the summation of the life work of Professor Andrews. It will undoubtedly stand for many years as the best work in a wide and difficult field. It views the American colonies in the 17th century as the frontier of Europe. The institutional thread is kept dominant, but the economic and social factors, in Europe especially, are given adequate treatment. The bestowal of the Prize upon Professor Andrews will not only crown this particular work, but will honor a valuable career in American history." [28]

Whatever favor the amateurs won from the hard-bitten professionals for their historical scholarship, it was only natural that the professionals would be happiest when they were able without prejudice to favor their own. Nevertheless, despite their dominance in the field of history, they still had to take second place to the journalists and assorted amateur scholars in biography during the 1933–1942 period. The greatest of these was a marvelously versatile Virginian, Douglas Southall Freeman, editor, historian, biographer, and teacher.

Whenever there is an evaluation of the Pulitzer Prizes in Biography, three names invariably rise to the top of the list—Henry Adams, Douglas Southall Freeman, and Samuel Eliot Morison. While Adams and Morison had so much in common as Harvard men and Bostonians of an older and far more proper school, Freeman was entirely different—a Southerner whose life was rooted in Virginia and whose outlook was shaped by the Southern point of view. It was no accident that his *R. E. Lee* won the Pulitzer Prize for 1935; all his life, in effect, he had prepared himself for this magnificent effort. Nor was it mere happenstance that his second prize came to him posthumously in 1958 for his seven-volume life of George Washington, the last volume of which was completed by John Alexander Carroll and Mary Wells Ashworth after his death in 1953. For Washington, too, was one of Freeman's heroes and he gave the latter part of his life to this biography. The prohibition against honoring works about Lincoln and Washington in the Pulitzer Prizes had meanwhile been removed.

Freeman lived by the clock and worked out his schedule to the minute to crowd all his activities into an abnormal working day. There was, in fact, never a waking moment when he didn't see to it that he was usefully occupied. It formed the pattern for his career. He was born in 1886 in Lynchburg, Va., was graduated from Richmond College in 1904, and took his Ph.D. from Johns Hopkins in 1908. He soon turned to newspaper work, paralleling his interest in historical scholarship, and in 1915 became the editor of the Richmond *News Leader*, a post he held until

1949. Between 1915 and 1934, he gave half the hours of his working day to *R. E. Lee*, the rest to the newspaper and assorted additional activities. The result was a four-volume biography, published in 1934, that remains the most definitive work on the great Southern general today and one of the major biographical works of this century.

The 1935 biography jury of Professor Richard Burton, Dr. Henry Seidel Canby of the *Saturday Review*, and Royal Cortissoz, chairman, placed it at the top of their list with the following comment:

"This is unquestionably the outstanding biography of the year. It is exhaustive in research and it portrays a figure of national import sympathetically but without prejudice. It does justice to the man and the soldier and, without being brilliant in style, it is clear and workmanlike in execution. Altogether Lee's best literary monument."

With the award of the Biography Prize, Freeman undertook to teach once a week at the Columbia School of Journalism, which in 1935 had become the first all-graduate institution of its kind in the country. For the eight years that he traveled each week during the school year from Richmond to New York, he preached the gospel of completeness and honesty in research, discipline, precision in writing, and respect for learning. But he did not let either his teaching or his newspaper work interfere with his own writing schedule, for the books continued to flow from his work room—the three-volume *Lee's Lieutenants* from 1942 to 1944, a biography of John Stewart Bryan in 1947, and the first of the volumes on Washington's life in 1948. At length, in 1949, he retired to devote himself entirely to his last great work—one of the giants of his profession and living proof that good journalism and good scholarship were compatible.[29]

The Biography Jury, a stable and conservative group, peaked for the 1934–1942 period with its selection of *R. E. Lee* in 1935. It wasn't particularly venturesome, picked respectable works, had relatively few arguments, and gave the Advisory Board no trouble by dutifully listing its choices in a preferred, but not inflexible, order. The fixtures were Cortissoz, the chairman for the entire period; Burton, from 1934 through 1940; Canby, from 1935 through 1941 except for 1940, when one of his books was in contention; and Hendrick, 1940 through 1942. Professor Harper of Princeton served in 1934, and the director of the New York Public Library, Dr. H. M. Lydenberg, in 1942.

The jurors were unanimous in choosing Tyler Dennett's *John Hay* in

1934; Ralph Barton Perry's *The Thought and Character of William James* in 1936; Allan Nevins' *Hamilton Fish* in 1937, termed a "remarkable work" by the jury; Ray Stannard Baker's concluding two volumes of his eight-volume *Woodrow Wilson, Life and Letters,* in 1940; and Ola Elizabeth Winslow's *Jonathan Edwards* in 1941. In 1938, when the jurors weren't sure they could give a second Pulitzer Prize to Marquis James for his two-volume *Andrew Jackson,* they recommended Odell Shepard's *Pedlar's Progress: The Life of Bronson Alcott,* upon which the Advisory Board obligingly voted two coequal prizes for each book. In 1940, Burton was enthusiastic about *Elihu Root* by Professor Philip C. Jessup of Columbia, but was finally persuaded to join Cortissoz and Canby in voting the prize to another Columbia professor, Carl Van Doren, for his *Benjamin Franklin.* The sole reversal, and it wasn't serious except to the author of the recommended book, was the Advisory Board's decision in 1942 to give the prize to Forrest Wilson's *Crusader in Crinoline: The Life of Harriet Beecher Stowe,* rather than the jury's first choice, Professor Arthur Hobson Quinn's *Edgar Allan Poe.*[30] The Stowe book had been a strong second choice; moreover, it was a trying time in American history, one that called for the spirit and determination of another Harriet Beecher Stowe. Whatever the reason for the Board's reversal, it did not make any difference to the jury. There was no protest and the same jurors were back on the job in 1943 to pick a wartime laureate in biography.

5
Poets Pleasant and Unpleasant

Governor Cross, the stern arbiter of the poetry awards for a quarter of a century, was a serious and dedicated man whose taste in verse was on the grim and hardheaded side, but even he experienced a few giddy moments of doubt. In his 1939 Poetry Jury report, he wrote that he and his associates, Professor Bliss Perry and the poet, Leonard Bacon, had thought briefly of honoring either the *New Yorker's* E. B. White or the prince of light poetry, Ogden Nash. But, he added, "The jury decided with considerable hesitancy to eliminate both Nash and White."

With his moment of weakness put firmly behind him, the governor joined his colleagues in recommending John Gould Fletcher for his *Selected Poems,* which won the 1940 prize. Fletcher was no reckless innovator but an Imagist of the old Amy Lowell school, a fixture in Ezra Pound's original Imagist anthology. It would be twenty-two years before the Pulitzer Prizes would get around to recognizing the poets of jaunty mien and lighter heart by bestowing an award on Phillis McGinley for *Times Three: Selected Verse from Three Decades*, the 1961 winner.

Governor Cross had few illusions about the quality of some of the poetry he judged. He wrote in his 1934 report, for example: "There is the usual percentage of poor verse. Above this class rise a few volumes of fierce attacks on the present social order. Then comes a larger percentage of rather good verse, some of it from young writers of promise."

In the latter class he put such poets as Robert P. Tristram Coffin, who had just published his *Ballads of Square-Toed Americans*. As for the prize itself, Governor Cross and his colleagues, Professor Perry and Brian Hooker, rejected Robinson Jeffers' *Give Your Heart to the Hawks and Other Poems* because they thought the work "very abnormal in its psychology and over-strained." They proposed a more conservative and less troubled poet, Robert Hillyer, for the 1934 award for his *Collected Verse*, which was duly confirmed by the Advisory Board.[31]

This was the manner of the judging for most of the 1934–1942 period, during which awards also went to Audrey Wurdemann in 1935 for *Bright Ambush*, Robert P. Tristram Coffin in 1936 for *Strange Holiness*, Marya Zaturenska in 1938 for *Cold Morning Sky*, Leonard Bacon in 1941 for *Sunderland Capture*, and William Rose Benet, brother of Stephen, in 1942 for *The Dust Which Is God*. The exceptional years were 1937 when Robert Frost won his third prize for *A Further Range* and 1940 when Mark Van Doren won an award for his *Collected Poems*.

Joining Governor Cross and Professor Perry for the judging in those years were Brian Hooker in 1934–1935, Leonard Bacon, 1936–1939, William Rose Benet, 1940–1941, and Louis Untermeyer, 1942. With the rest of the Pulitzer Prize judges, the poetry jurors had to take criticism now and then although the firing was never as severe and as concentrated in poetry because the target was neither as prominent nor as large as fiction and drama. Professor Arthur Mizener of Cornell took a fairly typical critical view when he praised most of the selections as "good," but went on:

> There are, nonetheless, some pretty odd choices even among the books of poetry. In 1935, the year of Marianne Moore's *Selected*

Poems and of Robert Penn Warren's *Thirty-six Poems*, the prize went to Robert P. Tristram Coffin's *Strange Holiness;* in 1938, our judges preferred Marya Zaturenska's *Cold Morning Sky* to Wallace Stevens' *Man With The Blue Guitar* and Allen Tate's *Selected Poems.* One could easily multiply examples of this kind.

The truth is that the judges have—with rare exceptions—limited themselves to regional poets who celebrate the area north of Jersey City and east of Albany. This narrow provincialism has forced them to give the prize to Robert Frost four times and to a handful of other poets two or three times, and into ignoring all the other good poets. Nonetheless, it is true—again, with some exceptions—that the poets the judges have honored have been good poets, so that there is a valid if narrow-minded defense to be made of them.

Another favorite target was Audrey Wurdemann's *Bright Ambush,* written when she was only 23 years old and selected even though Governor Cross reminded the Advisory Board that her work was "still experimental." It was one of the few calculated risks that the governor and his colleagues took, for they had been disposed that year to give the prize to Edwin Arlington Robinson's *Amaranth* but decided against it because he already had won three times. The critics, however, neither knew nor cared about such inner qualms; they had a field day with Malcolm Cowley leading the pack against Miss Wurdemann in these terms: "You would suspect from reading her that she was born somewhere in a provincial library, that she had moved no farther than from Elizabeth Barrett Browning to E. A. Housman, and that she sank every night into tender dreams after wrapping herself in the proofsheets of Edna St. Vincent Millay. Her book is written on the margins of others." [32]

The selections of Miss Zaturenska, wife of the poet Horace Gregory, and of Robert P. Tristram Coffin also were experiments designed to encourage younger poets. Regardless of the critical reception of these and other awards, the practice of selecting younger writers, dramatists, and poets continued to be a feature of the judging of the Pulitzer Prizes in all Letters categories, along with the easier and much more satisfactory business of honoring those who were already established.

Another consequential aspect of the work of Governor Cross and his colleagues was the submission to the Advisory Board of a number of judgments of leading American poets, some of whom later won prizes.

With the Board's membership as fixed as it turned out to be until the limitation on service that was adopted in 1954, such critical estimates sometimes could be of importance in helping to establish the general character and reputation of a poet.

There was, for example, a statement in the 1939 jury report on one of the most important of modern American poets, William Carlos Williams, based on his *Complete Collected Poems, 1906–1938:*

"This is a volume of over 300 pages of verse by William Carlos Williams, a practicing physician in Rutherford, N.J. It well represents the school of imagists of the last thirty years, now somewhat in decline. Some reviewers regard the book as the best volume of verse in the year 1938. Certainly, it contains many very fine poems. In other circumstances, Mr. Williams might qualify for the Pulitzer Prize."

That was John Gould Fletcher's year. Dr. Williams finally won in 1963 with *Pictures from Breughel.*

Robinson Jeffers, whose poetry was highly rated in several of the poetry reports, never did win an award and the following comment by Governor Cross in his 1941 report probably indicates the source of the jury's dissatisfaction: "Mr. Jeffers is one of the most forceful of all contemporary American poets. But his *Be Angry With The Sun and Other Poems*—like all his other verse-tales—runs into uncontrolled melodrama and presents a philosophy of life which is negative and abhorrent to most readers. Nevertheless, his work cannot be passed by lightly in any consideration of modern poetry."

Jeffers lost that year to William Rose Benet.

There was capsule criticism, too, of works by major poets that were given secondary consideration by various juries, including the following:

John Hall Wheelock's *Poems*, published in 1936: "It is a good volume, though rather narrow in subject, thought, and technique. It is a highly respectable volume with a dozen outstanding poems such as 'Earth.'"

Horace Gregory's *Poems*, published in 1941: "Mr. Gregory has worked out a rather interesting technique, somewhat resembling in his dialogue the shifts and interruptions of the radio. His best work, which is very interesting, is in his monologues."

Christopher LaFarge's *Each to the Other*, published in 1939: "It is one of the best long narratives that have been inspired by Stephen Vincent Benet's *John Brown's Body*. Perhaps it is better as a story than as a poem. It would nevertheless be worthy of the Pulitzer Prize."

John Ciardi's *Homeward to America,* published in 1940: "John Ciardi is a young poet of large promise. He is one of the most sane of the radicals." [33]

There is no poet in the long list of Pulitzer Prize winners, except perhaps for Robert Frost, who has had the influence on America's younger poets and writers that has been exerted in such a kindly way by Mark Van Doren. As a poet of stature himself and as a teacher of poets for well-nigh fifty years, he matched Frost in arousing an appreciation for the best in poetry and stimulating his younger colleagues both in the classroom and in later life. Among his students were such diverse personalities as Lionel Trilling, John Berryman, Louis Simpson, Allen Ginsberg, and Thomas Merton. He won his Pulitzer Prize in 1940 for his *Collected Poems,* one year after his older brother, Carl, had won the biography award for *Benjamin Franklin.*

Carl and Mark Van Doren were two of the five sons of a country doctor in Hope, Ill. Carl was born in 1885, Mark nine years later. Carl went to Columbia and obtained his Ph.D., then became a teacher there. Mark followed, becoming an assistant professor of English at Columbia after taking his Ph.D. there is 1920. But from then on, the literary pathways of the two Van Dorens separated, with Mark concentrating on criticism and on the collection of anthologies of poetry. He became literary editor of the *Nation,* serving from 1924 to 1928, and in the following decade published six volumes of his own poetry.

While critics have noted the influence of Frost on Van Doren's early work, he soon developed a quiet, persuasive, and highly individual style of his own. "The best of his work," Louis Untermeyer once wrote, "is valuable not only for its discipline but for its discernment." And the editors of *Poetry* magazine called him "solidly entrenched in the tradition of definite purpose framed in strict patterns . . . he has never been a slave to a vogue and never having been in fashion will never be out of it."

Whatever else there was in Mark Van Doren's poetry, he was above all else a realist. He could write, as he did with sober contemplation of a sunset in "This Amber Sunstream":

> Another hour and nothing will be here.
> Even upon themselves the eyes will close.
> Now will this bulk, withdrawing, die outdoors

In night, that from another silence flows.
No living man in any western room
But sits at amber sunset around a tomb.

Mark Van Doren wrote much more poetry after he won the Pulitzer Prize in mid-career, several novels, and considerable criticism. Yet, he always refused, gently but firmly, to be a judge of the awards; it was not a responsibility that he cared to undertake when he had so many other things to do. In a letter written from his home at Falls Village, Conn., shortly before his death, he recalled with pleasure the circumstances under which he was notified of his prize in 1940:

"That year I was here on sabbatical leave from Columbia, with my wife and children, and one day in the spring the radio was turned on, I think by one of my young sons, and to the astonishment of us all my name was at that very moment being spoken. The Pulitzer Prizes were being announced, and the prize for poetry was just then up for mention."

Governor Cross and his associates, Professor Perry, and William Rose Benet, had had little trouble placing Van Doren's *Collected Poems* at the top of the heap of forty-four volumes of poetry that year. In his report, the governor made this assessment:

"In his volume, Mr. Van Doren has brought together the best of his work covering many years and has added a group of new poems. The collection well represents the various phases of contemporary verse in content and technique. It is excellent throughout, though no one of the poems rises to the heights."

The runner-up was Muriel Rukeyser's *A Turning Wind, Poems,* but the governor put down the author with this comment, "She seems to cultivate obscurity for its own sake, though this may not be quite a just statement. The volume impressed me more on my first reading than after I had studied the main poems more carefully."

While the Pulitzer Prize did not materially affect Mark Van Doren's subsequent career, and did not perceptibly increase the sales of his award-winning volume, he was more generous than some of his contemporaries in assessing the importance of the award. "I have never ceased to hear about the prize from persons introducing me on the platform or from writers of biographical sketches about me," he commented in 1972. "It is clear to me that the Pulitzer Prizes continue to be respected. I continue to respect them myself, and to be glad that one of them came my way thirty-two years ago." [34]

6
The Prizes After Twenty-five Years

Although the composition of the Advisory Board had changed in the twenty-five years since the award of the first Pulitzer Prizes and the terms of the Plan of Award had been modified, the method of selecting the prize winners was still shaped in its essentials by President Butler. He cared greatly about the Letters prizes and personally supervised the selection of the juries in the various categories, which usually were proposed in the first instance by Fackenthal, who had become Provost of the University in 1937. The Advisory Board never interfered in this delicate operation, so far as the records indicate; nor was there any dependence on either the American Academy of Arts and Letters or its larger affiliate, the National Institute of Arts and Letters. Except for the early years, jurors had never been nominated by the Academy, and membership in either the Academy or the Institute had never been a prerequisite for selection for Pulitzer jury service. It merely had been desirable.

While the Letters juries therefore remained firmly in President Butler's grasp, he had long since delegated responsibility for the Journalism Juries to Dean Ackerman as the secretary of the Advisory Board. However, the president was careful to insist on regular reports from Ackerman to Fackenthal, who remained the actual administrator of the prizes. The journalism dean didn't mind. A native of Indiana, born in Richmond January 15, 1890 and a graduate of Earlham College, he had always referred to himself, by reason of alphabetical accident, as the "first graduate of the first class" at Joseph Pulitzer's school. He had been a correspondent for UP, the New York *Times* and the Philadelphia *Public Ledger* between 1914 and 1921, when he set up his own public relations firm and handled such accounts as Eastman Kodak, and had been assistant to the president of General Motors when he had come back to Columbia in 1931. He was a small, restless, aggressive bundle of energy who made the journalism school his personal province, but like everybody else at Columbia he was respectful of Butler's authority.

Like most Columbia faculty people and all members of the Advisory Board, Ackerman would have found it easier to call the President of the United States by his first name than to risk such intimacy with the president of Columbia University. Once, a new member of the Board timidly asked Butler if it was all right to smoke in the Trustees' Room. "Yes, yes," was the testy reply. "But no one ever does." [35]

After the abortive revolt by the Advisory Board over Hemingway's *For Whom The Bell Tolls*, nobody on the Board ever challenged Butler's decisions again. He remained the sole connecting link between the first Joseph Pulitzer, his successors, and the current membership of the Advisory Board. To add to his imposing stature as an authority on what the donor had desired, Columbia's president also could threaten, as he did in the Hemingway case, to persuade the university Trustees to disapprove of any Advisory Board action that was contrary to his liking. What eventually happened, in this extremity, was that a kind of mutual forbearance developed between Butler and the newspaper executives of the Board. He did not usually interfere in matters that were of primary concern to them, mainly the journalism awards, and they did not presume very often to intrude on decisions that were of major importance to him.

It was characteristic of both Butler and the newspaper executives that no special notice was taken at the Board's meeting on May 1, 1942, of the passage of twenty-five years since the announcement of the first awards. The Board, as a matter of unwritten but well understood policy, had never called particular attention to its work. In addition, counting both the awards that had been made in 1917 and those that were being voted on for 1942, it was actually the twenty-sixth judging of the prizes.

As a self-perpetuating body without limitation on the terms of service of its members, the Board had grown old and settled in its ways. For at the 1942 meeting, the junior member was Arthur Krock, who had been elected in 1939. The senior member was President Butler, who alone survived the original Board of 1912. Then came in order of seniority, with the dates of their first service, Arthur M. Howe of the Brooklyn *Eagle* and Robert Lincoln O'Brien of the Boston *Herald*, both 1919; Joseph Pulitzer of the St. Louis *Post-Dispatch*, youngest son of the Donor, 1920; Julian LaRose Harris, Columbus (Ga.) *Enquirer-Sun* and later the Atlanta *Constitution*, 1927; Frank R. Kent of the Baltimore *Sun* and Stuart H. Perry of the Adrian (Mich.) *Telegram*, both 1928; Kent Cooper of the Associated Press, 1930; Harold S. Pollard of the New York *World-*

Telegram, 1934; William Allen White of the Emporia *Gazette*, 1936; and Sevellon Brown of the Providence (R.I.) *Journal* and Walter N. Harrison of the Oklahoma City *Daily Oklahoman*, both 1937.

The Board's chairman was Joseph Pulitzer, who was elected at the beginning of the meeting in what became an annual rite whenever he was present. The minutes were kept by Dean Ackerman as secretary, but President Butler actually conducted much of the business of the session. The way in which the Board handled its membership problem in 1942 was fairly typical of the procedure it had adopted from the first. For when Butler reported the expiration of the terms of Howe, O'Brien, and White, all were promptly re-elected to additional four-year terms. Before another year had passed, however, O'Brien had to resign because of ill health.[36]

In voting on the prizes, the most marked change was in the journalism awards. Only three of the original prizes—Public Service, Editorial Writing and Reporting—remained on the list; two others, awards for a paper to improve the Columbia School of Journalism and for the best history of the annual services of the American press had been dropped. Those that had been added were for Correspondence, Editorial Cartooning, Telegraphic Reporting on National Affairs, Telegraphic Reporting on International Affairs, and Photography.

In Letters, the original prizes remained for Fiction, Drama, History, and Biography and Poetry had been added. On the recommendation of the Columbia Department of Music, which was forcefully presented by President Butler, the Board added a Music Prize in 1942, substituting it for the $1,500 Pulitzer Scholarship in Music that had been granted annually since 1917. The new award was to be given for the first time in 1943.[37]

The entire business, from start to finish, took sixty-five minutes beginning at 11 A.M. Actually, what the formal meeting amounted to was a close reading of all resolutions that had been worked out by the Board at an informal session the day before and a final vote of approval for all recommendations. Beginning with 1942, the Board regularized its meetings, which were set for the Thursday and Friday of the annual sessions in New York of the American Newspaper Publishers Association late in April.

There was one move, which had been reluctantly made in the previous year, that was a matter of obvious embarrassment to the university and the Advisory Board but everyone apparently accepted it as a sign of the times. This was the reduction of all prizes except Public Service in journalism and letters alike, to $500 each from the usual $1,000, never a munificent sum to begin with. Evidently, the yield of the Pulitzer Prize Fund, in general with other funds invested by the university, had been sharply cut by the Depression years and the extraordinary measure had to be undertaken to enable Fackenthal and Ackerman to keep the budget of the Pulitzer Prizes in balance.

From its subordinate role in the handling of the Pulitzer Prizes, the School of Journalism gradually had gained both authority and stature once Dean Ackerman made it an all-graduate institution in 1935. Almost the first thing he did, with the consent of Butler and Fackenthal, was to do away with the practice of waiting for journalism entries to come in voluntarily. While anything nominated by a responsible source was accepted for judgment, the Journalism Faculty also conducted a search, with the help of students of the school, for additional material that might be adjudged worthy of a prize. The association with the American Society of Newspaper Editors, informal and limited though it had been, also ended for the time being. From 1925 through 1934, one member of the A.S.N.E. had been mustered into service to work with members of the Journalism Faculty on the various Journalism Juries, but beginning in 1935 and continuing through 1946, Faculty members alone did the judging under Dean Ackerman's supervision.[38]

The reports that the Faculty turned out were voluminous and appeared to be designed to permit the Advisory Board to make its own selection of Pulitzer Prize winners. In any event, despite numerous instances in which Faculty preferences were not followed, there never was a protest. In the time of President Butler and Dean Ackerman, protesting at Columbia was both unfashionable and unproductive. It should not be imagined, however, that the membership of the Journalism Juries consisted of dreamy academics years removed from professional experience; on the contrary, by enlisting the adjunct Faculty of distinguished newspaper people who gave their extra time to the school, the balance of jury membership was heavily in favor of the working press.

The list of Journalism Juries for 1942 was reasonably typical of the Faculty people who did the spadework for the Advisory Board during a substantial part of the Ackerman regime. Ackerman himself was on the

Public Service Jury with Professor Roscoe Ellard and the critic, John Chamberlain. Herbert Brucker, the associate dean, and Richard L. Tobin of the New York *Herald Tribune* were on the Reporting Jury. For Correspondence, Robert E. Garst of the New York *Times* worked by himself. Brucker and Tobin handled the National Telegraphic Report Jury while Theodore M. Bernstein of the New York *Times* was the International Telegraphic Report Jury. For Editorials, the jurors were Professor Ellard and Chamberlain; for Cartoons, Professor Eleanor Carroll, and for Photography, Brucker, Ellard, and Richard F. Crandell of the New York *Herald Tribune*.

Considering that full-time Faculty members had a heavy schedule of teaching and committee work and that the downtown part-timers also had full-time newspaper responsibilities, the practice had its awkward side even though it had been suggested in the Pulitzer will. What made it possible was the relatively modest size of the journalism entries, no more than a few hundred at most each year, as well as the willingness of some of the more talented students to help. At least one student, Michael J. Ogden of the Class of 1932, in later years the executive editor of the Providence *Journal-Bulletin* and president of the American Society of Newspaper Editors, always liked to tell of his part in picking Pulitzer Prize winners.

Although the Journalism Juries of the era were not publicized any more than the Letters Juries were, there was no particular concern over keeping secret the identities of the newspaper judges. Nor was there any undue argument over the possibility that those with newspaper affiliations, past or present, might try to influence the voting in favor of a colleague. In the first place, the Journalism Jury processes, to a far greater extent than those of the Letters judges, often represented a screening of entries rather than any final selection. And in the second place, whenever charges of favoritism were made, they were usually leveled against members of the Advisory Board.

In one of the most celebrated cases, the posthumous selection of Will Barber of the Chicago *Tribune* for the Correspondence Prize in 1936, a Journalism Faculty jury without comment had listed Barber third and Webb Miller of United Press first in its report. Both were cited for their reporting of the Ethiopian War. When the decision for Barber became known, the United Press initiated a boycott against the Pulitzer Prizes that lasted eighteen years. While UP work frequently cropped up in jury reports during that period, it was invariably nominated by the Journalism Faculty; as far as the wire service itself was concerned, it made no nominations of its own and unofficially blamed Kent Cooper of the Associated Press for Miller's failure to win the prize. While the AP-UP argument was fairly common knowledge among professionals, it did not break into print until 1948 when Carroll Binder, the foreign editor of the Chicago *Daily News,* wrote a critical article in the *American Mercury* in which he also made charges of favoritism against Dean Ackerman.

The Board's response was to express its confidence in the dean's impartiality. It also accepted as a matter of record, but not for publication, a statement by Cooper in which he listed all Scripps-Howard news organizations under the general heading of United Press, a rather large assumption, and showed that the representatives of this general grouping and of the Associated Press each had won six prizes between 1933 and 1947. The most that the Board did with this compilation was to ask informally that it be brought to Binder's attention. As for the UP boycott, it continued.

There was also recurring dissatisfaction with the dominance of what critics called "the large Eastern and elite newspapers" in the awards for journalism. It was pointed out with considerable regularity that great newspapers, which were represented on the Advisory Board, also won numerous prizes. The problem was one that often concerned Joseph Pulitzer as chairman of the Advisory Board and caused him at one time to offer to restrict entries from Pulitzer papers or even bar them entirely. That, however, wasn't equitable or practical. If the Board was to stand for anything, it had to be thoroughly representative of American journalism, at the very least, and it also had to insist that the most influential forces in American literature should be represented on its Letters juries. If this meant that prizes would flow in inordinately large numbers to either organizations or persons who had been involved in the Pulitzer awards setup, then safeguards would have to be devised to protect the integrity of the prizes.

In answering a critic, Arthur Krock once agreed that large and powerful newspapers in all parts of the land had won a "notable and recurrent percentage of the journalism awards," but argued that this was due mainly to their superior resources, facilities, and wealth rather than to favoritism. He also pointed out that smaller newspapers had increasingly carried off by far the largest share of the prizes.[39]

Actually, favoritism was not a particular problem in the journalism awards during the 1934–1942 period. The Pulitzer awards organization was solid enough; moreover, despite criticism from the increasingly vocal outsiders, the integrity of the insiders as a whole was not substantially damaged either in journalism or letters. Its weakness was a comparative lack of change in its personnel, which often led to an undue amount of conservatism in prize giving and an unwillingness, in all save a few instances, to reflect minority views.

Fresh approaches to the swiftly changing patterns of the news, to say nothing of the upheaval in the standards of American literature, were needed. For example, the Advisory Board brushed aside a jury recommendation in 1941 for William L. Laurence of the New York *Times* for his disclosure that Columbia University scientists on May 5, 1940, had split the atom. Instead, the reporting prize for that year went to Westbrook Pegler, who wasn't even on the jury's list.[40]

There was no doubt, however, that for all their demonstrable frailties the Pulitzer Prizes had become an established American institution in their first twenty-five years. If they were almost constantly surrounded by controversy, both Columbia University and the Advisory Board had learned to live with their problems. Arguments rarely disturbed Joseph Pulitzer, the chairman of the Advisory Board. As he once said: "That they occur is evidence that the prizes are taken seriously. I believe it would be an unhealthy situation if the whole thing were cut and dried, for it's inevitable that active, conscientious men will disagree on the technique or execution of a projected idea. My father, I'm sure, would have preferred vigorous controversy to dull acceptance."

For the next twenty-five years of the Pulitzer Prizes, one irreversible change lay directly ahead—the retirement of President Butler. In 1942, he was 82 years old but stubbornly clung to all his responsibilities even though his closest associates knew regretfully that the time had come for a change. More often than not in the past, his supervision of the Pulitzer Prizes had been carried out to such details as the reading of the annual announcement of the awards to the press. He also had been interested in the annual dinners that Dean Ackerman had arranged for the benefit of Pulitzer Prize winners, even though few of them showed up. At their best, these dinners were impressive affairs at downtown hotels like the Biltmore; but gradually, interest in them wore off and they became dreary, ill-attended functions at the Men's Faculty Club at Columbia. In his prime, Butler would have done something about that; in his declining years, he no longer could worry about such details.

In one of his last memos on the Pulitzer Prizes, he wrote to Fackenthal on March 20, 1944, about the sheaf of reports of the juries in Letters that had been sent to him as usual in advance of the Board meeting. "I cannot read any of the books named," the memo said, "so there is no use sending them to me. From what I have heard of them, however, from others, I should say that American literature has fallen to a pretty low ebb and in fact is as poor as that now appearing in France and Great Britain. So far as I am concerned, the awards will have to be left to the Committee and the Advisory Board." [41]

The strong hand, showing the tremors of age, at last was slipping from the controls. The last meeting that President Butler attended was on April 27, 1945, but he appeared to have taken little part in the proceedings. During the following year, he retired as Columbia's president and was replaced on the Board by Fackenthal; in 1947, at the age of 85, he died.

No succeeding president of Columbia University sought to exercise the power that Nicholas Murray Butler had applied to the granting of the Pulitzer Prizes; instead, primary influence over the awards soon shifted to the newspaper members of the Board and, in particular, to its chairman.

The second Joseph Pulitzer, who had been born in New York at the height of his father's career, was then 62 years old and the driving force behind the St. Louis *Post-Dispatch*, which he had made into one of the greatest newspapers in the country. At four years of age, he had dedicated the cornerstone of the twenty-story Pulitzer Building, home of the New York *World*, and had survived them both. Beginning on the *Post-Dispatch* as a 21-year-old reporter who had the temerity to punch William Randolph Hearst for insulting his father, Joseph Pulitzer had risen steadily through the ranks and built the *Post-Dispatch*'s fortunes while his brothers, Ralph and Herbert, were losing the *World*. Always a modest man, he remained in the background of the Advisory Board's work until the turn of events thrust him into a leading role.

5
The Prizes in War and Peace 1943–1954

1
The Era of the Reporter

There was something for almost everybody in America to work for in World War II. For the Eastern liberals, the most devoted of the followers of the New Deal, there was the heady experience of giving battle to Hitler in the name of freedom and national survival. For the Midwest isolationists, there was the satisfaction of striking back at the Japanese, who had dragged the nation into a war it did not want. For the various ethnic groups—the Italians, Poles, Czechs, Hungarians, and all the rest—there was hope that the war would bring a better era to their former homelands. And for Christians and Jews alike, there was the eternal struggle against the anti-Christ for one and the anti-Semite for the other.

It was this unique combination of purpose toward a clear national objective—victory over the Axis—that shaped the public will and made of the combat reporter a trusted observer at the very least and, at best, a hero in his own right. Such status had not been conferred on American reporters since the time of Richard Harding Davis and they enjoyed it to the fullest while it lasted, which was not for long. From the beaches of Normandy to Moscow and beyond, and from Pearl Harbor to Hiroshima and Nagasaki, some two thousand reporters for American news organizations followed the day-by-day progress of the war by land, sea, and air.

Viewing these manifold activities with both professional pride and patriotic zeal, the Advisory Board did not wait very long to declare itself. Five months after Pearl Harbor, its membership came down on the side of the war effort even though a substantial number of the newspapers they represented had been against Roosevelt's third term and had fought the New Deal all the way. In a public statement explaining its 1942 Editorial Writing award to Geoffrey Parsons of the liberal Republican New York *Herald Tribune*, the Board said it was recognizing "an outstanding instance where political affiliation was subordinated to the national welfare, and a newspaper firmly led its party to higher ground." It also memorialized one of its outstanding members, William Allen White, upon his death in 1944, for his contribution "to the building of America's aspiration for liberty and peace." White, in the period before Pearl Harbor, had labored for intervention as the chairman of the Committee to Defend America by Aiding the Allies.[1]

It is no wonder, therefore, that the Board made it a point to honor distinguished war correspondence and other major war-related activities of the American press with no fewer than eighteen prizes in seven different categories plus three special awards. Of the winners, by all odds the greatest was Ernie Pyle.

Ernest Taylor Pyle was just an old-fashioned reporter in the pre-television age. Sometimes, he couldn't read his own notes and he never did look like much. His baggy, and usually dirty, correspondent's uniform hung on him like a used potato sack because his was scarcely an Olympian figure; he was small, scrawny, and unashamedly bald. His enunciation was poor, his language worse, for he loved the "God-damned infantry" and he expressed himself in vigorous and earthy terms that would send a sensitive television vice president into screaming tantrums.

When Pyle began his wartime service in Europe in 1942 at the age of 42, he was among the oldest of all the correspondents and he was deplorably subject to colds. Never for a moment did he glory in the false and brassy romance of war. He hated war with a convulsive, impassioned hatred. And yet, in World War II, he became the best-loved and most influential of all American war correspondents and he brought the war into the American home with mere words on paper as no one had been able to do it before.

Pyle was not much of a stylist. If anything, he deplored elegance. But he was no mere word mechanic either. He despised the journalistic dubs who thumbed through headquarters press releases in search of a jazzy lead to satisfy the headline hunters among American editors. To him, communiques were a nuisance, and more often than not he found that they covered up rather than revealed the truth. What he sought was no broad panorama of war action, no exclusive interviews with gilded generals, but the simple stories of individuals under fire. It was typical of him to write:

"Now to the infantry, the God-damned infantry as they like to call themselves. . . . I love the infantry because they are the underdogs. They are the mud-rain-frost-and-wind boys. They have no comforts, and they even learn to live without the necessities. And in the end they are the guys that wars can't be won without."

To those who read Pyle day after day in the hundreds of newspapers that printed his dispatches, the war was dreadfully real. Through the GIs he wrote about, they could picture for themselves what their own sons or husbands or fathers were undergoing. And that, to an American family, meant everything.

Although a journalism school building is now named after Ernie Pyle at his alma mater, the University of Indiana, he was no model of deportment to be held up as an exquisite example to aspiring students of journalism. He was delightfully human, a good and solid companion in a vexing and ever-demanding business. He was born in 1900 in Dana, Indiana, picked up the rudiments of journalism at the University of Indiana and worked on a string of newspapers in New York and Washington before he became a Scripps-Howard war correspondent in 1942. It wasn't long before he was annoying both the generals and the politicians, for directly after the Allied landing in North Africa he protested the American policy that kept Fascist officials in office. "Our enemies see it, laugh, and call us soft," he wrote.

With his eyes and ears, the American public followed the progress of American troops through Europe. Millions of readers rejoiced when he reported on the first hard-won victories in Italy, and later foreshadowed the massive invasion of Hitler's Fortress Europa. On March 21, 1944, Robert E. Garst and Theodore M. Bernstein of the New York *Times*, the

Columbia journalism faculty members of the Correspondence Jury, proposed him for the Pulitzer Prize in Correspondence. When it was announced on May 1, it was greeted with popular acclaim everywhere. For of the five hundred correspondents who were preparing at the time to cover D-Day, Ernie Pyle was No. 1.

Soon after the first troops landed in Normandy on June 6, he was on the beach with them. On July 25, 1944, when he reported the breakthrough that sent American arms racing into the heart of France, he was under fire and narrowly escaped death. And on August 25, 1944, when he rode into Paris in a jeep with the victorious French and Americans, he wrote: "I had thought that for me there could never again be any elation in war. But I had reckoned without the liberation of Paris. . . ." After that, he had enough and came home for a rest, but not for long. On April 12, 1945, when he was with the American 77th Division in the Pacific, he learned of President Roosevelt's death that day. And on tiny Ie Shima six days later, when he hit the beach with the GIs of the 77th, a Japanese sniper got him in the right temple.

Everywhere on the war fronts, the correspondents mourned him. And in the United States, the outpouring of national grief came from the White House and the humblest homes alike. For with Franklin Delano Roosevelt, Ernie Pyle had shared the trust and the love of a war-beleaguered people and he would not soon be forgotten.[2]

The Advisory Board recognized early in the war that it could not easily identify and reward every outstanding feat of combat reporting. Among two thousand correspondents, there were many who were outstanding and who gallantly conducted themselves beyond the call of duty. It was for this reason that a 1941 group award was authorized, a gesture toward the entire correspondents' corps; it was for this reason, too, that awards were spread through every conceivable category, with a special award in 1945 going to the artists who drew the war maps for the American press.

As for the individual awards that often were won at grave personal risk, not many evoked the kind of homage that accompanied Ernie Pyle's. In several instances, the reaction was somewhat mixed, to say the least. This was particularly true of reporters who in one way or another breached the tight security of the U.S. Navy.

Hanson W. Baldwin of the New York *Times*, an Annapolis graduate and a military specialist almost from the day he joined the *Times* in 1929, was among the first to face the Navy hard-liners. Shortly after he had won the 1943 Correspondence award for his reporting from the Southwest Pacific, he was secretly summoned before the Joint Chiefs of Staff in Washington and asked for his impressions. As he gave an account of specific American losses, an angry Navy four-striper protested that Top Secret information was being disclosed. Baldwin remarked that he hadn't published the material, and didn't intend to do so, but some time later he was blamed nevertheless for the leak that enabled the columnist, Drew Pearson, to publish a garbled version of the story. Following the *Times* correspondent's heated denial of responsibility, he received a belated Navy apology.[3]

The experience of George Weller of the Chicago *Daily News*, winner of the 1943 reporting award, was almost as trying. Weller had won the prize for a brilliant account of how a Navy Pharmacist's Mate had saved a sailor's life by performing an emergency appendectomy while under enemy waters in a submarine. However, the Navy was far from grateful. After a visit with Admiral Chester Nimitz at the Navy's Pearl Harbor headquarters, the correspondent was drawn aside by a Navy captain who said: "The next time you hit a story like this, do us a favor and skip it." [4]

A two-line note in the Pulitzer files memorializes a strange experience of a different kind that befell Ira Wolfert of North American Newspaper Alliance, winner of a 1943 reporting award for his coverage of the fifth battle of the Solomons in the Pacific. The note, from Dr. Fackenthal to Dean Ackerman, reads:

"I am placing your letter of May 17 in regard to Mr. Ira Wolfert in the hands of the Bursar for his information and attention."

What Dean Ackerman wrote will remain a mystery forever, for his letter cannot be found, but there is no doubt about the Bursar's action. Wolfert, a Columbia journalism graduate of 1930, still owed a small amount on his tuition, which was duly deducted from his $1,000 Pulitzer Prize check.[5]

The other war correspondents who won Pulitzer Prizes had better experiences, but the risks they took and the horrors they witnessed left an indelible impression on them for the rest of their lives. Beginning with the unsinkable Larry Allen, who was rescued from a torpedoed British warship and won a 1942 award, all the prizes bestowed on reporters featured strenuous action. Dan DeLuce of the Associated Press, a 1944 winner, crossed the Adriatic in a small boat in 1943 to become the first Allied war correspondent to join Tito's guerrillas in Yugoslavia. Mark Watson of the Baltimore *Sun*, a 1945 winner, was 57 years old when he dodged snipers' bullets while covering General Charles De Gaulle's triumphal entry into Paris. Homer William Bigart of the New York *Herald Tribune*, a 1946 winner, walked through the atomic wreckage of Hiroshima and saw the maimed and other survivors who were dying. Hal Boyle of the Associated Press, another 1945 winner, took refuge under a Sherman tank outside Rennes to watch General George S. Patton's forces crush Nazi resistance.

These seasoned correspondents knew what it meant to cover an "assignment in hell," a phrase used by a young UP correspondent, Walter Cronkite, after he had survived an air raid over Wilhelmshaven.[6] But it was not to one of this hard-bitten troop that the most crucial of war assignments came—the unleashing of the atomic bomb. The reporter who made it was a peaceful, meditative little man with the soul of a poet—William Leonard Laurence of the New York *Times*.

As a science writer who already had won a Pulitzer Prize, Laurence's principal interest during the war had been the secret strategy through which the United States, in a race with Germany, sought to unlock the fantastic power of the atom. He knew more about it than anybody outside those directly concerned with the research, and already had published material that worried the government.

Laurence had become a reporter by accident, which was the case more often than not with the newspapermen of his generation. He was a native of Lithuania who had emigrated to the United States in 1905, picked his last name off a Boston street sign, and somehow worked his way through Harvard College and Harvard Law School. In 1925, a Harvard colleague who also was a member of the gilded Long Island set, took him to the home of Herbert Bayard Swope for an evening of fun and games. He did so well at questions and answers that the huge Swope towered over him at the end of the party, while he was paying court to Ethel Barrymore, and demanded: "Who the hell are you? And why?" It was the beginning of Laurence's journalistic career, for Swope hired him on the spot for the *World*. He was then 37 years old.

From the *World*, after a painful breaking-in experience, the mild little

Harvard lawyer went to the *Times* where he made science his specialty. And once again, an unexpected benefactor played a part in his life— General Leslie R. Groves, the ruler of the secret atomic empire known as the Manhattan Engineer District. For as matters turned out, Groves needed a trustworthy journalist to prepare the press material that would have to be released with the dropping of the first atomic bomb. The *Times* let Laurence go on his Top Secret assignment, without really knowing what it was all about. And when he turned up at Los Alamos shortly before the first explosion of an atomic device at Alamogordo, N.M., the scientists who recognized him were panic-stricken until it was explained to them that he was now a part of their team.

Once Laurence's preparatory work was done, he was hustled to Tinian island in the Pacific but just missed riding on the first atomic mission over Hiroshima. He was still on Tinian when President Truman announced on August 6, 1945, that a bomb more powerful than twenty thousand tons of TNT had virtually wiped out Hiroshima, and had the satisfaction of knowing that his material gave the American people their first detailed report of the dawn of the atomic age. In its August 7 issue, his paper credited him (on page 5) with being the author of the story of the atomic bomb and the only journalistic eyewitness to the Alamogordo explosion.

On the following day, Laurence received his orders to fly with the second atomic bombing group—quite an assignment for a 57-year-old science writer who up to that moment had never heard a shot fired in anger. He was in one of the two B-29s that took off from Tinian on August 9 with the big atomic bomber, the Great Artiste, bound for Nagasaki. And at one minute after noon, as the bomb hit the doomed city, Laurence noted:

"A giant flash broke through the dark barrier of our arc welder's lenses and flooded our cabin with intense light. Observers in the tail of our ship saw a giant ball of fire rise as though from the bowels of the earth, belching forth enormous white smoke rings. Next, they saw a giant pillar of purple fire shooting skyward. . . . "

When Laurence landed that afternoon in Okinawa, his work as a war correspondent was almost over. He had become the only journalist in history to make an eyewitness report of the destruction of an entire city with a single atomic blast. By a unanimous vote of jurors, Advisory Board members and Columbia Trustees, he was awarded the Pulitzer

Prize in Reporting for 1946. Three decades later, his feat was still unique, and no one inside or outside journalism in his right mind ever wanted to see it repeated.[7]

What the press accomplished during World War II was by no means limited to war correspondents. Among the editorial cartoonists, editorial writers, and combat photographers, there were standouts, too, whose prizes testified to their magnificent performance under pressure. Three among them are particularly memorable in Pulitzer annals—Sergeant William H. Mauldin of *Stars and Stripes*, Hodding Carter of the *Delta Democrat-Times* in Greenville, Miss., and Joe Rosenthal of the Associated Press. Each in his own way left a bright landmark of achievement behind him in World War II that won him the admiration of his profession.

While Bill Mauldin was in the 45th Division, his cartooning attracted such attention that he soon was featured in *Stars and Stripes*, the wartime service newspaper, and his bleary-eyed, boozy-looking cartoon characters, Willie and Joe, became heroes to the troops. Any GI could identify with Willie and Joe. Through them, the troops could tell the brass what they thought of the way the war was being run; through them, too, the keen and sometimes cruel satiric sense of the humblest man in uniform could be brought to bear on the highest at headquarters. For Mauldin was a satirist of the first order. He was the Ernie Pyle of the drawing board; and like Ernie, he was an unwitting master of psychological warfare and an incomparable builder of morale.

The brass, of course, didn't see it that way. But they couldn't very well knock Mauldin's own soldierly credentials. He had caught a shell fragment at Salerno and received the Purple Heart. Yet, the combative General George S. Patton once became so enraged over Mauldin's work that the cartoonist narrowly escaped court martial proceedings. The petty persecution stopped, however, when Mauldin won the Pulitzer Prize for Editorial Cartooning in 1945, at age 23, for his "Up Front With Mauldin" series in *Stars and Stripes*.[8]

The services of Hodding Carter were of an entirely different order, for they were directed more toward the task of awakening the nation to its responsibility toward its own people, particularly minority groups. When he came home after his wartime service on *Stars and Stripes* after V-J Day, he wrote a series of deeply moving editorials in his own paper, the *Delta Democrat-Times*, based mainly on his own observations and experience. The finest of these, a plea for tolerance, was published on August 27, 1945, less than three weeks after V-J Day, and it was titled "Go For Broke." That was the motto emblazoned on the banner of the heroic wartime Japanese-American combat outfit, the 442d Infantry Regiment. What it meant to these natives of Hawaii was that they would make every sacrifice in the service of their country, no matter what their fellow citizens thought of their yellow skins and slanted eyes.

With other editorials, this one was submitted in the Pulitzer Prize competition for 1946 in Hodding Carter's folder. Floyd Taylor, then on the Columbia Journalism faculty and later a founder of the American Press Institute, read "Go For Broke" and passed it on to the Advisory Board with three other entries. There, one of the members read aloud from Carter's work:

"It is so easy for a dominant race to explain good or evil, patriotism or treachery, courage or cowardice, in terms of skin color. So easy and so tragically wrong. Too many have committed that wrong against the loyal Nisei, who by the thousands have proved themselves good Americans, even while others of us, by our actions against them, have shown ourselves to be bad Americans. . . . It seems to us that the Nisei slogan of 'Go For Broke' could be adapted by Americans of good will in the days ahead."

That was good enough for the Board. It recommended Carter for the 1946 Editorial Writing prize, which was duly awarded to him. Five years later, he was elected to Board membership and served with great merit for more than a decade.

If any one was able to catch the spirit of World War II in a single assignment on any particular day, it was Joe Rosenthal of the Associated Press, combat photographer extraordinary. He did it, as combat photographers must, with the bullets of the enemy still zinging from their suicidal redoubts. For him, the great adventure reached its climax on a mild February day in 1945 when he climbed Mount Suribachi on Iwo Jima under sniper fire and saw a party of Marines about to raise the Stars and Stripes on the mountain's topmost ridge. Up went the flagpole, the banner whipping in the breeze, the men straining to keep it solid in its rocky base, and Rosenthal clicked his shutter almost by instinct. It was not until his home office sent him congratulations on his spectacular picture, "Raising the Flag on Mount Suribachi," that he knew he had taken the greatest photograph of World War II.

When the Advisory Board met on April 27, 1945, it swept aside the technicality that only photographs taken in 1944 were eligible for the 1945 prize. Rosenthal's was the picture that had dominated the front page of almost every American daily newspaper, that had been reprinted abroad, that had touched off a wave of patriotic pride in American fighting men rarely matched in American history. It was awarded the 1945 Pulitzer Prize by acclamation. And twenty-eight years later, while Rosenthal was taking pictures for the San Francisco *Chronicle,* he wrote: "When someone today connects me with That Picture, I glow real down deep." [9]

While there were a dozen and a half Pulitzer awards for war correspondence and kindred subjects in World War II, there was only one for the halting and somewhat despairing story of the peacemaking. It went to James Reston of the New York *Times* in 1945 for his extraordinary coverage of the Dumbarton Oaks security conference of 1944, during which he became the first to publish private American, British, and Soviet documents on the shaping of the peace.

Not since Bismarck had lifted a tablecloth at the Congress of Berlin in 1878 to make sure he was not being spied upon by the diplomatic correspondent of the *Times* of London, Henri Stefan Opper de Blowitz, had any reporter so dominated a major diplomatic conference. For the New York *Times*, through the efforts of its correspondent, was able to produce the secret papers of the Dumbarton Oaks meeting day by day while it was in progress. The State Department protested to the *Times* and the Department of Justice set the FBI on Reston, but the flow of exclusive information remained unchecked.

"The documents are authentic, and the people have a right to know what they contain," said the *Times*. "It is their interests that are at stake in this meeting."

Had it not been for the uproar created by Reston's disclosures, the conference at the graceful old Georgetown mansion in the District of Columbia might have attracted little more than cursory attention. As it was, the publication of the secret papers touched off a wave of public enthusiasm for the United Nations. And when the Big Four finally announced their joint support of a new world peace-keeping organization, it was universally praised as the highest and most idealistic of war objectives.

There was more of John Calvin than Richard Harding Davis in the Scottish-born reporter who had engineered this diplomatic coup. Reston was quiet almost to the point of self-effacement, small and neat of figure, and almost painfully sober in attire. After graduating from the University of Illinois with a journalism degree in 1932, he had a few odd jobs before joining the Associated Press two years later. In 1939, while working in London for the AP, he shifted to the London bureau of the New York *Times* and worked through the blitz until he was assigned to the Washington bureau in 1941. The Dumbarton Oaks assignment, which at first had seemed so routine and unglamorous, thrust him into the first rank of American correspondents at home and abroad.

Reston was awarded the 1945 Pulitzer Prize for Telegraphic National Reporting for his Dumbarton Oaks coup. He went on to pile up many more honors, including a second Pulitzer Prize for National Reporting in 1957, and became Arthur Krock's successor as chief of the *Times*'s Washington bureau. Although he later concentrated on his column while serving as one of the *Times*'s top executives, he never quit being a reporter. And when he became a member of the Advisory Board in 1968, he was as fervent in his support of prizes for first-rate opposition reporters as he had been in going after exclusives of his own. But always—from the time of Dumbarton Oaks onward—his main interest as a newspaperman lay with the peacemakers rather than those who planned and waged war.[10]

The ghost of the ancient Hearst-Pulitzer rivalry was laid to rest during World War II with the granting of Pulitzer Prizes to Hearst newspapermen. The first was awarded in 1944 to Paul Schoenstein, city editor of the New York *Journal-American*, and his staff, for saving the life of a 2-year-old girl by obtaining for her the then rare drug, penicillin. The second went to Jack S. McDowell of the San Francisco *Call-Bulletin* in the following year for a successful campaign to encourage blood donations.

In public service, also, wartime initiative by the press was recognized, the Omaha *World-Herald* being awarded the 1943 gold medal for organizing a state-wide campaign to collect scrap metal. It was the patriotic stimulus of the war, too, that caused the Advisory Board to set aside a number of recommendations by the Journalism Faculty and recommend the New York *Times* for the 1944 gold medal for its nation-wide survey of the teaching of American history.

The fervor of wartime faded quickly enough. With the country clamoring to "bring the boys back home" even before the formal Japanese surrender aboard the *U.S.S. Missouri* in Tokyo Bay, the greatest military machine the world had ever seen was incontinently torn apart. From its leadership in the war effort, the press turned just as sharply to peacetime concerns and soon the storied battlefields from Omaha Beach to Bastogne and from Guadalcanal to Okinawa were but brittle memories.

The public service awards, in all their diversity, amply illustrate the manifold areas in which the press was most active. While the war was still on, newspapers in various parts of the country continued to maintain their traditional "watchdog" role over government, as was exemplified by the 1945 award to the Detroit *Free Press* for its exposé of legislative corruption and the Scranton *Times*'s 1946 prize for uncovering judicial malpractice in the Federal courts in its area. Once the war ended, the attack on grafting gathered force and became a primary concern of numerous leading newspapers. The Baltimore *Sun* won the gold medal in 1947 for exposing corruption in unemployment compensation. In 1948, after a coal mine disaster in Centralia, Ill., the St. Louis *Post-Dispatch* received the award for making such an issue out of lax and unenforced regulations that an Illinois governor was defeated for re-election and large-scale mine reforms were adopted. Two years later, the *Post-Dispatch* shared the award with the Chicago *Daily News* for a joint exposé of the presence of Illinois newspapermen on the Illinois state payroll. Another joint award went to the Miami *Herald* and the Brooklyn *Eagle* in 1951 for their crime reporting. In 1952, the *Post-Dispatch* won still another gold medal for its disclosure of corruption in the Internal Revenue Service. And in 1954, one of the earliest and largest of the new suburban newspapers, Alicia Patterson's *Newsday* of Garden City, N. Y., received the prize for revealing a combination of racetrack scandals and labor racketeering. The only gold medals in the 1942–1954 period that were not for war service or graft exposés went to two North Carolina weeklies in 1953—the Whiteville *News Reporter* and the Tabor City *Tribune*—for their campaigns against a revival of the Ku Klux Klan and to the Nebraska *State Journal* in 1949 for helping establish a presidential preference primary election in that state.

Crime and corruption were the principal preoccupations of numerous reporters, as well. In the reporting category, prizes were won in 1948 by George E. Goodwin of the Atlanta *Journal* for disclosing vote frauds, in 1949 by Malcolm Johnson of the New York *Sun* for a series about

"Crime on the Waterfront," in 1950 by Meyer Berger of the New York *Times* for his remarkable account of the mass murders in East Camden, N. J., in 1951 by Edward S. Montgomery of the San Francisco *Examiner* for a tax fraud exposé, and in 1952 by George de Carvalho of the San Francisco *Chronicle* for a series about a Chinese "ransom racket."

Since National and International Reporting categories had been established in 1948 out of the old Correspondence award and the two telegraphic reporting categories that replaced it, the Advisory Board set up two Local Reporting categories in 1953 to take the place of the old Reporting award. One was for reporting under deadline pressure, the other for the more time-consuming investigative and depth reporting procedures and other material that was not subject to daily deadline pressure. The result was renewed emphasis on investigative reporting.[11]

The first two years of the new local reporting divisions illustrated the difference between them. For in 1953, the Providence *Journal-Bulletin* won the deadline award for coverage of a bank robbery while in the same year the non-deadline prize went to Edward J. Mowery of the New York *World-Telegram & Sun* for clearing a prisoner serving a life sentence for a murder he had not committed. And in 1954, the deadline award went to the Vicksburg (Miss.) *Sunday Post-Herald* for covering a local tornado while the non-deadline prize was won by Alvin Scott McCoy of the Kansas City *Star* for a series that led to the resignation of C. Wesley Roberts as Republican National Chairman.

It did not take long for editors and reporters to see that the non-deadline category gave them an opportunity for the kind of work that television either could not or would not do very often, while the deadline division—once the bread and butter of the American newspaper—now lay very largely in the faster and more dramatic medium of television. It simply did not do for the press to pretend, as it had for so many years with radio, that television did not exist; from 1948 on, it was a major competitor and was bound to grow more powerful with the passage of the years.

The cold war abroad and its effect on civil liberties at home became another major source of concern for the American press in the post-World War II period. No fewer than four prizes were awarded between 1947 and 1950 for correspondence from the Soviet Union, the winners being Brooks Atkinson of the New York *Times* and Eddy Gilmore of the

Associated Press in 1947, Paul Ward of the Baltimore *Sun* in 1948 and Edmund Stevens of the *Christian Science Monitor* in 1950. In 1951, C. L. Sulzberger won a special award for interviewing Archbishop Stepinac. There was, in addition, a prize for Frederick Woltman of the New York *World-Telegram* in 1947 for his investigation of Communism in the United States.

It is one of the oddities of journalism that the articles about the Soviet Union that had the biggest impact, the Atkinson pieces, were written by a drama critic on wartime leave from his aisle seat and not a foreign affairs specialist. The reason the pieces created a stir when they were published on July 7–8–9, 1946, was that Atkinson gave his views of the American-Soviet postwar relationship in blunt language.

"Although we are not enemies, we are not friends," Atkinson wrote, "and the most we can hope for is an armed peace for the next few years. Where our interests lie, we have to apply equal power in the opposite direction. It is a pity, perhaps it will be a tragedy, that as a nation we have to live with the Russian nation in an atmosphere of bitterness and tension. But we have to. There is no other way."

Pravda angrily attacked Atkinson and the *Times* when the articles were published. *Life*, duly impressed, reprinted them. And, without even a struggle, they won for their author the last Pulitzer Prize for Correspondence—the 1947 award. A quarter-century thereafter, when a Moscow-Washington detente was being sought, the now-retired critic recalled that it took an order from the acting publisher, Major General Julius Ochs Adler, to get the series printed in the *Times*. He added:

"The Prize legitimized those articles about the 'paranoid' Russian government. I was grateful and still am. But there is something ironic about the fact that I received a Prize in a field in which, owing to the exigencies of the war, I was a temporary intruder." [12]

The impact of the cold war on the American public also was registered picturesquely in the work of the Pulitzer Prize cartoonists. There was, in 1946, Bruce Russell's drawing in the Los Angeles *Times* of a deepening chasm that separated the American eagle and Russian bear, surmounted by the caption: "Time to Bridge That Gulch." There followed, in 1948, Rube Goldberg's New York *Sun* cartoon entitled "Peace Today," showing the atomic bomb balanced between world peace and world destruction. And in 1954, with the death of the Soviet dictator Stalin, the Washington *Post* published Herblock's devastating cartoon of the hooded figure of Death saying: "You always were a great friend of mine, Joseph."

The cold war also had a predictable impact on the cause of civil liberties in the United States. While a conservative segment of the press championed the repressive anti-Communist campaign of Senator Joseph R. McCarthy Jr., there were stout-hearted newspapers that refused to be stampeded. Bert Andrews in the New York *Herald Tribune* won a National Reporting Prize in 1948 for revealing that the State Department had fired an employee as a security risk without even the semblance of due process of law. Two years later, the National Reporting award went to Edwin O. Guthman of the Seattle *Times* for clearing a professor of charges that he had attended a Communist training school. And when Nat S. Finney of the Minneapolis *Tribune* disclosed that the Truman administration was imposing secrecy on the ordinary affairs of government, he also was given a National Reporting award in 1948.

The most striking of the investigations of repression in American life was conducted by the Washington *Post*'s able correspondent, Edward T. Folliard, when he exposed an Atlanta hate group called the Columbians in 1946. It won him the National Telegraphic Reporting Prize in 1947 and the personal congratulations of President Truman. But more important, it marked the end of the Columbians; under a barrage of adverse publicity and multiple investigations, the hate outfit withered away and its leader was sent to jail for rioting.[13]

The coverage of affairs in the nation's capital during and after World War II brought Pulitzer Prizes to such correspondents as Dewey L. Fleming of the Baltimore *Sun* in 1944, Edward A. Harris of the St. Louis *Post-Dispatch* in 1946, C. P. Trussell of the New York *Times* in 1949, and Richard Wilson of the Cowles newspapers in 1954. But Folliard's particular contribution to journalism was that he helped broaden the concept of national reporting far beyond the limits of the District of Columbia and the political conventions.

It was difficult, and in all but a few dramatic instances, impossible to focus the attention of the American public on foreign news outside the war from 1942 to 1945 and the cold war for some time thereafter. The records of the Pulitzer Prizes, an index of public interest in the news, show that up to 1954 only two awards were given for reporting from the hemisphere of the Americas—in 1946 to Arnaldo Cortesi of the New

York *Times* for correspondence from Peron's Argentina and in 1953 to Austin Wehrwein of the Milwaukee Journal for a series on Canada. And up to 1950, with the exception of Pacific war coverage, there had been only one prize for the reporting of Asian affairs, an award to Price Day of the Baltimore *Sun* in 1949 for his series: "Experiment in Freedom—India and Its First Year of Independence."

Day, a small and soft-spoken Texan, had become a war correspondent for the Baltimore Sun in 1943 at the age of 36—a blazing introduction to the coverage of foreign affairs. Once the shooting stopped, he turned foreign correspondent on a roving commission that took him to India in 1948 when Mahatma Gandhi was trying to halt a bitter communal war by fasting and praying. On January 19, barely five months after Indian independence, the *Sun* published his historic interview with Gandhi in which the Indian leader said: "I no longer have plans. I may hold a prayer meeting tonight—but I may not be alive. Whenever I make plans, something—call it God, call in Nature—intervenes."

Eleven days later, Gandhi was assassinated by a Hindu fanatic in the peaceful garden of Birla House in New Delhi while at evening prayer. Day's articles, however, did far more than convey Gandhi's premonition of the end. They brought home to American readers the depth of the subcontinent's degradation; they signaled, in effect, a new trend in the history of Asia with the accession of Jawaharlal Nehru to primacy over India and a new force in world affairs with which the United States sooner or later would have to contend.

Day's career as a foreign correspondent ended in 1960 with his appointment as editor-in-chief of the Sun Newspapers, but his interest in India did not lapse. When he became a member of the Advisory Board on the Pulitzer Prizes in 1971, he invariably took a special interest in foreign correspondence in general and Asian affairs in particular.

For the second time in less than a decade, the United States was caught up in an Asian war on June 25, 1950, when North Korean troops surged southward across the 38th parallel and President Truman carried the aggression before the United Nations, at the same time ordering General Douglas MacArthur to lead the resistance. To the bewilderment of the American public and a large section of the American press, the country once again headed into a conflict for which it had no stomach and for which it had not prepared. It didn't seem to make much difference, except to the liberal-minded, that this time the United States was fighting under the banner of the United Nations.

The old correspondents of World War II and some of the younger ones of more recent vintage came streaming in. And so did the combat photographers. But the story they had to tell this time was disappointing and even tragic. For MacArthur's boastful predictions of victory were proved wrong, as was his assurance that the Chinese would not enter the war. Worse still, after making these statements to President Truman at their secret Wake Island conference on October 15, 1950, he began issuing belligerent declarations without authority. At length, on April 11, 1951, at 1 A.M., President Truman ordered MacArthur relieved as United Nations commander in Korea and replaced him with General Matthew B. Ridgway.

By that time, six combat correspondents had been nominated for the Pulitzer Prize in International Reporting by a new type of journalism jury, consisting of Virginius Dabney of the Richmond (Va.) *Times-Dispatch* and W. C. Stouffer of the Roanoke (Va.) *World-News*. They had supplanted the one-member juries of the Journalism faculty, along with editors in other categories who had accepted appointments offered by Dean Ackerman.

Their recommendations, dated March 21, 1951, and based on work done in 1950, were as follows:

> Keyes Beech, Chicago *Daily News*, for his graphic, concise, well-written, informed dispatches from the Korean war front. His work shows background, courageous willingness to state unpleasant facts, and great resourcefulness under the most trying and hazardous conditions.
>
> Homer Bigart, New York *Herald Tribune*, for his outstanding reports from Korea. Rather than take the easy way by writing far behind the lines, he wrote his vivid reports from the front. He went to extraordinary risks in gathering his facts.
>
> Marguerite Higgins, New York *Herald Tribune*, for fine front line reporting showing enterprise and courage. She is entitled to special consideration by reason of being a woman, since she had to work under unusual dangers.
>
> Relman Morin, Associated Press, for his on-the-spot articles from Korea, marked by good writing and excellent explanatory coverage.

Fred Sparks, Chicago *Daily News,* for his well-written dispatches, and especially the fine job of backgrounding.

Don Whitehead, Associated Press, for his superlative reporting, much of it under fire. He also scored major scoops.

It became the business of the Advisory Board to determine which of the six reporters, alphabetically listed in the report, should be given the prize. After considerable debate, however, the Board was unable to come to a decision and voted to give all six candidates individual Pulitzer Prizes—an unprecedented action in the history of the awards. When the university Trustees ratified the Board's recommendation, that was the way it was announced. And in the following year, Anthony Leviero of the New York *Times* received the National Reporting Prize for his exclusive disclosure of the Wake Island talks.[14]

Three other prizes were granted for outstanding correspondence in connection with the Korean War and the long and difficult peacemaking. They went to John Hightower, the Associated Press's diplomatic correspondent, in 1952; Don Whitehead of the Associated Press in 1953, his second award, for his report on President-elect Eisenhower's secret trip to Korea; and Jim G. Lucas of the Scripps-Howard Newspapers in 1954 for his reporting of the final Korean War cease-fire.

Hightower's prize was notable because it gave recognition to one of the most trusted of Washington correspondents, the confidant of a succession of Secretaries of State, and the most widely read writer on the diplomatic circuit. He was among the first to report the quarrel between President Truman and General MacArthur. He also made it clear that the basis of their dispute was MacArthur's continual challenges to Peking and President Truman's unwillingness to risk a war with China. And finally, three days before the President took his decisive action, Hightower wrote a piece predicting that the commander-in-chief would relieve the general of some or all of his power. It was on the basis of this record that the correspondent won the International Reporting Prize in 1952. Coincidentally, in that year, all the Pulitzer Prizes in Journalism were restored to their $1,000 level while the Letters, Drama, and Music awards continued at $500 for almost two more decades.[15]

One of the many arguments within the Advisory Board in the post-World War II years was over the status of the Wall Street Journal.

Joseph Pulitzer argued that the *Journal* was not a "secular" newspaper, meaning that it was not a newspaper of general circulation. That was true enough, for the *Journal* at the time was a financial newspaper with 100,000 circulation. Regardless of whether or not it was "secular," however, Pulitzer's associates maintained that the *Journal* was eligible under the Plan of Award and its staff members should be considered.

Although Pulitzer was the son of the donor of the prizes, he seldom received special treatment by the Board. He was still obliged to undergo the routine of being elected chairman each year when he was present. Moreover, in 1933, he had criticized Allan Nevins' *Grover Cleveland*, the recommended selection for the Biography Prize, for calling his father "brilliant, hot-headed, and irresponsible . . . intensely earnest, cocksure, and belligerent." Nevertheless, the Board had voted to give the prize to Nevins. Privately, perhaps to assuage Pulitzer's feelings, the Board called Nevins' attention to what it believed was "a mistake in fact or interpretation" in his biography and asked him "to reexamine the facts in connection with future editions." If Nevins did any reexamination, the result was not evident in the sixteenth printing of *Grover Cleveland* in 1964. His view of the first Joseph Pulitzer remained unchanged.

Pulitzer lost his fight against the *Wall Street Journal*, too. In 1947, William H. Grimes of the *Journal* won the Editorial Writing Prize and Vermont Connecticut Royster followed him by carrying off the same award six years later. Soon, *Journal* staff members were winning prizes in other categories as well. The old score was so far forgotten in 1968 that Royster, who had become the editor of the paper, was invited to join the Advisory Board and accepted, serving with Joseph Pulitzer Jr., then the chairman. By that time the *Journal* had become a great national newspaper with more than one million circulation.

Royster, born in Raleigh, N.C., in 1914, received his A.B. and membership in Phi Beta Kappa at the University of North Carolina in 1935, and in the following year joined the *Wall Street Journal*'s staff. It was not long before he was shifted from New York to Washinton. After four years on active duty with the U.S.Navy during World War II, he became the *Journal*'s chief Washington correspondent at the age of 31 and its editor thirteen years later.

If he knew about the Board's difference of opinion over the *Wall Street Journal*, he never let it bother him. For in 1973, he wrote: "We on the Board seem to be always arguing with each other, which I find inevitable in view of the fact that the Board is composed of strong-minded men. I have always been amused when, after some controversial award or other, I have been called by reporters trying to 'make something' of the differences of opinion. They want to treat that as something unusual, and preferably acrimonious, because nothing makes a better story than a good fight. Reporters rarely understand, or maybe they don't want to admit, that differences of opinion among any body of intelligent men— whether on the Pulitzer Board, in business, or in government—are routine and, indeed, healthy." [16]

Ordinarily, the Advisory Board paid more attention to the second Joseph Pulitzer than it did in the *Wall Street Journal* case. During the hottest of arguments, as William R. Mathews of the Arizona *Daily Star* liked to recall, the chairman would restore order with a mild rebuke, "Gentlemen! Gentlemen!" He was, Mathews said, "a model of patience, decorum, and dignity."

Other members of the Board had their ups and downs as well. Frank R. Kent of the Baltimore *Sun* once opposed the selection of Virginius Dabney for the Editorial Writing Prize on the horrendous ground that the editor of the Richmond *Times Dispatch* was an enemy of Senator Harry Flood Byrd. The Board did not regard that as a disqualification by any means and voted Dabney the 1948 award over Kent's objections. It was only later that the Baltimorean learned his estimate of Senator Byrd's editorial preferences had been wrong, but by that time it didn't matter. Dabney already had the prize.

Kent Cooper of the Associated Press also had his troubles. Usually, he was tireless in promoting the interests of his own staff people whenever it was opportune for him to do so, but in 1949 he voted with the rest of the Advisory Board for Nathaniel Fein's sports photo, "Babe Ruth Bows Out," in the New York *Herald Tribune*. After the prize was announced, Cooper learned that an AP man, among others, had made almost the same picture, for Ruth's last moments as a baseball player were scarcely private. The AP photo, however, was not considered.[17] Few news executives of Cooper's stature would have been in ignorance for very long about the work of their reporters, however.

To the members of the Advisory Board, and to the profession as a whole beginning with World War II, it was the reporter who counted. For in war and peace, and in the cold war years, the credibility of the newspaper in its struggle against the opposing media, both print and electronic, depended to a very large extent on what the reporter could deliver. He was not only a public servant; he was, in many respects, a public necessity.

2
The Troublesome Novel

The emotional, crusading fervor against the enemies of America that bulked so large in the nation's consciousness during World War II had a predictable impact on the American novel. Not since the Civil War had so many writers of consequence felt it to be their destiny to write about war in fictional form for the benefit of their countrymen, if not entirely for themselves. Perhaps the patriotic spirit was greater in World War I, but it didn't last as long. In World War II, the ideological commitment of the intellectuals was made years before the Nazis struck at Poland in 1939. Thus, the novelists had a long time to mull over their feelings and the books they produced about the conflict continued to reach the public years after World War II ended.

The first of the war books published in 1942 to win a Pulitzer Prize in Fiction was Upton Sinclair's *Dragon's Teeth*, which Joseph Pulitzer had called to the Board's attention at its previous meeting. It was a long over-due recognition of the old Socialist gadfly, then 64 years old, who had made literary history with such books as *The Jungle* and *The Brass Check*.

The jury's recommendation, although strong, was not unanimous. James Gould Cozzens' novel about justice in a democratic community, *The Just and the Unjust*, had one anonymous supporter among the three professional critics on the jury—Lewis Gannett, Maxwell Geismar, and John Chamberlain, chairman. But he did not press his objection to the report, which said: "The Lanny Budd sequence, of which *Dragon's Teeth* is a part, is Sinclair's best fiction by far."

There followed a soothing assurance that Sinclair was no longer the fiery Socialist of old and his story had nothing to do with the Marxist class struggle. *Dragon's Teeth*, the report went on, "is actually a story of well-meaning Americans waking up to the threat of the German system of ideas." With that, the Advisory Board and the university Trustees gave the 1943 Pulitzer Prize for Fiction to the oldest and most formidable critic of the American press, and he responded on his part with courtly expressions of pleasure.[18]

The same Fiction jury was so badly split over the 1944 award that the Advisory Board had to make the final decision. No juror favored Betty Smith's sentimental best-seller, *A Tree Grows in Brooklyn*, the popular choice. Geismar wanted Ira Wolfert's *Tucker's People*, but nobody else did. That left the final choice between Chamberlain's favorite, Martin Flavin's *Journey in the Dark*, and Gannett's selection, Christine Weston's *Indigo*, a story about India and therefore not as "American" as *Journey in the Dark*. The Board chose the Flavin book, the rather turgid tale of a millionaire who went to work in a defense plant during the war, and was severely criticized for it.[19]

The 1945 jury, on which Orville Prescott of the New York *Times* replaced Lewis Gannett of the New York *Herald Tribune*, also ran into trouble. They were split between Prescott's choice, John Hersey's *A Bell for Adano*; Geismar's preference, Joseph Pennell's *The History of Rome Hanks*; and Edith Pope's *Colcorton*. Chamberlain finally decided that, as between *A Bell for Adano* and *Rome Hanks*, he preferred the former.

A Bell for Adano, the story of an American Army officer who took over the government of a liberated Italian village and restored a precious church bell to the villagers, also ran into difficulty before the Advisory Board. There, one of the members, in an outburst of patriotic wrath, denounced the novel because he didn't like the way Hersey depicted General George S. Patton Jr. Hersey, a war correspondent, had had his own ideas about the blustering general and had put them in his book, but the Board's majority didn't hold that against him. The Pulitzer Prize in Fiction for 1945, accordingly, was voted to *A Bell for Adano*.

The book had been a best-seller before it won the prize. It later became both a play and a successful motion picture. Whether it was "a truly remarkable book" as Prescott had thought, however, remained for the judgment of future generations.[20]

The same jury was in even less agreement over the 1946 prize. This time the split was between Glenway Wescott's *Apartment in Athens*, Dan Wickenden's *The Wayfarers*, and Richard Wright's autobiography, *Black Boy*, which Prescott refused to consider as a novel. The Advisory Board passed the award for lack of definitive guidance from the jurors.

The 1947 winner, *All the King's Men* by Robert Penn Warren, was a welcome change from the uncertainties of the war years. It was the complex story of the rise and fall of an opportunistic country lawyer who became the virtual dictator of a Southern state and came to an untimely end through assassination. To many, the novel seemed to be a fictional retelling of the tragedy of Huey Long, the Louisiana "Kingfish," but it went far deeper than that. Possibly, its philosophical overtones kept it from being more than a moderately popular book until it won the Pulitzer Prize by courtesy of the jury and the Advisory Board. Then, the critics hailed the selection and most of them, even the youngest dissenters, have done so ever since.

Warren's reaction was modest. When a reporter asked him how he felt after he had won the prize, he replied, "I feel guilty about all the writers better than I am who have never received the Pulitzer Prize."

As a novelist and poet, Warren's career was one of the most distinguished in modern American literature. He was born in 1905 in Guthrie, Ky., graduated summa cum laude from Vanderbilt in 1925, took his master's from California at Berkeley in 1927, and won a Rhodes scholarship for study at Oxford in 1930. His teaching career began at Southwestern College in Memphis in 1931, after which he taught at Vanderbilt for three years beginning in 1931 and at Louisiana State University for eight years beginning in 1934. It was here that he lived through the turbulent era of Huey Long's empire that gave him the basis for his prize-winning novel.

Throughout his early academic career, Warren had been writing superior verse and had achieved recognition as a poet. It helped him win a Guggenheim Fellowship and, in 1944-45, while he was a professor at the University of Minnesota, brought him the coveted chair in poetry of the Library of Congress. He was back at the University of Minnesota, teaching a class on a pleasant early May afternoon in 1947 when a colleague, Professor Tremaine McDowell, entered and asked to make an announcement. It was Warren's first news that he had won the Pulitzer Prize that year. In 1950, he shifted to Yale, where he remained for much of the rest of his career, winning a Pulitzer Prize in Poetry in 1958 for *Promises: Poems 1954-1956*. He received many other awards, as well, and published numerous other volumes of poetry and prose.

To most established writers, it has always been difficult to determine what effect, if any, the Pulitzer Prize has had on their careers. In Warren's case, there was something tangible. As he put it long afterward,

"The first one got my novel made into a movie." Before *All The King's Men* received the award, it had gone begging in Hollywood at a price as low as $15,000. The rumor was that the film executives feared the prospect of legal action, a threat that also may have been made against another novel that recalled Huey Long's career.

"But a few days after the Prize," Warren wrote, "I had a call from Lambert Davis at Harcourt Brace, with news that negotiations were under way and all that remained was some haggling about the figure. The long-range result was that I could give more time to my work, and teach only when and if I wanted to." [21]

There was another, and strikingly different, success story behind the award of the 1948 fiction prize to a comparatively unknown writer, James A. Michener, for a book of short stories entitled *Tales of the South Pacific*.

In the annals of the Pulitzer Prizes, there has never been a less likely winner than *Tales of the South Pacific*. If odds had been quoted against it during the 1947 publishing season, it would very probably have been in the range of 100–1. For Michener up to that time had not written anything that had brought him to public attention other than a textbook. He was a native of New York City, born there in 1907; a summa cum laude graduate of Swarthmore, 1929; a teacher at prep schools, Hill and George, and later at Colorado State College. Just before World War II, he worked briefly for the publishing house of Macmillan and later, while with the Navy in the Pacific in 1944–45, he began writing some short stories about what he heard and saw.

There were a lot of entertaining characters in Michener's stories—a French planter who had taken refuge on a Pacific island and lived with a native; a cheerful, open-hearted American nurse from Little Rock; a native harridan called "Bloody Mary" who peddled her merchandise to the Seabees and had a beautiful daughter; a romantic young Navy officer from Philadelphia; and the usual complement of raucous Seabees, nurses, pilots, and assorted camp followers. Nobody thought of it as great fiction, but it had character and substance and it was fun. However, except for two fortuitous circumstances, it never would have been brought to the Advisory Board's attention.

The first was the Board's appointment of a committee—John S. Knight, William R. Mathews and Robert Choate—to do a complete redraft of the Pulitzer Prize Plan of Award, effective in 1947. On the basis of their work, the Board in that year adopted a revised formula for the fiction prize which for the first time made short stories eligible. It read:

"For distinguished fiction published in book form during the year by an American author, preferably dealing with American life."

The second circumstance was the willingness of a major critic, Orville Prescott of the New York *Times*, to back a newcomer's book of short stories for the 1948 fiction award. As Prescott recalled the experience: "I did serve on the jury which chose Michener's *Tales of the South Pacific* and I was personally responsible for nominating it and urging it. I and the other judges felt it was a poor year for fiction and here was a wonderful new talent. Unfortunately, Mr. Michener has not lived up to his early promise."

Arthur Krock was Michener's strongest advocate at the Board meeting of April 23, 1948. Mrs. Alice Roosevelt Longworth, another of Michener's champions, had urged Krock to read the book and he did so. "I nominated Michener, gave my reasons, and the Board accepted them," Krock wrote. "That prize initiated the public and critical awareness of Michener that assured his subsequent literary prominence and success."

It did all of that, despite the inevitable negative critical reaction that accompanied the award to a book of romantic short stories about the war by a newcomer to the American literary scene. When Oscar Hammerstein II put Michener's *Tales* together, wrote the lyrics to Richard Rodgers' tuneful score and worked with Joshua Logan to present the musical *South Pacific* in 1949, all the argument stopped and the rush for the almost unobtainable tickets began. President Carlos P. Romulo of the United Nations General Assembly, finding that the lack of tickets for *South Pacific* was a major social issue among the wives of the delegates that year, scored a theatrical coup of his own by producing the stars, Ezio Pinza and Mary Martin, to sing their well-remembered love songs in the grand ballroom of the Waldorf Astoria. *South Pacific*, too, won the Pulitzer Prize—it was for drama in 1950. This time, there were no sour notices; everyone was pleased. And when Rodgers and Hammerstein protested that Logan had been left out of the Pulitzer Prize honors, Dean Ackerman obligingly wrote in his name as a winner. A quarter-century later, Michener's tales were a part of American folk-lore—a movie that played to world-wide audiences and kept turning up on television.[22]

Three non-New York book critics—Joseph Henry Jackson of the San
Francisco *Chronicle*, Frederic Babcock of the Chicago *Tribune* and the
chairman, David Appel of the Philadelphia *Inquirer*—came together as
the Fiction Jury for 1949. They placed four books before the Board for
the award for that year—*Guard of Honor* by James Gould Cozzens, *The
Naked and the Dead* by Norman Mailer, *The Ides of March* by Thornton
Wilder, and *The Young Lions* by Irwin Shaw. Appel wrote: "The above
listing is not made in order of preference, but each of the books recommended received the vote of at least two of the three jurors. The first
two titles were unanimous choices."

It came down to a great newcomer, Mailer, with a tough and uncompromising war novel that was one of the best for World War II, and
the well-established Cozzens, who had been considered by another Fiction Jury. Cozzens' World War II story of embattled whites and blacks
at an air base had had a good critical reception but it was not a best
seller. Mailer, ever outspoken and profane, had won both critical acclaim
and a place on the best seller lists. The Board chose Cozzens as the superior novelist that year. It was, on the whole a defensible choice in view
of Cozzens' literary reputation and his record of achievement; through
hindsight, the selection of Mailer would have given early recognition to a
coming leader of American literature. But the Board, in this instance,
didn't have 20–20 rear vision.

"As for the *The Naked and the Dead*" Mailer wrote long afterward, "I
don't know if it was even considered seriously. I had come out all ten
thumbs and ten big toes for Henry Wallace, and for all I know may have
been considered a fellow-traveler or a Communist dupe. Or perhaps the
language of the book repelled the judges. Promiscuous use of the word
fug was thought of as strong waters in those days. I am afraid it took Jim
Jones and *From Here to Eternity* to set the spelling straight." [23]

The 1950 selection by the same Fiction Jury was a well-regarded
Western, A. B. Guthrie Jr.'s *The Way West*, about which there was little
argument. But in 1951, when all juries were reduced to two members
each, evidently an economy move, there was unpleasantness over the
recommendation by Messrs. Appel and Jackson of John Hersey's *The
Wall*, which dealt with Hitler's extermination of the Jews. The jurors
had told the Board that they believed only the Hersey book was worthy
of the prize that year. When Ackerman asked for alternatives, they proposed Conrad Richter's *The Town*, Robert Penn Warren's *World Enough*

and Time, and Max Steele's *Debbie*, but they still insisted on *The Wall* even though it did not deal with the American scene. Appel wrote:

"Both Mr. Jackson and I would like to point out that there have been times when the prize was not awarded to a novel of American subject matter, notable *The Bridge of San Luis Rey* and *The Good Earth*, and in latter years such choices as *A Bell for Adano* and *Tales of the South Pacific* did not deal specifically with the American scene."

The Advisory Board was not impressed. For its own reasons, it voted for *The Town* and Messrs. Appel and Jackson quietly retired from the Fiction Jury.[24]

Ackerman, who now was responsible for administering all the Pulitzer awards, turned next to Professors Eric P. Kelly of Dartmouth and Roy W. Cowden of the University of Michigan as the 1952 Fiction Jury. In their report, Cowden chose Herman Wouk's *The Caine Mutiny* while Kelly was for *Jenkins's Ear* by Odell and Willard Shepard. James Jones's best-selling *From Here To Eternity* was given short shrift by Cowden, who wrote that "quite aside from its lack as a work of art, it is, in my opinion, in very bad taste."

The Advisory Board settled for Wouk's novel, but in later years he had mingled views about the prize. He realized, of course, that "coterie" writers thought the novel award "of little value, and even rather disreputable"—which he attributed in part to "too many dull choices and the slighting of some outstanding novels." He concluded:

"Prize juries are only human, and they tend to be hidebound in one way or another. I am sure that every critic who sneers at the Pulitzer Prize would be overjoyed to win one. It remains the most famous American literary award." [25]

Kelly and Cowden split again in their 1953 report. Kelly at last gave the Board a belated chance to honor Ernest Hemingway for *The Old Man and the Sea*. Cowden disagreed, being for Carl Jonas' *Jefferson Selleck*. Kelly wrote of the Hemingway book:

"Although short, this book contains all the elements that make a novel excellent. . . . It is well written, well planned, and possesses the beauty that only a real work of art can have."

Ackerman remarked long afterward that he had lobbied for the acceptance of *The Old Man and the Sea*, but he really didn't have to work very hard. There was no other realistic choice for the Board and the honor to Hemingway was long overdue. The 1953 prize to *The Old Man and the*

Sea, therefore, was no surprise. It had been printed in full in *Life* magazine before its publication in book form and had been the choice of most of the nation's book critics in a poll taken by the *Saturday Review*.

Hemingway wrote to Charles Poore of the New York *Times* not long after the announcement:

"Mary and I were down the coast (of Cuba) anchored off Megano de Casigua. . . . When we caught the prize news on the evening newscast, Miss Mary made some martinis for both of us and we opened some special cheese for supper to celebrate. Miss Mary said I was her Pulitzer Prize-winning husband and had they given it to me for being a good boy for nearly three years or what? I told her I had never understood the Pulitzer Prize very well but that I had beaten Tony Pulitzer shooting and maybe it was for that."

There was never a word of reproach from Hemingway about his previous experiences with the Pulitzer Prizes. He had a little fun with the award, calling it the "Pullover Prize" and the "IgNoble Prize," but there was no doubt that he was pleased. He was awarded the Nobel Prize for Literature the following year. Shortly thereafter, he told Harvey Breit, an interviewer, "Anyone receiving an honor . . . must receive it in humility." [26]

Apparently, Professor Cowden was displeased by the award because he dropped off the Fiction Jury for 1954, being replaced by Professor Harris F. Fletcher of the University of Illinois, who worked with Kelly. They were in such disagreement that neither duplicated the other in any of the first five books each recommended. Kelly liked *Ramey* by Jack D. Ferris and *The Sand of Karakorum* by James R. Ullman while Fletcher recommended, as his first two, Myron Brinig's *The Street of the Three Friends* and Wright Morris' *The Deep Sleep*. Kelly alone mentioned Saul Bellow's *The Adventures of Augie March* under a heading, "Best Sellers," saying, "The book is readable, but unless one is willing to abandon the idea of man trying to work out some object for himself in the battle that he engages in, one cannot put too high a premium upon a piece of work of this sort which certainly is not general." To confuse the issue still further, Kelly sent in a personal memo a week after his formal report, asking to have Ben Lucien Burman's *The Four Lives of Mundy Tolliver* placed first on his list of five. The Burman book, however, wasn't mentioned in Fletcher's report. With that kind of a split among its experts, the Advisory Board passed the 1954 award. [27]

The World War II books were running out. A few had been done about the Korean War, and there would be a bit more of them. But by and large, the day of the belligerent novelists was just about over. There would be revivals of interest in the World War II period, to be sure, but when it came new novelists would be taking up old themes and putting them between new covers.

3
The Theater Looks Up

During the era of World War II and thereafter, the famous men who had brought world leadership to the American theater passed slowly from the scene. Sidney Howard, so brilliant and urbane at his best, died in 1939. Maxwell Anderson, Robert E. Sherwood, and Elmer Rice already had attained their peak and did comparatively little in the theater once the nation went to war. The master craftsman, George S. Kaufman, kept on going until 1961 but his best work, too, was long since over. The giant of them all, Eugene O'Neill, surmounted illness and despair during the war period to write two of his finest plays, *The Iceman Cometh*, and *Long Day's Journey Into Night*, before his death in 1953.

It was a time for new talent and fresh ideas. Some already had come forward, as witness Thornton Wilder's debut in the theater with *Our Town* and William Saroyan's genial and hopeful if largely formless plays. Greater figures were waiting in the wings—Tennessee Williams and Arthur Miller. And the new partnership of Oscar Hammerstein II and Richard Rodgers was embarking on a glad venture that would make the American musical theater a beautiful and shimmering thing. To those who mourned the passing of the great ones of the past and cried out that the theater was dead, there was a ready answer. Broadway, somewhat shabbier and more commercial than inspirational, was still vibrant and alive. New faces and new figures were replacing the illustrious pillars of the drama. The theater, once again, was looking up.

In the darkest time of the war, the fall of 1942, when the nation had need of uplift and courage, Thornton Wilder presented a dazzling new play on the indestructibility of mankind, *The Skin of Our Teeth*. Against the background of all of human history, he took a family of bright and unusual characters though every kind of disaster from the Ice Age to the havoc of modern war. And at the end, he offered hope and the simple message that life would go on. This "fantastic comedy," as he called it, ran for a year on wartime Broadway against the competition of mindless amusements from peep shows to booming night clubs.

The Pulitzer Drama Jury of Professor Phelps, Mrs. Colum, and W. Somerset Maugham unanimously recommended *The Skin of Our Teeth* to the Advisory Board in glowing terms. "This has vitality," Maugham wrote, "a gay and fantastic invention, and it is almost consistently entertaining." Mrs. Colum called it "that rare thing—a combination of drama and theater of a very high degree." Phelps simply presented the verdict, which was promptly accepted, Messrs. Pulitzer and Krock dissenting. It brought Wilder his third Pulitzer Prize, his second in the drama.

In 1944, with Maugham as the Drama Jury chairman and Mrs. Colum and Glenway Wescott as members, there was little to recommend. Mrs. Colum wanted to pass. Wescott and Maugham proposed John Van Druten's *The Voice of the Turtle*, a light comedy, or nothing. What the Board did was to pass the prize, but at the same time it took the unprecedented step of announcing a specal award for *Oklahoma!* by Richard Rodgers and Oscar Hammerstein II. This was evidently done on the Board's own initiative for there was no mention of *Oklahoma!* in the jury report.

The recognition that came to the team of Rodgers and Hammerstein was no mere endorsement of a reigning success. For *Oklahoma!* represented something new on the American stage, a musical in which there was an artistic determination to portray character and plot and in which the songs grew out of the circumstances of the story. The tryout in New Haven was so discouraging that one wag observed: "No legs, no jokes, no chance."

What Hammerstein had done was to make a play with music out of Lynn Riggs's novel, *Green Grow the Lilacs*, and Rodgers had written an adult, superior score. Everybody including the authors had their doubts about *Oklahoma!* when it opened at the St. James Theatre in New York, but the reception it received from a wartime audience guaranteed its success. It ran for 2,212 performances.

The success of Rodgers and Hammerstein was no accident. Both were experienced in the theater and both had been outstanding before forming their partnership for *Oklahoma!* At the time the show opened, Hammerstein was 48, Rodgers 41. Both were New Yorkers and had attended Columbia College. Hammerstein, the grandson of the celebrated showman, Oscar Hammerstein, had such early successes as *Rose Marie*, which he did with Rudolf Friml in 1924, *The Desert Song*, with Sigmund Romberg in 1926, and *Show Boat* with Jerome Kern in 1927. Rodgers had done successful shows with Lorenz Hart, beginning with the *Garrick Gaieties* in 1925 and including *The Girl Friend* and *A Connecticut Yankee*. Once *Oklahoma!* sealed the new relationship between Rodgers and Hammerstein, they went on to a notable series of musical plays including *Carousel*, *South Pacific* and *The King and I*.

Theirs was a special relationship. Hammerstein, big and suave and kindly in everything he did, was the "cock-eyed optimist" whose lyrics often had a kind of worldly uplift to them. Whatever he wrote, he sweated over, sometimes for days at a time. He never ceased to marvel at the facility with which Rodgers would set the lyrics to music, sometimes in a matter of minutes. As an amateur pianist, Hammerstein knew the values of music although he was no composer himself. As for Rodgers, he appreciated story values and was in on every bit of such discussions. While the special award for *Oklahoma!* and the Pulitzer Prize for *South Pacific* did not materially affect them, they were, as Rodgers wrote, "greatly honored by the award and extremely happy to have received it." Characteristically, Rodgers always felt, too, that it had been "shameful" to omit George Gershwin's name from the prize that was given to *Of Thee I Sing*.[28]

A new and striking figure came to the Drama Jury during the 1945 season—Professor Oscar James Campbell, the small, wiry, and immensely learned head of Columbia's English Department and an authority on Shakespeare. He joined with his Columbia colleague, Joseph Wood Krutch, and Mrs. Colum, the chairman that year, in a unanimous report favoring Mary Chase's comedy, *Harvey*. It was an amusing fantasy about a genial alcoholic and his invisible companion, a six-foot rabbit called "Harvey." All three jurors liked it.

Laughter and relief from anxiety were qualities of importance in the closing months of World War II. While Frank Bacon's long-running alcoholic comedy, *Lightnin'*, had been passed up for a Pulitzer Prize in its early years, the subject matter no longer was disagreeable. The Advisory Board without dissent voted the 1945 Pulitzer award to *Harvey*, which ran for 1,775 performances on Broadway, went into the movies, and survived as a staple on television.[29]

Although two successive Pulitzer Prize juries had taken no notice of them, the two most impressive postwar dramatists had made their bow on Broadway. There was some reason not to make mention of Arthur Miller, for his first Broadway production, *The Man Who Had All the Luck*, died after four performances in 1944. But in 1945, Tennessee Williams' lovely and poetic play, *The Glass Menagerie*, opened on Broadway on the last day of the Pulitzer season, March 31, after thirteen successful weeks in Chicago. It was, in Williams' words, a "memory play"—a recollection of the trials and the tenderness of an insecure life with his sister and his mother while he was growing up.

Pulitzer juries traditionally have been sensitive about holding their reports as long as possible in March, usually over the protests of the Advisory Board, in order to see new plays, particularly by new dramatists. This was as true of the 1945 jury as it had been of others. Mrs. Colum's report was dated April 3, as was Professor Campbell's, and Professor Krutch's report was dated April 2. Krutch alone mentioned *The Glass Menagerie*, saying he was seeing the play that night and adding, "If, as seems unlikely, I should wish to put it first, I shall send you a supplementary report." There was no supplementary report, so *Harvey* took the prize over *Dark of the Moon*, by Howard Richardson and William Berney, the runner-up. It remained for the Critics Circle to pin their annual award on *The Glass Menagerie* on April 10, Williams' first recognition as a masterful playwright.

The same jury gave belated recognition to the talents of the authors of *Life With Father*, Howard Lindsay and Russel Crouse, by recommending their play, *State of the Union*, in 1946. But in 1947, inexplicably, there was no award in a season that featured Arthur Miller's first great success, *All My Sons*, as well as Eugene O'Neill's *The Iceman Cometh*, Lillian Hellman's *Another Part of the Forest*, and the two imaginative and tuneful musicals, *Brigadoon* and *Finian's Rainbow*. The Critics Circle had no difficulty bestowing its prize on Arthur Miller for drama and *Brigadoon* for musical shows. It gave the critics' organization a proud distinction, for the successive awards to Miller and Williams served notice on the nation that two major theatrical talents had arrived. The Pulitzer Prizes were to recognize them in due course, a tactical delay that seemed to bother Miller unduly but did not upset Williams in the slightest. Both were to make history in the theater.

An all-Columbia jury consisting of Professors Campbell, Krutch, and

Maurice J. Valency recommended Williams' *A Streetcar Named Desire* for the first of his two Pulitzer Prizes in 1948. The tenderness of *The Glass Menagerie* was missing here, but Williams' poetic ability to avoke character was much in evidence. The tragedy of Blanche duBois, the aging Southern belle who loses her suitor and is raped by her brutal brother-in-law, came alive with raw and startling force at the Ethel Barrymore Theatre when it opened on December 3, 1947. Jessica Tandy as Blanche and Marlon Brando as Stanley Kowalski, the brother-in-law, contributed to its success but it was Williams who dominated the enthusiastic reviews. Even twenty-six years later, at a Broadway revival, Walter Kerr of the New York *Times* was still ecstatic, writing that "Mr. Williams' play has always seemed to me the finest single work yet created for the American theater." The Pulitzer Prize for Drama in 1948 served to confirm his genius. His second prize in 1955 was for *Cat on a Hot Tin Roof*.

Like Eugene O'Neill, Thomas Lanier Williams had a trying, unhappy childhood, torn between his Southern Belle of a mother and his harsh and demanding father. He was born in Mississippi in 1914, reared in St. Louis, and attended the University of Missouri and Washington University before his father forced him to become a clerk in a shoe factory. After such treatment, he left home as soon as he could, worked at anything he could find, and turned up eventually in Greenwich Village in New York as a waiter. All the time he was trying to write plays and short stories with little success, but things changed when he enrolled in a New School playwriting seminar, working with Theresa Helburn and Professor John Gassner of Yale. There was no doubt of his genius, but at first his luck was all bad. His first play, *Battle of Angels*, produced by the Theatre Guild, closed in Boston during its tryout and the Guild apologized for having put on an "obscene" production. The success of *The Glass Menagerie* changed all that, however.

Looking back over his accomplishments in 1972, he wrote:

> I would say that only the first award, a Critics award for *The Glass Menagerie*, had a slightly disturbing effect, since I was abruptly turned into a person of public interest and, well, it was initially somewhat unnerving.
>
> But as for the two Pulitzers, any privacy which I had once possessed having been thoroughly relinquished—or exorcised?—they were both occasions for great rejoicing in my heart despite the disappointment of invidious workers at the same craft.

One thing has always puzzled me in relation to myself and the Pulitzer jury, and that is just how they arrived at the conclusion that *Harvey* out-classed *Menagerie* in '45—but that is what the French call *vieux jeux* and let us look to the future.[30]

The same all-Columbia jury recommended Arthur Miller's *Death of a Salesman* for a Pulitzer Prize in 1949, but it was by a split decision even though the critics were unanimous in praising the play. Professors Campbell and Valency were for Miller's work, but Professor Krutch preferred Tennessee Williams' *Summer and Smoke*, which had closed after a comparatively short run. Campbell's recommendation was even stronger than those of most of the critics, for he wrote:

"I strongly recommend that the prize be given to *Death of a Salesman* by Arthur Miller. This tragedy is by all odds the most notable American play of the season. Indeed, I am inclined to regard it as the best modern American tragedy of the last decade. In a sense, it is the tragedy of every one who plays an important part in our acquisitive civilization. . . . The Pulitzer award would add to its already great prestige by crowning so distinguished a work by a young American playwright."

Valency, too, called *Death of a Salesman* the year's outstanding play although he didn't think it a "great" one. "It is," he wrote, "open to very grave objections from the point of view of intellectual content, style, and construction. Nevertheless, it is an extremely powerful play and I believe it will have consequences in the development of a sphere of drama which has not previously been practiced with conspicuous success in this country."

The story of the decline, failure, and eventually the death of Willy Loman, the salesman, attracted Broadway audiences from the night it opened, February 10, 1949, at the Morosco Theatre, where it ran for 742 performances. But the Pulitzer Prize didn't bring Miller any particular satisfaction, for he thought he should have had it for *All My Sons*, his earlier work, and he credited the Critics Circle with starting him on his way to the top.

Miller was only 34 when he won his Pulitzer. He was a New Yorker, born in the city in 1915, and had begun writing plays as a student at the University of Michigan, from which he was graduated in 1938. From the beginning, Miller was a social crusader, a critic who saw the flaws in

American society and never hesitated to point them out. He was a dramatist who was deeply concerned with the life of his time and who did not let himself be deterred from writing what he thought because of a fury of conservative criticism. His play, *The Crucible*, which later became an opera, was a protest against the evils of McCarthyism, from which he suffered to some extent although it never really affected his career. A later work, *Incident at Vichy*, was an attack on anti-Semitism and the manner in which the Nazis used it. If there was any *Long Day's Journey Into Night* among Miller's works, it was *After the Fall*, which he wrote after the failure of his marriage to the movie star, Marilyn Monroe. It was, perhaps, the most human of all his plays, although it won no awards.[31]

If there was any single factor of importance in the works of both Miller and Williams, it was the shattering of nearly all the remaining conventions that bound the American drama to the historic forms of other generations. They served also to remove some, but not all, of the remaining inhibitions that had caused Pulitzer juries in the past to hesitate to offer outstanding dramatic works as prize recommendations for fear of offending the sensibilities of either the Advisory Board or the Columbia Trustees. In at least one instance, the award of the Pulitzer Prize to *Cat on a Hot Tin Roof* in 1955, the Advisory Board took the initiative despite the lingering prejudice against the use of offensive language on the stage.

The Advisory Board overruled its experts on the Drama Jury twice in succession in 1950 and 1951. In 1950, the Columbia team of Professors Campbell, Krutch, and Valency ran into trouble because they recommended Gian-Carlo Menotti's *The Consul*, which as it turned out was also the first choice of the Music Jury and the eventual winner of the Pulitzer Prize in Music that year. The Advisory Board, in a thoroughly musical mood, decided on its own that the Pulitzer Prize in Drama for that year should go to *South Pacific*, which was great theater. During the following year, a two-member jury of Professors Campbell and Valency recommended a dramatization of Herman Melville's novel, *Billy Budd*, by Louis O'Coxe and Robert Chapman, but the Advisory Board refused to accept it for undetermined reasons. The award was passed for 1951. The team of Campbell and Valency, which was to remain together through

1955, had better luck in the following year with its recommendation of Joseph Kramm's psychological tragedy about mental illness, *The Shrike*, the 1952 drama winner.[32]

William Inge, a protege of Tennessee Williams, had the brightest year of his career in 1953 when his play, *Picnic*, won the Pulitzer Prize. The recognition that came to him both for this work and an earlier play, *Come Back, Little Sheba*, caused him to be linked for some years with Williams and Arthur Miller as the leading dramatists of the postwar era in the United States. Inge specialized in plays about commonplace people who were involved in complicated situations that were at once comic and dramatic. *Picnic* was that kind of work—a play about a good-looking drifter who creates an uproar in a small Kansas town, seduces a girl who thought of herself as perfectly proper while everybody is off on a community picnic, and runs away from the consequences.

Campbell and Valency, in their report, called it a "notable" play and added: "Though the characters are commonplace, they are portrayed with insight and in such a way as to create the situations and the illuminating scenes. It is an expertly composed piece, beautifully written and American to the core."

Inge, who was born in Independence, Kansas, in 1913, had graduated from the University of Kansas in 1935, taught for five years at a women's college and served as a drama critic for the St. Louis *Star-Times* during World War II. The young critic's life was changed by an interview he had sought with Tennessee Williams in 1945, while the dramatist was visiting his parents in St. Louis. The two men found a community of interest in the theater. Williams encouraged Inge to work on a play, *Farther Off from Heaven*, and recommended it to Margo Jones, who was running an experimental theater in Dallas and agreed to produce it. That play led to Inge's first Broadway success, *Come Back, Little Sheba*, in 1950 and later to *Picnic*. Another small town play about ordinary people, *Bus Stop*, further advanced his career in 1955. That was followed two years later by *The Dark at the Top of the Stairs*, but from then on Inge's career was almost at a standstill. After working in Hollywood for some years, he confessed to utter frustration, saying:

"I must admit that I am getting awfully tired of the public arts. The frustrations, the anxieties, the pressures—the whole thing takes far more from a man than it gives him." [33]

Professors Campbell and Valency picked a happier winner in 1954,

John Patrick's comedy about military government on Okinawa, *The Teahouse of the August Moon.* They called it "an altogether delightful comedy, a fantasy about the impact of the East and West on each other." The Advisory Board gladly recommended it for the Pulitzer Prize in Drama that year, which pleased most of the critics. *Teahouse* became quite a property over the years that followed, running for 1,027 performances at the Martin Beck Theatre in New York, delighting movie audiences all over the world, and attaining a place on television's late, late show.[34]

In comedy, as in drama, the American theater showed itself to be vibrant with fresh talent and new ideas in the postwar world. The Pulitzer Prizes served to encourage its progress.

4

History—The Broader View

A dynamic young historian, fully equipped with the crusading fervor of an early New Dealer and the brilliant style of an eminent Victorian, burst out of academic life toward the end of World War II. He was Arthur Meier Schlesinger Jr., a summa cum laude graduate of Harvard in 1938 and the son of a Harvard historian. His pathbreaking work, which he published at the age of 28, was *The Age of Jackson*, in which he imposed a New Dealer's view of the class struggle on the Jacksonian movement. Embellishing the line of Charles A. Beard's economic approach to American history, Schlesinger laid down the thesis that a loosely knit confederation of laboring men, farmers, and intellectuals provided Andrew Jackson with the power to fight the bankers and businessmen of his time.

Even in wartime, Schlesinger's view of Jacksonian history created a stir. His adherents lavishly praised his work while the conservative historical community attacked his "present-mindedness," then an academic sin. Despite this ideological split, the Pulitzer History Jury of Guy Stanton Ford, James Phinney Baxter III, and Thomas J. Wertenbaker, professor of history at Princeton, unanimously voted for Schlesinger's work for the 1946 history award. Their report concluded that *The Age of Jackson* will survive "and date a new approach by future scholars" to the Jacksonian era.

The jury's prediction was amply fulfilled following Schlesinger's re-

ceipt of the Pulitzer Prize, the first of two he has won. For despite the
ebbing of the progressive spirit among major historians and the rising
doubt about the thesis of class struggle as an explanation for the turmoil
of the Jacksonian age, the young historian's work did become a guidepost
for scholars. Like Turner and Beard, he promoted controversy and stimulated thought, an invaluable asset in the process of broadening the
view of American history.[35]

There was one other significant addition to American historical literature in the wartime Pulitzer Prizes—the award of the 1944 prize to Merle
Curti's *The Growth of American Thought*. As an intellectual history, written by a student of Turner, it also took the view that democracy was an
eternal struggle on behalf of the common man. The jury—Messrs. Ford,
Baxter, and Arthur Meier Schlesinger Sr.—accepted it as a "path-
breaking work." The same jury successfully proposed Esther Forbes's
Paul Revere and the World He Lived In for the 1943 prize, even though it
was as much biography as it was history. But in 1945 it came a cropper
when the Advisory Board again intervened.

The jury had proposed *Lee's Lieutenants, Vol. III*, by Douglas Southall
Freeman, who already had won a Pulitzer Prize. But the Board voted instead for Stephen Bonsal's *Unfinished Business*, a diary of the Peace Conference of World War I, written by a former war correspondent. It
wasn't a popular decision. The Board's prejudice in favor of one of its
own, a widely known newspaperman, did not sit well with many historians, even though the jury itself made no public protest.[36]

The process of broadening the view of American historians continued
apace in the post-World War II period. One of the most influential pro-
nouncements came from Professor Roy Franklin Nichols of the University of Pennsylvania. In an essay in the American Historical Review in
1948, he called on historians for a "declaration of intellectual independence" and warned them not to let themselves be subordinated in the
general view of social sciences. That same years, Nichols' own major historical work, *The Disruption of American Democracy*, was published, with
salutary results. A jury of Dr. Baxter, Merle Curti, and Dean Theodore
C. Blegen of the University of Minnesota unanimously recommended it
for the 1949 history award.

Nichols was teaching in England at Cambridge University and his
wife was lecturing at the University of Birmingham when the news of
the award came from Columbia University, where both had established

some sort of a record in 1923 by receiving their Ph.D. degrees at the same commencement. Although he wrote many more books and became dean of Pennsylvania's graduate school, the historian never forgot the effect of his 1949 prize. "It was inspiriting in the finest sense," he wrote almost a quarter-century later, "encouraging me to continuing production of other books in the fields of my special interests. . . . The award was a continuous pleasurable experience, which probably had a happy effect, whether or not I stopped to think of it thus, through the many years of my writing of articles and books." [37]

There were other notable awards in the postwar period—Baxter's *Scientists Against Time* in 1947, Bernard DeVoto's *Across the Wide Missouri* in 1948, Oliver W. Larkin's *Art and Life in America* in 1950, R. Carlyle Buley's *The Old Northwest, Pioneer Period 1815–1840* in 1951, Oscar Handlin's classic study of European immigration to America, *The Uprooted,* in 1952, and George Dangerfield's *The Era of Good Feelings* in 1953. Nearly all of these works, in one way or another, served to broaden the field of the American historian and the best of them, particularly Handlin's book, set high standards for innovative scholarship.

The balance of responsibility for historical literature had long since swung toward the academics whose work was very largely subsidized by their universities or by private foundations and away from the non-institutionalized writers of the type of Douglas Southall Freeman and Carl Sandburg. But now and then, one of the unaffiliated would turn up in the mass of academic literature with a work that simply demanded attention. Bruce Catton, a former newspaperman and former public official, was such a historian and the book that brought him prominence was his study of the last year of the Civil War, *A Stillness at Appomattox*.

The two-member jury in history for 1954, Professors Curti and Schlesinger Sr., were understandably conditioned to think of the fine work of their fellow professionals—the massive and authoritative study by William L. Langer and S. Everett Gleason, *The Undeclared War;* Clinton Rossiter's *Seed-time of the Republic;* and Perry Miller's *The New England Mind from Colony to Province.* But they did include Catton's book with this comment:

"*A Stillness at Appomattox* is the story of the last desperate year of the Army of the Potomac, ending with Lee's surrender and the downfall of the Confederacy. It is a moving book, with good character portraits and vivid portrayal of the sights, sounds, and feelings of the battlefield. The scholar will find little new in it, but few scholarly accounts approach this one in re-creating the human side of the war."

Catton had previously published two other books about the Civil War, *Mr. Lincoln's Army* and *Glory Road*, but he was by no means a national figure at the time. Mostly, he had been a newspaperman, born in Petoskey, Mich., in 1899, a student at Oberlin, a reporter successively on the Cleveland *News*, Boston *American*, and Cleveland *Plain Dealer* before becoming a Washington correspondent for Newspaper Enterprise Association. During the war, he had been director of information for the War Production Board and later the Department of Commerce, and remained in government service while he made his uncertain beginnings as a historian.

It was Catton's good fortune that William Granger Blair, a reporter for the New York *Times*, happened to read *A Stillness at Appomattox* and was so enthusiastic about it that he urged his stepfather, Arthur Krock, to get the book at once. That was two days before the Board meeting of April 23, 1954, but Krock did his homework, was impressed by *A Stillness at Appomattox*, and nominated it for the Pulitzer Prize in History for 1954 over the jury's choice, *The Undeclared War*. The Board voted for Catton, without dissent, thus recognizing a new and unaffiliated historian and continuing the long line of nonprofessionals that had begun with Henry Adams to leave their mark on the Pulitzer Prizes.

There was still another surprise in the Catton story. The historian learned of his prize when a young woman phoned him and asked him if he could appear on the Dave Garroway television show next morning. When he asked why, she replied quite innocently, "Didn't you win a Pulitzer Prize or something?" Thinking she had made a mistake, Catton then phoned his editor at Doubleday to ask what was going on. The response: "Oh, yes. Haven't you heard?" It was, the historian recalled, one of the oddest experiences of his life.

As for the prize itself, Catton had these reflections:

"It certainly had a profound effect on my own life. It not only opened doors that otherwise would have been closed; it somehow gave me the courage to keep on going and more or less confirmed me in my notion that the kind of work I was doing was worth while." [38]

That same year, Catton became the editor of *American Heritage* magazine, realizing Allan Nevins' dream of a quality magazine that would popularize history. And one of Catton's special projects for *American Heritage*, its Picture History of the Civil War, won a Pulitzer Prize special citation in 1961.

In biography, too, a small group of devoted professional historians and their nonprofessional rivals achieved new standards of excellence. They turned their backs on the cold, impersonal minutiae of academic historical research to bring a warmer, more human quality to history. Indeed, biography became a distinctive feature of American humanistic studies in the 1940s and 1950s because the leading biographers often gave their work an engaging literary flair that was lacking in much of academically produced history.

It fell to the oldest—and certainly one of the finest—of practicing historians, Samuel Eliot Morison, to set an example for most of his younger colleagues in the research and the writing of biography. He was Boston-born in 1887 and all Harvard in background—a graduate of Harvard College in 1908, holder of a Ph.D. in 1912, and a teacher beginning in 1915 for four decades. Even before he began his academic career, he wrote a biography of Harrison Gray Otis in 1913, and continued steadily thereafter to produce works of high quality in both history and biography. It was his custom, as a historian born with a love of the sea, to retrace painstakingly the routes of the seafaring heroes of whom he loved to write—a practice that gave both added substance and a remarkable authenticity to his biographies. Two of these, the Christopher Columbus story entitled *Admiral of the Ocean Sea* and *John Paul Jones*, won Pulitzer Prizes in Biography in 1943 and 1960 respectively.

The usual stern and sober-minded jurors in biography had a little fun with their recommendation of the Columbus story because of the requirement in the Plan of Award that it should teach "patriotic and unselfish services to the people, illustrated by eminent example," and that it must be "American." Messrs. Cortissoz, Hendrick, and Lydenberg, the 1943 jury, wrote as follows in their report:

> "Let it be admitted at the outset that Columbus was not a citizen of the United States. But the terms of the prize specify that it is to be given to a "distinguished American biography teaching patriotic and unselfish services to the people," and surely Columbus is thereby made eligible as a subject. After all, he invented us, was, in a sense, our onlie begetter, and that was some service to the peo-

ple. Furthermore, this biography of him, we unanimously agree, is whole parasangs ahead of everything else submitted.

It is the work of a finished scholar who is also a sea-faring man. He has absolutely mastered his subject and has brought to his treatment of it a warm, humanizing touch. . . . [The book] has had no comparable predecessors and it is unlikely to have any worthy successors. Mr. Morison has done his task superlatively well and the jury unhesitatingly commends his book for the award.

Morison, ever the proper Bostonian, accepted this honor as he did the many others that came to him, with an Olympian graciousness. Looking back long afterward on his two Pulitzer awards, he wrote: "They did not have the slightest effect on my subsequent career, which would have been the same, prize or no prize." [39]

Another of the more notable Pulitzer Prizes of the period went to the diplomatic historian, Professor Samuel Flagg Bemis of Yale, in 1950 for his *John Quincy Adams and the Foundations of American Foreign Policy*. Bemis, one of Channing's students, was, like Morison, a historian of an older generation. He brought to biography a lucid and readable style and an expertness in archival research that studded his work with fresh insights. His two-volume Quincy Adams biography became the standard in the field.

The 1943–1954 period was distinguished, too, by such biographical works as Robert E. Sherwood's *Roosevelt and Hopkins*, the 1949 winner; *Charles Evans Hughes* by Merlo J. Pusey, the winner in 1952; and *The Autobiography of William Allen White* which received the 1947 award. Other Pulitzer Prizes in biography went to Carleton Mabee's *The American Leonardo: The Life of Samuel F. B. Morse*, in 1944; Russel Blaine Nye's *George Bancroft, Brahmin Rebel*, in 1945; the John Muir story, *Son of the Wilderness*, by Linnie Marsh Wolfe, in 1946; Margaret Clapp's *Forgotten First Citizen: John Bigelow*, in 1948; Margaret Louise Coit's *John C. Calhoun: American Portrait*, in 1951; David J. Mays's *Edmund Pendleton 1721–1803*, in 1953; and Charles A. Lindbergh's story of his 1927 solo flight to Paris, which bore the same name as his little aircraft, *The Spirit of St. Louis*, in 1954.

True to its custom, the Advisory Board did not always take the first choice of its juries, notably in the cases of the Lindbergh and Muir books which were listed as alternative selections.[40] Nor did the juries always take into consideration the niceties of the Board's relationships with the outstanding personalities of the era. For among the also-rans in the 1949 History Jury report, submitted by Messrs. Baxter, Blegen, and Curti, was a rather rough disqualification of a historical work by the then president of Columbia University, General Dwight David Eisenhower, entitled *The Crusade in Europe*. Despite their warmly expressed admiration for Eisenhower as a general and as a person, they declared his book to be "something less than a major contribution to American history" although they ranked it ahead of General Pershing's World War I Pulitzer Prize winner, an award the jury termed "a great mistake."

While Eisenhower technically became a member of the Advisory Board when he assumed the Columbia presidency, he never attended a meeting. In 1949, Provost Albert C. Jacobs summoned the Board to its annual session and attended in place of the general, so it is probable that he never knew the History Jury's opinion of *Crusade in Europe*. The 1946 Biography Jury, consisting of Messers. Hendrick, Lydenberg, and J. Donald Adams of the New York *Times*, did a great deal better for Eisenhower, recommending Kenneth S. Davis' full-length biography, *Soldier of Democracy*, for the prize in that year. But the Advisory Board, for its own reasons, preferred the John Muir story in that instance. The upshot was that General Eisenhower, despite his brief tenure as a Columbia president, was never a giver nor a recipient of a Pulitzer Prize.

There was, however, one occasion on which he became a defender of the award. At a dinner for new faculty members at Columbia in 1950, he heard Professor Oscar James Campbell attack an ABC television program, "Pulitzer Prize Playhouse," because it was sponsored by Schlitz beer. Through the William Morris Agency, Columbia's agent then as now for anything on television having to do with the Pulitzer Prizes, the program had brought a $100,000 Schlitz endowment to the awards and the journalism school. The good-natured Eisenhower smiled broadly at Campbell's remarks and, in his own welcoming speech, said he liked beer but couldn't have as much as he wanted because he had to watch his waistline. Then he added:

"I see nothing wrong with the $100,000 Schlitz endowment for the Graduate School of Journalism. If Tiffany's had made a grant of this kind, everybody would be in favor of it and nothing would be said. But frankly, I prefer beer to diamonds." [41]

That was the extent of General Eisenhower's association with the Pulitzer Prizes. He was a pleasant stranger, briefly passing through academe.

5

Poets—Modern and Not So Modern

While Karl Jay Shapiro was on active duty in the South Pacific in World War II, he found the time to write verse that was put together and published under the title, *V-Letter and Other Poems*. It won the Pulitzer Prize for Poetry in 1945 on the recommendation of the jury, Messrs. Cross, Canby, and Untermeyer, although Shapiro, then 32 years old, protested profusely that he was "no war poet" and seemed to be more embarrassed than proud of being in uniform. Obviously, he was no Joyce Kilmer nor Rupert Brooke; rather, he was a rebel, an angry man at constant war with convention. In short, a modern poet.

The view that was attributed to him in 1941 amplified his position as follows: "Today American poetry suffers from the dictatorship of criticism. . . . Our poetry has the task of destroying the government of critics and of making a wholesale return to the anarchy of experience."

It was no great surprise, therefore, when Shapiro began attacking his poetic godfather, T. S. Eliot, in the years after the war and reveling in a rediscovery of the great poet of self, Walt Whitman. Obviously, since the young poet devoted so much time to his crusading against those who he thought put shackles on poetry, his own output suffered. In his later years, therefore, he became far less typical of the modern poet in America than his more distinguished and productive fellow Pulitzer Prize winners, Robert Lowell, who received his first award in 1947 for *Lord Weary's Castle*, and Theodore Roethke, the 1954 winner for *The Waking*.

All three poets dwelt deeply, sometimes to an embarrassing extent, on personal experience. All three were highly moralistic, sitting in judgment on man's fate. Shapiro, for example, wrote—in the view of the Poetry Jury—of the "change wrought in a man's spirit and view of life and death by his experiences at the front." In *Lord Weary's Castle*, published six years after his conversion to Roman Catholicism, Lowell's style was metaphysical and permeated with the doctrine of the Church of Rome.

Roethke, the most subtle and in many ways the most admired of the moderns of his day, was, as Louis Untermeyer put it, "that rare thing, a poet who is original without being freakish."

In the 1954 jury report, which he submitted for himself and Alfred Kreymborg, Untermeyer presented this analysis of the most modern of the moderns: "His imagery is sometimes bizarre and often brusque, but it is always logical and never less than stimulating. He is essentially a lyric poet and, although his lyrics are not conventionally rhythmical, they have enough music to make them traditional and just enough dissonances to make them modern. . . . Of the so-called younger poets, Roethke has the most striking combination of boldness and discipline." [42]

Governor Cross's juries, and those headed by Messrs. Canby and Untermeyer, who succeeded him beginning in 1948, did not appear to worry about the kinds of poets they honored. What interested the jurors was excellence and established ability, so it was no surprise that they gave Robert Frost his fourth prize in 1943 for *A Witness Tree*, Stephen Vincent Benet his second for *A Western Star* in 1944, Archibald MacLeish his second in 1953 for *Collected Poems, 1917–1952*, and Carl Sandburg his second for *Complete Poems* in 1951.

Everybody recognized the primacy of W. H. Auden, one of the truly great poets of the century, but there was hesitation over granting him an award until he became an American citizen. Then, speedily, he was given the 1948 Pulitzer Prize in Poetry for *The Age of Anxiety*. Upon his death in 1973, he was accounted by some critics to be "the leading poet of his generation," and "a pre-eminent master of modern English verse." [43]

Now and then, the Poetry Juries would venture out of their established orbit to recognize some bold, attractive, and innovative newcomer. Such was the case in 1950 when Messrs. Canby, Kreymborg, and Untermeyer turned aside from their admiration of such established figures as Frost, Auden, and William Carlos Williams to recognize Gwendolyn Brooks, the first black person to win a Pulitzer Prize. She received the award for her poetic work, *Annie Allen*. The report said:

"Some years ago, Gwendolyn Brooks, a Negro writer of unusual ability, published *A Street in Bronzeville*, which made a great impression on all its readers and had what is unusual for poetry today—a wide sale. In 1949 she published *Annie Allen*, a much better book, and indeed, in our opinion, the outstanding volume of the year if you exclude Robert Frost. No other Negro poet has written such poetry of her own race, of her own experiences, subjective and objective, and with no grievance or racial criticism as the purpose of her poetry. It is highly skillful and strong poetry, come out of the heart, but rich with racial experience."

Gwendolyn Brooks was born in Topeka in 1917 but grew up in Chicago, attended school there and was graduated from Wilson Jr. College. Her *Annie Allen* was born out of her own experiences on Chicago's South Side, from childhood to womanhood, and included characters she knew there. The varied lyrics and ballads in the book, modestly called notes, were developed into a single short narrative called "The Anniad." Alfred Kreymborg called it "not only brilliant but profound in its tragic and tragi-comic implications.

Miss Brooks's ability as a poet had been recognized before she won her Pulitzer, for she was the recipient in her earlier years of two Guggenheim Fellowships and a grant from the American Academy of Arts and Letters. Thereafter, in 1969, she became the Poet Laureate of Illinois and a poet of the first rank in America. But she did not stand aside from the struggle of her people when it reached a violent pitch in the 1960s; like the younger black artists, writers, and poets, she became a part of the black revolution. It did not bother her that some of the black activists regarded her new activities with puzzlement in view of her status as a Pulitzer Prize winner.

"For me," she wrote in 1972, "the award had the effect of a doctorate, enabling me to teach in universities and colleges. It has been an 'open sesame' to much in this country. It has also—formerly—abashed and puzzled certain young people, who considered it 'establishmentarian'!"

In her autobiography, *Report from Part One*, she thought deeply of her old life style and the changes that time and circumstance had made in it. These were her reflections:

"I—who have 'gone the gamut' from an almost angry rejection of my dark skin by some of my brainwashed brothers and sisters to a surprised queenhood in the new black sun—am qualified to enter at least the kindergarten of new consciousness now. New consciousness and trudge-toward-progress. I have hopes for myself." [44]

There were other departures from the norm—a prize in 1949 for Peter Viereck's first volume of poetry, *Terror and Decorum*. And there were disappointments, too, such as the 1946 prize that the Advisory Board passed because the jury recommended a prize for Auden before he became a citizen, with a posthumous volume of Emily Dickinson's poetry as an alternative choice. But perhaps the most popular poetry prize of the decade went to an elderly and unpretentious woman who was one of the most influential and best-loved poets of her time, Marianne Craig Moore.

No poet in America was ever quite like Marianne Moore. To her fellow poets, she was a supreme imagist whose verse was, in T. S. Eliot's opinion, a part of the small yield of durable poetry in this unhappy age. To the public, she was a much-admired personage—a trim, grey-haired figure in tricorn hat and dark cape who appeared regularly at functions as varied as charity balls and baseball games.

Miss Moore was born in Kirkwood, Mo., in 1887, graduated from Bryn Mawr, moved to New York and became a librarian, and at the age of 38 won the Dial Award for her volume of poetry, *Observations*. From that time on until she won the Pulitzer Prize in 1952 for her *Collected Poems*, and thereafter, she was recognized as a major American poet. In the 1952 jury report for Alfred Kreymborg and himself, Louis Untermeyer called her "a perfectionist among craftsmen" and went on:

"Miss Moore's power is intellectual and, in the later poems, spiritual. She does not attempt panoramas, for she is a miniaturist, a worker in verbal tapestries, a designer whose details carry surprising information and even more surprising intensity. Her skillful use of multiple quotations (credited in a noteworthy 'Note on the Notes') accomplishes a kind of poetic montage, delicate but not frail, intricate but not obscure."

Was Marianne Moore a modern poet? To such questions, she usually replied lightly: "I'm a happy hack." Actually, she defied classification. "The only reason I know for calling my work poetry," she once said, "is that there is no other category in which to put it." The 120 poems she wrote before her death at the age of 84 have become a part of the nation's literary heritage.[45]

6
The First Music Prizes

When Joseph Pulitzer came to the United States a little more than a century ago, he found much of it a musical no man's land with scant interest in opera, outside the European immigrant communities, or any of the other larger forms of musical composition. There were no native composers of significance except those like Stephen Foster who thrived on folk melody, nor was there very much hope for musical education and training in the academic centers of the era. Pulitzer could only sigh for the urbanity and musical knowledge of the Europe he had left behind him, for he had come to a country almost without a musical history. Here, he would not soon find the equivalent of the famous musical organizations of the old world; nor, for that matter, would he ever find the American equivalents of his favorite composers, Beethoven, Wagner, and Liszt.

Pulitzer loved music. Throughout his life, he was never too weary to have his secretaries read to him about the composers and musicians he admired. Moreover, when he so desired, he could have the accomplished Dr. Friedrich Mann, who was usually with him in his declining years, play Beethoven on the piano. The publisher supported worthy musical causes throughout his career and bequeathed $500,000 to the New York Philharmonic Society, as well as the funds for the Pulitzer Music Scholarship that became, after twenty-five years, the Pulitzer Prize in Music. It remains today the only major prize for American composers in the larger musical forms, including opera and ballet.

At the time of Pulitzer's death in 1911, the foundations for the growth of a distinctively American form of musical composition had been laid by Edward MacDowell, Horatio Parker, and George W. Chadwick. It was still subordinate as a native musical idiom to the operetta music of Victor Herbert and Reginald DeKoven, the blues popularized by W. C. Handy, and the catchy rhythms of jazz. But before 1920, Harvard, Columbia, and the University of California became centers of competent musical instruction and training under the supervision of French-trained American composers. And by 1930, such native composers as Charles Ives and Carl Ruggles found younger talent in profusion emerging from the widening academic musical community to join them. From Harvard and Columbia, the cause of musical education was taken up by almost every other major university in the land and three impressive music schools were founded—Eastman in Rochester, Curtis in Philadelphia, and Juilliard in New York. Nadia Boulanger, the great Parisian teacher, used to tell her gifted American students of the 1920s and 1930s, "Watch out! American music is about to take off just like Russian music did in the 1850s." And it did.

It is noteworthy that, among the American composers of opera who now came to the fore, there were two who had held the Pulitzer Music Scholarship for study in Europe, Douglas Stuart Moore and Samuel Barber. By the time the Pulitzer Prize in Music was established, there were at least thirty thousand musical organizations in the country that were performing symphonic repertory in public—quite a change from the single group, the New York Philharmonic, that existed in 1842. In a remarkably short time, American music had come of age.

The Russian-born composer, Nicolas Nabokov, wrote: "America is gradually becoming the homing ground for all kinds of musical activities and a guest-house for some of the world's best and most advanced minds in the field of the arts, and especially music." The American composer, Virgil Thomson, said it in simpler fashion: "American is something a musician need not be ashamed to be." [46]

The first two winners of the Pulitzer Prize in Music—William Schuman in 1943 and Howard Hanson in 1944—were leaders in the American musical establishment but the third, Aaron Copland, was something special. He was, in the words of Leonard Bernstein, "the best we've got." For while Schuman became the head of the Juilliard School after winning his prize and later the president of the Lincoln Center for the Performing Arts, and while Hanson set high standards as the director of the Eastman School of Music, it was Copland who had the greater impact on American musical composition. In sheer volume and diversity of output, few then or now could match him; moreover, in addition to producing some of the most notable American works of his time, he was a veritable mobilization agent for the cause of American music among people in all walks of life. He demonstrated, in many ways, that American composers could be the equal of, if not superior to, their European contemporaries.

Copland was born in Brooklyn in 1900, graduated from Boys High and studied the piano under Victor Wittgenstein and Clarence Adler. Later, he studied composition with Rubin Goldmark and Nadia Boulanger. Before he was 25 years old, he had written his First Symphony, and a Dance Symphony. From then on, his compositions streamed from his studio in all their remarkable variety while he held numerous teaching posts, ranging from the New School to Harvard. He did ballet, opera, scores for films, chamber music, and intricate works for orchestra, all of admirable quality. His *Appalachian Spring*, for which he won the 1945 Pulitzer Prize in Music, remains the only ballet score in the Pulitzer list. It was written for and presented by the Martha Graham dance group at the Library of Congress in Washington, D.C.

The jury of Otto Luening, Henry Cowell and Chalmers Clifton, chairman, all composers, wrote in this fashion of the prize-winning work:

"The best stage music of the year. It is very simple, using fragments of Springfield Mountain and other American folk tunes interwoven and developed with great elegance and deftness, showing great experience with the orchestra, and with musical materials. Above all, it is an entirely satisfactory vehicle for the dance."

Copland was 45 at the time, well established as a composer, and detected no particular impact on his career after he received the prize. "Needless to say," he wrote, "the naming of *Appalachian Spring* was of great help in giving the ballet and its score wider dissemination." [47]

Another pathbreaking innovation in the early history of the Music Prize was the award to Virgil Thomson in 1949 for his music for the film, *Louisiana Story*, the first and until now the only film score that has been so honored. Prizes had been given in the three preceding years for more conventional works—in 1946 to Leo Sowerby, in 1947 to the old master, Charles Ives, for a work that had been written years earlier, and in 1948 to Walter Piston. The jury of Chalmers Clifton, Henry Cowell, and Beveridge Webster split 2–1 in favor of the Thomson work, with Webster favoring Copland's music set to the scenario of John Steinbeck's *The Red Pony*.

"This [film] is a simple, direct account of the drilling of an oil well in the Louisiana bayous and the reactions of a 'Cajun' family to the presence of engineers, skilled mechanics, and complicated drilling apparatus in their quiet countryside," the report said. "Thomson's music, transparent and refined in texture, is of telling assistance in dramatizing and humanizing an everyday mechanical process, reinforcing the action or lack of action, without interference. It opens a wide field for the composer who has this kind of talent."

There was no doubt of Thomson's talent and genius for innovation. He was born in Kansas City in 1896, graduated from Harvard in 1922 and, like so many of his talented colleagues, studied with Nadia Boulanger in Paris. Among his many important works was his pioneering opera, *Four Saints in Three Acts*, written in 1934 to a libretto by Gertrude

Stein. With its success, he pursued the effort to create American opera as a musical form that was not dependent upon the limitations of foreign languages and old-style dramaturgy. Invariably, his question was, "Can it be put on the stage?" and he was a tough critic, both of his own work and that of others, having been the New York *Herald Tribune*'s music expert for fourteen years. One of his other major operas was *The Mother of Us All*, produced in 1947, also with a Stein libretto. It was such work that established him as an American composer of the first rank in the same line as Ives, Ruggles, Edgard Varese, and others who followed them.[48]

No leading American composer was more adept in his use of native materials, or more enthusiastic in his pursuit of them, than Douglas Moore. By training, background, and inclination, he was deeply devoted to the advancement of American music. And like Aaron Copland, he was as tireless in the necessary activities of rallying public and institutional support for American composers as he was in maintaining the flow and the quality of his own compositions. As the president of the National Institute of Arts and Letters in 1947, and in 1960 as the president of the American Academy of Arts and Letters, his prestige in the community of the arts was enormous and his influence in the cause of music education was unsurpassed.

The background of the Moore family was rooted in colonial America. Douglas Moore himself was descended from Miles Standish on his mother's side, and he lived on the land originally occupied by his family in 1640 in Southold Town, Long Island, where he was born in 1893. He took his baccalaureate degree from Yale in 1915 and a degree in music two years later from the Yale Music School, leaving as a memento an original composition entitled, *Good Night Harvard*. There followed an interregnum during World War I, in which he served as a lieutenant (j.g.) aboard U.S. destroyers in the Atlantic. In 1921, he resumed his music education at the Schola Cantorum in Paris, studying composition with Vincent d'Indy and Ernest Bloch. He later became the music director of the Cleveland Art Museum and in 1925 won the Pulitzer Music Scholarship, which enabled him to return to Paris for further study. In the following year, he joined the Columbia Music Faculty under the pioneering Daniel Gregory Mason, rose through the academic ladder to professor and chairman of the department in 1940, and in 1943 became the MacDowell Professor of Music, a post he held with distinction for twenty years.

Douglas Moore's principal interest throughout his career was American opera. His first was *White Wings* in 1935, eleven years after his first music was publicly performed. In the following year, he completed *The Headless Horseman* and in 1938 produced one of his most enduring and successful works, *The Devil and Daniel Webster*, with libretto by Stephen Vincent Benet. His most ambitious opera, *Giants in the Earth*, based on the novel by O. E. Rolvaag with libretto by Arnold Sundgaard, won the 1951 Pulitzer Prize in Music. In their report, Chalmers Clifton and Norman Lockwood, the jurors, wrote:

"In no opera by an American is there music of such freshness, beauty and distinctive character. The music has a life of its own apart from its appositeness to the text."

The Moore opera that went most frequently into repertory, as it turned out, was *The Ballad of Baby Doe*, based on the life of a fabulous Western mining princess, in which the composer gave full sway to his melodic gifts. His concluding works, true to his training and his interests, remained persuasively American—the tuneful and amusing *Gallantry*, which he called his "soap opera," in 1958; *The Wings of the Dove*, in 1961; and *Carrie Nation* in 1967.[49]

Gian-Carlo Menotti, too, distinguished himself as a Pulitzer Prize-winning composer, first with *The Consul* and later with *The Saint of Bleecker Street* in 1955. Although he was an Italian citizen at the time, he was eligible under the terms of the music award, which until 1974 specified that the works of foreign composers resident in the United States could be considered. Menotti came to the United States in 1928, studied at the Curtis Institute, taught there for many years, and composed most of his many operas while he was in this country. Perhaps the most familiar and enduring is his opera for NBC television, *Amahl and the Night Visitor*, first produced in 1951.[50]

The winners in 1952 and 1954, Gail Kubik and Quincy Porter respectively, were honored for symphonic music. There was no prize in 1953 because the jury was split between three contending works, arrived at a tentative decision by a narrow margin on a preferential ballot, and failed to convince the Advisory Board of the prize-winning qualities of any of them.[51]

Chalmers Clifton, as the jury chairman for seventeen years beginning in 1943, had the assistance each year of some of the outstanding figures in the world of American music, including Aaron Copland and Howard Hanson in 1946, Wallingford Riegger in 1953, and Robert Ward in 1954. Where possible, the juries attended performances of works that were nominated in New York. Outside the city, the main reliance was recordings either on acetate or tape with infrequent use of radio broadcasts when available. As the major work in American music settled more and more into the realm of the universities, colleges, and music schools throughout the land, a process that continued into the 1970s, it became necessary for juries to rely almost entirely on tapes to make their judgments. The performance of new American music in its larger forms was too widespread and too frequent for any jury to attempt coverage in person. The intensity and diffusion of the creative process was a tribute to the vigor of American musicianship; if the Pulitzer Prize in Music could be said to have had a modest part in stimulating this movement, the award was amply justified.

7
The Old Order Passes

The Advisory Board formally severed its connection with Columbia's Graduate School of Journalism in 1950. In a resolution adopted at its meeting on April 18 of that year, the Board changed its name from the Advisory Board of the Graduate School of Journalism to the Advisory Board on the Pulitzer Prizes. Through this symbolic act, the Board confined its scope to "the control of the annual selection of the winners of the Pulitzer Prizes, and of the jurors who screen the material, and of the form in which the public announcements are made." The university's Trustees ratified the change on October 2, 1950.[52]

Four years later, the Board, acting on a motion by Arthur Krock, decided to limit the service of its members to three terms of four years each. Under the resolution of April 23, 1954, an entirely new Board came into being within a relatively short time and some of the oldest and most influential figures in its history were phased out of membership.[53] In that year, too, Dean Ackerman voluntarily gave up his responsibilities for the Pulitzer Prizes in view of his approaching retirement and I became the Board's secretary and the administrator of the awards, at the same time remaining a full-time teaching member of the Journalism Faculty.

Quite by chance, the university's representation on the Board also had changed during this particular period. Grayson Kirk, who as Provost had represented President Eisenhower at Board meetings from 1950 on, now was the university's president; in that capacity, his tenure on the Board began formally in 1953. As a professional historian and a specialist in foreign affairs who had been one of the officers of the organizing conference of the United Nations in San Francisco, President Kirk, by disposition, character, and training, was far removed from the authoritarian posture of President Butler. The new president, always urbane and unruffled, took the lead in persuading the second Joseph Pulitzer to continue to conduct the affairs of the Board in his accustomed fashion. It was not Dr. Kirk's disposition to interfere with the Board's work, although he did on occasion, as the years passed, present the university's position on Pulitzer Prize matters with clarity and persuasion. He generally preferred, however, to leave all except issues of major policy to the newspaper membership of the Board, and to respect the guidance of its leadership.

Here, too, there was a change. At the 1954 meeting, Joseph Pulitzer Jr., the son of the chairman and the grandson of the Donor of the prizes, had been invited to attend the 1955 session as an observer. But with the death of the second Joseph Pulitzer on March 30, 1955, the Board's chairmanship unexpectedly became vacant. Arthur Krock, as always, rose to the occasion by proposing a resolution within a few days under which Joseph Pulitzer Jr. would succeed his father as the Board's chairman at the 1955 meeting. It was circulated by wire and unanimously adopted.

Krock, too, wrote the memorial resolution adopted by the Board in honor of the long service of the second Joseph Pulitzer:

> Joseph Pulitzer, the late editor and publisher of the St. Louis *Post-Dispatch*, inherited a great newspaper tradition. This he steadily enhanced throughout his professional career, elevating and protecting the standards of publication implicitly imposed by the First Amendment on American journalism as its special responsibility to the people. In elevating and protecting these standards, he exemplified them through his newspaper in such a way that the people appreciated whence and why they came and what they were.

Great as was the prestige of the *World* of New York City, and despite the advantage it enjoyed in acquiring national fame because it was published in the Metropolis, the St. Louis *Post-Dispatch* under Joseph Pulitzer the Second kept pace with the *World* under his equally dedicated elder brother.

Though this was a notable contribution to the life of the United States, Joseph Pulitzer, in the opinion of these associates, left a greater heritage—shining personal character, humility in the possession of power, and compassion for the unfortunate. He hated cant, sham, injustice, and corruption and was incapable of any of these. He was of the few gifted with both humor and a sense of consecration. His companionship was as inspiring as it is irreplaceable, and we shall miss it and be the poorer always for the fact that it is no more.[54]

Dr. Fackenthal, whose gentle administrative guidance had been of such importance to the Prizes during his long tenure as secretary of the university, provost, and finally acting president, had been saluted in similar fashion at the end of his service in 1948. The other veterans of the Board, as they concluded their tenure, also were honored with ceremonial resolutions and Arthur Krock was given a citation, his fourth recognition in the records of the Pulitzer Prizes. Dean Ackerman retired from Joseph Pulitzer's school, which he had done so much to revive and expand into an all-graduate institution, in 1955 and was replaced in 1956 by Edward W. Barrett, a former editorial director of *Newsweek*.

The last links with Joseph Pulitzer, the donor of the prizes, and Nicholas Murray Butler, the recipient on behalf of the university, had now been severed.

6
A Change in Direction for the Prizes 1955–1965

1
The New Board

There were few outward signs of change in the Pulitzer Prizes under their new leadership. The Advisory Board, with its new name, proceeded steadfastly to carry out the policies it had pursued for many years. If there was to be a change in its essential character, it would come slowly. Both President Kirk and Joseph Pulitzer Jr., the new chairman, needed time to familiarize themselves with the Board's operations, its philosophy, and its essential relationships to its juries, the university's Trustees, and the university itself. Neither one was in a mood to rush into untested innovations; for that matter, no innovative proposals were pending and none were likely to be considered seriously during the period when the Board's membership was in a transitional state. The one step which the new leadership took, almost without discussion, was to inaugurate the practice of obliging any Board member with an interest in a particular prize to leave the conference room while it was being discussed and voted upon.

Fourteen Pulitzer Prizes were awarded in 1955, plus the three traveling scholarships for graduates of the journalism school and the art scholarship that had been in the original Plan of Award. These consisted of eight journalism awards—Public Service, Local Deadline or General

News Reporting, Local Investigative or Special News Reporting, National Reporting, International Reporting, Editorial Writing, Editorial Cartooning, and Photography, with each carrying a $1,000 stipend except for the gold medal for public service. In Letters, the list continued to be confined to Fiction, Drama, History, Biography, and Poetry, with a separate prize for Music, each carrying a $500 stipend.

The Plan of Award remained very largely what it had been at the time of the 1947 write-through. In 1951, the term "the most" had been eliminated from the public service formula, making it read "for distinguished and meritorious public service," in conformity with the rest of the list. And in 1954, after the temporary elimination of the qualification that the drama winner shall represent "in marked fashion the educational value and power of the stage," the second Joseph Pulitzer had protested and then persuaded the Board to restore the omitted text. The prohibition against biographies of Lincoln and Washington was finally dropped in 1963.

During the decade ending in 1965, there was only one addition to the prize list—an award for general non-fiction that began in 1962 and was listed at $500 with the rest of the Letters prizes. The drama formula was finally changed to read: "For a distinguished play by an American author, preferably original in its source and dealing with American life." And the art scholarship became a fellowship in critical writing. The one other change was a marked disposition by the Board to eliminate special awards, except in the most extraordinary circumstances, because of the feeling that they "diluted" the already large regular prize list.

The secrecy that had blanketed the non-journalism juries was lifted just a bit in 1959 with the university's release of the names of all the jurors who had served in Letters, Drama, and Music during the first forty years of the awards. There were 102 persons in all, but, despite the years of protests over undue secrecy, the list was not published anywhere although it was fully distributed to the media. Thereafter, despite two private polls of non-journalism juries to obtain their permission to publicize their names with the announcement of the awards, secrecy in that department was technically maintained. While a majority favored disclosure, an obdurate minority protested so vigorously that the Board made no change in its policy. The Journalism Juries, of course, continued to be made public at the time of their service.[1]

In the period since 1917, when national awards of the character of the

Pulitzer Prizes were a distinct innovation, many new ones had come into being. In literature, the National Book Awards began in 1950 under the sponsorship of the book publishing industry. In the theater, the Critics Circle prizes of 1935 now had rivals of their own, the Antoinette Perry awards, the Tonys as they were called. In history, the Bancroft Prizes at Columbia University and the Parkman award both had standing and prestige. In poetry, the Bollingen Prize was much sought after. In music, the New York critics had an award for a few years. And in journalism, Sigma Delta Chi, the professional journalistic organization, and a host of others offered numerous prizes.

The Pulitzer Prizes had competition. Yet, in their first forty years, leaders in motion pictures, radio, television, and magazines continually proposed new Pulitzer awards in their particular fields. In general, the response invariably was a polite negative with the courteous explanation that the Pulitzer organization did not feel it should compete with established prizes in these areas. And so, the motion picture industry developed the glamorous Oscars, television its Emmys, and magazines their National Magazine Awards. Any reporter, writer, artist, or musician in the United States who wanted to compete for an award had a wide field from which to choose.

Necessarily, in view of competition and rising costs, pressures grew on the Pulitzer Prizes to limit their nominations and streamline the judging of prizes to make it less time-consuming and less cumbersome. But to all suggestions for a more elite competition, the Board reaffirmed the Plan of Award. It was still possible, as it had been from the beginning, for anybody to make a nomination for a Pulitzer Prize in any category. Anything published in a United States daily or weekly newspaper during a given year was eligible for consideration the following year. And in the book field, with the inclusion of the wide open general non-fiction category, literally any book published in a given year also was eligible for the next year's competition. In drama, even though the qualification for a New York performance had been eliminated from the text, it remained implicit in the operations of the jurors because there was neither sufficient time nor funds to fly them all over the country. But quite literally any play that opened on or off—or even off-off—Broadway between April 1 and March 31 was viewed by the Drama Jury. Musical performances were considered for the same period, although tapes were usually necessary to insure a proper hearing by the jury.

What this meant, as the competition for the Pulitzer awards increased in volume, was that anywhere from 600 to 700 individual exhibits were submitted in the journalism competition and 500 to 600 books. Depending on the number of openings in the theatrical season in New York, the jury probably saw anywhere between 35 and 60 performances while the music tapes were usually in excess of 50. The old practice of advertising the Pulitzer Prize competition was therefore abruptly halted in 1955; instead, a brief reminder of the respective deadlines was issued to newspapers and book publishers, the sources of the vast majority of the nominations. Repeated appeals were made to all nominators to submit only the best available works, but the volume continued to creep upward despite the small monetary rewards that were attached to the prizes. Even with a substantial increase in the value of the Pulitzer Prize Fund's securities from their low levels of the Depression years, it was not possible to restore the non-journalism awards to $1,000 each until 1968.

Service on the various juries, therefore, meant principally a lot of hard work, which for the non-journalism jurors carried a token stipend of $250 each and nothing at all for those who judged the bumper crop of journalism entries annually. Like the members of the Advisory Board, whose expenses had always been paid either by themselves or their organizations, the members of the journalism juries met their costs in the same fashion. True to the first Joseph Pulitzer's wish, the bulk of the prize fund went for the prizes and scholarships and the expense of administering them.

The new leadership of the Pulitzer Prizes tended to be on the moderate side, reflective rather than demonstrative, and given to conciliation when there were widely opposing points of view within the Board. This was not a policy on which there was conscious agreement among the new president of Columbia, the new chairman of the Advisory Board, and the new administrator; it was, in fact, never discussed but arose mainly out of the character, training, and disposition of the three men.

There was nothing on the surface to indicate that they would so quickly find common agreement on most matters of substance and procedure, for their backgrounds were diverse and their interests were varied. Grayson Louis Kirk, born in 1903 in Jeffersonville, Ohio, had graduated from Miami of Ohio and taken his Ph.D. from the University of Wisconsin in 1930. After a dozen years of teaching at Wisconsin and Columbia, he became a professor of government at Columbia in 1943 and succeeded Albert C. Jacobs as Provost in 1950. As President Eisenhower's chief of staff at Columbia, Dr. Kirk ran the university during the general's frequent absences and was a natural choice to succeed him when he became president of the United States in 1953. Joseph Pulitzer Jr., born in 1913 in St. Louis, had graduated from Harvard in 1936 and spent ten years on the staff of the St. Louis *Post-Dispatch* before being made associate editor in 1948. He succeeded his father as editor and publisher of the paper in 1955. As for myself, I was a native New Yorker, born in 1906, a 1927 graduate of the Columbia School of Journalism, and had been a working newspaperman in New York, Washington, and abroad for more than twenty years before becoming a professor of journalism at Columbia in 1950.

Eight of the twelve newspaper members of the Advisory Board completed their service within the next three years. They were Sevellon Brown of the Providence *Journal-Bulletin*, who served from 1938–1956; Robert Choate of the Boston *Herald*, 1943–1958; Kent Cooper of the Associated Press, 1931–1956; Gardner Cowles Jr. of the Des Moines *Register-Tribune*, 1947–1958; John S. Knight of the Knight Newspapers, 1944–1958; Arthur Krock of the New York *Times*, 1940–1954; William R. Mathews of the Arizona *Daily Star*, 1943–1956; and Stuart H. Perry of the Adrian (Mich.) *Telegram*, 1928–1956.

Replacing them were Turner Catledge of the New York *Times*, beginning in 1955; Barry Bingham of the Louisville *Courier-Journal*, Norman Chandler of the Los Angeles *Times*, Paul Miller of the Gannett Newspapers, and Louis B. Seltzer of the Cleveland *Press*, all beginning in 1956; and Erwin D. Canham of the *Christian Science Monitor*, Kenneth MacDonald of the Des Moines *Register-Tribune*, and W. D. Maxwell of the Chicago *Tribune*, all beginning in 1958.

The remaining members of the Advisory Board continued their service as follows: Hodding Carter of the *Delta Democrat-Times*, Greenville, Miss., 1949–1961; J. D. Ferguson of the Milwaukee *Journal*, 1952–1961, and Benjamin M. McKelway of the Washington *Evening Star*, 1951–1959. Chairman Pulitzer, being specifically exempt from the limiting resolution of 1954, was elected to permanent membership following the completion of his third term.

The reconstituted Board was more liberal in its relationship with its jurors, as was made evident in a twenty-four-page policy statement that was made public in 1957, but it was just as insistent as its predecessors on obtaining precise and reasoned judgments for the respective choices of the juries. While the policy statement dealt primarily with the Journalism Jurors, it was obvious that the same position would have to be taken with respect to those who judged Letters, Drama, and Music. Under the heading, "The Power of Juries," the policy statement said:

> The Plan of Award specifies that juries are to submit "from two to five recommendations, without necessarily indicating their order of preference." * This is not an inflexible rule, since juries sometimes find more than five exhibits worthy of final consideration. As many as a dozen have been passed to us. On extremely rare occasions, a jury has recommended but one exhibit for a prize.
>
> Moreover, there is no set procedure for the listing of jury recommendations in the order of preference. Where a jury has strong convictions, we are always deeply interested in a report that gives the reasons supporting its position. But where an order of preference has been listed without explanation or elaboration, we are often honestly puzzled and therefore have to review the judging. In the event of a split jury verdict, therefore, it is much better to list the finalists without expressing a preference; or, if a juror insists, majority and minority reports may be submitted.
>
> While we are charged under the will of Joseph Pulitzer with responsibility and authority, in making our nominations to the Trustees of Columbia University, to select, accept, or reject the recommendations of jurors, we find that we are placing increasing reliance on their judgment. But in a minority of cases there may be disagreements, although a complete reversal has become relatively rare. We do not give public explanations of our position out of consideration for the feelings of those who may be involved; in any case, we feel that such statements would serve no good purpose.
>
> There is but one inflexible rule in the judgment of the Pulitzer Prizes. Like the members of the juries, the individual members of the Advisory Board take no part whatever in either the discussion or judgment of any exhibit that may even remotely involve a conflict of interest. We feel that a larger number of exhibits and an ever-widening participation in the work of the Pulitzer juries by distinguished editors from all parts of the nation are additional guarantees of disinterested judgment.[2]

Accordingly, the Board gradually abandoned the practice of limiting juries to two members in any category in the belief that it was no guar-

* Now it is three to six recommendations.

antee of diversity of view. In Letters, Drama, and Music, over the years, the Board's conviction grew that a three-member panel was ideal. But in journalism, because of the tremendous volume of reading that had to be done in a comparatively short time when all jurors assembled at Columbia University, the five-member jury became standard. It was the Board's policy to rotate juries frequently, so that from one-third to one-half of the journalism panel consisted of new faces each year and the same juror rarely worked in any category for more than a year at a time. While the same policy applied to the non-journalism juries, there was an understandable tendency here to retain the services of specialists and expert critics for as long as possible. With the passage of time, the practice diminished but it continued through several of the reconstituted Advisory Boards.

The old relationship between the Advisory Board and organizations of distinguished specialists and other personages was now ended. There was no reliance whatever by the Board on the American Academy of Arts and Letters or the National Institute of Arts and Letters. The membership of the juries on Letters, Drama, and Music was now based on recommendations by Pulitzer Prize winners, former jurors, and leading specialists in the respective fields; only rarely, and then with obvious reluctance, did any member of the Advisory Board make suggestions. Even President Kirk, in an almost complete reversal of President Butler's practice, offered no proposals except when he was asked and then he usually confined himself to the fields he knew best, history and biography. He was always reluctant to ask members of the Columbia faculty to serve, realizing how awkward it would be if a Columbia professor won their recommendation.

With the abandonment of the art scholarship, the Board's relationship with the National Academy of Design also lapsed. The Faculty of Journalism at Columbia continued to exercise the Board's powers in recommending the annual appointment of three leading graduates to Pulitzer Traveling Scholarships (changed to Fellowships when the grants reached $3,000 each in 1969). But otherwise, its relationship to the Pulitzer Prizes ended with the exception of my participation in the work.

In the field of journalism, the Board's historic reliance on the membership of the American Society of Newspaper Editors for most of its jurors and chairmen continued indefinitely but without any formal arrangement between the two organizations. It simply turned out, in preparing the annual lists of jurors based on recommendations from Pulitzer Prize winners, former jurors, and others, that by far the largest number were also ASNE members.

From 1924 to 1935, with the assent of the Board, Dean Ackerman had had one member of the ASNE serving with jurors of the Journalism Faculty in each journalism category but that practice lapsed. Next, he centered on the procedure of letting one- or two-member juries of the Faculty judge each category without any outside experts and used students to prepare summaries of the exhibits. In 1943 and 1944, the Board resumed its relationship with the ASNE by electing to membership the respective ASNE presidents for those years, Roy A. Roberts of the Kansas City *Star* and John S. Knight of Knight Newspapers. But in 1947 and 1948, when the current presidents of ASNE were invited to name the juries directly, and no Faculty people participated, the policy changed again and Roberts resigned from the Board in the latter year. The ASNE-designated juries continued through 1949, but in the following year the Board resumed control of the journalism jury appointments and retained it thereafter. Thus, the ASNE members served in succeeding years as individuals, without regard to any responsibilities they may have had to their own organization, and even ASNE presidents and other officials willingly accepted invitations to participate in the work of the journalism juries. Indeed, it would have been difficult if not impossible to have assembled a panel of fifty outstanding journalism judges without them, once the prizes expanded to their current scope.

The reconstituted Advisory Board, while considerably more diversified both politically and geographically, remained very much its own master. Until 1959, it continued the practice of meeting on the April Thursday of "Newspaper Week" to make its judgments and then formally ratified them in the Trustees' Room on the following day. But in that year, it began the current practice of holding a one-day meeting in April in the *World* Room of the Journalism Building at Columbia, which was graced with the old stained-glass replica of the Statue of Liberty that had been taken from the *World* building on Park Row before it was torn down. The stained glass was the only remaining memento for the Advisory Board of the donor of the prizes.

2
The Press as Leader

"One of these days it will be Monday," Ralph McGill wrote in the Atlanta *Constitution* during 1953. And on May 17, 1954, Monday finally came—the Monday that a segregated South had dreaded for so many years, the Monday on which the United States Supreme Court handed down its decision desegregating the schools. McGill was ready for it, but not many others were; certainly, not the schools in the South nor their administrators, not even the bench and bar and the governors of the states that were directly affected.[3]

The great Georgian sometimes despaired even of his own profession because so few were willing to provide the leadership that this time of peril and change in American society so desperately required. And yet, between 1955 and 1965, no fewer than ten Pulitzer Prizes were granted for distinguished journalism dealing with the nation's massive racial crisis—one for public service, two for reporting, six for editorial writing, and there was a special citation as well. This was more than all the prizes that had been given between 1917 and 1954 for crusades against the Ku Klux Klan and ruthless lynch law.

One of the first to stand up against the social pressure to nullify desegregation in the South was Buford Boone, editor of the Tuscaloosa (Ala.) *News*. When student rioters on February 6, 1956, forced the withdrawal of the first black student at the University of Alabama, Boone rebuked the community in these harsh terms:

"We have had a breakdown of law and order, an abject surrender to what is expedient rather than a courageous stand for what is right. Yes, there's peace on the university campus this morning. But what a price has been paid for it!"

That editorial, "What a Price for Peace," brought Boone the Pulitzer Prize for Editorial Writing in 1957. What happened in Tuscaloosa, however, was only the beginning of a shameful campaign in some of the finest and loveliest cities of the South. What it finally came down to, in the fall of 1957, was the use of Federal troops by President Eisenhower to restore order in Little Rock, Ark.

Governor Orval Eugene Faubus of Arkansas had forced the issue by leading the opposition to the enrollment of nine Negro children at Central High School in Little Rock. Early in September, he even called out the National Guard to surround the then empty school on the pretext that violence was threatened. The White Citizens Councils, the lineal descendants of the Ku Klux Klan, were jubilant. But the 85-year-old publisher of the *Arkansas Gazette*, John Netherland Heiskell, was not. He chose to stand with his editor, Harry S. Ashmore, in a campaign for decency in Little Rock. The issue, as Ashmore saw it in an editorial on September 9, 1957, was basic:

"Somehow, some time, every Arkansan is going to have to be counted. We are going to have to decide what kind of people we are—whether we obey the law only when we approve of it, or whether we obey it no matter how distasteful we may find it. And this, finally, is the only issue before the people of Arkansas."

On a turbulent morning two weeks later, Relman (Pat) Morin of the Associated Press was outside Central High School in a glass-enclosed telephone booth when a shrieking mob forced its first black students to leave their classes. What Morin did in that epic report of September 23 won him the Pulitzer Prize for National Reporting, his second Pulitzer award. But even more important, his first-hand description of the riot almost certainly played a part in President Eisenhower's decision to move Federal troops into Little Rock that day.

Order was finally restored in the city. But the segregationists turned venomously on the *Arkansas Gazette*, their main enemy, and cut its revenue by $2 million through advertising and circulation boycotts. Eventually, Ashmore left his post in order to relieve the newspaper of some of the pressure. But before he did so, he and the *Gazette* shared a rare honor—a double Pulitzer Prize; in 1958, he won the editorial writing award and the paper was given the public service gold medal.[4]

Throughout the years of turmoil in Dixie, Ralph McGill had been thundering defiance in the columns of the Atlanta *Constitution* against the violent segregationists. In return, he was threatened. His wife, chronically ill, was abused. Their home was the target for all manner of senseless outrages. But McGill resolutely maintained his position. It wasn't in him to quit.

Despite his crusading fervor, Ralph McGill neither looked nor acted like a champion of social reform. He was a generous and kindly man, a lively companion, and an incomparable storyteller. But he was also, for all his days, an inveterate defender of the weak and the helpless. He had been born in Tennessee in 1898, attended Vanderbilt, served in World War I, and begun newspaper work as a sports writer for the Nashville *Banner* in 1922. It was only when he came to the Atlanta *Constitution* in 1931 that he lifted his sights beyond the starry-eyed world of sports to the realities of life and experienced the first Ku Klux Klan demonstration against him. Nevertheless, in 1942, he became the *Constitution*'s editor and its featured columnist.

Once the Supreme Court ordered the desegregation of the schools, McGill followed the course of events in Dixie with mounting anger— from Tuscaloosa to Little Rock and beyond, from bombings and burnings in Florida, Alabama, and South Carolina to his native Tennessee where a fine new high school at Clinton was destroyed. In mid-October 1958 when he came home, his wife told him that The Temple, home of Atlanta's largest Jewish congregation, had been ripped apart by a bomb. McGill was appalled and outraged. He went to his typewriter and in twenty minutes produced an editorial, "One Church . . . One School," that ran in the *Constitution* on October 15, 1958. He wrote:

> This is a harvest. It is a crop of things sown. It is the harvest of defiance of courts and the encouragement of citizens to defy the law on the part of many Southern politicians.
>
> It is not possible to preach lawlessness and restrict it. When leadership in high places fails to support constituted authority, it opens the gates to all those who wish to take law into their hands. The extremists of the citizens' councils, the political leaders who in terms violent and inflammatory have repudiated their oaths and stood against due process of law, have helped unloose this flood of hate.

The editorial brought Ralph McGill the Pulitzer Prize for Editorial Writing in 1959. Although he was the recognized leader of liberal opinion in the South, it was characteristic of him to say, when he heard the news, "I never thought I'd make it." Two years later, he was invited to join the Advisory Board on the Pulitzer Prizes.[5]

The conflict over segregation in Virginia brought Pulitzer Prizes to Mary Lou Werner of the Washington *Evening Star* for her year-long reporting of the conflict and to Lenoir Chambers, editor of the Norfolk *Virginian-Pilot*, for his editorial writing. Miss Werner won in 1959, Chambers in 1960.

When the focus of the struggle shifted to Mississippi in 1962, with rioters demonstrating against the admission to the University of Mississippi of its first black student, James Meredith, a small-town editor defied both the mob and the State government. The editor, Ira B. Harkey Jr., won the 1963 Pulitzer Prize for Editorial Writing, but with it came a bullet through the front door, the violent opposition of the segregationists, and such pitiless financial pressure that he had to sell his paper, the Pascagoula *Chronicle*, and leave the South.

Another small-town publisher in Mississippi, Hazel Brannon Smith, was no less vigorous in her opposition to the White Citizens' Councils but she managed to ride out the storm that almost destroyed her best property, the Lexington (Miss.) *Advertiser*. She won the Pulitzer Prize for Editorial Writing in 1964 and the plaudits of her neighbor, Hodding Carter of Greenville, who called her "The Fighting Lady." [6]

It remained for the Gannett Newspapers to round out the decade following the Supreme Court's historic decision by combining their efforts to produce a series, "The Road to Integration," which cited the positive accomplishments that had been achieved even though it did not gloss over the failures. The special citation, awarded to Gannett by recommendation of the Advisory Board in 1964, was the first ever given to any newspaper group.

If the first decade of the massive American racial crisis did nothing else, it placed a heavy—perhaps too heavy—burden of leadership on the press, a responsibility that even the best and the bravest newspapers were not designed to discharge. But even more difficult times lay ahead, when the flames of burning cities in the latter 1960s threatened to spread all over the land in an outbreak of fierce and intractable civil strife.

The growth of massive racial conflict overshadowed the postwar struggle for the protection of civil liberties, which had been dealt such body blows by the activities of Senator Joseph R. McCarthy Jr. For despite McCarthy's downfall after he had failed to prove his charges of subversion within the Army during televised hearings from April 22 to June 17, 1954, and despite his censure by the United States Senate, his evil spirit lingered on. In Herblock's prize-winning portfolio of cartoons for 1954, there is a drawing of a great tree with a rotten apple on it shaped in McCarthy's sullen features—an apt commentary on the spirit of the times. For many an American continued to have his loyalty questioned and there were few who were willing to offer a defense.

It took a 28-year-old reporter for the Washington *Daily News,* Anthony Lewis, to clear an obscure employee of the U. S. Navy, Abraham Chasanow, of charges by anonymous informants that he was a security risk. Lewis forced the Navy to vindicate Chasanow on September 1, 1954, five months after his dismissal.

When the Pulitzer Prizes were announced the following May, Lewis was being interviewed for a job by a New York *Times* executive. At a crucial moment, someone held up a sign behind Lewis' back: "Better grab this guy. He's just won a Pulitzer Prize."

The 1955 award for National Reporting changed Tony Lewis' career in other ways, as well. For, as a reporter for the New York *Times,* he specialized in covering the law, studied at Harvard for a year, and in 1963 won a second Pulitzer Prize for his coverage of the United States Supreme Court.[7]

Another National Reporting award in the field of civil liberties went to Howard Van Smith of the Miami (Fla.) *News* for his defense of Florida's migrant workers. There also were two editorial writing prizes during the 1955–1965 decade for outstanding work in civil liberties. In 1961, William J. Dorvillier of the San Juan *Star* won for his attacks on clerical interference with the 1960 gubernatorial elections in Puerto Rico. And in the following year, the award went to Thomas R. Storke, editor and publisher of the Santa Barbara (Calif.) *News-Press,* for his battle against the far-right John Birch Society.

During the decade beginning with 1955, no fewer than nine persons won awards in what had been one of the most neglected fields of American journalism—labor reporting. Of these, the most unusual went to Lee Hills, executive editor of the Detroit *Free Press* for his "inside story" of the secret negotiations of the United Automobile Workers with Ford and General Motors over a new principle in collective bargaining—the guaranteed annual wage.

Hills was a shrewd and hard-working mixture of reporter, editor, manager, and lawyer, born in 1906 in Granville, N.D., educated at the University of Missouri's Journalism School and Oklahoma City University Law School, and former member of the staffs of newspapers in the South and Midwest before he joined the Knight group in 1942. From the Miami *Herald,* where he served for nine years, he went on to the Detroit *Free Press* in 1951.

Only one Pulitzer Prize had previously gone to a Detroit newspaper-man for writing about the labor story in the nation's automobile cap-ital—Royce Howes, a *Free Press* associate editor, who won in 1955 for an editorial, "The Cause of a Strike." What Hills did was to turn re-porter and run a daily story on Page 1 of the *Free Press* for three weeks under the standing head: "A Look Behind the UAW-Auto Curtain." He worked through his own sources, developed his own interviews, and at the end was able to assure his readers: "We have tried to cut away the underbrush and tell you exactly what is going on and what it means to you."

For his effort, Hills won the 1956 award for Local Reporting under deadline pressure, one of the few editors in Pulitzer Prize annals to do so. And in 1970, when he was president of Knight Newspapers, he became a member of the Advisory Board.[8]

Other labor reporters who were honored included Wallace Turner and William Lambert of the Portland *Oregonian*, who won in 1957 for expos-ing corruption in the Teamsters Union; Clark Mollenhoff of the Des Moines *Register-Tribune* in 1958 for an exposé of labor racketeering; J. Harold Brislin of the Scranton (Pa.) *Tribune* in 1959 for a campaign against labor violence; and Nathan G. Caldwell and Gene S. Graham of the Nashville *Tennessean* in 1962 for disclosing undercover cooperation between the United Mine Workers and management interests. In 1958, Bruce Shanks of the Buffalo *Evening News* won for his cartoon, "The Thinker," showing a union member in the grip of racketeers.

Pulitzer Prize juries also ventured into widely varying fields of the news in this era. The Los Angeles *Times* won the public service gold medal in 1960 for exposing the illegal narcotics traffic between the United States and Mexico. In the same year, local reporting prizes went to Jack Nelson of the Atlanta *Constitution* for uncovering the miserable condition of some of Georgia's mental institutions and to Miriam Otten-berg of the Washington *Evening Star* for exposing a used car racket in the nation's capital. The Chicago *Daily News* was awarded the 1963 public service gold medal for its campaign to provide birth control services in the public health programs in its area. Also in the field of public health, Tom Little of the Nashville *Tennessean* won the 1957 cartooning prize for a provocative cartoon in favor of Salk vaccine to prevent polio.

The expanding problems of localities and states were twice recognized during the decade—in 1958, when George Beveridge of the Washington

Evening Star won a local reporting prize for his series, "Metro, City of Tomorrow," and in 1965, when the Hutchinson *News* received the public service gold medal for forcing reapportionment of the Kansas Legislature. Financial scandals brought two other prizes to *Wall Street Journal* reporters—Edward R. Cony in 1961 for exposing a timber deal, and Norman C. Miller Jr. in 1964 for breaking the multi-million-dollar "Salad Oil Swindle." In sports, Max Kase of the New York *Journal-American* won a special citation in 1952 for uncovering corruption in basketball, and Arthur Daley of the New York *Times* won a local reporting prize in 1956.

In foreign affairs, relations between post-Stalinist Soviet regimes and the West dominated the news and the prize-giving for the 1955–1965 decade. Harrison E. Salisbury of the New York *Times* came out of Moscow in 1954 with a sensational series in which he told of the last hours of Joseph V. Stalin, who died on March 5, 1953; the vain effort of Lavrenti P. Beria to capture the government; and the rise of the mercurial Nikita S. Khrushchev. The series won for Salisbury the 1955 foreign reporting prize and ushered in the period, somewhat misnamed, of "the thaw." Two American journalistic feats, one by Lauren K. Soth of the Des Moines *Register-Tribune* and the other by William Randolph Hearst Jr. and two associates, helped to some extent to create a more relaxed atmosphere temporarily between Washington and Moscow. And both performances won Pulitzer Prizes in 1956.

Soth, ruminating over Khrushchev's impatient demand on Soviet economic managers for a corn-hog economy like that of Middle America, dashed off an editorial on February 9, 1955, inviting Russians to come to Iowa to see how it was done. That summer, much to Soth's surprise, the Russian delegation showed up. "It was certainly luck that this turned out to be the beginning of a series of cultural exchanges with the Soviet Union," he said afterward. Lucky or not, he won the editorial writing award for 1956.[9]

The Hearst team—so named by Bill Hearst himself—came to Moscow during the worst part of the winter of 1955. The big, good-looking, and highly articulate son of Pulitzer's bitterest rival, then 47 years old and the publisher of the New York *Journal-American*, was accompanied by his editorial associate, Frank Conniff, and the Hearst European manager, J. Kingsbury Smith. At that time, no more than a handful of American resident correspondents were permitted to file and they were severely restricted on what they could report. But for the Hearst team, all restrictions were removed. Khrushchev and his associates wanted better relations with the United States and were delighted to have such devoted anti-Communists convey their message.

Khrushchev, too, was ready to show who was boss. For while the Hearst team was in Moscow, he unceremoniously dumped Georgi Malenkov as premier and replaced him with the old soldier, Marshal Nikolai A. Bulganin. The pudgy Khrushchev was content, for awhile, to run the show from his party post as first secretary of the Central Committee, CPSU. He made the Hearst team's visit so fruitful, and with his associates provided so much headline news, that it became the dominant foreign story in the American press.

The Pulitzer Prize for foreign reporting for that year, however, was not concluded routinely. Some of the jurors and Advisory Board members argued against the recommendation of the Hearst team on the ground that resident correspondents, not traveling writers, should be honored. But the fight for the Hearst team was led by the chairman of the Advisory Board, Joseph Pulitzer Jr., and that made the difference. The sons of the old New York newspaper rivals had met once or twice, by chance, but theirs was a bare acquaintance. In any event, the Hearst team won the 1956 International Reporting Prize on its own merit. And it finally disposed of the notion that Hearst entries were unwelcome in the Pulitzer competition.[10]

The time of the Khrushchev "thaw" in Moscow, like Mao Tse-tung's brief loosening of ties in Peking during the "hundred flowers" period, had disagreeable results for the leadership. First Poland, then Hungary, staged uprisings based on national discontent in 1956. In Budapest, Russell Jones of the United Press became the last American to report the suppression of the Hungarian Freedom Fighters by the Red Army from October 29 to December 3. The United Press, having ended its boycott of the Pulitzer Prizes with the advent of the new directorate for the awards, promptly nominated Jones for the International Reporting Award of 1957 and he won it—the first Pulitzer honor for the wire service.

In Poland, the time of the "thaw" proved just as illusory for Abraham Michael Rosenthal, the New York *Times*'s correspondent. He was 36 years old when he arrived in Poland in 1958, fresh from service in India.

He had been with the *Times* since his graduation from the City College of New York in 1944, had served with distinction for eight years at the United Nations, and now faced the test for the first time of operating under a restrictive regime.

It didn't take Rosenthal long to make a name for himself with his Polish dispatches. On August 31, 1958, the *Times*'s Sunday magazine led off with his classic, "There Is No News From Auschwitz." The Poles should have been grateful, but they were not; for Rosenthal, digging at the roots of their regime, was publishing some disagreeable truths as well. On November 11, 1958, he was ordered to leave Warsaw by a Foreign Ministry official who told him that he had written too deeply about Poland's internal affairs and that the government "cannot tolerate such probing reporting." The truth of his dispatches was not questioned.

Rosenthal, one of a group of correspondents who brought the New York *Times* the 1958 Pulitzer Prize for International Reporting, won his own award in 1960 for his Polish dispatches, plus the additional material about the country that appeared in 1959 following his expulsion.[11]

The reverberations of the East-West conflict produced uprisings in Africa, Asia, and Latin America as well as in Eastern Europe, all of them tough jobs for American correspondents. In the Congo, once the panicky Belgians withdrew in 1960 and chaotic fighting spread through the unhappy land, the veteran Lynn Heinzerling of the Associated Press so distinguished himself with his cool and accurate reporting that he won the Pulitzer foreign reporting prize for 1961.

In Cuba, the position of American correspondents was even more difficult, for an aura of heroism had been cast about Fidel Castro. There were many who simply would not believe that Castro was anything but a native folk hero, resisting the cruelties of the Batista regime, and they denounced all suggestions that he was a covert ally of the Soviet Union. It remained for two reporters from the New York *Daily News*, Joseph Martin and Philip Santora, to disclose Castro's true political alliance in a series of articles in which they predicted his eventual victory over the government of Fulgencio Batista. For their work, they won the 1959 International Reporting prize. Four years later, in 1963, Hal Hendrix of the Miami (Fla.) *News* won the award for his disclosures, at an early stage, that the Soviet Union was installing missile launching pads in Cuba and sending in large numbers of MIG-21 aircraft—the opening phase of the great Missile Crisis of 1962 during which Khrushchev lost his nerve and eventually his power.

There were two other prizes of unusual significance during this critical period in relations between the Soviet Union and the United States. The first was the 1962 Pulitzer Prize to Walter Lippmann for his interview with Khrushchev while he was the premier of the Soviet regime. Essentially, the interview merely provided a peg for the long overdue recognition of Lippmann's superior contributions to American journalism, which also brought him a special citation in 1958. The second was the 1965 award to the financial editor of the Philadelphia *Bulletin*, J. A. Livingston, for his reports on the growth of the spirit of financial independence among Soviet allies in Eastern Europe and their desire for better trade relations with the West.

While most Americans were preoccupied with the developing racial crisis at home and the increasing tensions with the Soviet Union abroad, the United States was slowly becoming involved in the Vietnam War— the third Asian conflict for American armed forces within a generation. The alarm bells should have been ringing as early as 1954, when the French gave up their Indo-China empire at Geneva and a powerful faction in the American government pressed for direct intervention at that time. But when President Eisenhower refused to act, a kind of foggy optimism settled over the editorial departments of the nation's newspapers. And in academe, the principal professorial concern appeared to be over the docility of the students—the "silent generation," as they were called.

The only outcry of warning that attracted attention in the American press came from a veteran cartoonist, Daniel R. Fitzpatrick of the St. Louis *Post-Dispatch*. On June 8, 1954, the paper published his prophetic drawing of Uncle Sam, bayoneted rifle in hand, pausing at the brink of a quagmire labeled "French Mistakes in Indo-China." The caption was a challenge to American policy-makers: "How Would Another Mistake Help?" It won the Pulitzer Prize for Cartooning for 1955.[12]

Unhappily, the American public paid no attention to the warning and the American government, from 1961 on, began to increase its support for the South Vietnamese regime of Ngo Dinh Diem with funds, arms, and troops disguised as "advisers." When the handful of American correspondents in Saigon tried to write about American involvement, however, they were harassed and maligned and told brusquely by the American military to "get on the team."[13] The showdown came when Diem's regime hailed its building of strategic armed hamlets against the Vietcong as a great success and orchestrated a series of victory predictions in both Saigon and Washington. The correspondents, for the most part, said it simply wasn't so and proved their point.

In the tight struggle that developed between press and government, Diem lost out and was discredited in the eyes of the Kennedy administration. On November 1, 1963, he was overthrown by a military uprising in Saigon that had at least the tacit approval of the United States. In the aftermath, both Diem and his brother, Ngo Dinh Nhu, were killed by the rebels, ushering in a period of fear and uncertainty in Saigon. For their leading roles in the coverage of the Vietnam War and the downfall of Diem, Malcolm Browne of the Associated Press and David Halberstam of the New York *Times* shared the Pulitzer Prize for International Reporting in 1964. Another outstanding correspondent, Neil Sheehan of United Press International (formed in 1958 by a merger of United Press and International News Service), would almost certainly have shared Pulitzer honors that year if he had not been in Japan at the time of the coup against Diem. It was a circumstance to which the jurors repeatedly referred in studying his otherwise impressive exhibit submitted by UPI.

This first prize for war correspondence in Vietnam was matched in the following year by the first award for combat photography in the conflict, which went to Horst Faas of the Associated Press, the first of two that he was to win. From that time on, for the next eight years of American participation in the struggle, there wasn't an announcement of the Pulitzer Prizes that did not contain at least one prize for outstanding journalistic performance that dealt with Vietnam.[14]

The Pulitzer Prizes continued to reward newspapers and their staffs in the 1955–1965 period for uncovering graft and corruption at all levels of government. The Columbus (Ga.) *Ledger* won the 1955 public service gold medal by exposing corruption in neighboring Phenix City, Ala. In the same year, two Texas journalists, Mrs. Caro Brown of the Alice *Daily Echo* and Roland Kenneth Towery of the Cuero *Record*, won local reporting awards, the former for helping destroy a grafting political machine and the latter for exposing a Veterans' Land Program scandal. In 1956, the public service gold medal went to another small daily, the Watsonville (Calif.) *Register-Pajaronian*, for cleaning up the corrupt office of a prosecutor. Three years later, another offensive against civic corruption brought a gold medal to the Utica (N.Y.) *Observer–Dispatch* and the Utica *Daily Press*.

Public service became a journalistic article of faith among numerous small newspapers in the 1960s, often with astonishing results. In 1960, the Amarillo (Texas) *Globe-Times* not only exposed a breakdown in local law enforcement but also led an election campaign that swept lax officials from their posts. And in the following year, the Panama City (Fla.) *News-Herald*, with an editorial staff of only six persons, bravely attacked entrenched power and corruption in its region with resultant reforms. In each case, the newspapers concerned won the public service gold medal. An even more spectacular feat was performed by Oscar Griffin Jr., the editor of the Pecos (Texas) *Independent and Enterprise*, in developing and publishing the evidence that caused the collapse of the financial empire of Billie Sol Estes, a Texas financial wizard with White House connections, and sent him to jail. On the quieter side, John R. Harrison succeeded in bringing better housing to Gainesville, Fla., through his editorial campaign in the Gainesville *Sun*. Griffin won a local reporting award in 1963 while Harrison was given an editorial writing award in 1965.

The larger newspapers, too, stepped up their efforts in the major areas of public service. Charles L. Bartlett of the Chattanooga *Times* published grave and detailed disclosures that reflected on the official conduct of Harold E. Talbott, President Eisenhower's Secretary of the Air Force, and forced his resignation in 1955. Bartlett won the award for National Reporting in 1956. In the following year, the Chicago *Daily News* won the Public Service gold medal for having uncovered a $2.5 million theft by Orville E. Hodge, the Illinois State Auditor, and produced the evidence that helped put him in prison. An exposé of laxity and mismanagement in New York State's public welfare services brought a local reporting award to Edgar May of the Buffalo *Evening News* in 1961. And in 1962, George Bliss of the Chicago *Tribune* also was rewarded with a local reporting prize for disclosing scandals in the Metropolitan Sanitary District of Greater Chicago, with resultant reforms.

Vance Trimble of the Scripps-Howard Newspaper Alliance took on the Congress of the United States as a major assignment in 1959, leading to the publication of numerous hitherto unreported examples of nepotism. It won him the National Reporting award in 1960. In 1964, the public service gold medal went to the St. Petersburg (Fla.) *Times* for attacking illegal acts and excessively costly operations of the Florida Turnpike Authority with salutary results. That same year, the Philadelphia *Bulletin*'s James V. Magee, Albert V. Gaudiosi, and Frederick A. Meyer won a local reporting award for publishing evidence of local police collusion with numbers racket operations, leading to a thorough Police Department shakeup. Gene Goltz of the Houston *Post* also received a local reporting award in 1965 for uncovering governmental corruption in Pasadena, Texas. And the prize for National Reporting that year went to Louis M. Kohlmeier of the *Wall Street Journal* for a series of articles that traced the growth of the fortune of President Lyndon Baines Johnson and his family.

Taken as a whole, such widespread and continuous activity by the American press could not help but have its effect on the processes of government. At the local and state level, certainly, public officials got the message that nobody was immune from scrutiny by tough and persistent investigative reporters, backed by determined editors and publishers. The pity of it was that the word didn't get through to the highest offices in the land in the nation's capital, where within less than a decade a scandal was to shake the institution of the Presidency itself to its foundations in one of the saddest periods in American history.

With the rise of the newspaper of public service and the development of television as an effective medium for the coverage of spot news, many an editor feared that the press was losing its primary function—the telling of the news. And yet, during the 1955–1965 period, numerous Pulitzer Prizes were won by newspaper reporters either because they were at the center of the news, and television wasn't, or because they did a better job.

In 1957, for example, the Salt Lake *Tribune* won a local reporting prize for its coverage of an air crash over the Grand Canyon, which took 128 lives. This was an assignment in which a team of fast-moving reporters had to cover immense difficulties of distance and terrain. The following year, the Fargo (N.D.) *Forum* also won a local reporting award for its coverage of the tornado of June 20, 1957, during which it issued a complete news edition with casualty and damage lists five hours after the disaster. In 1961, a local reporting prize went to Sanche de Gramont of the New York *Herald Tribune* for his exclusive account of the death of the baritone, Leonard Warren, on the stage of the Metropolitan Opera House. In 1962, Robert D. Mullins of the *Deseret News*, Salt Lake City, was similarly honored for his coverage of a Wild West-type murder and kidnapping at remote Dead Horse Point, Utah. A local reporting prize went to Sylvan Fox, Anthony Shannon, and William Longgood of the New York *World-Telegram and Sun* in the following year for their coverage of a local air crash in which 95 persons died. And in 1965, one of the most unusual local reporting prizes went to Melvin H. Ruder of the weekly *Hungry Horse News* in Montana for arousing his community to the danger of a disastrous flood—a warning that ultimately saved many lives.

It remained for the veteran wire service reporter, the 50-year-old Merriman Smith of United Press International, to perform the hardest task that can come to anyone in American journalism—the dispatch of the first news of the assassination of a President of the United States. Smith, a White House correspondent for twenty-two years, was in Dallas with President John Fitzgerald Kennedy on November 22, 1963, for what was supposed to be a routine public appearance. The UPI correspondent was in the fourth car of the presidential motorcade with other reporters—a vehicle that was equipped with a mobile radio telephone. When he heard gunfire as the Kennedy car passed the ugly red brick building of the Texas School Book Depository and saw the big bubble-top Presidential limousine suddenly dash away at high speed, he fought for the radio telephone, got through to his office, and at 12:34 P.M. reported the shooting. Five minutes later, after Smith had seen the President's body outside Dallas' Parkland Hospital, he flashed the news of the death.

There were many feats of outstanding reporting in Dallas on that somber day and Smith was never ahead of his colleagues by very much. But when he finally was able to get to a typewriter himself, and set down his account of the assassination of President Kennedy, it turned out to be a classic of American journalism.[15] The correspondent always deprecated his feat, telling his associates, "The piece wrote itself." He was awarded the Pulitzer Prize in National Reporting for 1964. Two days later, Robert H. Jackson of the Dallas *Times-Herald* photographed Jack Ruby's murder of the suspected killer, Lee Harvey Oswald, before 50 million television witnesses—the Pulitzer Prize picture of 1964.

The Warren Commission later made much of the journalistic misconduct of that day, and bench and bar used it to try to check the ability of the press to cover the judicial process. But eventually, the press emerged from that chastening experience to exert its leadership once again when the Watergate affair besmirched both the White House and an important segment of the legal profession as well.

3
New Novelists, New Arguments

The reconstituted Advisory Board faced none of the obstacles of its predecessors during the 1955–1965 period, particularly in fiction. The terms of the Plan of Award were now clear: "For distinguished fiction in book form during the year by an American author, preferably dealing with American life." There was no longer any feeling that the Pulitzer Prize novel must be wholesome. Nor was there any Nicholas Murray Butler to threaten a Trustees' veto of any novel that reflected what he considered to be deplorable morals and used regrettable language. Not once during his long association with the Board did President Grayson Kirk take any leading part in the continuing argument over the values of the American novel. He was primarily a historian and he remained in his own bailiwick.

It was, therefore, entirely a matter of judgment that had to be resolved between the respective members of the Fiction Juries each year and the members of the Advisory Board. And since both included some of the most respected figures in American journalism and critical opinion, there should not have been many arguments. But there were, from the early years of the chairmanship of Joseph Pulitzer Jr., even though he seldom took the initiative in opening discussion on the reports of the Fiction Juries.

There was no clear motivation for the Board's rather critical approach to the fiction reports. The mid-Victorian spirit wasn't running rampant here, as had been the case in the earlier years of the Advisory Board. There was a genuine willingness to seek out and reward the new talent that had emerged in the post-war generation of American novelists. The question that seemed to stump the Board more often than not was the choice it had to make among the newcomers, based on a particular novel that was recommended by the jurors. Every Board member at the oval table beneath the glowing Statue of Liberty window knew quite well that the fiction category had been the most criticized of all the Pulitzer awards and that the selection in fiction, accordingly, would be given the closest scrutiny. It probably made the Board as a whole more careful and reserved in its judgments than it otherwise would have been during at least a part of the decade.

One other circumstance had to be taken into account in handling the Letters categories as a whole. The members of the Board realized there had been considerable criticism in the past that their predecessors had not read the books upon which they passed judgment. With anywhere from fifteen to thirty recommended books to be read by each Board member if he intended to make an individual assessment of the Letters jurors' reports, it was obvious that the work load was heavy though not unreasonable. The Board had always taken on an even heavier and more intensive reading assignment without protest in the case of the journalism categories. To make certain of a closer contact with the work of the Letters jurors, the Board gradually developed a system of consultative committees among its own membership, each of which was charged with intensive reading in one category and the responsibility for working with the jurors when differences of opinion developed. The system was extended to drama and, during Vermont Royster's service on the Board, to music because he had formerly been a member of a symphony orchestra. In the words of the announcement of the new procedure in 1961: "The appointment of committees is not intended to confine any member of the Board to a particular channel but merely to insure that each prize area is thoroughly covered not only by a jury but by the Board itself." [16]

Four of the younger novelists received Pulitzer Prizes during the 1955–1965 decade. A posthumous award went to James Agee's *A Death in the Family* in 1958. Robert Lewis Taylor won in 1959 for *The Travels of Jaimie McPheeters*, Harper Lee in 1961 with *To Kill a Mockingbird*, and Shirley Ann Grau in 1965 with *The Keepers of the House*. The Lee and Grau books were first choices of the jurors, the Agee and Taylor books were not. In all four cases, there was considerable discussion in the Advisory Board about the merits of the newer novelists, as well as the sharp comments of the jurors about the qualities of reigning novelists.

The case of *The Keepers of the House* served to illustrate the general approach of both the jurors and the Board. In their report, Lewis Gannett of the New York *Herald Tribune* and Maxwell Geismar, another outstanding critic, agreed on Miss Grau's novel as the best of the year. "With it," Gannett wrote, "she emerges as, since the death of William Faulkner, the major Southern writer—and perhaps the regional qualification is unnecessary. No other novel of the year compares with it in the quality of the writing." He ranked the book over Saul Bellow's *Herzog*,

which he called "overwritten and undisciplined . . . a pretentious bore."
While Geismar did not put Miss Grau in a class with Faulkner, he also
liked her work better than *Herzog*, of which he said, "I think it is close to
scandalous to have such a mediocre book, aimed plainly at sales rather
than at art, considered so highly." He dismissed another entry, Louis
Auchincloss' *The Rector of Justin*, also a best-seller, as "the kind of a novel
to which the Prize has been awarded in the past." There was no dissent
in the Advisory Board.[17]

Irita Van Doren, editor of the New York *Herald Tribune* Sunday
Books section, and John Barkham, critic of the Saturday Review Syndicate, both recommended Harper Lee's tender first novel over such
better-known novelists as William Styron and his *Set This House on Fire*
and John Updike with *Rabbit, Run*. The report commented: "Both lav-
ished major talents on minor themes." It went on:

"Fortunately, however, the stream of new talent which constantly re-
vitalizes American fiction produced at least two novels of unusual distinction. The first and more ambitious of these was *To Kill a Mockingbird*,
by Harper Lee. Set in her native Alabama, the book sums up in its
seemingly artless tale the pride and shame that are integral to Southern
living." The second choice was John Hersey's *The Child Buyer*. Again,
the Advisory Board agreed.[18]

Often, in the past, when jurors had recommended best-selling novels
by writers of repute, the Board had accepted their verdict without a
murmur. But in 1958, in the case of James Gould Cozzens's *By Love Possessed*, the Board revolted even though Cozzens had already won a Pulitzer Prize and the case for his novel was put most persuasively by John
K. Hutchens, former critic of the New York *Herald Tribune*, and Professor Robert Gorham Davis, then of Smith College. Instead, the Board itself picked James Agee's notable short novel, which had been mentioned
with a number of others in the report. Frequently, in the past, such rash
interventions had caused furious reaction but this time there was nothing
but praise.[19] It was an unaccustomed position for the Advisory Board to
be in, but it didn't last long.

The intervention in favor of Taylor's Mark Twainish novel, *The
Travels of Jaimie McPheeters*, in 1959 received only mixed notices at best.
The jury of John K. Hutchens and Professor Carlos Baker of Princeton
had urgently recommended a Pulitzer Prize for John O'Hara, one of
America's major novelists who had never been given such an award dur-

ing a long and outstanding career. There was no argument within the Board on O'Hara's merits; the doubt extended only to the book that was recommended, *From The Terrace*. In the end, the doubts prevailed, O'Hara lost the prize, and Taylor won.[20]

The only time during the decade that the Board went to the length of setting aside a jury's report entirely and substituting its own judgment was in 1960, when the prize went to Allen Drury's highly politicized novel, *Advise and Consent*. John K. Hutchens and Thomas B. Sherman, book critic of the St. Louis *Post-Dispatch*, had recommended Saul Bellow's novel, *Henderson the Rain King*, which they called more of an allegory than a conventionally patterned novel. "It is," they wrote, "the chronicle of one man—who symbolically is the perpetually restless Everyman—in search of his identity, of personal salvation." The Board liked Drury's melodramatic tale of conflict in Washington better, even though it hadn't been mentioned in the fiction report. The only member who sat silent throughout the debate was Drury's boss at the time, Turner Catledge, the executive editor of the New York *Times*. He never did say whether he was merely being neutral or didn't like the book.[21]

The Board recognized two veteran novelists during the decade, MacKinlay Kantor and Edwin O'Connor, both on the recommendations of juries, and passed the award twice, once over the opposition of a jury. Kantor won in 1956 for his bumper novel of the Confederate Civil War prison stockade, *Andersonville*, and O'Connor followed in 1962 with *The Edge of Sadness* after his better-known *The Last Hurrah* failed to take the prize in an earlier year.

Francis Brown, editor of the New York *Times* Sunday Book Review, and Professor Carlos Baker put *Andersonville* ahead of John O'Hara's *Ten North Frederick* and Robert Penn Warren's *Band of Angels*. They called it a "historical novel in the grand manner (which) recaptures the tragedy and drama not only of the prison stockade from which it takes its name, but of the Civil War itself." The report also called attention to Kantor's thirty-year career as a writer, during most of which he had been a student of the Civil War, and concluded, "For sweep of subject-matter, for depth of understanding, for skill of narration, this novel would be great in any year and surely in 1955 was unsurpassed."

Irita Van Doren and John Barkham selected O'Connor's novel of Irish-American life, with its respectful portrait of a middle-aged priest, over Carson McCullers' *Clock Without Hands* and William Maxwell's *The*

Chateau. This was their evaluation of the winning work: "It is impressive in manner as well as matter, solidly constructed, tightly plotted, peopled with credible (and in some cases memorable) characters and written with unfaltering warmth and sympathy." They passed up the most discussed work of the year, J. D. Salinger's *Franny and Zooey,* as not a novel at all but two segments of an ongoing work. And they expressed disappointment in such works as John Steinbeck's *The Winter of Our Discontent,* John Dos Passos' *Midcentury,* and Bernard Malamud's *A New Life.*

One of the reasons for the Advisory Board's failure to recommend an award in 1957 was the statement of the jurors, Francis Brown and Carlos Baker, that the previous year had been "a poor one for the American novel." Out of ninety novels submitted to the jury, the report went on, "most of them could not by any stretch of the imagination be regarded as serious contenders for that (Pulitzer) award or any other." Then, pointing out that the year was not wholly lacking in novels of distinction and merit, the jurors named Elizabeth Spencer's *The Voice at the Back Door* as the best of the lot with *The Last Hurrah* as an alternative. The Board couldn't work up much enthusiasm for either work after a thorough reading of the report and passed.

Lewis Gannett and Maxwell Geismar recommended no award for fiction in 1964, saying in their report: "More than ninety novels were nominated by their publishers this past year. The judges have read most of them (and a few others recommended by various critics but not presented by their publishers) and have carefully considered them all. A few seem to us to be more original, or more distinguished in other ways, than some of the titles which have in the past received Pulitzer awards, but no one of them imposes itself upon us as demanding recognition as 'distinguished fiction published in book form by an American author, preferably dealing with American life.' " The Board took them at their word and passed again.[22]

William Faulkner was recognized twice during the 1955–1965 period, after he no longer needed it, for he had been awarded the Nobel Prize in 1949. In each instance, that of *A Fable* in 1955 and a posthumous award to *The Reivers* in 1963, the judgment was that of the Advisory Board rather than its respective Fiction Juries. It was the Board's way, through the only means at its command, of showing its respect for Faulkner's stature as an American novelist and its appreciation, however tardy, of the permanence of much of his work. If the Board's position was awkward in this respect, it was scarcely more so than the body of American literary judgment which had failed in general to recognize Faulkner until he had first won his reputation in Europe.

Faulkner was 32 years old when he published *The Sound and the Fury*, the first of his major works about the South. During the next twenty years he wrote *As I Lay Dying, Sanctuary, Light In August, Absalom, Absalom!, The Unvanquished*, and *Intruder in the Dust*. None had been recommended by Pulitzer Prize juries, or even considered for that matter; furthermore, it is doubtful if the Board's membership in that era would have supported a judgment for Faulkner, except possibly in the late 1940s when he had finally begun to penetrate American mass consciousness. Faulkner won the Nobel Prize at 52, his first Pulitzer Prize at 58, and he died at 65 in 1962 after completing his second Pulitzer Prize novel. It was regrettable that the Board had to pass up the well-considered selections of younger novelists in order to pay Faulkner its long overdue tribute, but no one ever made any public protest.

Francis Brown and Carlos Baker recommended Milton Lott's rousing Western novel, *The Last Hunt*, for the fiction prize in 1955 and placed *The Fable* second. Writing of Faulkner's account of the revolt of a French army unit in World War I, their report said with engaging frankness, "There are portions of this novel which seemed to us to be close to greatness but I think we are agreed that it fails ultimately because of its inability to communicate with the reader. We also have a feeling that Faulkner has done better in the past and that it would be a mistake to give him a Pulitzer award for something less than he has done before."

Irita Van Doren and John Barkham recommended Katharine Anne Porter's *Ship of Fools* for the 1963 fiction award and placed *The Reivers* second. But they wrote so warmly and so movingly about Faulkner's book that the Board's members had second thoughts about the best-selling *Ship of Fools*. The report commented:

> As it happened, 1962 was also the year which saw the publication of William Faulkner's *The Reivers*, his last novel and also one of his most appealing. A genial comedy of three Mississippi innocents on a visit to Memphis, it contains a minimum of the rhetoric and moralizing which characterized Faulkner's later writing. *The Reivers*, is, in fact, a sunny interlude (the last, alas) in the shaping of the vast Yoknapatawpha saga, in which Faulkner for once sounds

relaxed, as though he were yarning to a circle of friends in that soft, elliptical drawl of his. *The Reivers* has been described as 'a perfect book for that last goodnight,' and we agree.

The Board did, too, in voting Faulkner his posthumous prize.[23] In 1966, the fiftieth anniversary year of the Pulitzer Prizes, Katharine Anne Porter won for her *Collected Stories*. But Milton Lott never did win, although one of his later novels, *Dance Back the Buffalo*, was also given respectful attention.

4
The Drama's Time of Troubles

Tennessee Williams' outspoken play about a Southern plantation family, *Cat on a Hot Tin Roof*, involved the reconstituted Advisory Board in a lively argument in 1955 at the outset of the chairmanship of Joseph Pulitzer Jr. At issue were all the old prejudices against gamey language and displays of immorality on the stage which had animated President Butler and the Board members of his day. To be sure, they had considered themselves more as guardians of the purity of the American novel, and had been relatively liberal within their lights in accepting the more venturesome reports of their drama juries. But they hadn't come up against anything quite like *Cat on a Hot Tin Roof* which, even to jaded Broadway critics, was something special in free-wheeling dramaturgy. To quote Jack Gaver of United Press International: "There is more and rougher dialogue of a sexual nature—a lot more and a lot rougher—than in any other American play ever produced on Broadway. Much of it is completely unnecessary."

That was not the only objection in terms of an older Pulitzer view of the stage as a place of inspiration and uplift. The play itself was the main issue. The self-described "cat on a hot tin roof," Maggie, a childless wife with an alcoholic husband, is sexually frustrated and worried about a former homosexual incident in her husband's life. She also is concerned because her father-in-law, "Big Daddy," a cancer victim although he doesn't know it, is likely to leave his estate to an older son rather than her husband. In the struggle that ensues, the characters taunt, insult, and lie to each other with Maggie still hoping at the end for pregnancy and fulfillment.

Despite its faults, the major New York critics liked the play. Brooks Atkinson of the New York *Times* thought it a "stunning drama." Walter Kerr of the New York *Herald Tribune* called it "beautifully written." John Chapman of the New York *Daily News* didn't care for the "dirty talk" but conceded there was a "great deal of fine theater" in the play. However, the Pulitizer Drama Jury of Professors Oscar Campbell and Maurice Valency found it both "obscure" and "annoyingly pretentious" and recommended instead *The Flowering Peach* by Clifford Odets. Although he had been a major American playwright for many years, he had never received a Pulitzer Prize and the jury thought his play, a fantasy based on the story of Noah, "original in conception, poetic in execution." Unfortunately, *The Flowering Peach* closed on the Saturday night before the Advisory Board's annual meeting on April 29, 1955, which was a mark against it.

Pulitzer, the new chairman, had seen *Cat on a Hot Tin Roof* and thought it worthy of the drama prize. He had little patience with the arguments against its extravagant language and unpleasant sexual themes, but based himself entirely on its effectiveness as a piece of realistic theater. The reconstituted Board, after considerable discussion, went along with him and voted for *Cat on a Hot Tin Roof*. This time, there was no Nicholas Murray Butler to threaten to invoke the veto power of the university Trustees, so Williams won his second drama award. It was the first and last time that the third Pulitzer took the lead in any discussion of the drama prize, although he often expressed his views with vigor and conviction as a member of the Board's consultative committee on the drama.[24]

The verdict for *Cat on a Hot Tin Roof* didn't settle the long-standing argument over obscenity and sexual permissiveness on the stage. It broke out all over again eight years later with Edward Albee's *Who's Afraid of Virginia Woolf?* as the issue, but this time the results were explosively different. By 1970, when Charles Gordone's *No Place To Be Somebody* made *Virigina Woolf* sound like kindergarten talk, the social view of the theater had changed to such an extent that there was hardly any comment at all because the Gordone play won the Pulitzer Prize.

During the four years after the jury upset that marked the prize award to *Cat on a Hot Tin Roof*, the Advisory Board accepted the word of its experts without question. There was no room for argument about the first three—*The Diary of Anne Frank* by Albert Hackett and Frances Goodrich, *Long Day's Journey Into Night* by Eugene O'Neill, and *Look Home-ward Angel* by Ketti Frings. As for Archibald MacLeish's *J.B.*, the first poetic drama to win a Pulitzer Prize, the stature of its author was such that no one on the Board opposed the innovative award.

The O'Neill play, by all odds, was the finest of the decade and per-haps of the century as well. Certainly, it was the greatest of the drama-tist's own works, wrenched out of his inner being in the last years of his life, and produced after his death as an autobiographical record of a tragic American family. John Mason Brown, one of the finest of Ameri-can critics who served on the jury that year with Professor Campbell, had this to say in its report:

> It is a monumental work, overwhelming in its power. No matter how the dialogue may read, it adjusts itself (as was so often the case in O'Neill's writing) admirably to the speaking needs of the actors. Moreover, O'Neill faces the anguish of a period in his own family life with the same unblinking courage with which throughout his career he faced the tragic sorrows of the world. In many years of theatregoing, I must confess I have never seen a play more nakedly autobiographical than this one. Inevitably, its exploration of the misery of O'Neill's own life adds to its fascination.

To this, Professor Campbell added the comment: "In brief, we believe that the Pulitzer award has seldom gone to so great a play as *Long Day's Journey Into Night*." With that verdict, the Board agreed.[25]

Brown and Campbell also recommended Mr. and Mrs. Hackett's dra-matization of *The Diary of Anne Frank*, even though it was an adaptation of the little Jewish girl's poignant story of how she and her family strug-gled to survive in Nazi-occupied Holland. The jurors wrote:

> We are well aware that under the terms of the award the prize should go "for the American play, preferably original in its source and dealing with American life," etc. etc. *The Diary of Anne Frank*, we realize, does not deal with American life and is a dramatization. But we feel, and strongly feel, that its merits, sensitivity, and im-portance are such that they justify ignoring the qualifying clause that begins with "preferably". . . . More than being a brilliant and poignant reminder of the agonies through which the world has re-cently gone, it is a statement, courageous and immensely human, of the need of all of us in our daily lives to live not merely with death but above it.

There was no dissent from the Board in 1956.

The case of *Look Homeward Angel* presented the Board with still another dramatization, this one of the outstanding novel by Thomas Wolfe that had failed to win a Pulitzer Prize. In the words of Professor John Gassner of the Yale Drama School, John Mason Brown's associate on the 1958 Drama Jury, "In honoring this play, the Committee would be honoring both Ketti Frings, the playwright, and Tom Wolfe, the novelist, commending an excellently performed job of dramatization, no small task in this case, and encouraging the American theatre." It was an ingenious argument and it won the Board's approval. Neither the jury nor the Board considered Leonard Bernstein's musical evocation of the Romeo and Juliet theme in a New York setting, *West Side Story.*

Gassner and Brown both were for MacLeish's *J.B.* in 1959. As a modern allegory based on the theme of the Book of Job, it represented hard going for Broadway audiences despite the recommendation of Brooks Atkinson, who wrote in his review for the New York *Times: "J.B.* is one of the memorable works of the century as verse, as drama, and as spiritual inquiry." In the jury's report, Brown appended the comment: "This may well prove extravagant as praise and hurried as prophecy. But certainly no other play of this or many seasons has attempted to come to grips with so large and universal a theme and succeeded in stating it in terms more eloquent, moving, and provocative." Gassner added: "*J.B.* is the first poetic drama of genuine distinction to have been written by an American poet who has remained American in every fiber of his thought and artistry." [26]

The Board put up no argument and MacLeish won his third Pulitzer Prize. But its sense of independence was rising after four years of meek submission and its docility was near an end. Broadway had entered into its time of troubles. The great minds and strong hands that had built the American theater were slowly vanishing from the scene. Only a few now remained. And not many new ones were coming along. The problem for the Board, as always, was whether to honor the playwrights of distinction and established excellence or to take a chance on newcomers or innovative specialties.

Messrs. Brown and Gassner urgently recommended Lillian Hellman's *Toys in the Attic* for the 1960 Drama Prize. Gassner saluted her for the integrity and distinction of her work as an American dramatist for more than twenty-five years, concluding, "The Pulitzer Prize should go to her as a means of honoring both her present and past contributions to our theater." Brown praised the "driving muscularity of mind and unflinching attitude towards life which have distinguished her work," then went on to discuss her current play in these terms: "It may not be her best work, but certainly it is by all odds the best play of this season."

The almost entirely new Advisory Board, from which all but two of the 1954 membership had been phased out, didn't particularly care for *Toys in the Attic*. The argument of those who opposed it was that it really did not, as Brown had conceded, represent Miss Hellman's best work. There was some discussion about passing the award, but the Board was reluctant to do so. However, it was also unimpressed with the alternatives in the Brown-Gassner report and the state of the Broadway theater in general until someone mentioned a new musical, *Fiorello!* Nearly everyone at the big oval table had seen it and enjoyed it, recalling as it did the lively and somewhat delirious era when Fiorello H. LaGuardia, the "Little Flower" of song and story, had ruled New York's City Hall. *The Sound of Music*, the Rodgers and Hammerstein sugar-sweet musical, was also on Broadway at the time but nobody paid attention to it during the discussion. *Fiorello!* carried the day and won the 1960 Drama award.

For Jerry Bock, the composer; Sheldon Harnick, the lyricist; and Jerome Weidman and George Abbott, the authors of the book, the news was as unexpected as it was happy. "I think we all shared a special thrill with that news," Bock wrote, "in that we never considered such a prospect or, if some of us had thought about it, we were so immersed in *Tenderloin* at the time that it was rarely, if ever, referred to. The announcement to us was a joyful shock, an ecstatic intrusion, that is if joy and ecstasy may be measured by whooping, jumping, hand-clapping, and hugging. We rushed to the producer's office to view the telegram informing us of *Fiorello!*'s prize and exulted evermore."

To this Harnick added the observation, "*Fiorello!* made me solvent. This was a brand new feeling and I wasn't used to it. So when George Abbott suggested that we give the financial part of the award to some worthy charity rather than splitting it four ways, I was among the first to splutter a protest. I had been financially insecure for going on ten years and for me, at that time, charity definitely began at home."

All the collaborators agreed that the surprise award gave them a lift and stimulated their work for some time thereafter. Perhaps, in a vague way, it might have had something to do with the events in Sholom Aleichem's Russian village of 1905 called Anatevka, which came to life for six years on Broadway beginning in 1964 with the opening of the musical, *Fiddler on the Roof.* But that was another story. In general, the Board's spur-of-the-moment decision was well received despite a certain amount of criticism that Miss Hellman, one of Broadway's illustrious ones, had once again been passed over. Messrs. Brown and Gassner both registered the strongest kind of protest privately, but agreed to serve again the following year.

Brown wrote to me that he had enjoyed *Fiorello!* but had never mentioned it for the prize because he didn't believe it to be in a class with *Of Thee I Sing* or *Oklahoma!* Yet, though he was "deeply upset" by the Board's verdict, he didn't question its right to disregard the jury's recommendation of *Toys in the Attic.* He argued, however, that some means would have to be taken to reduce if not entirely eliminate the conflict between the Board and its juries. As he put it:

> The Advisory Board consists of a very distinguished group of representative Americans whose judgment as non-professional theatergoers has an interest and value of its own. If they are understandably tired of disagreeable plays and want something light, pleasant, and wholesome instead, they are certainly within their rights to choose the latter. But critics have to judge by different standards than their own pleasure—I mean in the ordinary sense of being entertained or cheered. Though, God willing, they don't take themselves seriously, critics have to take the theater seriously and believe in its importance. Hence, they cannot pass over the painful merely because it is painful, and must think as professional observers in terms of careers, craftsmanship, language, ideas, etc. This is where the conflict is bound, at times, to arise between the Board and the Jurors.

What Brown proposed was that the jurors should be publicly identified and set down as dissenting from the Board's selection in a year in which they were overruled. He pointed out that the secrecy that supposedly blanketed the identities of the Drama jurors was an amiable fiction along Broadway and that, in consequence, "Jurors, as serious critics, should not be put in a position of approving of something of which they did not approve." [27]

While the Board did not go along with Brown's specific proposal, both he and Gassner were given assurances that their reports would not in the future be so abruptly disregarded. During the next two years, all went well between the Board and the Brown-Gassner team. In 1961, the jury recommended *All the Way Home*, Tad Mosel's dramatization of James Agee's Pulitzer Prize-winning novel, *A Death in the Family*, which the Board accepted. For the following year, with somewhat more enthusiasm, the Board also agreed on the jury's choice of the Frank Loesser–Abe Burrows musical, *How to Succeed in Business Without Really Trying*.

The stock of native American drama on Broadway was sinking. Messrs. Brown and Gassner recognized all the symptoms in their report for 1963, calling the season "drably undistinguished" and mourning that "most of the new American plays have wallowed in every form of despair, drug addiction, and deviation." After such an unpromising beginning, however, he joined with Gassner in recommending Edward Albee's *Who's Afraid of Virginia Woolf?* and offering no second choice. The play, by an outstanding new American dramatist, was an alcoholic embellishment of a searing marital conflict, a theme celebrated with European flourishes by August Strindberg in *The Dance of Death*. Brown wrote:

> Although I can't pretend that *Who's Afraid* makes for a pleasant evening in the theater, I do know it provides an unforgettable one. If it is an experience which is in part an ordeal, this is precisely what Mr. Albee meant it to be. With his unblinking view of life, he slashes savagely into his characters' innermost selves. Some critics have described him as being a new Strindberg or O'Neill. Such a judgment seems to me premature, though I understand what they mean. Like O'Neill, he shrinks from no horror; like Strindberg, the war he declares between men and women is brutally fierce. But Mr. Albee already has an identity of his own.
>
> His play is a game played with undismayed candor by an older couple in the presence of a younger couple, all four of whom are drenched in alcohol. In terms of dialogue that is at times hilariously funny and at times abrasively revealing, it is a study in hatreds and frustrations, of impotence and jealousy, and with doing away with illusion (in this case, an imaginary son who is at last killed off). In the course of all this Mr. Albee proves to have a power for summoning extraordinary interest and excitement in a play which is both over-long and weak in its pivotal point.

Although I have my reservations, these by no means keep me from recognizing the rare qualities of *Who's Afraid of Virginia Woolf?* In it Mr. Albee proves to be a young man who, having already done much, will unquestionably do more and has just now done a great deal.

Gassner's verdict was even more positive, for he wrote: "Although Mr. Albee's play has easily detectable flaws, it is a slashing and penetrating work by the most eminent of our new American playwrights. . . . I see no insuperable objection to the work on the grounds of immorality, lubricity, or scatology once one reflects that we cannot expect the vital plays of our period, whether we like the period or not, to abide by Victorian standards."

When the Advisory Board met on April 25, 1963, there was a predictable split. The terms of the Drama Prize still were: "For the American play, preferably original in its source and dealing with American life, which shall represent in marked fashion the educational value and power of the stage." Although the so-called "uplift" provision had been tacitly ignored in awarding the prize to *Cat on a Hot Tin Roof* eight years earlier, only President Kirk, Chairman Pulitzer, and Benjamin McKelway of the Washington *Evening Star* remained on the Board in 1963—and McKelway had been absent at the 1955 meeting. The reconstituted Board debated the issue earnestly, with the opponents of the Albee play pointing out that it did not match up with the terms of the award and the advocates basing themselves on the jury's recommendation. But in the end, *Who's Afraid of Virginia Woolf?* lost by a narrow margin and the Board decided against any other award, hoping the jurors would not be too displeased. But they were.

About thirty minutes after the announcement on May 6, 1963 that there had been no drama award, Brown telephoned me to say that he and Gassner were resigning from the Drama Jury. Both were naturally displeased over the rejection of *Who's Afraid of Virginia Woolf?* in such abrupt fashion. But in addition, Brown pointed out that the theater was in a difficult position and the prize therefore could well have been awarded to the Albee play as an "encouragement." Gassner, equally polite, telegraphed his resignation but there the amenities ended.

To the press, Brown announced his resignation and Gassner's in these terms: "This is a case of advice without consent. They have made a farce out of the drama award." To which Gassner added: "After we were overruled in 1960, we stipulated that if the Trustees overruled us on future occasions and gave the award to a play other than the one we selected, then the Trustees would have to announce what our selection was. This year's decision seems to be an indirect way of getting around our vote."

Of course there was no secret about *Toys in the Attic* being the selection of the jurors in 1960. Nor did the deliberations of the Advisory Board itself remain a private matter, for the Board members quickly enough talked back to the angry jurors. Sevellon Brown III, associate editor of the Providence *Journal-Bulletin* and a Board member since 1961, argued for the Board's majority that the play "was pretentious, did not conform to the terms of the award, and was not a good play." He added, "We did not vote against it because it was controversial or shocking." However, W. D. Maxwell, editor of the Chicago *Tribune*, left no doubt of his own position. The Albee work, he said, was a "filthy play." And Louis B. Seltzer, editor of the Cleveland *Press*, made a general attack on all plays that "reek with obscenity" and "offend good taste." It was like a page out of the Board's Butlerian past.

Reporters for some years had been polling all members of the Board after controversial decisions and this time was no exception. In this manner, it came to the public's attention that Benjamin M. McKelway of the Washington *Evening Star* had voted against the Albee play without having seen it, a circumstance that further inflamed the Board's inveterate critics. They brushed aside McKelway's explanation that he had every right to accept the judgment of some of his colleagues on the Board who *had* seen the play. It wasn't right, they insisted; nobody should condemn a play without seeing it.

The formalities of a severance of relations between the jurors and the Board were accomplished in a quieter atmosphere. As a purely technical matter, John Mason Brown and John Gassner both recognized that their appointments as jurors had lapsed on March 1, 1963, so they actually didn't have anything from which to resign. However, Brown wrote to the Board:

> Since I have not been reappointed, I realize that I am in no position to *resign* as a Pulitzer Prize Drama Juror. Even so, I ask you not to reconsider me. I do not challenge the right of the Advisory Board or the Trustees of Columbia University to ignore a juror's recommendation. It was with full knowledge of this right that I have served. But, inasmuch as my recommendations have been

disregarded twice since 1956, it seems to me that my usefulness to the Board has ceased. Clearly, its approach to the theatre and mine are different.

I have enjoyed serving as a juror and working with John Hohenberg and John Gassner. I believe deeply in the Pulitzer Prize for Drama and all that the prestige it carries can mean for the theatre. Hence, it is with genuine regret that I send you this letter.

There were two consequences of the unpleasantness over *Who's Afraid of Virginia Woolf?* during the following year. The first was a recommendation by a Special Committee on the Drama Award to drop the "uplift" clause, beginning with the 1964 season, and wording the terms of the Drama Prize as follows:

"For a distinguished play by an American author, preferably original in its source and dealing with American life."

The committee—President Kirk, Chairman Pulitzer, and Erwin D. Canham of the *Christian Science Monitor*—concluded with a reference to the provisions of the Pulitzer will: "Your committee recommends the change in the wording of the Drama Award and believes it to be fully in keeping with the testator's long-range purpose since it would, in the testator's language, be 'conducive to the public good' and it is 'rendered advisable . . . by reason of change in time.' "

The second consequence was not as formal and it wasn't intended to be binding, but it was first suggested by Barry Bingham of the Louisville *Courier-Journal* at the 1964 meeting as a helpful procedure and later endorsed by Chairman Pulitzer and several others. Put very briefly, what all Board members were expected to do henceforth was to abstain from passing judgment on any book they had not read and any play they had not seen. This procedure was nowhere noted as a formal resolution, but over the ensuing decade it was accepted by all Board members as readily as the custom of leaving the room during discussion and action on any matter involving a conflict of interest.[28]

A new jury consisting of Professor Maurice Valency of Columbia, Elliot Norton, critic of the Boston *Record American*, and Walter Kerr, critic of the New York *Herald Tribune*, took over in 1964 but found nothing to recommend. "The Jury took into consideration the salutary effect of the Pulitzer Prize upon the state of the theater," the report said, "and it was agreed that as a matter of principle it is preferable in doubtful cases to make rather than to withhold an award. It was, accordingly, with the greatest reluctance that we came to the conclusion unanimously that no play has been presented this season either on the Broadway stage or off Broadway which merits the Pulitzer Prize and that, in consequence, no award should be made in the drama for the current year."

As if it hadn't been bad enough to pass the drama prize two years in a row, the fiction and music awards also were omitted in 1964. These circumstances caused a stir, but scarcely an uprising of the intensity and duration of the demonstration of 1963. In 1965, the same jury unanimously recommended Frank D. Gilroy's autobiographical play about a soldier's homecoming, *The Subject Was Roses*—a well-deserved honor for a young playwright. It was, the jury reported, the only play worthy of consideration—a wry commentary on the position of the Broadway theater. The report went on to point out that *Roses* was no smashing box-office success, saying:

> *The Subject Was Roses* opened at the Royale Theatre on May 25, 1964, too late for consideration by this jury. It is still running. But although this play received superb reviews, and was extremely inexpensive to produce and operate, it can in no sense be considered a box-office success; and its long run must be attributed not so much to the support of the Broadway audience as to the gallant efforts of the management, the author, and the actors to keep it running at considerable cost to themselves in the way of reduced royalties and salaries during periods of stress.

The Board readily agreed to a Pulitzer Prize for *The Subject Was Roses*. When Gilroy was notified later by a radio commentator who neglected to tell him that the conversation was on the air, there was considerable confusion. "I always thought it symbolic and fitting," he wrote, "that our conversation was interrupted by one of my sons clamoring to have a kite rescued from a tree." [29]

On that note, a decade of troubles for the American theater phased into a period of adjustment to new social realities. For the Advisory Board, too, the changing social order meant that it would have to reexamine its standards as well as its beliefs.

5
The Importance of Biography

J. D. Ferguson, editor of the Milwaukee *Journal*, came to the Advisory Board's meeting on April 26, 1957, with a highly personal recommendation for the Biography Prize. He recognized quite well that the Biography Jury had proposed two outstanding works, Alpheus T. Mason's *Harlan Fiske Stone: Pillar of the Law* as its first choice and James MacGregor Burns's *Roosevelt: The Lion and the Fox* as an alternative. The jurors in the category were both respected experts—Dr. Julian P. Boyd, the editor of the Thomas Jefferson Papers, of Princeton, and Professor Bernard Mayo of the University of Virginia. And yet, Don Ferguson was greatly taken with a book that neither of the jurors had mentioned, *Profiles In Courage*, by John Fitzgerald Kennedy, then a senator from Massachusetts.

Kennedy had written the book during a long and painful convalescence after an operation in 1954 to relieve a war-aggravated back injury. At the Hospital for Special Surgery in New York and later at the Kennedy home in Palm Beach, Fla., the young senator did his research for the profiles of such courageous men as John Quincy Adams, Daniel Webster, Edmund Ross of Kansas, George W. Norris of Nebraska, and others who had captured his imagination. He wrote slowly in bed, and later beside the swimming pool in Palm Beach, using heavy white paper in a hard-covered lawyers' notebook. To be sure, he had aid in his research. The Library of Congress was helpful in providing him with books while such old friends in Washington as Theodore Sorensen and Arthur Krock gave him advice. But he did his own writing for the first draft and dictated the second draft to a secretary.

Ferguson came across the book soon after it was published in 1956 with a foreword by Allan Nevins. As it went to the top of best-seller lists, the Milwaukee editor recommended it to friends and took it home to his family. Nor was he alone among the editors of prominent papers in his admiration for Kennedy's work. Erwin D. Canham of the *Christian Science Monitor*, who was not then a member of the Advisory Board, wrote: "That a United States Senator, a young man of independent means with a gallant and thoughtful background, should have produced this study is as remarkable as it is helpful. It is a splendid flag that Senator Kennedy has nailed to his mast. May he keep it there." In Washington, naturally, Arthur Krock was also beating the drums for his friend but Krock, too, was not an Advisory Board member at that time.

At first, the discussion of the Biography Jury's report before the Board was aimless and it seemed likely that its first choice might be accepted until Ferguson intervened. He leaned across the big table in the Trustees' Room at Columbia, the sunlight glinting on his white hair and gold-rimmed spectacles, and told his colleagues how impressed he had been with Kennedy's book. "I read it aloud to my 12-year-old grandson," he said, "and the boy was absolutely fascinated. I think we should give the prize to *Profiles in Courage.*"

Others around the table who had read the book were equally impressed, and in that particular year the Board was considerably more conservative than it is today. The upshot of the discussion was a majority vote to upset the jury's recommendations and bestow the prize on Kennedy's book. With the concurrence of the university's Trustees, therefore, the 1957 award for a distinguished American biography "teaching patriotic and unselfish services to the people" went to *Profiles in Courage.*

Kennedy was no amateur writer. At 23 years of age, he had written a book about prewar Britain entitled, *Why England Slept.* At the organization conference of the United Nations at San Francisco, he had represented the New York *Journal-American* and other Hearst newspapers as a special correspondent. Nevertheless, in rumor-conscious Washington, gossip soon began circulating that Kennedy had not actually written his Pulitzer Prize-winning book and that good friends like Sorensen had done a ghost-writing job for him. After some months Drew Pearson, whose journalistic batting average for accuracy wasn't very high, picked up the rumor and used it on a broadcast over the American Broadcasting Company's network. Although ABC immediately issued a statement of disavowal and Kennedy also denied the story, it created a minor tempest. A few indignant letters even came to the Pulitzer Prize office, asking whether the award would be reconsidered or canceled altogether.

It did not take me very long to make an investigation of the circumstances and determine, on my own responsibility, that Pearson's charges were wrong. On January 7, 1958, I wrote as follows to Senator Kennedy:

"I have received several inquiries regarding Drew Pearson's remarks over the ABC Television Network. Beyond answering them with a copy of the enclosed statement given to me by the American Broadcasting Company, I have taken no action and do not intend to do so. I thought you would like to know about this."

Kennedy replied three days later:

"I am very grateful to you for your letter of Jan. 7 and the position you are taking as expressed therein.

"All of us regret that this situation has occurred—although I suppose it is not unusual in either the worlds of politics or literature."

There was a handwritten note below the familiar scrawled signature: "I have an appointment with Mr. Pearson Tuesday and I hope at that time the matter may be settled for good and all."

It was, eventually, with Pearson's published concession in his column that Senator Kennedy had written *Profiles in Courage*. There was a footnote to the incident, which was recorded by Kennedy's biographer, James MacGregor Burns, one of the unsuccessful contenders for the senator's prize. He noted that the Gallup Poll showed a four point rise, from 41 to 45 percent, in Senator Kennedy's favor over Senator Estes Kefauver for the Democratic Presidential nomination after the Pulitzer Prize announcement. The previous poll had been taken in January 1957.

"Since the only relevant and significant event in the four-month interim was the Pulitzer award," Professor Burns wrote, "it seems possible that literary honors carry more weight with the public than has been commonly thought."

In any event, three years later, John Fitzgerald Kennedy became the first Pulitzer Prize winner to be elected President of the United States. He always cherished the award, not only because it increased the value of his other writings, but also for the intangible merit of its literary distinction.[30]

Biography became even bigger news in 1962 when the Advisory Board voted overwhelmingly for W. A. Swanberg's *Citizen Hearst*. The jury, consisting of Professor C. Vann Woodward of Yale and Orville Prescott of the New York *Times*, had split, Woodward being for Mark Schorer's biography, *Sinclair Lewis*, and Prescott urging the selection of *Citizen Hearst*. Prescott wrote:

> *Citizen Hearst* is a long, solid, impressively detailed work which is based upon massive research. It contains all the information any reasonable person could want to know about an extraordinary, a controversial, and a fascinating man. Hearst may have exercised a lamentable influence in American journalism. Nevertheless, he cut a wide swath across American life. Mr. Swanberg writes about him with objective good judgment and prancing vigor. . . . This is a book which is a pleasure to read. It provides much information about our recent past and much insight into a now vanished social

era. Since Mr. Swanberg is also the author of two earlier, excellent American biographies, *Sickles the Incredible* and *Jim Fisk*, this seems to me the appropriate time to honor his finest book and by implication his whole career."

Professor Woodward, undeterred by Prescott's fourth place ranking of the Lewis biography, insisted that it was "one of the most penetrating and revealing" studies ever written of an American man of letters. He called *Citizen Hearst* an "entertaining and colorful" book, but went on:

> What troubles me is that the book represents a limited effort and inconclusive results. The author admits that it is an "incomplete picture" and that he had "access to only a scattering of the thousands of letters Hearst wrote and received," still in the possession of the family. Also disturbing is the fact that he did not consult available private papers of public figures with whom Hearst was associated. While the book has merit, I seriously doubt that it measures up to the standards of the prize, certainly not those set up by recent selections.

The only real question when the book came before the Advisory Board was how large the majority for *Citizen Hearst* would be. Everybody around the table had read it and enjoyed it, more or less. All technicalities were swept aside in the discussion, for the jury hadn't brought up the idealistic terms of the award and no member of the Board thought of doing it. Members with such widely varying interests as Erwin D. Canham of the *Christian Science Monitor*, W. D. Maxwell of the Chicago *Tribune* and Benjamin M. McKelway of the Washington *Evening Star* spoke up for the Swanberg book. Joseph Pulitzer Jr., the chairman, certainly had no objection to giving the prize to a biography of his grandfather's old foe and was among those voting for it. Norman Chandler of the Los Angeles *Times*, who cast his first ballot for the Lewis biography, changed his vote when *Citizen Hearst* emerged as an overwhelming choice and made the selection unanimous. Thus the Board meeting of April 26, 1962, went off without a harsh word.

It was quite a different story, however, when the Columbia Trustees met on the traditional first Monday in May, which that year fell on the seventh. For forty-six years, the Trustees had routinely listened to a report of the recommendations of the Advisory Board and then voted without comment to accept them. Their powers had been strictly defined by a succession of lawyers for the university, who interpreted the will and the agreements based on it to mean that the Trustees could only accept or reject what the Board had handed them. From time to time, an eminent member of the Trustees would complain privately that he did not relish being a "rubber stamp." And particularly in the hiatus after the years of Butler's dominance, a Trustee would raise questions in the meeting about one of the awards, usually in drama and occasionally in fiction but never in biography.

In fact, the meeting of the Trustees on the Pulitzer Prizes had become so routine that the university's publicity office almost always informed reporters they could expect the announcement at about 3:30 P.M., Eastern Daylight Time, thirty minutes after the Trustees convened. Sometimes, the verdict would come after only fifteen minutes, which made it possible for the late afternoon editions in the Eastern time zone to carry the news along with radio and television. Consequently, the entire announcement, including the text of the citations and biographical material and pictures of the winners, was prepared in advance and held for release. When the telephone call came from the Trustees' Room that all awards had been accepted, there was a mad scramble for the press packets, reporters rushed to open telephone lines in the Journalism Building and the bulletins started tumbling off the wire service printers in newspaper and broadcasting offices all over the land and abroad.

The big news for much of the afternoon of that particular May 7 was that nothing happened. More than fifty reporters, plus cameramen and a few operatives from radio and television stations, waited in the Journalism Building long past the usual hour without any sign of activity. But at the publicity office, upon receiving word from the director, Robert C. Harron, Miss Nancy Carmody was furiously re-typing a press release and a crew under the direction of John Hastings was frantically revising the press packets. What had happened was that President Kirk had advised me at 3:25 P.M. that the university's Trustees had approved all awards except Biography.

Except to a few insiders, the details of the Trustees' action never did get around and only piecemeal reports reached print. But in all truth, the decision to reverse the Advisory Board for the first time in forty-six years hinged on the question of whether *Citizen Hearst* fitted the definition of the Biography Prize as it then existed: "For a distinguished American biography or autobiography teaching patriotic and unselfish services to the people, illustrated by an eminent example." One of the Trustees remarked quite casually to his colleagues that he believed the Swanberg book didn't "fit" with the definition of the prize. The discussion was relatively brief, but it swung the Trustees against the recommended biography.

When the Pulitzer Prize announcement finally was made at 4:23 P.M. and the press packets were released in revised form, the reporters were told by a university official: "The university Trustees decided today to make no biography award. This is the only explanation that can be made now pending notification of the Advisory Board members by the university." A few minutes later, with President Kirk's approval, I sent the following telegram to all Board members: "I am instructed to notify you that the Columbia Trustees awarded no Pulitzer Prize in Biography today, while approving all other Advisory Board recommendations. It was the sense of the Trustees that the Advisory Board recommendation for biography was not entirely consistent with the Plan of Award."

Through the simple expedient of telephoning to numerous members of the Advisory Board, Peter Kihss of the New York *Times* reported next day on Page 1 of the newspaper that *Citizen Hearst* had been turned down by the Trustees for the Biography Prize. The Advisory Board members took their reversal calmly enough, with Ralph McGill and others expressing approval of what had been done in view of the terminology of the Plan of Award. Nothing at all was heard from the jurors immediately, although Professor Woodward later asked privately not to be considered again for Pulitzer jury service.

As for Swanberg, he was thoroughly professional about the incident. It was, he said, a "high distinction to be the only man in history to be turned down for a Pulitzer Prize by Columbia's Trustees." He was then 54 years old and had had a long and successful career as a writer following his graduation from the University of Minnesota in 1930. The rejection didn't hurt too much, for the unexpected burst of publicity had sent the sales of *Citizen Hearst* soaring.

Even the Hearst family was stoical about the affair. William Randolph Hearst Jr. had not been pleased by the biography, but he thought the Trustees' rejection unfair. "After all," he said, "everything my Pop learned about journalism came right from old man Pulitzer."

There were two post-mortems. On December 7, 1962, by mail ballot, the Advisory Board accepted a revision of the terms of the biography award as follows: "For a distinguished biography or autobiography by an American author published during the year, preferably on an American subject." And eleven years later, Swanberg's biography of Henry Luce won the Pulitzer Prize by unanimous vote of the jurors, the Advisory Board, and the Columbia Trustees.[31]

Two other Biography Jury reversals occurred during the 1955–1965 period. In the case of William S. White's *The Taft Story* in 1955, the Board set aside a long and very complete jury report by Julian P. Boyd and Bernard Mayo, partly at Arthur Krock's suggestion. In 1960, when a jury consisting of Francis Brown of the New York *Times* and Professor C. Vann Woodward recommended Margaret Leech's *In the Days of McKinley* first and Samuel Eliot Morison's *John Paul Jones* second, the Board ruled that the Leech work properly belonged in the history category and voted it the Pulitzer Prize in History, leaving *John Paul Jones* as the winner in Biography. In so doing, the Board reversed a History Jury consisting of Dr. John A. Krout, provost of Columbia University, and Dean Roy F. Nichols of the University of Pennsylvania graduate division, who had proposed Henry F. May's *The End of American Innocence*. Messrs. Brown and Woodward wrote of Miss Leech's book:

> Here is a first class and fascinating performance. McKinley, his wife, and the world in which they moved are brought alive in Miss Leech's sympathetic but not uncritical reconstruction of an era. The portrait of the President is new, and that of his wife unforgettable. . . . Miss Leech's story, told with literary skill and scholarship of a high order, has a freshness that accounts in part for her achieving what many might regard as impossible: she makes William McKinley a flesh-and-blood man; she makes him interesting and understandable. Because she writes with great felicity her biography, although perhaps overlong and at times too detailed, is a reading delight, an exciting experience.

Of Morison's *John Paul Jones*, the report said, "It is a good book, written with the excellent style that one expects from Morison and with his customary superior scholarship." [32]

The other winners, all of them eminent examples of the biographers' art, were unanimous selections of both juries and the Advisory Board. Professors Boyd and Mayo picked Talbot Hamlin's *Benjamin Henry Latrobe* in 1956 and the seven-volume Douglas Southall Freeman biography of George Washington in 1958. Arthur Walworth's *Woodrow Wilson* won in 1959. Francis Brown and Professor John M. Gaus of Harvard chose David Donald's *Charles Summer and the Coming of the Civil War* in 1961. The second and third volumes of Leon Edel's biography of Henry James were recommended by Orville Prescott and Professor Eric F. Goldman of Princeton in 1963. Walter Jackson Bate's *John Keats* received the votes of Roderick Nordell of the *Christian Science Monitor* and Edward Weeks of the *Atlantic Monthly* in 1964. John Barkham and Professor Henry Steele Commager of Amherst selected Ernest Samuels' three-volume biography of Henry Adams in 1965.

The prizes for these major works emphasized the emergence of professionally written biography from the long shadow of historical scholarship and the importance of the biographer in American literary pursuits. The manner in which some of the awards were received served to illustrate the rising popularity of biographical writing. Professor Donald, for example, was teaching at Princeton at the time he received his award for the first volume of his Charles Sumner biography and became a campus hero, the toast of champagne parties and the recipient of a standing ovation from a class of 350 Princeton undergraduates. Professor Samuels' prize at Northwestern brought him a major pay increase and a testimonial dinner given by President James Roscoe Miller. Professor Bate at Harvard also received numerous other awards for his *John Keats* but wrote: "I can say that these awards never meant as much to me as the Pulitzer." [33]

For sheer excitement, the historians could not contend with the biographers in the 1955–1965 decade although numerous worthy works were produced, including some that broke new ground. The dominant historical figure in the group was Richard Hofstadter, whose reputation was assured with the publication of his *The American Political Tradition and the Men Who Made It* in 1948, and confirmed by his two Pulitzer Prizes in later years. Brilliant younger scholars came to the fore, including Sumner Chilton Powell and Irwin Unger. Specialists, too, were rewarded for new works, among them Paul Horgan, George F. Kennan, Bray Hammond, Leonard D. White, Margaret Leech, and Herbert Feis. Constance McLaughlin Green, daughter of Andrew C. McLaughlin who received the 1936 Pulitzer Prize in History, won her own history award in 1963 with *Washington, Village and Capital, 1800–1878*. And the dean of all American historians, Lawrence H. Gipson, was rewarded in 1962 for his life's work with a prize for *The Triumphant Empire: Thunder Clouds in the West.*

Except for the single reversal in 1960, the History Juries had their own way without even an argument from the Advisory Board. Professors Arthur Meier Schlesinger Sr. and Merle Curti recommended Paul Horgan's *Great River: The Rio Grande in North American History* in 1955. For three years thereafter, the History Jury consisted of Dr. Harry J. Carman, for many years the dean of Columbia College, and Professor C. Vann Woodward, who chose Hofstadter's *The Age of Reform* in 1956, Kennan's *Russia Leaves the War: Soviet-American Relations, 1917–1920* in 1957 and Bray Hammond's pathbreaking banking history, *Banks and Politics in America* in 1958. Dr. John A. Krout and Dean Roy F. Nichols served as jurors from 1960 through 1963, recommending Herbert Feis's *Between War and Peace: The Potsdam Conference* in 1961, Gipson's work in 1962, and the Green history of Washington in 1963. Powell's specialized monograph, *Puritan Village: The Formation of a New England Town*, was selected in 1964 by Professors Lawrence H. Chamberlain of Columbia and Elting E. Morison of M.I.T. And in the following year, Professor Richard B. Morris of Columbia and Paul Horgan picked Unger's *The Greenback Era.* The White prize in 1959 was for *The Republican Era: 1869–1901.*

For sheer impact on American historical studies and influence on contemporary historians, there was no one quite like Richard Hofstadter. In addition to his prize-winning *The Age of Reform*, the outstanding new historical work published in 1955, he won a Pulitzer Prize in the new category of General Non-Fiction in 1964 for his *Anti-Intellectualism in American Life* and that was a pleasurable surprise for him. He hadn't expected much recognition for it, being a modest man without any mark of the painful ego that so afflicts much of university scholarship.

Hofstadter was easy-going, quiet, and relaxed in manner, with little of the fussiness of the old-fashioned scholar about him. He was born in Buffalo in 1916, received his B.A. from the University of Buffalo in 1937, his M.A. from Columbia in 1938 and his Ph.D. from Columbia in 1942. His life-long teaching association with Columbia began in 1946, leading to his appointment as a professor of history in 1952. By that time, through his *American Political Tradition*, he was well established. While he thought well of Charles A. Beard and was no admirer of Amer-

ican business, he became one of the most penetrating critics of the progressive viewpoint. He felt a "lack of confidence in the American future"
and commented incisively on what he called the American "democracy
in cupidity." But liberals could take scant comfort from his writing, for
he pointed out in blunt fashion "the rudderless and demoralized state of
American liberalism." He saw little to be gained in staying with the
populist interpretation of the American past and he didn't believe very
much in the frequent postwar proclamations of an American renaissance.
The tide, he thought, was going the other way, particularly during the
McCarthy era, which deeply affected him.

Hofstadter was not one to accept simplistic theories about the flow of
history. If anything, he went in too much for the complexities of historical influence. He studied the Marxist interpretation of history with its
overwhelming emphasis on economic influence, but rejected it. Nor was
he ever much impressed with so-called American "pragmatism," which
he felt to be a form of intellectual bankruptcy. In his later years, he
wrote:

> No doubt it is, more than anything else, the events of our time,
> and among these some of the most ominous and appalling, that
> have launched students of society upon a restless search for new
> methods of understanding. But the work of other intellectual dis-
> ciplines has also made the present generation of historians more
> conscious of important aspects of behavior which our predecessors
> left largely in the background. An increasing interest of philoso-
> phers, anthropologists, and literary critics in the symbolic and
> myth-making aspects of the human mind has found its way into
> historical writing, and with it has come a growing sensitivity to the
> possibilities of textual analysis. . . . This does not mean that the
> material interests of politics can be psychologized away or reduced
> to episodes in intellectual history. It means only that historians and
> political scientists have always worked, implicitly or explicitly,
> with psychological assumptions; that these ought to be made as
> conscious as possible; and that they should be sophisticated enough
> to take ample account of the complexity of political action.

The body of Hofstadter's work illustrates his preoccupation with the
complex, but it also demonstrates that he had the breadth of mind, the
background, and the literary skill to give it focus and meaning. After his

death, a younger historian, Christopher Lasch, mourned the decline of the art of history in these terms:

> Our generation has seen too many brave beginnings, too many claims that came to nothing, too many books unfinished and even unbegun, too many broken and truncated careers. As activists, we have achieved far less than we hoped; as scholars, our record is undistinguished on the whole. It is not too late to achieve something better, but it is no longer possible to be complacent about our accomplishments or the superiority of our own understanding of American society to that of the generation before us, whose finest historian was Richard Hofstadter.

It was, in fact, one of the low points of professional historical scholarship, a time of doubting and testing for the younger historians, a moment of truth for the older ones.[34]

While it was entirely happenstance that caused the Advisory Board to pick this particular period for the inauguration of a General Non-Fiction Prize, the move was symbolic in a way. For beginning with 1962, the award recognized valued works that were compounded in part of journalism, history, philosophy, political action, depth psychology, and literature. It was a format that fitted Hofstadter's own philosophy of history and it soon came to rival the history category in both influence and importance. Aptly enough, Hofstadter's second Pulitzer Prize was in this field, although it could just as well have been judged in the older and better established category of history.

The Advisory Board wasn't quite certain how it wanted to define General Non-Fiction but finally agreed on a catch-all description: "For a distinguished book by an American which is not eligible for consideration in any other existing category." That wording set off an annual avalanche of books of all descriptions, from cook books to travelogues, explorations in journalism to belles lettres, a collection that was bound to try the patience and the judgment of the most devoted judges. As things turned out, the Advisory Board had to make its own decisions during three of the four initial years of the prize because of jury disagreements.

The selection of the first non-fiction prize winner, Theodore H. White's *The Making of the President 1960*, went a long way toward setting the pattern for the category. The jury of Roderick Nordell and Edward Weeks had split, with Nordell urging the choice of the White book and Weeks plumping for Jane Jacobs' *The Death and Life of Great American Cities*. The Advisory Board had little trouble making up its mind that White should have the prize for what turned out to be the first of a series of penetrating histories of modern presidential campaigns. Nordell called it "masterful" and "absorbing" and concluded: "A discerning reporter and supple writer, Mr. White coolly explores the problems of the system, conveys a kind of hardheaded idealism about it, and portrays the people involved in it with clarity, humor, and compassion."

The announcement of the first non-fiction prize was well received by the critics, not the least of whom was the central character of the book, President Kennedy, who wrote to White: "It pleases me that I could at least provide a little of the scenario for the book." As for the usually articulate author, he was stumped for once. "I can't really say what the prize meant to me," he wrote, "except that, once you have received the Pulitzer Prize, people feel that you should wear a grey beard and a necktie and they immediately put you on a shelf. All the other awards I have received since have been for television and magazine pieces. Once you have a Pulitzer, there's nothing left to look forward to."

There was no argument at all about the 1963 winner, Barbara Tuchman's expert recital of the events leading up to World War I, *The Guns of August*. It was easily the first choice of the jury of Hodding Carter and Lewis Gannett, the unanimous selection of the Board, and a great favorite with the public. The only unusual part of it was that Mrs. Tuchman received the news of her first Pulitzer Prize while she was under the dryer at her hairdresser's, an unliterary moment in a remarkable life. As for the effect of the prize on her career, she wrote later: "I can say definitely that it has been by far the most important recognition, as I am sure other recipients will agree, that an American writer can enjoy."

Hofstadter's 1964 winner, *Anti-Intellectualism in American Life*, wasn't an automatic choice. The jurors, John Barkham and Paul Horgan, offered the Board two other books as well—Stewart L. Udall's *The Quiet Crisis* and James Baldwin's *The Fire Next Time*. But they told the Board that Hofstadter's work was "one of the truly distinguished books of the year" and praised it so highly that it won unanimous acceptance.

For 1965, there was another divided jury. Roderick Nordell wanted the prize to go to Howard Mumford Jones's scholarly *O Strange New*

World: American Culture—the Formative Years. His fellow juror, Charles Poore of the New York *Times*, proposed an award posthumously for Ernest Hemingway's *A Moveable Feast.* On balance, the Board was impressed with Nordell's argument that honoring Jones's cultural history would also "honor a man who has given a lifetime's distinguished contribution to American letters." [35]

The common theme that ran through all four winners of the non-fiction prize, therefore, was historical. Each of the works could easily have gone in the category of American history, even Barbara Tuchman's, for *The Guns of August* reverberated with deafening impact in Washington, D.C., and eventually drew the United States into its first global war. The difference, if any, was that most histories included in General Non-Fiction tended to be more relevant to the college generation of the 1960s than the usual type of academic historical studies. Thus, the response to the latest Pulitzer Prize, for those who took the trouble to think about it, constituted still another danger signal for the professional historians. If the book-reading public was more interested in biography and non-fiction in general, the effect would be felt soon enough in the enrollments for historical studies in the nation's great universities.

6

Poetry and Music: Rewards of Fame

In a brief assessment of the Pulitzer Prizes in Music toward the end of 1972, Aaron Copland wrote: "As I look down the list, I see no name of a composer who is not well known, and certainly sufficiently played. In other words, there are no brand new discoveries hitherto unheard of before being crowned with a Pulitzer. This would seem to indicate that a composer's general reputation may put him in a favorable light when being considered by his peers." [36]

For the decade between 1955 and 1965, Copland's observation was particularly sound. There were four composers during that period who were to be double winners. Gian-Carlo Menotti won his second prize in 1955 for *The Saint of Bleecker Street.* Samuel Barber, a former Pulitzer Music Scholarship holder, took the prize twice in five years—in 1958 with his opera *Vanessa* and in 1963 with his Piano Concerto No. 1. In 1960, Elliott Carter won the first of his two prizes for his Second String

Quartet. And in 1961, Walter Piston received his second prize for his Symphony No. 7.

The other awards for the decade also went to composers of known quality and distinction—Ernst Toch in 1956 for his Symphony No. 3, Norman Dello Joio in 1957 for *Meditations on Ecclesiastes*, John LaMontaine in 1959 for his Concerto for Piano and Orchestra, and Robert Ward in 1962 for his opera, *The Crucible*, based on Arthur Miller's play of the same name.

The juries, too, consisted of composers and musicians who had been long and favorably known. Chalmers Clifton, the conductor, continued as chairman through 1960, serving with Professor Willard Rhodes of Columbia and Irving Kolodin of the *Saturday Review* in 1955, Miles Kastendieck of the New York *Journal-American* and Aaron Copland in 1956, Kastendieck and William Bergsma of the Julliard School in 1957, Norman Dello Joio and Professor Paul Henry Lang of Columbia in 1958, Quincy Porter and Kastendieck in 1959, and Lang in 1960. In 1961, the jury consisted of Lang and Robert Ward, in 1962 Lang and Bergsma, and in 1963 and 1964, Kastendieck and Kolodin.

All selections were routinely approved by the Advisory Board until 1964, when Kolodin was against giving any award and Kastendieck somewhat hesitantly put forward Menotti's opera, *The Last Savage*, which he conceded was "no masterpiece" but "good entertainment." The Board decided in favor of Kolodin and withheld the prize for the second time in the history of the award.[37] Even so, that would have caused little comment except that the prize also was passed the following year, with embarrassing results.

An entirely new Music Jury was recruited for the 1964–1965 season in an effort to widen the circle of composers and musical works that were then being considered. It was not something that was casually undertaken, for both President Kirk and Chairman Pulitzer deeply believed in diversity and hoped that new faces and new names would come to the top. The jurors, none of whom had ever served before, were Ronald Eyer of *Newsday*, Winthrop Sargeant of the *New Yorker* and Thomas B. Sherman of the St. Louis *Post-Dispatch*. In their report, they declared unanimously for no award—but with a strikingly original difference. They wanted an appropriate citation for Duke Ellington for his "many notable contributions to American music over a period of thirty years or more."

The Board, which did not pretend to be expert in the field of American music in its larger forms, had trouble with the report, for it began, as Eyer wrote it: "My fellow jurors and I have come to the unanimous decision that no major musical composition by an American composer performed for the first time in this country during the past season—of which we were aware—was worthy of a Pulitzer Prize award, within our understanding of the qualifications for that award."

In proposing Ellington, Eyer went on:

> In lieu of a seasonal award, therefore, we respectfully suggest that an appropriate citation of some sort be given to the American composer, pianist, and conductor, Edward K. ("Duke") Ellington, who has made many notable contributions to American music over a period of thirty years or more with compositions of high artistic quality couched mainly in the idiom of jazz. . . . Though its language is jazz, Ellington's work should not be confused with that of commercial, popular, or show composers. It has true artistic quality, with roots in the traditional music of his race, and it has a strong influence on the music of a whole generation, both in this country and elsewhere.

To this, Winthrop Sargeant added his own high estimation of Ellington's work, saying that he had been the first to propose the special award. But, like Eyer, he asked the Board not to consider the lone new Ellington work of the season, *Far Eastern Suite*, which both did not consider comparable to the best of his output. Had the jury found it possible to recommend *Far Eastern Suite*, there is little doubt that Ellington would have been awarded the Pulitzer Prize in Music for 1965. Instead, what the jury sought was a recognition of a distinguished career in music— something that could have also been applied to Igor Stravinsky, Roger Sessions, and other great ones who had not previously received Pulitzer Prizes.

The Board mulled over the problem for some time but finally denied both the award and the special citation to Ellington. All the niceties of the Board's position simply could not be explained to the satisfaction of those who were outraged, beginning with the jurors themselves. On May 5, 1965, two days after the formal announcement of no award for music, the protests began with the publication in the New York *Times* of the news that Ellington had been denied a special award. The Duke himself was too much the professional to be upset, saying, "Fate's being kind to me. Fate doesn't want me to be too famous too young." He was then 66 years old.

A member of the jury, who preferred at the time to remain anonymous, had leaked the story but neither he nor his colleagues talked of resigning. What happened next also came from an anonymous source, a Board member who asked not to be identified, and protested:

"The jury was a craven goddam jury. They expressed contempt for contemporary composition and then threw in a special recommendation. If they thought Ellington was worth it, why didn't they give him the Pulitzer Prize itself?"

That did it. On May 13, Eyer and Sargeant resigned and complained in a letter to the Advisory Board of "an attack on us in the public prints by an anonymous member of your body as a 'craven goddam jury.' "

Sherman, the remaining juror, said he saw no sense in resigning from a post to which he had not been reappointed; in any event, he announced he had voted for Benjamin Lees for the prize and Ellington for a special citation but his prize recommendation had been rejected by his colleagues.

The unrepentant Ralph McGill, who now emerged as the jury's anonymous critic, followed up with another salvo from Atlanta: "I will confess that the report of the jury did seem to me to be intellectually dishonest in that it recommended in the strongest terms that no prize be given and yet at the same time suggested that a citation be given to Ellington. It seems to me preposterous and sort of contradictory."

Sevellon Brown III,* another Board member, argued that the jury had made a weak recommendation. Another of his colleagues, W. D. Maxwell, said that if the Board "couldn't decide on anything worth while to give a prize to, it seems outside limits to give a weaker prize as a citation."

The two protesting jurors maintained that they had given "the best advice" of which they were capable, that they proposed the special citation for Ellington's career because they had found no single new piece worthy

---

* Son of Sevellon Brown, an earlier Board member.

of a prize, that the Board had given many such citations in the past and should have granted this one. But since their proposal had been rejected without explanation and since they felt they had been vilified in the newspapers, they felt their position was untenable and the Board's action "intolerable." They therefore decided to "disassociate ourselves from any action taken by you in this matter."

While the Advisory Board took its lumps in the controversy, the jurors did not escape criticism, either. William Schuman, the former Pulitzer Prize winner in Music who had become the president of the Lincoln Center for the Performing Arts, joined with such eminent figures as Aaron Copland and Elliott Carter in attacking the jury's "conservatism" and calling the refusal to grant a prize "utterly preposterous." Schuman termed the award "a potent symbol to the American people" but then took the Board itself to task in these terms:

"For the past two years, the Advisory Board has done harm to the cause of American music by its failure to make an award in either year. If there were no Pulitzer Prize for music, the world of music would be in a better state than it is in a year when no award is given. The negative effect of the no-prize discourages public acceptance of new music and is a black eye for our composers."

It remained for Irving Kolodin in the *Saturday Review* to report that one of the protesting jurors had not read the terms of the music prize citation: "For a distinguished composition in the larger forms of chamber, orchestral, or choral music, or for any operatic work including ballet, performed or published by a composer of established residence in the United States." Kolodin commented:

"I yield to no one in admiration for Ellington's distinctions, and he is without doubt a resident, but large forms are precisely what he is *not* distinguished for. The citation may be all wrong, muddle-headed, and outmoded, but that is the rule of the road the jury members agreed to follow when they accepted appointment—had they bothered to read it."

Throughout the unseemly row, Ellington acted with exemplary grace and good humor and notably increased his stature through his forbearance. It was Columbia's Board of Trustees that finally righted the balance in his favor in 1972 by awarding him an honorary doctorate for his services to American music and the distinction of his career. When the granting of the Music Prize resumed in 1966, it was Aaron Copland's observation that the jurors eventually appeared to be more "daring" in making awards to "far out" composers.[38] Perhaps Duke Ellington had something to do with that, too. He died on May 24, 1974.

There were no public outbursts about the state of American poetry during the 1955–1965 decade, at least as far as the Pulitzer Prizes were concerned. Mainly, that was attributable to the practice of the Poetry Juries, like those in music, to give most of their recommendations to some of the most illustrious people in the field. Wallace Stevens, Richard Wilbur, Robert Penn Warren, Stanley Kunitz, William Carlos Williams, and John Berryman were unanimous choices of both the jurors and the Board and few could quarrel with the selection of any one of them. Elizabeth Bishop, who gracefully admitted her debt to Marianne Moore, also won an award as did one of the major writers of light verse, Phyllis McGinley. The only young poets to be recognized during the decade were W. D. Snodgrass, Alan Dugan, and Louis Simpson, which was quite a distinction for them, considering the strength of the veteran opposition.

Simpson's reaction to his victory was typical of the younger winners. Because of the preponderance of older and more famous poets who had received the Pulitzer Prize, he was quite literally astonished when he was told he had won in 1964 for his fourth volume of verse, *At the End of the Open Road*. He should not have been. He was then 41 years old, held a Ph.D. from Columbia where he had studied with Mark Van Doren, and already had won the Prix de Rome and two Guggenheim Fellowships. Yet, when a reporter appeared at the door of his office at the University of California in Berkeley on the first Monday in May, 1964, and asked what he thought of "the Pulitzer," he replied, "I think it's a good thing." Even when the reporter told him he had won the Pulitzer Prize in Poetry, he was sure a mistake had been made. But finally, when the congratulations came rolling in, he realized he had become a celebrity. "Editors who had never read my poems were willing to pay me a thousand dollars for a column of prose on any subject," he recalled. "The book that won the prize did a brisk sale, for poetry. The publishers of my subsequent books have not failed to print 'Winner of the Pulitzer Prize' on the jacket, so that prospective buyers will think that this is the book that won the prize." [39]

As was the case with music, the various Poetry Juries during the decade consisted of major poets and critics of poetry and did not vary greatly from accepted norms. From 1955 through 1961, Louis Untermeyer and Alfred Kreymborg picked a succession of winners without difficulty except for two instances in which they disagreed. Their unanimous choices were Wallace Stevens in 1955 for *Collected Poems*, Elizabeth Bishop in 1956 for *Poems—North and South*, Richard Wilbur in 1957 for *Things of This World*, W. D. Snodgrass in 1960 for *Heart's Needle*, and Phyllis McGinley in 1961 for *Times Three: Selected Verse from Three Decades*. The split verdicts came in 1958, when Untermeyer was successful in urging the selection of Robert Penn Warren for *Promises: Poems 1954–1956* over Richard Eberhart, and in 1959, when Kreymborg's candidate, Stanley Kunitz's *Selected Poems 1928–1958*, was chosen over e. e. cummings.

For the remainder of the decade, all selections were unanimous and supported by plentiful evidence in strong reports. For 1962 and 1963, a jury of Messrs. Untermeyer and Kunitz picked respectively Alan Dugan's first published volume, *Poems*, and William Carlos Williams' *Pictures from Breughel*, which actually was a tribute to Williams' long and fruitful career. The team of Kunitz and Wilbur picked Simpson's work without opposition for 1964 and settled on John Berryman's 77 *Dream Songs* for 1965.

There wasn't much here to ruffle the surface. What criticism there was came from poets and critics who pointed out, with varying degrees of indignation, that not all the celebrated figures in American verse had yet been recognized. To the juries yet to come, in consequence, this poetic problem became identical with those in the other literary prizes— whether the awards should go to eminent literary figures or to newcomers who really needed the encouragement.[40]

For the far-sighted, there was indeed scant satisfaction in a pat list of Pulitzer Prize winners of established reputation. To journalists, it didn't matter so much, for youngsters were always coming along to shatter precedent and knock holes in the established order. But where were the young O'Neills, Wilders, Warrens, Frosts, MacLeishes, and Coplands to be found now and encouraged with a major award? It was to this problem that the Advisory Board addressed itself as the Pulitzer Prizes approached their fiftieth anniversary.

7
The Prizes: Present and Future 1966–1974

1
After Fifty Years

For the guests of honor at the fiftieth anniversary dinner of the Pulitzer Prizes, there was a priceless ticket of admission. It was a Pulitzer Prize.

Almost two hundred of the three hundred surviving winners of the award attended. They came to the Plaza Hotel in New York from all parts of the land and abroad on the warm and pleasant evening of May 10, 1966—a reminder of the first Joseph Pulitzer's faith in the magical qualities of the number 10. On the dais were nineteen double winners of the Pulitzer Prize with President Kirk of Columbia, Chairman Pulitzer of the Advisory Board, and Maurice T. Moore, chairman of the university's Trustees. The speakers, strictly limited to five minutes each, were five Pulitzer Prize winners—Aaron Copland, Archibald MacLeish, Arthur M. Schlesinger Jr., James Reston, and Robert Penn Warren. The party, a once-in-a-lifetime event, was planned and executed under the direction of the Advisory Board and paid for entirely by savings from the annual income of the Pulitzer Prize Fund.

Governor Nelson A. Rockefeller of New York State came to extend his tribute to the guests in an informal way, as did Mayor John V. Lindsay of New York City. But for once they did not attract much attention, for this was a nostalgic evening—a celebration of the rewards of excellence. At one time, it had been planned to invite John Fitzgerald Kennedy to deliver the main address as the most eminent of Pulitzer Prize winners; instead, he was represented by his mother, Rose Kennedy, and his brother, Senator Robert Francis Kennedy, who smoked a big cigar and thoroughly enjoyed himself. The current President of the United States, Lyndon Baines Johnson, was so displeased by the opposition of Pulitzer's St. Louis *Post-Dispatch* to the Vietnam War that he would have nothing to do with the party at the Plaza.

It didn't bother anybody. Among the oldest of the surviving winners who attended were the 88-year-old novelist, Upton Sinclair; the 86-year-old historian, Lawrence Henry Gipson; and the 79-year-old biographer, Samuel Eliot Morison. The younger ones, such as Peter Arnett of the Associated Press, a 1966 winner, hurried in from the treacherous terrain of Vietnam.

The arts and literature were well represented. Elmer Rice, Richard Rodgers, and Marc Connelly were among the theatre group, while the novelists included Katharine Anne Porter, Herman Wouk, and John Hersey. Richard Hofstadter, Barbara Tuchman, Margaret Leech, and Paul Horgan were among the historians; Samuel Flagg Bemis, Merlo J. Pusey, and Ernest Samuels, the biographers. Douglas Moore drove halfway across the country to be with the composers, including William Schuman, Howard Hanson, and Robert Ward. And the poets were represented by a large delegation, among them Gwendolyn Brooks, Richard Eberhart, Stanley Kunitz, and Phyllis McGinley.

The journalists, of course, outnumbered all, and that would have pleased the first Pulitzer who sought in his own lifetime to elevate journalism, "regarding it as a noble profession and one of unequalled importance for its influence upon the minds and morals of the people." There were editors such as Ralph McGill, Lee Hills, Hodding Carter, William Randolph Hearst Jr., Vermont Connecticut Royster, and Virginius Dabney. The old war correspondents were there, headed by Homer Bigart, Harrison Salisbury, Relman Morin, and Don Whitehead. And the foreign correspondents also turned up, from Edgar Ansel Mowrer, who had been expelled from Germany before World War II, to A. M. Rosenthal, who had been expelled from postwar Poland. There were many who had made their reputations in national affairs, including Meriman Smith, Anthony Lewis, Vance Trimble, and Oscar Griffin.

And there were numerous investigative reporters, from Alvin Goldstein, who had broken the Loeb–Leopold case, to Edward R. Cony, who had uncovered one of the latest financial scandals. The cartoonists were amply represented, including Herblock, William H. Mauldin, and Vaughn Shoemaker. And the photographers were headed by the latest winner, Kyoichi Sawada, a combat lensman who was so soon to lose his life in Vietnam.

Many of the winners brought their wives or husbands. At the tables in the Plaza's ballroom and later during informal visits that went on for hours in and around the bar, they also met publishers and jurors, members of the Advisory Board and the Columbia Trustees, and selected members of the Columbia faculty. It was, in all, an overflow crowd of more than six hundred and fifty persons, a gathering that was unlikely to take place again under such auspices for the remainder of the century.

President Kirk set the tone for the evening with his congratulations to the winners, his thanks to the Advisory Board, and his tactful acknowledgment of fifty years of criticism: "Well, I am a believer in human fallibility but as I look over this magnificent audience tonight I am confident that each of approximately two hundred of our guests, plus their wives or husbands, knows that in at least one instance the judges exercised impeccable and flawless judgment."

For the present, he sought no elaborate justification of the awards and made no promises for the future, saying:

> The existence of these prizes, and the national prestige which they have achieved, is one more demonstration of the fact that man does not live by technology alone. No matter how great our devotion to the machines which now perform our menial daily tasks and which have opened up a glimpse, however banal, of the world's horizons to the humblest citizen, we know that in the inexorable judgment of time, a nation will be remembered not by its technical artifacts but by its cultural achievements. If recognition is not extended to those worthy of it, how shall these achievements be known?

The same mild, low-key estimates of achievement came from each of the five main speakers. For Aaron Copland, a "charter member of the revolutionary generation of the 20s," the message of the evening was that a new musical revolution was in progress from which he expected new art forms to emerge "in ways we never dreamed of." Robert Penn Warren, too, promised new life for the novel and took no stock in the frequent proclamations of its death. "Certainly the novel will change, as it discovers new insights and encounters new materials," he said. "But this is only to say that it will be renewed by the continuing challenge of life. The novel may even leave the printed page, if the age of Gutenberg is really over, but it could still be a novel."

To Arthur Meier Schlesinger Jr., the flowering of biography and the rise of intellectual history were the important new factors in his field. But as a historian, his was a tempered optimism, for he said: "A nation informed by a vivid understanding of the ironies of history is, I believe, best equipped to live with the temptations and tragedy of power; and, since we are condemned as a nation to the role of power, let a growing sense of history temper and civilize its use."

It remained for the poet and dramatist, Archibald MacLeish, to attempt an evaluation of the Pulitzer Prizes after 50 years—a modest but perceptive judgment: "What these awards have done for many in this indifferent world of ours—this particularly indifferent American world—is somehow to *include* them. We need, most of us, a sign of recognition . . . recognition that we exist. That we are there. Among those who went before and those who will come after."

Typically enough, it was only the journalist, James Reston, who brought the harsh realities of the night inside the Plaza's ballroom: the great American tragedy that was in the making in Vietnam, the ruthless outbreaks of civil disorder that were setting the nation's largest cities aflame. He said:

> The balance of political power in America is not running with the press or the Congress but with the President. He now has more power to make war, to tolerate or create the conditions that lead to war, than ever before. . . . We are going to have to use blunt instruments and have some tough characters around.
>
> Somewhere there is a line where the old skeptical, combative, publish-and-be-damned tradition of the past in our papers may converge with the new intelligence and the new duties and responsibilities of this rising and restless generation. I wish I knew how to find it, for it could help both the newspapers and the nation in

their present plight, and it could help us believe again, which in this age of tricks and techniques may be our greatest need.

Throughout the evening, curiously enough, there was no celebration of the accomplishments of the great ones of the past; indeed, the references to them were made only in passing. And yet, they were as much a part of the fiftieth year of the Pulitzer Prizes as the living, for without them it might not have come to pass. To those with a sense of history, the prizes were inextricably bound up with Eugene O'Neill and Henry Adams, Edith Wharton and Sinclair Lewis, Frederick J. Turner and Vernon Louis Parrington, Robert Frost and Edna St. Vincent Millay and Edwin Arlington Robinson, Carl Sandburg and Marianne Moore, Hemingway, Steinbeck, and Faulkner, Maxwell Anderson, Robert E. Sherwood, and Douglas Southall Freeman, Henry Watterson, Herbert Bayard Swope, and William Allen White—yes, and Nicholas Murray Butler and Frank Diehl Fackenthal. They were as much a part of the festive scene as if they had been present.[1]

All too soon, the night of celebration and self-congratulation was over. Before two more years had passed, Reston's fears for the future had been realized. In the aftermath of the 1968 Tet offensive in Vietnam, which cruelly revealed how groundless American hopes for victory had been, civil disorders reached fighting pitch in the nation's principal cities and revolution swept every major campus in the land.

At Columbia, a red flag flew from the Mathematics building and student strikers paralyzed the campus until the New York police, with a violent demonstration of sheer force and passion, smashed the antiwar movement at the university. The backlash from the Columbia faculty resulted in President Kirk's retirement and, at about the same time, the resignation of Dean Barrett from the journalism school in protest against the policies of the university's Trustees.

The work of the Pulitzer Prizes continued without significant change even though there was a full-fledged student strike at the time of the announcement of May 7, 1968, with a few flareups in the two succeeding years. The only discernible effect was to concentrate somewhat more responsibility in the administrator's office than had been customary in the past. President Andrew Wellington Cordier, the richly talented peacemaker, United Nations specialist, and dean of the School of International Affairs, was much too busy keeping Columbia going between 1968 and 1970 to do more than to maintain contact with the judging process and the Advisory Board.

With the inauguration in 1970 of President William James McGill, the former chancellor of the University of California at San Diego and the former chairman of Columbia's Psychology Department, the prizes once more became a major responsibility of the president's office—but with a difference. Both as an experienced administrator and as a psychologist, Dr. McGill very soon realized that a subtle shift of relationships was taking place between the Advisory Board and the university's Trustees. What had happened was that the essential conflict between the law and the press, the guarantees of a free press and a fair trial, which had gone on for much of the 1960s, inevitably had had an effect on the differing viewpoints of the Trustees and the Advisory Board. The lawyers among the Trustees, in particular, simply did not see some issues in the same light as the journalists of the Advisory Board and sought some way to express themselves on matters of importance.

Dr. McGill was not thrust into the middle of this developing argument without preparation. He was a born New Yorker with an acute political sense and he had had long experience at Columbia as a faculty member. At the time he became president, he was 48 years old—a stocky, cheerful figure with a crisp crew cut who came surging into Columbia's doleful and resentful academic community at a low point in the university's history. Not since an early president of King's College had been forced to flee to a British warship in New York harbor at the outbreak of the American revolution had there been so much ferment at Columbia against what was loosely, and often hatefully, described as the Establishment.

It was a heavy burden for the new president to bear, but he proved equal to it. By nature, he was a scholar—A.B. from Fordham in 1943, M.A. from Fordham in 1947, and Ph.D. from Harvard in 1953, with membership in Phi Beta Kappa and Sigma Xi tucked in for good measure. After joining the Columbia faculty in 1951, he developed gradually as an administrator; a year after becoming a professor of psychology in 1960, he assumed the chairmanship of the department. In 1965, he transferred to San Diego as a professor and became the chancellor there three years later at a time when Professor Herbert Marcuse was under violent attack by rightist elements. Despite divergent political sympathies, Dr.

McGill stood up for academic freedom in the case of the patron saint of the New Left—a factor that was much in his favor when he came to Columbia.

During the interim between President Kirk's departure and the beginning of President McGill's service, the Pulitzer Prize office in the Journalism Building had been operating with the friendly encouragement of both President Cordier and Professor Richard T. Baker, the acting dean of the journalism school. Beginning in 1970, it also had received the sympathetic support of the new dean, Elie Abel, former diplomatic correspondent of the National Broadcasting Company and a member of the foreign correspondents' team that brought the 1958 Pulitzer Prize for International Reporting to the New York *Times*. President McGill soon added to this his own pledge that the integrity of the prizes would be one of his major concerns and that he intended to see that the entire judging process would continue to be safeguarded. In his first conversation with me after his inauguration, he made it plain that he would not interfere in the selection of Pulitzer Prize winners and would tolerate no interference by anyone else.[2] It was a pledge that he kept at considerable cost to himself.

2
Press versus Government

Harrison E. Salisbury of the New York *Times* landed in Hanoi at dusk on December 23, 1966, after a short flight from Vientiane aboard an ancient aircraft of the International Control Commission. American bombers had raided the North Vietnamese capital as recently as December 13 and 14 and he was given a prompt escorted tour of the damage, which had included civilian areas as well as military targets. The articles that he wrote then, and the others that followed a number of additional tours behind enemy lines, created a furor when they were published in the New York *Times*.

Until Salisbury's departure from Hanoi on January 17, 1967, he dominated the war news. To the antiwar movement, he became a hero; to the crusty desk warriors at the Pentagon, little better than an enemy agent. He was accused of having given aid and comfort to North Vietnam. And his critics singled out in his dispatches some errors of fact which, they charged, were due to relying too much initially on North Vietnamese sources.

Salisbury was then 58 years old—a competent veteran who had come up through the ranks of the United Press following his graduation from the University of Minnesota, joined the New York *Times* in 1944 as its Moscow correspondent and won the 1955 Pulitzer Prize for foreign reporting. He was, of course, by no means the only correspondent on whom the American government did not look with favor. At least four other Pulitzer Prize winners were viewed with suspicion—David Halberstam and Malcolm Browne, the co-winners in 1964; Peter Arnett, the plucky New Zealander who had to put up with scandalous attacks on his integrity as an Associated Press correspondent in Saigon and won the 1966 award; and even the intrepid Kyoichi Sawada of UPI, the 1966 photography winner, whose pictures didn't include the kind of propaganda the American embassy desired.

What the government thought, however, obviously made no difference to the International Reporting Jury for 1967. The five editors, headed by Michael J. Ogden of the Providence *Journal-Bulletin*, had a lot of top-flight correspondence to consider in addition to Salisbury's. High on the list of exhibits were the work of John Hughes of the *Christian Science Monitor*, with his exclusive account of the frightful purge in Indonesia following an abortive Communist coup; Ward Just and Stanley Karnow of the Washington *Post*; Paul Grimes of the Philadelphia *Bulletin*; and Hugh A. Mulligan and Fred S. Hoffman of the Associated Press.

After two days of deliberation, the jury voted 4–1 for Salisbury and sent this verdict on to the Advisory Board: "Enterprise, world impact, and total significance outweigh some demerits in on-the-spot reporting."

When the Advisory Board met on April 14, 1967, at Arden House, Harriman, N.Y., Erwin D. Canham of the *Christian Science Monitor* was absent in South Africa and the New York *Times*'s executive editor, Turner Catledge, was not in the conference room during the debate over the foreign correspondence prize. With Chairman Pulitzer presiding and ten other members present, a majority of six was required to recommend an award and it was apparent from the outset that the vote would be close.

Those who opposed Salisbury argued that he was not entitled to special credit for having been the first reporter from the United States to be invited to Hanoi, that he had failed to give the sources of casualty figures in his initial articles, and that there were other reportorial deficiencies in his work. The case for Salisbury, as it was argued before the Board, emphasized the reporter's accomplishments in forcing the Defense Department to concede that civilian casualties were inevitable in the wide-ranging American bombing campaign and in bringing to the American public a firsthand view of North Vietnam at war.

Despite Chairman Pulitzer's championship of Salisbury's cause, the vote went against the *Times* correspondent, 6–5, and in favor of John Hughes of the *Christian Science Monitor*. But next morning, when I was asked to give the Advisory Board a fuller report of the work of the jury, which I obtained by telephone from its chairman, Mike Ogden, the debate was renewed. On a motion for reconsideration of the previous day's action, a secret ballot was taken. The result remained 6–5 in favor of Hughes and against Salisbury.

When the decision went to the university's Trustees on the afternoon of May 1, the issue was debated for more than an hour and the prize announcement accordingly was held up until 4:29 P.M. Between the unexpected delay and the publication in the St. Louis *Post-Dispatch* of an authoritative account of the Advisory Board meeting, the reporters had all they could handle and raised no questions—with me, at least—about the Trustees' action.

It soon became known, however, that much the same split had occurred among the Trustees as the one that had developed within the Advisory Board. While Arthur Ochs Sulzberger of the New York *Times* did not participate in the Trustees' debate, the case for Salisbury was put so strongly by his advocates that the Trustees for a time thought of reversing the Advisory Board even though the university's counsel had repeatedly warned them that they had no authority to do so. Eventually, under the influence of the chairman, Maurice T. Moore, the Trustees by a close vote upheld the Advisory Board's decision.

Salisbury said only: "I put the judgment of the editors of the *Times* ahead of any other criteria." And Catledge held his peace until, several years later in his autobiography, he accused some of his Board colleagues of making their decision "on political rather than journalistic grounds." The charge was promptly denied.

When the 36-year-old, Welsh-born Hughes was informed by the Associated Press in Hong Kong that he had won the Pulitzer Prize, his response was, "Give me a minute to think. I'm sort of stunned." He recovered soon enough, going on to become the *Monitor*'s managing editor in a short time and, in 1970, its editor.

There was still another journalism jury reversal in 1967 that kicked up a fuss. The Advisory Board turned down a National Reporting Jury recommendation in favor of the columnists, Drew Pearson and Jack Anderson, for their disclosures of the financial dealings of Senator Thomas J. Dodd of Connecticut, and selected instead a *Wall Street Journal* exposé by Stanley W. Penn and Monroe Karmin of links between American crime and gambling in the Bahamas. When there was a public protest by one of the jurors, Paul Sann of the New York *Post*, the Board members were not in the least contrite. As the Board's position was put by Newbold Noyes Jr., editor of the Washington *Evening Star*, "The juries are not supposed to be awarding prizes. They're supposed to whittle down the entries from, say, about one hundred to maybe five or six. They are not requested to give us their preference, but sometimes they do." [3]

No one can say exactly what combination of circumstances created the forces that turned public opinion in the United States against the Vietnam War. But certainly, an aggressive, 33-year-old free-lance reporter, Seymour M. Hersh, had something to do with it when he exposed the My Lai tragedy and at least a part of the evidence that led to the conviction of Lieut. William L. Calley Jr. for his part in the slaughter of South Vietnamese villagers there. If the critical public reaction in the United States after the Tet offensive of 1968 obliged President Johnson to retire, the shock of My Lai at the very least put the succeeding Nixon administration on the defensive.

The Chicago-born Hersh, a graduate of the University of Chicago and a former Pentagon correspondent of the Associated Press, had heard about My Lai from former members of Calley's army unit. With a $2,000 grant from a small foundation, the free lancer interviewed other participants during 40,000 miles of travel in this country. He put together his evidence carefully and gave his series to a struggling new syndicate, the Dispatch News Service, which was operated by a friend and neighbor, 24-year-old David Obst. Hersh's first My Lai article was run by thirty-six newspapers, including the St. Louis *Post-Dispatch*, which put it on Page 1 on November 13, 1969. As he poured out his horror tale, the tone of public opinion changed from incredulity to shock. Obst, despite his youth and inexperience, knew enough to get his nomination of Hersh before the International Reporting Jury promptly, with the result that it unanimously recommended him for the 1970 Pulitzer Prize in that category. Its four members, under the chairmanship of Carl T. Rowan, the columnist, wrote in their report:

> In the face of disbelief and disinterest on the part of many news-papers, and operating with limited resources, Hersh showed initiative, enterprise, and perseverance to break the My Lai story—a story that shook the nation and had vast international repercussions.
>
> In pursuing his story to the point that the topmost officials in the United States, South Vietnam, Great Britain, and other countries became publicly and directly involved, Hersh's performance met the high journalistic standards for which Pulitzer recognition is traditionally granted.

No member of the Advisory Board even raised a question about Hersh's right to the award. The recommendation was voted unanimously, and without discussion, and ratified without dissent by the University Trustees. It was a measure of the change that had come about in American public opinion in the three years since the uproar about Salisbury's first-hand reports of American air raid damage to Hanoi.[4]

There were other worthy performances during those three years, both in the United States and in South Vietnam, that resulted in Pulitzer Prize awards. William Tuohy of the Los Angeles *Times* won the 1969 International Reporting prize for his Vietnam war correspondence. John Fetterman of the Louisville *Times and Courier-Journal* received a local reporting prize in the same year for his poignant account of the homecoming and burial of an American soldier who had been killed in Vietnam. Edward T. Adams of the Associated Press and Toshio Sakai of United Press International won awards for their combat pictures. But none of them carried the impact of Hersh's disclosures.

Not until May 4, 1970, when National Guardsmen fired into a crowd of student antiwar demonstrators at Kent State University, was there another war-related event that created so much public revulsion. The swift and dramatic reporting of the events at Kent State that day by the Akron *Beacon Journal* brought the newspaper the 1971 Pulitzer Prize for General Local Reporting. And John Paul Filo, a 21-year-old photographer for the *Valley Daily News & Daily Dispatch*, of Tarentum, Pa., that same day snapped the Pulitzer Prize-winning spot news photograph of the following year—a weeping girl, her arms outstretched, kneeling beside the body of a student who had just been shot to death. Just four years later, as a testimonial to the swiftly changing spirit of the times, a photography prize was won by Slava Veder of the AP for his emotion-charged picture of the reunion of a returning American prisoner of war with his family.

The historically combative relationships between a free press and a representative government in a democratic society extended far beyond the Vietnam War in the trying period beginning with 1966. In the coverage of race relations, civil liberties, wrongdoing in high places, and such new areas as the protection of the ecology, the leaders of the press—both large and small—often found themselves in conflict with the government.

It was no long-haired, radical newcomer but one of the oldest and most respected newspaper editors in the land, John Shively Knight, who played a leading role as a government critic. He frequently attacked the secretive conduct of the Vietnam War and also wrote vigorous dissents against the erratic course of governmental economic policies. He was one of the first to predict disaster when President Johnson escalated the conflict in Vietnam. And as early as 1967, he warned:

"The nation is over-committed, our resources strained, the treasury bare, inflation out of hand, and each of us must be prepared for an uncertain future of war, higher taxes, and personal sacrifices for an indeterminate period."

For his editorial leadership, as well as for his entire career as the guiding spirit of the Knight Newspapers, John Knight at 74 years of age received the 1968 Pulitzer Prize for Editorial Writing. The award was one of three in that year for the Knight group, the other two going to the Detroit *Free Press* for its coverage of the Detroit riots of 1967 and to Eugene Gray Payne, editorial cartoonist of the Charlotte *Observer*.[5]

It was a far cry from Knight's sophisticated criticism of an errant government and an unpopular war to Marse Henry Watterson's patriotic yawps against the Kaiser that had brought him the first wartime Pulitzer Prize for Editorial Writing. It was also a measure of the change that had come to the Pulitzer Prizes themselves. In place of the stolid conservatives of other days, a number of liberal-minded editorial writers who were highly critical of government now were winning prizes, among them Robert Lasch of the St. Louis *Post-Dispatch* in 1966, Eugene Patterson of the Atlanta *Constitution* in 1967, Paul Greenberg of the Pine Bluff (Ark.) *Commercial* in 1969, and Philip L. Geyelin of the Washington *Post* in 1970. And in the new Commentary category, beginning in 1970, liberal columnists won top honors—Marquis Childs of the St. Louis *Post-Dispatch* in 1970; William A. Caldwell of the *Record*, Hackensack, N.J., in 1971; Mike Royko of the Chicago *Daily News* in 1972; and David S. Broder of the Washington *Post* in 1973.

The development of the racial crisis in the great cities of America had a lot to do with the way both juries and Advisory Board members now looked at the course of events. No thoughtful American, certainly no concerned American journalist, could fail to be affected by such outstanding feats as the Los Angeles *Times*'s coverage of the Watts riots in 1965, Haynes Johnson's reporting of the 1965 crisis centered about Selma, Ala., and the Detroit *Free Press*'s coverage of the 1967 riots there, all of which won Pulitzer Prizes in the following years.

In pictorial journalism, too, the racial conflict registered a powerful impact on the Pulitzer Prizes, particularly after the adoption of separate awards for news and feature photography in 1968. In that year, Moneta Sleet Jr., of *Ebony* magazine, won the first feature picture award with his funeral photograph, taken as a member of a press pool, of the widow and child of the Rev. Dr. Martin Luther King Jr., the assassinated black leader. The mark of violent racial strife also was imprinted on the awards by Jack R. Thornell's AP picture of the shooting of James Meredith in Mississippi, the 1967 photo winner, and Steve Starr's picture, also for AP, of armed black students marching from a Cornell University building, the 1970 winner.

It was scarcely an accident, in so highly charged an atmosphere, that the American press began to react sharply to violations of civil liberties. Local Investigative Reporting prizes were won in 1966 by John A. Frasca of the Tampa *Tribune* for helping to free a man who had been wrongfully convicted of robbery, and in 1967 by Gene Miller of the Miami *Herald* for developing the evidence that freed two persons who had been wrongfully convicted of murder. In 1968, the Riverside (Calif.) *Press-Enterprise* was awarded the public service gold medal for exposing a corrupt court's handling of the property of an Indian tribe. Two years later, Harold Eugene Martin of the Montgomery *Advertiser* was awarded the

Local Investigative Reporting prize for uncovering a commercial scheme through which Alabama prisoners had been used for drug experiments. And in 1972, Richard Cooper and John Machacek of the Rochester (N.Y.) *Times-Union* won the prize for General Local Reporting with their disclosure that hostages in the Attica prison riots had been accidentally killed by police bullets and not, as State officials had said, by convicts who had slashed throats.

Pictorial journalism made its contribution in this field, too. In 1969, Dallas Kinney of the Palm Beach *Post* attacked Florida's harsh migrant labor camps in a superb portfolio, "Migration to Misery," which won the 1970 Feature Photography award. In the following year, Jack Dykinga of the Chicago *Sun-Times* won the same prize with a portfolio showing conditions in a state school for the retarded.

One of the most heartening developments in this immense revival of concern over civil liberties was the manner in which small city dailies reacted, often in defiance of prevailing public sentiment. Horance G. Davis Jr., of the Gainesville (Fla.) *Sun* won the 1971 Editorial Writing prize for his editorials in support of the peaceful desegregation of Florida schools. In the next year, the same prize went to John Strohmeyer of the Bethlehem (Pa.) *Globe-Times* for an admirable campaign to reduce racial tensions there. Such editors provided leadership in their communities when local officials were fearful and sat on their hands.

Inevitably, the spirit of the times also brought about a vast increase in campaigns for better government. In every year from 1966 on, at least one award was granted for outstanding work in this field, and sometimes two or three.

Newspapers, editorial writers, and investigative reporters continued to exercise the "watchdog" function of the press with telling effect in local government. The Los Angeles *Times* won the public service gold medal in 1969 for exposing wrongdoing within the Los Angeles City Government Commission. In the next year, *Newsday*, in Garden City, N.Y., captured the gold medal for its three-year inquiry into the secret land deals of crooked politicians in eastern Long Island. In 1971, William Jones of the Chicago *Tribune* took the Local Investigative Reporting award for uncovering collusion between police and some of Chicago's largest private ambulance companies to restrict service in low income areas. The Boston *Globe* in 1972 won the same award, bestowed on a reportorial team headed by Timothy Leland, for bringing to light widespread corruption in Somerville, Mass. And in Pittsfield, Mass., Roger Linscott of the *Berkshire Eagle* won the 1973 Editorial Writing prize for successfully opposing an unnecessary highway project.

Twice in 1974, the "watchdogs" of the press carried off Pulitzer Prizes. *Newsday* won its third public service gold medal for a monumental series on the illegal narcotics traffic and governmental failures to halt it. And F. Gilman Spencer of the *Trentonian* in Trenton, N.J., won the Editorial Writing award for his courageous campaign to focus public opinion on the scandals in New Jersey's state government.

The courts came in for special attention during this period. Beginning with the Warren Commission's attack on the news media for their conduct at the time of the Kennedy assassination, both judges and bar committees had been highly critical of the press and more sensitive than usual to editorial comment. The formation of voluntary press-bar committees and the drafting of voluntary codes of conduct had helped lessen tensions without doing much to solve the central issue of free press and fair trial. Nor did all this activity deter the press from continuing its surveillance of the courts and those who were nominated to high judicial posts.

Pulitzer Prizes had been won in the past by reporters who produced the evidence that sent judges to jail. But now, any Pulitzer award in this area was almost certain to kick up a fuss among judges and lawyers. Nevertheless, they kept coming. In 1966 the Boston *Globe* won the public service gold medal for its successful campaign to prevent the confirmation of Francis X. Morrissey, an ally of the Kennedys, as a Federal District Judge in Massachusetts. Two years later, Howard James of the *Christian Science Monitor* won a National Reporting prize for his critical series, "Crisis in the Courts." And in 1969, when President Nixon nominated Judge Clement F. Haynesworth Jr. to the United States Supreme Court, William J. Eaton of the Chicago *Daily News* made such damaging disclosures of his background that he could not be confirmed. Eaton won the 1970 National Reporting award for his work.

The defense of the nation's natural resources also brought Pulitzer Prizes to crusading newspapers and reporters. In 1967, the Louisville *Courier-Journal* and the Milwaukee *Journal* won public service gold medals in this field, the former for standing against the Kentucky strip mining industry and the latter for its fight against water pollution in

Wisconsin. Robert Cahn of the *Christian Science Monitor* was awarded the 1969 National Reporting prize for his campaign to protect the national parks. And in 1971, the Winston-Salem (N.C.) *Journal and Sentinel* took the public service gold medal for blocking a strip mining operation in the Carolina hill country.

There were prize-winning campaigns in other areas of public interest, as well. Nathan K. (Nick) Kotz of the Des Moines *Register* and Minneapolis *Tribune* won a National Reporting prize in 1968 for his campaign against unsanitary conditions among some meat packers, which helped in the enactment of the Federal Wholesome Meat Act of 1967. Albert L. Delugach and Denny Walsh of the St. Louis *Globe-Democrat* were awarded the Local Investigative Reporting prize for 1969 for their campaign against fraud within the St. Louis Steamfitters Union, Local 562. The Chicago *Tribune* received a local reporting award in 1973 for a widespread drive against voting frauds that helped insure clean elections in 1972. And, in one of the most unusual campaigns in Pulitzer annals, the weekly Sun Newspapers of Omaha won the 1973 local investigative prize for establishing the vastness of the financial resources of Boys Town, Neb., leading to reforms in its annual charitable solicitations.

The Pulitzer Prize juries and the Advisory Board also were prompt in recognizing new and effective approaches to the more familiar aspects of the news, particularly in the reporting of crime. J. Anthony Lukas of the New York *Times* won a 1968 local reporting prize for his painstaking reconstruction of the double life of a socially prominent girl who had been murdered in New York's East Village with a drifter. Three years later, a National Reporting award went to Lucinda Franks and Thomas Powers of United Press International for the same kind of a documentary on the life and death of a girl revolutionary, entitled, "The Making of a Terrorist." For his coverage of a mountain manhunt for a deranged sniper who had terrorized his community, Robert V. Cox of the Chambersburg (Pa.) *Public Opinion* won a local reporting prize in 1967. And in 1970, Thomas Fitzpatrick of the Chicago *Sun-Times* also received a local reporting award for his story about a violent night in Chicago with a gang of youthful radicals, members of the Students for a Democratic Society. Four years later, two *Sun-Times* reporters, Arthur M. Petacque and Hugh F. Hough, won a local reporting prize for uncovering new evidence that led to the reopening of efforts to solve the 1966 murder of Valerie Percy. A New York *Daily News* reporter, William Sherman, uncovered a multi-million dollar swindle in the administration of Medicaid in New York City. And a California free lance photographer, Anthony K. Roberts, won a photography prize with his pictures of the slaying of an alleged kidnaper in Hollywood—the first news photos he had ever taken.

New ground was broken in foreign correspondence, too, despite the national preoccupation with Vietnam. After more than fifty years of Pulitzer Prizes, an award finally went in 1968 to a correspondent for his coverage of the ever-troubled Middle East—Alfred Friendly of the Washington *Post*, who won for his reporting of the six-day war of 1967. The first award for correspondence from South Africa went to Jimmie Lee Hoagland of the Washington *Post* in 1971. The coverage of the sixteen-day Indo-Pakistan War of 1971 resulted in awards in 1972 for Peter R. Kann of the *Wall Street Journal* in International Reporting and Horst Faas and Michel Laurent of the AP for News Photography. And the first prize for correspondence from China was voted in 1973 to Max Frankel of the New York *Times* for his extraordinary eight days and nights of solo coverage of President Nixon's China visit of 1972—a feat that included many columns of news plus his innovative "Reporter's Notebook." It was an effort that ranked with the finest of the prizes for foreign correspondence in Pulitzer annals. Innovative foreign correspondence, also for the New York *Times*, brought the 1974 prize to Hedrick Smith, chief of the newspaper's Moscow bureau.

The new prize for criticism was a long overdue recognition of the growing importance of cultural affairs as a special field of journalism. Only the wealthiest and most powerful newspapers, which included most of the large ones, could afford to maintain their own critics in such varied fields as books and drama, movies and television, art and architecture, and music. It was scarcely a surprise, therefore, that the initial prizes for criticism went to Ada Louise Huxtable of the New York *Times* in 1970 for her architectural criticism, Harold C. Schonberg of the New York *Times* in 1971 for his music criticism, Frank Peters Jr. of the St. Louis *Post-Dispatch* in 1972 for his music criticism, Ron Powers of the Chicago *Sun-Times* in 1973 for his television criticism, and Emily Genauer of Newsday Syndicate in 1974 for her art criticism. What jurors and Advisory Board members hoped for was that the prizes for such critics would encourage younger newspaper people to go in for critical writing in years to come.

The Board had its troubles meanwhile with one of the oldest of the Pulitzer Prizes—the award for cartooning. It had been passed in 1960, 1965, and 1973, a sure sign of difficulty, and more often than not the Board now failed to cite a single outstanding cartoon but based its recommendation on the entire exhibit of a cartoonist.

When Cartoon Juries came up with a good choice, the Board usually accepted it. This was the case with Don Wright of the Miami *News* in 1966, Patrick B. Oliphant of the Denver *Post* in 1967, Eugene Gray Payne of the Charlotte *Observer* in 1968, John Fischetti of the Chicago *Daily News* in 1969, Thomas F. Darcy of *Newsday* in 1970, Paul Conrad of the Los Angeles *Times* in 1971, his second award, Jeffrey K. Mac-Nelly of the Richmond *News–Leader* in 1972, and Paul Szep of the Boston *Globe* in 1974. But when juries refused to act, as happened in 1973, the Board also accepted the negative verdict.[6]

However much the Board was concerned over the slump in editorial cartooning, or the encouragement of critical writing for the press, these were strictly subsidiary interests. The spreading conflict between press and government was the central issue. And the Board, in common with the university's Trustees, could not help but be affected by it. For in 1972 and 1973, the turn of events became crucial. This was no longer a matter of a correspondent going behind enemy lines and embarrassing the government. Now, the confrontation was between the government and two of the greatest newspapers in the land.

The publication of the Pentagon Papers was the issue that led to the first direct test of strength between press and government in modern times—a conflict that had the strongest repercussions in the judging of the Pulitzer Prizes for 1972. Most of the documents, which consisted of forty-seven book-length volumes totaling more than 2.5 million words, had been obtained by the New York *Times* through the efforts of Neil Sheehan, who had become its Pentagon correspondent after leaving UPI. The top secret project, commissioned in mid-1967 by the then Secretary of Defense, Robert Strange McNamara, was a detailed record of American involvement in Vietnam, Laos, and Cambodia from the end of World War II until May, 1968.

After the *Times* had published the third of nine articles in this series on June 15, 1971, the Federal Court in the Southern District of New York granted the government a temporary order restraining publication. In the government's view, further publication would have done "immediate and irreparable harm" to national security.

It was not until June 30, when the United States Supreme Court rejected the government's position, that publication was resumed. The high court, in an unsigned ruling, voted 6–3 in favor of the New York *Times* and the Washington *Post*, which had begun its own publication of the documents on June 19. It held that "any system of prior restraints of expression comes to this court bearing a heavy presumption against its constitutionality," that the government had to show justification for such suppression, and that it had failed to do so.

The *Times*, alone among the newspapers that had published the Pentagon Papers in whole or in part, entered two exhibits in the judging of the Pulitzer Prizes for 1972. One consisted of more than fifty full-size pages, the text of its nine articles plus supporting materials, which was nominated in the public service category. Another was the basis for the nomination of Neil Sheehan in both the National and International Reporting categories.

When the Pulitzer Prize Journalism Juries met at Columbia University on March 7–8–9, 1972, the chairmen held a preliminary session, as was customary, to pass on matters of classification. Without the participation of Miss Charlotte Curtis of the New York *Times*, who headed the Cartooning Jury, the chairmen consolidated the *Times*'s Pentagon exhibits in the Public Service category. After examining eighty exhibits for two days, the Public Service Jury, under the chairmanship of Stuart Awbrey, editor and publisher of the Hutchinson (Kansas) *News*, unanimously reached the following verdict on March 9:

"A gold medal is recommended for the New York *Times* and for Neil Sheehan for the remarkable journalistic feat which has come to be known as the Pentagon Papers. . . . It is fortuitous that the Pulitzer Prizes can recognize the accomplishments of both the newspaper and of a persistent, courageous reporter, and thus can reaffirm to the American people that the press continues its devotion to their right to know, a basic bulwark in our democratic society."

When the Advisory Board met on April 13, with Chairman Pulitzer presiding, eight other members were in the *World* Room with him to vote on the public service award—Benjamin C. Bradlee, executive editor, Washington *Post;* Wallace Carroll, editor and publisher, Winston-Salem (N.C.) *Journal & Sentinel;* John Cowles Jr., president and editorial chairman, Minneapolis *Star & Tribune;* Price Day, editor-in-chief, Baltimore *Sun;* William B. Dickinson, executive editor, Philadelphia *Bulletin;* Sylvan Meyer, editor, Miami *News;* Newbold Noyes Jr., editor, Washington *Evening Star;* and Vermont Royster, contributing editor, *Wall Street Journal.* Those whose exhibits were before the Board in that category (there were six finalists in all) left the room as usual—James Reston of the New York *Times,* Lee Hills, president and executive editor, Knight Newspapers, Inc., and Robert J. Donovan, associate editor and columnist, Los Angeles *Times.* President McGill did not attend the meeting but was host to the Board at the annual luncheon at the President's House, 60 Morningside Drive, New York.

Once all other considerations were put aside, the Board found itself in complete agreement on the major point at issue—that the Pentagon Papers should have been published. It therefore voted unanimously to recommend the award of the public service gold medal to the New York *Times* "for the publication of the Pentagon Papers." It was, in effect, recognition of the dominant responsibility of the *Times's* publisher, Arthur Ochs Sulzberger, in the decision to disclose the hitherto secret Pentagon file. The question of the source of the papers, and Neil Sheehan's role in obtaining them for the *Times,* was made secondary. Members of the Board also pointed out informally that, while individuals had been mentioned in the past in connection with the public service prize, none had ever shared the gold medal because it was restricted to newspapers under the terms of the Plan of Award.

When the National Reporting Jury's recommendations for Jack Anderson were discussed, however, the troublesome question of sources cropped up again. The columnist's sources to secret government policy-making documents during the Indo-Pakistan War of 1971 bothered some members of the Board a good deal more than anything in the Pentagon Papers case. However, a five-member jury, headed by George N. Gill, managing editor of the Louisville *Courier-Journal,* already had recommended the Anderson Papers as "an excellent example of investigative reporting into the manner in which foreign policy decisions are made by the government." The Board, by a decisive though not unanimous vote, accepted the jury's verdict and recommended Anderson for the National Reporting award.

President McGill was now committed to take the recommendations for the New York *Times* and Anderson before the university's Trustees, together with the balance of the Board's 1972 prize slate. But the president's position, in this respect, was unique, for he had done something that none of his predecessors had ever undertaken. At his annual luncheon for the Journalism Jurors on March 8 at Faculty House, Dr. McGill had assured them he would support the decisions upon which they and the Advisory Board agreed and see that they were enacted by the Trustees. He repeated this pledge to safeguard the integrity of the judging process before the Advisory Board at his April 13 luncheon.

With the reorganization of the university's governance following President Kirk's retirement, a new factor had entered into the final action on the Pulitzer Prizes. For much of the history of the awards, only the Trustees had acted on the Advisory Board's slate. But since 1970, with the creation of the University Senate, its Faculty-Student Committee on Prizes had been represented at a meeting of the Trustees' executive committee preparatory to the final session of the Trustees. As matters turned out in 1972, it was a Columbia faculty member who first questioned the New York *Times* and Anderson awards because both involved the publication of secret government documents.

The Trustees included a number of distinguished lawyers and one jurist, Federal Judge Fredrick van Pelt Bryan, who took no part in the discussion and voting because the Pentagon Papers case had been an issue in the Federal courts. Another abstainer was the *Times*'s publisher, Arthur Ochs Sulzberger, a Columbia Trustee just as his father had been. The remainder of the twenty-two–member Board of Trustees decided to explore their Pulitzer Prize problem at a special meeting on Sunday, April 30, at the Columbia University Club. From 8 to 11:15 P.M., they argued the case for and against the two major recommended awards and twice voted them down. However, on each occasion, President McGill insisted on reconsideration and the Trustees turned to other means of showing their displeasure. The solution which they finally agreed upon was to disassociate themselves from both major awards by pointing out that the primary responsibility rested with the Advisory Board under the terms of the will of the first Joseph Pulitzer. All the other awards were approved.

The draft statement, worked over by the lawyers on the Board of Trustees and the university's counsel, John Wheeler, was completed next morning, given to me by President McGill and included in the press packets assembled by John Hastings, the university's public relations director. The Trustees, at their regular meeting beginning at 3 P.M., took no further action and the Pulitzer Prize announcement was made at 4:10 P.M.[7]

This was the text of their statement:

> By the terms of the Will of Joseph Pulitzer and the agreement between the Pulitzer executors and the University, under which the Pulitzer Prizes are awarded, the Trustees of Columbia University may act only on the recommendations of the Advisory Board on the Pulitzer Prizes. While the Trustees may accept or reject a recommendation, they may not substitute an award of their own choice. The Advisory Board on the Pulitzer Prizes, however, may accept or reject the recommendations of the Pulitzer juries, appointed by the Advisory Board, or substitute the Advisory Board's own recommendations.

> The Advisory Board is comprised of eminent journalists. It has the major role in all phases of the selection process, and its judgments are to be accorded great weight by the Trustees. In the Trustees' deliberations on the 1972 Pulitzer Prizes, a majority of them had reservations about the timeliness and suitability of certain of the journalism awards. Had the selections been those of the Trustees alone, certain of the recipients would not have been chosen. The decision to accept all of the Advisory Board's recommendations this year was arrived at, in large part, in consideration of the prescribed and historic role of the Advisory Board.

There was no doubt, of course, that the prizes for the New York *Times* and Anderson were the ones singled out for adverse comment, as newspaper and wire service dispatches quickly reported. But it didn't disturb Sulzberger, who accepted the *Times*'s thirty-eighth Pulitzer Prize—and its third public service gold medal—with these words: "All of us on the *Times* are deeply proud of this award for the Pentagon Papers. It is important to us today and it will be important to us always."

Anderson, too, was pleased, saying: "The Pulitzer Prize is the Academy Award of journalism, so I have to be both pleased and proud to receive it." [8]

A. M. Rosenthal, the *Times*'s managing editor and himself a Pulitzer Prize winner, called the whole experience of the Pentagon Papers a "roller coaster of emotion." He wrote in retrospect:

As the time drew near for the Pulitzer Prize announcements, I think every one of us felt that this was a special thing, special even for the Pulitzer Prizes. If we won it, we felt, it would be not only an endorsement for the *Times* and an honor for the *Times*, but an endorsement and an honor for the traditions of newspapering that brought about the publication of the Pentagon Papers. . . .

Until the end, I had believed and hoped that if Neil [Sheehan] did not get it himself, he would be mentioned by name in the citation for the Public Service Award but it didn't work out that way. When the announcement came through about the *Times* winning it, there was great jubilation, mixed with a certain sense of disappointment that Neil had not been mentioned.[9]

It was the second time Sheehan had lost a Pulitzer Prize that most of his colleagues thought he had earned, the other having been the 1964 International Reporting award. In any event, he received numerous other prizes, including the annual distinguished service award of the Columbia Graduate School of Journalism for 1972.

While much of the comment on the 1972 Pulitzer Prizes was laudatory, except for a few editorial sideswipes at the Trustees, the White House was pained by the outcome. Much had been made by White House sources of statements by Dr. Daniel Ellsberg, former Pentagon official, that he had been the source of the Pentagon Papers; however, neither the New York *Times* nor Sheehan had ever made any disclosure as to the source of their documents. One of the most outspoken White House critics, Patrick J. Buchanan, a speech writer for President Nixon and a Columbia journalism graduate of 1962, called the prizes for the New York *Times* and Anderson "appalling" and "atrocious."

It wasn't the first critical reaction against the Pulitzer Prizes by the Nixon administration. In 1970, Vice President Spiro Agnew, in the wake of the rejection of Judge G. Harrold Carswell for the United States Supreme Court, had said: "Pulitzer Prizes are not won by exposing the evils of Communism as readily as by discrediting American elective officials. Tons and tons of innuendoes designed to smear officials are printed every day."

It remained for Clayton Fritchey to rebut the Agnew charge in his column in the Washington *Evening Star*. Fritchey pointed out that more than a score of Pulitzer Prizes had been won for the exposure of Communist activities in the United States and abroad and that other awards had gone to numerous newspapers and reporters for digging up the evidence that helped convict public officials who had betrayed their trust. He wrote:

"No journalist can look back over these prizes for the last fifty years, as I have just done, without some pride in his profession. It is hard for me to imagine what democracy would be like in the United States if the press shied off from investigating official wrongdoing." [10]

It was a curtain-raiser to Watergate and associated scandals, including the forced resignation of Vice President Agnew after he had confessed to fraud in his income tax returns.

Until the Washington *Post* decided to investigate a break-in at Democratic National Headquarters in the Watergate complex in Washington on June 17, 1972, it didn't seem to be much of a story. The White House called it a "third-rate burglary attempt" and wouldn't even comment on it. Much of official Washington shrugged it off as a bad political joke, a mere caper.

But the *Post* and two of its young and energetic investigative reporters, Carl Bernstein and Robert Woodward, took the case seriously. For the five masked men who were arrested at Watergate at 2:30 A.M. with a lot of wire tapping equipment had the closest ties to the highest figures in the Republican Party. The *Post* disclosed the White House's involvement on June 20 by showing that a long-time CIA operative, E. Howard Hunt Jr., had links to both the suspects and to President Nixon's special counsel, Charles W. Colson. The *Post* also traced the culpability of a former CIA and FBI agent, James W. McCord, who had been among those arrested and who was shown to have links to the Attorney General's office.

Soon, the *Post* was able to establish that a $100,000 contribution to President Nixon's re-election campaign had been "laundered" by Mexican banks and found its way into the bank account of one of the Watergate suspects. It was the first indication that a cover-up campaign was under way. Former Attorney General John N. Mitchell, who had headed the Nixon re-election campaign, precipitately resigned. As the summer went on, the *Post* uncovered a widespread campaign of political sabotage against the Democrats that had been financed by secretly contributed Republican funds.

It made sensational reading, but the *Post*'s investigation did not stir up the nation-wide concern that its editors had expected. Few other papers even bothered with the Watergate inquiry or, if they did, gave it half-hearted treatment. As for the news magazines and television, they ignored Watergate with the exception of a handful of reporters almost as lonely as Bernstein and Woodward for the *Post*.

Two other reporters, Robert Boyd and Clark Hoyt of the Knight Newspapers in Washington, accounted for another major political development that summer. Acting on a tip, they produced documented evidence that Senator Thomas Eagleton of Missouri, the Democratic candidate for Vice President, had a history of psychiatric therapy that he had concealed from the head of the Democratic ticket, Senator George McGovern of South Dakota. When the reporters told McGovern about the story in advance of publication, he arranged for a press conference in which Eagleton admitted his past medical record and stressed his complete recovery. Yet, despite the scoop that failed, the Missouri senator soon retired from the Democratic ticket.

Somehow, the Eagleton incident overshadowed the Washington *Post*'s continuing Watergate inquiry. The Democrats did little with it. And just before election day, the White House press secretary, Ronald L. Ziegler, accused the *Post* and its reporters of "shabby journalism" and "a blatant effort at character assassination." It didn't make any difference to the *Post*. Bernstein and Woodward remained on the job.

By January 1973 the long campaign at last began to make headway. Five of those involved in the break-in pleaded guilty. Two others went to trial. The first White House official who had been linked with Watergate lost his job. The first resignation came from the Committee to Re-Elect the President. And a Senate inquiry began under the direction of Senator Sam J. Ervin Jr. of North Carolina.

By March 8 and 9, 1973, the Watergate case was beginning to crack but the Pulitzer Prize Journalism Juries failed to give their top recommendation either to the Washington *Post* or its investigative reporters, Bernstein and Woodward. The committee of jury chairmen shifted the exhibit for the reporters out of National Reporting and consolidated it with the newspaper's own exhibit in Public Service. And when the Public Service Jury reported its recommendations, the Washington *Post* was third behind the entries of the Chicago *Tribune* and the New York *Times* in other campaigns.[11]

Then came the big break. On March 21, James W. McCord wrote a letter to Federal Judge John J. Sirica disclosing the cover-up effort. Two days later, Judge Sirica gave stiff sentences to the convicted conspirators but implied he would be lenient if they talked. On April 5, McCord implicated former Attorney General Mitchell, John W. Dean III, counsel to the President, and Jeb Stuart Magruder, former deputy campaign director of the Committee to Re-Elect the President. Next, Dean implicated the President's two highest aides in the White House, H. R. Haldeman and John D. Ehrlichman. The President himself, pale and shaken, announced that all members of his staff would cooperate with the Ervin Committee but, at the same time, he cast the blanket of executive privilege about them.

Now, there was no question about the importance of Watergate and the big black headlines portending a national crisis were flaring across the land. The Washington *Post*, Bernstein, and Woodward no longer were alone. And the paper's publisher, Katharine Graham, no longer had to wonder out loud why the other papers weren't digging into the case. Everybody was on it once the cover-up had blown sky high, even the news magazines and television.

It was in this charged atmosphere that the Advisory Board met at Columbia on April 12. The same membership as in 1972 met around the black oval table in the *World* Room under the lighted Statue of Liberty stained glass window, only this time Messrs. Bradlee and Reston were out of the room and Messrs. Cowles and McGill were absent. Within a few minutes after Chairman Pulitzer had declared himself in favor of the Washington *Post* for the public service gold medal, all nine Board members in the room agreed to reverse the Public Service Jury.

The only question that remained was what to do about the Chicago *Tribune*'s fine campaign against vote frauds, which was resolved by voting it a local reporting award in place of another recommended Washington *Post* entry. A second prize was voted to David S. Broder of the Washington *Post*, who had been the choice of the Commentary Jury. And in National Reporting, Robert Boyd and Clark Hoyt were rewarded with a prize, which they shared, for their work in the Eagleton case.[12]

On April 30, a week before the meeting of the university Trustees, Haldeman, Ehrlichman, and Dean resigned their White House posts, Attorney General Richard G. Kleindienst was replaced by Elliot L. Richardson, who had been Secretary of Defense, and President Nixon was obliged to go on television to defend himself. At about the same time, the trial of Dr. Daniel Ellsberg in Los Angeles over the Pentagon Papers case collapsed when it became known that two convicted Watergate conspirators had broken into the office of his psychiatrist on September 3–4, 1971. It was the first of the "White House horrors," a term coined by former Attorney General Mitchell, to come to public attention. There would be others.

One additional development occurred in the Watergate scandal before the Trustees met. Ron Ziegler, the White House press secretary, apologized on May 1 to the Washington *Post* and its reporters, Bernstein and Woodward, for having accused them of "shabby journalism." Ziegler admitted mistakes had been made and added, "I was overenthusiastic." [13]

When the Trustees met on May 7, therefore, the Washington *Post*'s major role in breaking the Watergate conspiracy had been fully acknowledged, even by its worst enemies. The Trustees, with little discussion, approved all prizes recommended by the Advisory Board and put before them by President McGill, thus causing the list of awards to be released before 3:30 P.M.

Because the gold medal for the Washington *Post* had been so widely anticipated, it was no surprise. But the outpouring of gratification over the award was enormous, nevertheless, and it was not confined to the press by any means. There was satisfaction in both houses of Congress, in the academic community and even from the usually mute public at large. As for the Public Service jurors, all wrote to me, in response to a note explaining the reason for their reversal, that they would have acted exactly as the Advisory Board did under the circumstances.

Howard Simons, the *Post*'s managing editor and a 1952 graduate of Columbia's journalism school, expressed the newspaper's gratification, saying: "The gold medal brings singular honor to this newspaper and especially to its young and hard-digging reporters, Bob Woodward and Carl Bernstein. Coverage of the Watergate affair was a newspaper-wide effort and receiving the Pulitzer Prize is a newspaper-wide joy. Receiving a second Pulitzer Prize—for the commentary of David Broder who is the best political reporter in the country—makes it a double joy."

Whatever criticism there was of the award centered on the failure to mention the roles of Woodward and Bernstein in the citation, which read simply that the Public Service gold medal had been won by the newspaper "for its investigation of the Watergate case." Having been out of the room during the debate on the Public Service category, James Reston had not known of the exclusion of the two reporters until afterward but he soon asked for reconsideration, by mail or telegraphic ballot if necessary. However, as had been the case with Neil Sheehan in the Pentagon Papers story, the terms of the award for public service still barred joint recognition for individual gold medals. Woodward and Bernstein won the Sigma Delta Chi, Drew Pearson, Heywood Broun, and George Polk awards for their Watergate investigation. And their publisher, Mrs. Graham, received the annual award of Columbia's journalism school. As for the executive editor, Ben Bradlee, he shared in the freedom of information award bestowed upon the newspaper by the Associated Press Managing Editors.[14]

For the 29-year-old Bernstein, a copy boy for the Washington *Evening Star* at 16 and a *Post* reporter at 22, and for Woodward, a 30-year-old Yale graduate and Navy veteran who had joined the *Post* in 1971, there was no time either for jubilation or afterthought. The Watergate scandal became so dominant in the news that both reporters and editors were working harder than ever. For the trail of guilt led directly to the White House, as the struggle over the Watergate tapes made clear. And by firing the Watergate special prosecutor, Archibald Cox, and thereby forcing the resignation of Attorney General Richardson, President Nixon himself became the central issue in a case that would reverberate in history.

In 1974, Jack White of the Providence *Journal-Bulletin* won a National Reporting prize for his disclosure that the President had paid minimal Federal income taxes in 1970 and 1971. James R. Polk of the Washington *Star-News* received a co-equal national award for his account of alleged irregularities in the financing of the campaign to re-elect the President in 1972. And some of the most trenchant pieces in the winning exhibit of Edwin A. Roberts Jr., of the *National Observer*, the laureate in Distinguished Commentary, dealt with the Watergate scandal.

Scant wonder, then, that President Nixon felt obliged to take a crack at the Pulitzer Prizes before the National Association of Broadcasters in Houston on March 20, 1974, saying that "people don't win Pulitzer Prizes by being for, they usually win them by being against." That, however, had not been the case with such winners as John Fitzgerald Kennedy, Dean Acheson, General Charles A. Lindbergh, and many a public-spirited newspaper. Considering the whole range of Pulitzer Prizes over six decades, they were scarcely so simple to categorize.

For those who feared that the press now was accumulating too much power by challenging the authority and the integrity of the Presidency itself, there was a ready answer. It had been given long ago in these trenchant terms:

"Another lesson I want to impress upon you all is that we shall not increase the power of the Executive any further; if this is to be a government of the people, for the people, by the people, it is a crime to put into the hands of the President such powers as no Monarch, no King, or Emperor ever possessed. He has too much power already." [15]

The author was the first Joseph Pulitzer and his view was expressed to Frank Cobb of the New York *World* in a letter of March 8, 1909, four days after the indictment of the newspaper on charges that grew out of its attack on President Theodore Roosevelt in the Panama Canal case. Pulitzer won his fight against the power of the Presidency when the indictment was dismissed as groundless. It was fitting that the prize bearing his name would continue to encourage the press long after his death to stand firmly against the sins of arbitrary government.

3
Modern Fiction and Its Problems

"It was, on the whole, an undistinguished year for fiction, a complaint we fear is becoming recurrent," wrote John Barkham and Maxwell Geismar in their Fiction Jury report for 1966, the fiftieth year of the Pulitzer Prizes.

What they were looking for was a single work that "stood out as a discovery or beacon," but they did not find it. Turning aside from the usual long list of novels that had been submitted, they discovered their compensation for the year in the *Collected Stories* of the venerable Katherine Anne Porter. For her "chaste and controlled style, her subtle sensibilities, and the power of her moments of revelation," they recommended her for the 1966 Fiction Prize. The Advisory Board, which had not included among its number many admirers of the modern American novel in recent years, promptly agreed with them. It was compensation of a kind for the gentle, 75-year-old Miss Porter, whose career as a writer had spanned forty years and whose *Ship of Fools* had failed to win the Pulitzer

Prize in 1963. But it was also a commentary on the state of the American
novel when a book of short stories was selected for the fiction award in
the fiftieth year of the Pulitzer Prizes.

The 1967 Fiction Jury had somewhat better news for the novel, although it had to disregard the Pulitzer preference for a book about the
American scene to do it. The unanimous choice of Elizabeth Janeway,
Melvin Maddocks of the *Christian Science Monitor* and Maxwell Geismar
was Bernard Malamud's novel about Jewish persecution in Czarist Russia, *The Fixer*. Geismar, the chairman, wrote:

"The jury recognized the fact that in an age notable for novels of self-
pity, Mr. Malamud has taken the raw material of still another victim–or
an 'anti-hero,'–and turned him into a heroic figure: twentieth century
and authentic. With a kind of wry passion, Malamud denies the modern
parlyzing fear that personal goodness cannot survive the evil of history;
and in doing so brings to the American novel a new and tough sense of
possibility."

Malamud, who was teaching at Harvard at the time, didn't believe the
first reports that he had won the Pulitzer Prize for *The Fixer*. He had
thought the novel was ineligible because of its foreign setting. But even
after his publisher reassured him that he was, indeed, a Pulitzer Prize
winner, he remained unimpressed. He had, as he pointed out in a brief
commentary some years later, already won two National Book Awards.

"From the point of view of literary merit," he wrote, "I think more of
the National Book Award. I am, however, aware that the Pulitzer Prize
is the better known award and received a good deal of publicity.

"I imagine I would value the Prize a good deal more if more books of
literary merit were chosen. Turning down Saul Bellow and Eudora
Welty after their books were nominated by the Advisory Committee
diminished the importance of the Pulitzer Prize for me."

If the decision of the Board in favor of Malamud failed to kindle
any critical bonfires, the split vote of the 1968 jury against William
Styron's *The Confessions of Nat Turner* was even more of a disappointment.
John K. Hutchens was for the Styron book, the story of an ill-fated
revolt of Negro slaves in Virginia in 1831, but Maxwell Geismar and
Melvin Maddocks were for Isaac Bashevis Singer's *The Manor*, a family
novel of the Polish "shtetls" of a century ago. While Geismar and Maddocks conceded that Hutchens' opinion was dominent among American

critics for that year, they also pointed to strong minority criticism of Styron's use of historical material and his central view of slavery. However, they could not persuade the Board to accept their choice and Styron's book won the 1968 Fiction Prize. It created no excitement, however, for the first great wave of its popularity already had subsided.[16]

An entirely new Fiction Jury consisting of Edmund Fuller, Raymond Walters Jr. of the New York *Times,* and P. Albert Duhamel of Boston University picked a real surprise for 1969—N. Scott Momaday's *House Made of Dawn.* Momaday, a 35-year-old Indian poet and teacher at the Santa Barbara campus of the University of California, was so little known that some of the senior editors at Harper & Row, his publisher, didn't immediately recall the novel when it won the Pulitzer Prize. It was the tale of the tragedy of an Indian who returned to his reservation after World War II and could no longer cope with his old life.

Momaday refused to believe the news at first. And the New York *Times* reported, "If the 35-year-old author was surprised, the publishing community seemed stunned at the selection of the relatively unknown author for one of the most coveted literary prizes in the country."

The reasoning of the jury, which was accepted by the Advisory Board, put the case for Momaday in this way:

"Our first choice is N. Scott Momaday's *House Made of Dawn* because of its, in the words of one of the members of the jury, 'eloquence and intensity of feeling, its freshness of vision and subject, its immediacy of theme,' and because an award to its author might be considered as a recognition of 'the arrival on the American literary scene of a matured, sophisticated literary artist from the original Americans.' "

The Board's membership wasn't exactly ecstatic but it went along with *House Made of Dawn.* Some years later, in a general criticism of all the novels that have won Pulitzer Prizes, John Leonard of the New York *Times* called Momaday's work "safe," which put it fairly high in his catalogue of disapproval. The jurors had thought, mistakenly in Leonard's view, that they were breaking new ground.[17]

The 1970 jury report began on an even more forbidding note. John Barkham, John Brooks of the *New Yorker,* and W. G. Rogers, the AP's book reviewer for many years, observed with chilling candor, "It cannot be said that fiction in 1969 recovered from the ground it has lost to nonfiction in recent years. The general standard of the entries impressed us as good but far from epochal, technically competent, with themes and styles suitably varied. All too many, however, substituted sophistication for vitality."

It was scarcely the kind of an estimate that was calculated to send the Advisory Board into ecstacies; historically, such estimates had frequently resulted in jury reversals or skipped awards and 1970 was no exception. The Board viewed with distinct reserve the list of novels that included John Cheever's *Bullet Park* and Joyce Carol Oates's, *Them*, the latter being the jury's choice. Of *Them*, the report said: "In the words of one juror, *Them* is a combination of American dream and American nightmare. Miss Oates has Dreiser's understanding of our society and much of his strength but she writes better."

The Board was much more interested in the report's estimate of Jean Stafford's *Collected Stories*, one of two collections that were favorably discussed, the other being Peter Taylor's. Of Miss Stafford, the report said: "Her range in subject, scene, and mood is remarkable, and her mastery of the short story form is everywhere manifest. She is wonderfully skilled in digging out drama where others would see only drabness. She builds to strong climaxes with the littlest of steps. In short, a gifted writer, secure in her technique, who prefers the miniature to the mural."

In the estimate of the Board's consultative committee and the full membership as well, it was no contest. The 1970 Pulitzer Prize for Fiction went to Jean Stafford.[18]

For 1971, the Fiction Jury ran headlong into the mire of indecision. P. Albert Duhamel, Elizabeth Janeway, and Lon Tinkle of the Dallas *News* couldn't decide on a "single, unanimous, persuasive choice," as they put it, and submitted an alphabetical list of three novels: *Losing Battles*, by Eudora Welty, *Mr. Sammler's Planet*, by Saul Bellow, and *The Wheel of Love* by Joyce Carol Oates. No particular enthusiasm was expressed for any of the three. The Board seriously discussed recognizing Eudora Welty for her lifelong achievements as a leading American writer, but was put off by the Jury's estimate of *Losing Battles* as "lacking in the freshness of some of her earlier work." The award was regretfully passed.

Thus, during a six-year period, the Pulitzer Prize in Fiction went to two accomplished short story writers, two older novelists for moderately successful works, and one newcomer, and was passed once for lack of a solid jury recommendation. It wasn't a particularly noteworthy assessment of the American novel. For 1972, a Fiction Jury consisting of Jean Stafford, John Barkham, and Maurice Dolbier of the Providence *Journal-Bulletin* also began on a low note in their report:

> It may have been a bad year for the economy, but writers continued to write and publishers to publish, and on the whole it was a good if not great year for books.
>
> Fiction, however, fared indifferently, and your jury was disappointed that the overall level of the entries submitted was no higher than it was. The omens had been for an exceptional year with new novels by major writers like John Updike, Mary McCarthy, Bernard Malamud, Robert Penn Warren, Joyce Carol Oates, Wallace Stegner, and Walker Percy—an impressive constellation of luminaries. But the result was a Barmecide feast. In the words of one juror, Maurice Dolbier, "A lot of the big ambitious ones fell on their big ambitious faces."

In that category the jury put *Rabbit Redux* by John Updike, Bernard Malamud's *The Tenants*, and Joyce Carol Oates's *Wonderland*. They found much to admire, however, in *The Autobiography of Miss Jane Pittman* by Ernest Gaines, *Love in the Ruins* by Walker Percy, and *Angle of Repose* by Wallace Stegner, the latter being their unanimous choice for the 1972 fiction award. The report said of the Stegner novel:

"Gentility and frontier exigence inform, and grate on, each other in this saga of the pioneer West, whose real setting is the human soul. A novel in the true American grain built around a memorable woman character, *Angle of Repose* impressed the jury as a solidly conceived, handsomely crafted work of fiction which fulfilled in manner and matter the requirements for a Pulitzer Prize."

It was enough to convince the Board and give the 1972 fiction award to the 63-year-old Stegner, a Stanford professor and a leading American writer for many years. But for the second year in a row, the *New York Times Book Review* blasted the Pulitzer Prize in Fiction with John Leonard proclaiming the Stegner book to be "forthright, yes; and morally uplifting; and middlebrow" and, of course, "safe." The *Book Review*'s Christmas summary that year had featured Updike's *Rabbit Redux*.

Stegner had mixed feelings about the whole business, as might have been expected. He wrote later: "Living the width of a continent away from what calls itself headquarters, I don't suppose the Pulitzer Prize is going to change my reputation substantially. After all, there have been some fairly odd choices over the last forty or fifty years. Maybe I'm one of them. If I am, I guess I'm not going to fret too much, or spend a lot of time trying to persuade unconvinced critics that the judges were right and they wrong. Je m'en fiche. But I can tell you that the prize gave this provincial novelist a great thrill. I value that prize, deserved or otherwise." [19]

For 1973, at last, the Pulitzer Prize in Fiction went to Eudora Welty and this time there was no quibbling, either from the Pulitzer Prize organization or the critics. Happily, the announcement of the award coincided with a state-wide celebration of her career proclaimed by the governor of Mississippi. It was, in effect, a Welty festival. Herman Kogan, chairman of the Fiction Jury and editor of the Chicago *Sun-Times Books*, conceded that while he was taken by Miss Welty's *The Optimist's Daughter* as a "narrative gem," he kept her at the top of his list because she had never received a Pulitzer Prize although she was "surely one of our finest writers." The other two jurors, Edmund Fuller and Professor Guy Davenport of the University of Kentucky, agreed with his position although they did not regard *The Optimist's Daughter* quite as highly as he did. As Fuller put it, "An award to this book would have to be considered fully as much an award to her cumulative body of work." In Davenport's opinion, she was "probably the best writer of fiction in the USA today." The Advisory Board showed no hesitation and this time had no regrets.

But in 1974, the Board was again in the unhappy situation of choosing between no award and the Fiction Jury's selection of Thomas Pynchon's *Gravity's Rainbow*, which the Board found to be turgid, confused, and overwritten. Benjamin DeMott, Elizabeth Hardwick, and Alfred Kazin, the jurors, protested the Advisory Board's decision to pass the award in strong terms and stood by their report, in which they had written, "No work of fiction in 1973 begins to compare in scale, originality, and sustained intellectual interest with Mr. Pynchon's work."

So, there appeared to be no end to the problems of selecting a distinguished work of American fiction for a Pulitzer Prize. Aside from the basic questions of determining artistic merit and literary values, the sheer volume of books that swamped the fiction judges every year was a complicating factor. As Guy Davenport put it, too much trash was submitted by publishers.

Taking the long view, Herman Kogan wrote:

> The problem of whether to limit the number of entries has
> always vexed jurors and the problem is obviously difficult to solve
> satisfactorily. From my experience as an editor of a book review
> supplement I know well the vagaries and stupidities of many book
> publishers who try to atone for their failure to promote or advertise
> books by sending them off to the Pulitzer Prize offices. Some au-
> thors are easily assuaged, and even impressed, by this kind of cop-
> out and, indeed, I know of several who never fail to mention, in
> biographical data, that their books were 'nominated' for a Pulitzer
> Prize.
>
> I don't know if the Advisory Board or the Trustees of Columbia
> University will want to take action to limit entries—what a howl
> would arise from the publishers!—but I pass along the suggestion
> that some discussion be considered of ways to keep jurors from
> having to wade through so many obviously worthless works to get
> to the good ones.[20]

Although the Advisory Board had long recognized the seriousness of
that particular problem, it was reluctant to change the democratic nature
of the system of entries in the mid-1970s. It was probable that the judges
would have to resort to much stronger action before any different system
could be seriously considered. But even if such technical changes eventually did come about, the day would never dawn when critics would be
satisfied. For any major award in American fiction, particularly the Pulitzer, was a veritable lightning rod that projected nakedly toward the
storm clouds that hovered over the nation's literature in the declining
years of the twentieth century. If it was no guarantee of perpetual safety,
it was at the very least a warning against complacency and it was well
worth watching for signs of danger.

4
The Tough Theater

There was no disguising the decline of the American theater during the
first part of the 1970s. Beginning in 1966, the Pulitzer Prize in Drama
was passed no less than four times on the doleful recommendation of a
succession of knowledgeable juries. While a few new theaters were built,

many more old ones were torn down or remained dark. Broadway itself became a sleazy honky-tonk thoroughfare, infested with pornography shops and petty thievery and loitering prostitutes. For the commuting audiences and those from farther out of town, who had helped sustain the theater through hard times in the past, the fear of muggers and other assorted forms of big city violence was a deterrent to pleasurable theater-going. Worse still, the new playwrights of quality were lamentably few in number and their kind of theater did not always please the older generation and the talkative theater parties, the two groups that were best able to face up to soaring ticket prices.

Still, there was a continual argument that, even in a poor season, a Drama Prize should be awarded. Brendan Gill of the *New Yorker*, a faithful and talented jury chairman, once exclaimed: "I do not approve of NOT giving a prize." [21] But many of his colleagues differed. In the 1966 report, Professor Maurice Valency wrote for himself and his colleagues, Walter Kerr and Elliot Norton:

> It is our opinion that the artistic standards which have so far governed the award of the Pulitzer Drama Prize should on no account be compromised by our natural desire to make, rather than to withhold, the award in a relatively poor season. Unlike the Critics' Prize which is conferred, ostensibly, on "the best play of the year," the Pulitzer award is made in accordance with a continuing conception of excellence in the theatre. This cannot, and should not, vary with the quality of the plays presented in any given season, and it is our opinion that the standard should be upheld regardless of all other considerations relative to the function of the award. It is, accordingly, our unanimous recommendation that no award be made in the drama for the current year. [22]

The point of view was interesting, but not necessarily valid for all time. Each jury had made up its own mind over the years on the basis of circumstances; as for the Advisory Board, it had never made any pronouncement on the subject and was unlikely to do so. Its position was reserved, also depending on circumstances. But for 1966, the jury's recommendation against an award was accepted.

Edward Albee's *A Delicate Balance* was the winner of the 1967 drama award, but he nearly rejected it. The 39-year-old playwright was still upset by the refusal of the Advisory Board to honor *Who's Afraid of Virginia Woolf?* In accepting the prize, he said that it "is in danger of losing its position of honor and could, forseeably, cease to be an honor at all." True to the position first taken by President Butler in the Sinclair Lewis case, neither Columbia nor the Advisory Board took any formal notice of Albee's protest. Once the prize had been voted, that was it.

Conceivably, Albee might not have received the award at all if the prize had not been passed so many times. *A Delicate Balance*, his ninth play, by no means became a roaring success like *Who's Afraid of Virginia Woolf?* It had opened at the Martin Beck Theatre on September 22, 1966, and closed January 14, 1967, long before the drama report for that year was handed in on April 1. Walter Kerr in the New York *Times* had called it a play that was offered on "an elegantly lacquered empty platter." It wasn't typically Albee; nor was it a part of the tough new theater that was taking shape mostly off Broadway. Actually, it was rather mild—a middle-aged Eastern couple in a typically American suburb being upset by the advent of another couple who were pursued by nameless fears.

Elliot Norton and Richard Watts Jr., two of the jurors, were for it "as the only play of American origin this season that was worthy of recommendation." But the chairman, Maurice Valency, was not impressed, although he wrote that his "lack of enthusiasm was not so serious as to preclude a unanimous decision in accordance with the judgment of the majority." The Board accepted the verdict, which was announced May 1.

Albee voiced his displeasure two days later at a news conference in the Cherry Lane Theatre, during which he attacked the Advisory Board for not accepting the judgment of its expert juries. But finally, he said, he would keep the prize for three reasons:

"First, because if I were to refuse it out of hand, I wouldn't feel as free to criticize it as I do accepting it. Second, because I don't wish to embarrass the other recipients this year by seeming to suggest that they follow my lead. And finally, because while the Pulitzer Prize is an honor in decline, it is still an honor, a considerable one."

John Mason Brown, one of the two jurors who had been overruled in the case of *Who's Afraid of Virginia Woolf?*, took an understandable pleasure in Albee's award. "We were right then and we are right now," he said. "Edward Albee is a demonstrated career talent—as opposed to the fly-by-night boys—and I found *A Delicate Balance* the most fascinating new American play of the season." [23]

For 1968, once again, there was no award. Walter Kerr, the chairman, wrote that he, Richard Watts Jr. of the New York *Post*, and Henry Hewes of the *Saturday Review* had found nothing worthy of a prize. The new American plays, he wrote, were "middling affairs," including such works as *The Price* by Arthur Miller, *The Prime of Miss Jean Brodie* by Jay Allen and *Plaza Suite* by Neil Simon. David Merrick and Richard Barr, both leading producers, criticized the repeated failure to award Pulitzer Prizes for Drama but the jury was very firm about its point of view, particularly after being upheld by the Advisory Board. Watts summed it up for his colleagues: "There was nothing good enough among the American plays to deserve a prize."

The prize winner for 1969, Howard Sackler's *The Great White Hope*, based in large part on the story of the first black heavyweight boxing champion, Jack Johnson, gave recognition to a new playwright and a form of respectability to the development of the tough new theatre. While Brendan Gill, Richard Watts Jr., and Walter Kerr voted unanimously for the violent and realistic drama, their choice was not easily arrived at. The season had been a good one, for a change, with such attractions as *1776*, *Ceremonies in Dark Old Men*, and *The Boys in the Band*. Kerr concluded for the jury:

"*The Great White Hope* is not only American and topical in its subject matter, it is an ambitious play of considerable actual size. In the end it seemed more substantial and more secure than any of the other candidates."

The Advisory Board went along with the jury. When the prize was announced on May 5, the 39-year-old, New York-born Sackler said, "It's probably the greatest honor that can be conferred." He had worked for four years on the play, his first success.[24]

The tough drama really came into its own in 1970 with the Pulitzer Prize award to Charles Gordone's *No Place To Be Somebody*. It was the first time in Pulitzer annals that a black playwright had been honored and it was also the first time that an off-Broadway production had won the prize. Nothing like it had ever been seen—or heard—by the few members of the Advisory Board who had a chance to go to a battered old ex-neighborhood movie house on upper Broadway, the Promenade Theatre, between the time the drama report was written on March 27 and the Board meeting on April 9. The play was what is known to the trade as a "saloon drama" but it had nothing in common with so celebrated an example as Eugene O'Neill's *The Iceman Cometh*. The 45-year-old Gordone, a veteran actor, had called his play a "black-black comedy" dealing with racial conflict, gangsterism, and sexual relations. The action was searing, the language fairly burned the ears. But Messrs. Kerr, Watts, and Gill, the jurors, would hear of nothing else for the prize.

As Kerr put it in the 1970 report, the jurors discussed various alternatives in what had admittedly been a poor season, but none gathered more than a single vote. "Once *No Place To Be Somebody* was proposed, however, agreement came very quickly," he wrote. "I might stress that this is in no sense a compromise choice. We all admire the play very much and feel it may be one of our more just and fortunate selections. The facts that it originated off-Broadway and is the work of a black playwright played no part in the determination though these things do add some interest after the fact."

Joseph Pulitzer Jr., the Advisory Board's chairman, journeyed to the Promenade Theatre as soon as he came to New York, saw the play on a night when about fifty persons were in the audience, and came away satisfied that it was a suitable prize winner. At least one of the other Board members who went to the Promenade was not as enthusiastic. When the Drama Prize was discussed at the April 9 meeting, therefore, the chairman became the chief advocate for *No Place To Be Somebody*.

"The language is pretty bad," one member observed. "Are you sure you are really for this play?"

"I really am," the chairman responded.

"Well," was the resigned reply, "it's your prize."

This was at least one instance in which the Board honored the unacknowledged practice under which members did not vote for or against a play they had not seen or a book they had not read. With the approval of the Board and later the university Trustees, *No Place To Be Somebody* turned out to be a very real surprise selection. It received almost unanimous critical acclaim, a source of pleasure and satisfaction to a new playwright.[25]

In 1971, the team of Kerr, Watts, and Gill chose another new playwright, Paul Zindel, for his awkwardly named off-Broadway play, *The Effect of Gamma Rays on Man-in-the-Moon Marigolds*. It dealt with the courage of a teen-age girl, living with a slatternly mother and an epileptic sister, and her faith in humanity despite her own difficult life. The title was based on her school essay on experiments with the effect of atomic energy on plant life.

Zindel, a 35-year-old writer from Staten Island, N.Y., had competition from another new playwright, John Guare, for his *The House of Blue Leaves*. Kerr wrote for the jury: "If we chose the Zindel play, more conventional in style, it was because it is a more perfectly formed work, always under control. *Blue Leaves* is still a bit ragged in certain ways, whereas *Marigolds* is firmly shaped, clearly accomplished." This one was easier for the Board to take, being somewhat less than tough and based on a more sympathetic view of human nature. Although compassion wasn't in much favor in the early 1970s, *Marigolds* came through as a reasonably popular winner of the Pulitzer Prize in Drama.

Once again, in 1972, the award was passed by vote of the jury, consisting of Messrs. Kerr and Watts and Judith Crist, the critic of *Cue* Magazine and the former editor of the arts for the New York *Herald Tribune*. Kerr wrote in the jury's report that various possibilities had been considered, including *Moonchildren, Twigs, Follies*, and the antiwar play, *Sticks and Bones*. He added: "No one of these, however, could muster more than one reasonably firm vote and *Sticks and Bones* received none. Even those on the committee who were willing to live with a choice were unwilling to try to press that choice on the others, reflecting the obvious slackness of the present theatrical situation. Reluctantly but probably sensibly, we agreed to pass for this year."

The report was dated April 5, but before it even reached the Pulitzer Prize office Joseph Papp, producer of *Sticks and Bones*, was demanding a meeting with President McGill to protest its verdict against his play. It was the only time in Pulitzer Prize annals that any producer had tried to intervene in the judging process, but the attempt had no effect on the outcome. Papp was politely informed that the prize would be determined in the normal manner and it was. The Advisory Board accepted the jury's recommendation and passed the award for the fifth time in a decade and the eleventh time in the history of the Pulitzer Prizes.[26]

The 1973 winner, Jason Miller's *That Championship Season*, honored still another new playwright and a drama that had started off-Broadway as a production of Joseph Papp's New York Shakespeare Festival. Miller's success was one of those improbable romances that always bring new life to the downtrodden in the theatre—the story of a 34-year-old, New York-born playwright whose play had been rejected for a Broadway production but who had won through anyway because of sheer talent and persistence.

That Championship Season was the story of the fateful reunion of a championship high school basketball team with an old and demanding coach, who had shaped and twisted their lives through his win-at-any-cost philosophy. It was tough theater of a different kind, a drama of decaying character and frustrating hopes, but it drew enthusiastic audiences during its long run, first at the Public Theatre downtown and beginning September 14, 1972, at the Booth Theatre.

Brendan Gill, the Drama Jury chairman for 1973, wrote to the Advisory Board: "It has turned out, pleasantly enough, that my colleagues George Oppenheimer and Elliot Norton and I were in immediate enthusiastic agreement on the play that should be given the Pulitzer—*That Championship Season*, by Jason Miller. It then turned out that we were not in agreement about any second choice, although *The River Niger* would have gained two of the three votes. No play seemed to us to come within voting reach of these two; but *That Championship Season* was clearly much the favorite over *The River Niger*."

It was the favorite, too, when the Advisory Board met and carried off the Pulitzer Prize in Drama without a struggle.[27]

For 1974, a jury consisting of Clive Barnes of the New York *Times*, Glenna Syse of the Chicago *Sun-Times*, and Douglas Watt of the New York *Daily News* recommended no award and the Board agreed.

It had long been contended, mainly by critics and editors outside New York, that what was produced on Broadway and off Broadway could no longer be considered a true measurement of the American theater. Boston, Chicago, Los Angeles, Minneapolis, Dallas, and Washington, D.C., all claimed now, to a greater or lesser degree, to be representative of the true American drama. However, no new American play that opened elsewhere had failed thus far to reach Broadway and win consideration for a Pulitzer Prize. In fact, *The Great White Hope* had not been considered during its original run at the Arena Stage in Washington, D.C., but had become a popular Pulitzer Prize winner once it was performed on Broadway.

The Advisory Board was all for branching out as soon as it became necessary—and feasible—to do so. But in the mid-1970s, the Drama Prize was still anchored to New York City although out-of-town critics more and more participated in making judgments on winners for the benefit of the Advisory Board.

5
Historians, Biographers, and Journalists

In a lighthearted reflection on the downbeat trends of the modern age, James Reston once observed that things were getting a little mixed up in the writing business. "The journalists," he said, "have been winning Pulitzer Prizes for history, and the historians have been winning prizes for journalism, and it has even been suggested occasionally that we [the journalists] have been winning prizes for what was really fiction." [28] He could have added, as well, that novelists of the first rank were masquerading as reporters by presenting books of non-fiction in fictional guise.

This blurring of the lines was almost a regular feature of the Pulitzer Prizes in History, Biography, and General Non-Fiction from 1966 on. With a few major exceptions, scholars and statesmen joined the journalists in the development of subjects that were deemed relevant, an academic code word of the period, to the topsy-turvy nature of the times. And the journalists, without so much as a by-your-leave, draped themselves in the trappings of scholarship on occasion and presented consequential biographies and current histories. The Advisory Board became so accustomed to this continual switching of literary chairs that relatively few jury verdicts were overturned, and then only for what seemed to be compelling reasons.

The biographers, whatever their literary derivation, concentrated for the most part on figures of current interest. The line began with *A Thousand Days*, the 1966 winner, in which the historian, Professor Arthur Meier Schlesinger Jr., produced a notable work of *grand reportage* about the Kennedy administration, in which he had been a leading figure. The jury of Professor Henry Steele Commager and Barbara Tuchman split, with Commager favoring Schlesinger's book and Mrs. Tuchman urging the selection of Van Wyck Brooks's *Autobiography*. While Commager conceded that Schlesinger's work was more history than biography and that it lacked perspective, he said the author had rendered "a signal service to all of us in providing us with a record so full, so rich, so illuminating." The weakness of the Brooks work, admittedly, was that it had all been published before in separate volumes. The Board, therefore, voted Schlesinger his second Pulitzer Prize for *A Thousand Days*.[29]

For the rest of the biography list in that period, there were only minor arguments or none at all. Among the dominant works that won prizes were George F. Kennan's *Memoirs, 1925–1950*, in 1968, Professor T. Harry Williams' *Huey Long* in 1970, Joseph P. Lash's *Eleanor and Franklin* in 1972, and W. A. Swanberg's *Luce and His Empire* in 1973. The Mark Twain revival prompted Justin Kaplan to write a new biography of the great American humorist, *Mr. Clemens and Mark Twain*, the 1967 winner, and Professor Lawrance Thompson crowned his life's work with his Pulitzer Prize-winning *Robert Frost: The Years of Triumph*, in 1971. There was one surprise victor, Benjamin Lawrence Reid's biography of a wealthy art patron and collector, *The Man From New York: John Quinn and His Friends*, in 1969. And there was general satisfaction over the 1974 selection, Louis Sheaffer's *O'Neill, Son and Artist*, the second volume of his biography of the dramatist, which had taken sixteen years to produce.

The juries were studded with Pulitzer Prize winners, including Professor Ernest Samuels in 1967, 1968 and 1972; Professor Walter Jackson Bate in 1968 and 1971; Dean Roy F. Nichols in 1967; Arthur Walworth in 1970; and Barbara Tuchman in 1971 in addition to her previous service in 1966. Among those who served on these juries from the academic community were Dr. Lyman H. Butterfield of Harvard, 1968; Dr. Julian P. Boyd of Princeton, 1969; Professor Louis Morton of Dartmouth, 1969; President Mason W. Gross of Rutgers, 1970; Professor Boyd C. Shafer of Macalester College, 1972; and Professors W. Frank Craven of Princeton and Charles M. Wiltse of Dartmouth, both 1973. John Barkham was the chairman in 1967, 1969, 1971, and 1973, while Dr. Butterfield headed the jury in 1968, Norman Cousins of the *Saturday Review* in 1970, and Herman Kogan in 1972.

The strong guidance that these jurors gave to the Advisory Board in their reports was invaluable in making the final determination of the awards. The 1968 report, for example, called Kennan's *Memoirs* a book that "one can expect to see written only a few times in a generation. That it will take its place among the great books in a great tradition seems unquestionable." In the 1971 report, Thompson's *Frost* was presented as a work that "plowed fresh ground" and showed the supposedly loveable poet in a more realistic light. "Was there ever such a gap," the jurors asked, "between the tortured, driven, jealous, conniving, yet always creative and sympathetic figure and the sturdy, homespun, New England poet so familiar in his public role?" It was, they concluded, a "major biographical work" that deserved the Pulitzer Prize.

Of Lash's *Eleanor and Franklin*, Herman Kogan wrote in the 1972 report that summarized the jury's views: "We agree that the reason for the choice is that the book, despite a kind of 'official' sponsorship by the Roosevelt family, is a historical work of the first importance that treats its subjects with candor, sympathy, and understanding and shows them 'with warts and all.' We agree, too, that it has been exhaustively re-searched and that new insights into the subjects have been afforded us by the author."

The jury of John Barkham and Professors Craven and Wiltse in 1973 unanimously recommended Swanberg's biography of Luce as "the first full-length portrait of a man whose magazines have exercised a profound influence on journalism in this country and abroad." The report con-cluded: "The book has aroused some controversy for its critical attitude to Luce, in particular for his breach of the traditional barrier between news and views. Nevertheless, the jury feels that Swanberg has grappled with a difficult but important subject and demonstrated the power that can be exercised by news media in the hands of a strong, dedicated, self-willed man." Strong objections to the Swanberg work had been ex-pressed in reviews in the New York *Times* and the *Wall Street Journal*, among others, but these did not sway the jurors. Nor did they influence the Advisory Board's majority, which accepted the jury report at face value.

Swanberg's reaction was graciousness itself in view of his previous rejection by the university's Trustees. He wrote to President McGill: "You will understand that I have never been at once so gratified and so grateful as I am at the selection of *Luce and His Empire* for the Pulitzer Prize in Biography. My deepest thanks to all who took part in the selec-tion." For Kennan, his second Pulitzer Prize was, he wrote, "the oc-casion for great pride and rejoicing," as the first had been. And for Lash, the New York *Post*'s United Nations correspondent who turned historian and biographer, his Pulitzer "represented the pinnacle for me in the way of recognition." He added, "Whenever I am introduced, it is as 'Pulitzer Prize-winning author Joseph P. Lash,' and whenever I am asked, 'Where do you go from here?' my reply is, 'I have nowhere to go but down.' "

Perhaps the most excitement of all came to Professor Williams, who had given up hope that his *Huey Long* would win the prize on the day of the announcement in 1970 and had gone to his doctor's office to have his ears washed out. When he returned to his office at Louisiana State University, people were shouting and a colleague breathlessly informed him, "Your book won the Pulitzer Prize. The news services have been trying to get you." There was a deluge of messages and phone calls, but Professor Williams managed somehow to inform his wife, taught part of a night class, then celebrated.[30]

For the historians in the sixth decade of the Pulitzer Prizes, new figures came forward, new leaders were developed in familiar fields and new subject areas were opened up. Whatever the state of mind of the student population of the colleges and universities of the land, the historians tried by every means at their command to advance the state of their art. If there was disagreement and controversy, it could not be helped. The rise of the professional historians in America, with their widely divergent views and loyalties, made arguments inevitable.

The controversy over the Pulitzer Prize in History for 1966 was a case in point. Margaret Leech, twice a Pulitzer Prize winner herself, and Professor Henry F. Graff of Columbia had recommended Professor Richard B. Morris' highly regarded narrative of the peace that followed the American Revolutionary War, *The Peacemakers*, while Professor Oscar Handlin of Harvard, also a Pulitzer Prize winner, had recommended a posthumous award for the greatly respected Professor Perry Miller of Harvard for *Life of the Mind in America*. The Morris work was called "a masterly specimen of the historian's craft based on monumental research in public and private archives here and abroad and presented with seasoned judgment and lively characterization." Miller's book was presented as "a major contribution to the understanding of religion, law, and science in nineteenth century society." The Advisory Board, at its annual meeting, picked Miller of Harvard over Morris of Columbia.[31]

In the following two years, younger historians were unanimously selected, primarily for the originality of their research and their presentation. Dr. Lyman Butterfield, Dr. Julian Boyd, and Professor Henry Steele Commager picked a new study of the exploration of the West, *Exploration and Empire*, by a Texas historian, William H. Goetzmann, in 1967. For 1968, Dr. Boyd, Professor Harold C. Syrett of the City University of New York, and Professor Louis Morton recommended a prize for Professor Bernard Bailyn of Harvard for *The Ideological Origins of the American Revolution.* Goetzmann's work was called "a most remarkable achievement for a young man . . . a tremendous book in its own right, tremendous in size, in imagination, and in interpretation." As for Bailyn, his award was based on the jury's opinion that his was a "work of such originality, distinction, and enduring value for the understanding of the Revolution as to make it pre-eminent among all the nominations for the award."

The 1969 prize for *The Origins of the Fifth Amendment* by Professor Leonard W. Levy, then of Brandeis University, was a standout for several reasons. The topic was one of overriding importance for both press and public, being so much in the news. The issue that frequently arose over legal actions that invoked the Fifth Amendment was widely misunderstood. And finally, Professor Levy himself, as a historian who was much preoccupied with the law and civil liberties, had impressive qualifications as an expert who was well able to deal with so troublesome a subject.   /

Professors Commager and Samuels, with Bruce Catton as chairman, wrote as follows of his work: "Our unanimous choice for the History Prize is Leonard W. Levy's book, *The Origins of the Fifth Amendment.* This struck all of us as a most distinguished work, thoroughly researched, and in its findings reflecting mature consideration and balanced judgment. It covers this particular aspect of our history so thoroughly and competently that the job need not be attempted again; in addition, it is a landmark book which must be examined by anyone who seeks a real understanding of this important issue."

When the news of the award reached Brandeis, Professor Levy was at a faculty meeting with twenty-five of his colleagues who gave him a standing ovation. The newspaper and radio interviews followed and, most impressive of all for the Levy children, TV cameras were set up in their home by the local station. Whether or not the Pulitzer Prize had anything to do with it, he was offered eight college presidencies within two years. "There are a lot of established scholars," he wrote. "There are few who have won a Pulitzer. Because it sets one apart, it carries with it a burden; it establishes in others great expectations. It creates a standard that one must live up to." [32]

What Professor Levy didn't mention was that the prize in and of itself also created a standard for subsequent juries, and in 1970 that standard was met and even raised a few notches with the selection of Dean Acheson's *Present at the Creation: My Years in the State Department*. This was no wooden narration of past glories, set down with ghostly help by a tired ex-office holder who surmised that he should be well thought of by the people. Nor was it a prize-winner on the order of General Pershing's memoirs, to be looked down on by professional historians. The saturnine former Secretary of State had no need to apologize to anybody, journalist or historian, for what he had to write and how he chose to write it.

A jury consisting of Catherine Drinker Bowen, J. Russell Wiggins, former editor of the Washington *Post*, and Dr. Lyman H. Butterfield as chairman recommended Acheson's work because it was "wonderfully informative and enlightening" and "magnificently told." The report summed up the book in this way:

> Here is notable literary distinction, also an honesty that is not hidden by the irony, the sophistication, and truly elegant wit. There is about Acheson a quality patently American, as there was about the colleagues he so much admired: Harry Truman and George Marshall. And there is about these memoirs of a great public figure, written in the classic manner, an air of gallantry and high emprise, of magnanimity, too, which even those who disagreed with him on great issues than (or for that matter now) cannot fail to recognize and respond to.[33]

The Acheson book was a winner, too, before the Advisory Board, where not all the membership by any means was cast in a mold of fervent admiration for the former Secretary of State. That was not a consideration in the vote. Nor was the matter of political partisanship an issue in the selection of the 1971 prize winner, Professor James MacGregor Burns's *Roosevelt, The Soldier of Freedom, 1940–1945*. Professors Morton and Levy were for it because, as they wrote in their report, it was "a distinguished work of history whose focus is President Roosevelt" and "constitutes a major contribution" to the World War II period. Dr. Boyd, the third member of the jury, wanted instead to honor an ongoing biography of Harvard graduates, but the Board expressed its preference for the Burns work.[34]

For 1972 and 1973, there were unanimous jury votes respectively for Professor Carl N. Degler's *Neither Black Nor White*, which dealt in part with the Brazilian experience in order to throw light on the question of slavery in the United States, and Professor Michael Kammen's *People of Paradox: An Inquiry Concerning the Origins of American Civilization.* Degler, a Stanford University historian, was selected by a jury consisting of Professors Morton, Craven, and T. Harry Williams. Kammen, a young history professor at Cornell, was picked by a jury that included Professors Syrett, Levy (then at the Claremont Graduate School in California), and Harold M. Hyman of Rice University.[35] It was a far cry from the early days of the Pulitzer Prizes when jurors and winners in history and biography often came from a narrow triangle in the northeastern United States.

In 1974, Professors Morton and Shafer joined with a newcomer to the History Juries, Professor Willie Lee Rose of Yale, to recommend Daniel J. Boorstin's *The Americans: The Democratic Experience,* the third volume of his major historical work. It won with ease. Historians also won special awards—James Thomas Flexner in 1973 for his four-volume *George Washington,* and Garrett Mattingly in 1960 for *The Armada.* A historical novelist, Kenneth Roberts, was similarly honored in 1957.

Theodore H. White, the first winner of the General Non-Fiction Prize, warned in 1971 that the award "has become a diffuse and catch-all category which may bloat in a few years to meaninglessness." He was the chairman of the Non-Fiction Jury that year and his fellow-jurors, Herman Kogan of the Chicago *Sun-Times Books* and Robert Cromie, book critic of the Chicago *Tribune,* agreed with him.

This was White's suggestion:

> Over the years American writers from Henry Adams and Lincoln Steffens through Vincent Sheean and John Gunther, to John Hersey and Norman Mailer, have developed a genre of contemporary reportage in book form which is, I think, one of the great prides of American letters. No other country, not even the French with their books of "temoinage," can match the quality of American reports on contemporary life.
>
> The award for General Non-Fiction should, I believe, thus be sharpened to an award given specifically for reportage of the present and the near past; it need not in any sense conflict with the scholarly award you now grant in history.[36]

The point was one calculated to appeal to the editors and publishers on the Advisory Board, if not particularly to the president of Columbia

University. To illustrate it, the jury unanimously proposed John Toland's *The Rising Sun* as the 1971 Non-Fiction Prize winner—a work that was, as the report put it, "a magnificent study of World War II as seen by the Japanese." The Advisory Board agreed, which was *ichidai* (extremely great) news in Japan when the announcement came. Toland's wife, Toshiko, and their two-year-old daughter, Tamiko, were staying with her parents in Tokyo at the time and were literally besieged by enthusiastic neighbors and the press with shouts of "Omedeto" (Congratulations) and "Yokattawane" (How wonderful!). Toland himself first heard about his good fortune in Duesseldorf, where he was researching a biography of Hitler, and received his congratulations from a leader of the bomb plot against the Fuehrer as well as from many others.[37]

Despite the popularity of the Toland award, and the reasonableness of White's suggestion for making it a kind of model for a Non-Fiction Prize, the Advisory Board couldn't see it that way. There already were eleven awards in journalism and only seven for books, drama, and music in the Pulitzer Prize list. It would not do, most Board members agreed informally, to create still another prize to celebrate the accomplishments of the journalists in book form. They would always win their share and perhaps more, it is true; yet, the Board wanted the prize to remain open for nominations of all kinds even though it invited the danger of as many as two hundred entries annually.

The winners from 1966 on illustrated the Board's view at the time of what the Non-Fiction Prize should be. On the recommendation of a jury of Roderick Nordell and Edward Weeks, the 1966 award went to a nature book, *Wandering Through Winter*, by Edwin Way Teale. For 1967, a jury of August Heckscher, Richard Hofstadter, and Robert Manning, editor of the *Atlantic*, selected a scholarly work, *The Problem of Slavery in Western Culture*, by Professor David Brion Davis of Cornell. The jurors called it a "major intellectual contribution" to the Western view of the worth of the individual. Yet, had the Non-Fiction Prize been restrictive, the book would not have been eligible. And Professor Davis, lecturing to a class in Hyderabad, India, would not have been hailed by his students as a teacher who had won an honor worthy of mention by the BBC.

The 1968 winner, too, owed its success to an open competition. It was Will and Ariel Durant's tenth and concluding volume of *The Story of Civilization*, entitled, *Rousseau and Revolution*. The jury of John Barkham,

Bruce Catton, and P. Albert Duhamel had favored David Kahn's *The Code Breakers*, but one juror was quoted in the report in support of the Durants' work as "an enduring achievement in the popularization of history." The Board intervened and recommended the prize for the elderly historians.

For 1969, the Board came up against a seemingly insoluble jury split. Norman Cousins, the chairman, was for *So Human An Animal*, in which the scientist, Rene Dubos, had been "remarkably successful in building a bridge between humanism and science." But Cousins' academic colleagues, Professor David Brion Davis and Professor Benjamin DeMott of Amherst, wanted the prize for Norman Mailer's *The Armies of the Night*, the novelist's recreation of the 1968 antiwar demonstration at the Pentagon. Cousins was against it. The academics wouldn't budge. For Davis, the work raised "public reporting and sociological analysis to a level of high art." For DeMott, no great admirer of Mailer before he read the book, it was "more gripping, intellectually stimulating, and finely made than any other work that fell to us to judge."

In this extremity, the Advisory Board voted two coequal Non-Fiction Prizes, one for Dubos and the other for Mailer. The scientist took it in stride but Mailer, who was running for Mayor of New York in the Democratic Primary Election at the time, used it as propaganda and donated the prize money to his campaign fund. Nothing much happened to help make a politician out of Mailer despite that. As the 44-year-old author recalled:

"Since the coverage of our campaign remained superficial, I used to try to shame newspaper reporters by telling them that if they honored me with the highest award of their profession, they in turn made it difficult for me to respect the award since they were covering our campaign so abominably. Needless to say, if these pep talks had any effect, it never got through to the city desk."

As for *The Armies of the Night*, he refused to define it as journalism, history, or fiction. "This may sound modest or pompous," he said, "but it was just writing." [38]

For 1970, once again, the Non-Fiction Prize veered off into academic territory and a subject far removed from current interest—the origins of Mohandas K. Gandhi's theories of non-violence and an analysis of the first massive strike movement he led in India after World War I. The volume, *Gandhi's Truth*, by the Harvard psychologist, Erick H. Erikson, was the unanimous choice of a jury of Raymond Walters Jr., Herman Kogan, and Lon Tinkle.

Another Advisory Board intervention brought the Non-Fiction Prize for 1972 to one of the most admired and widely read books of the year, Barbara Tuchman's *Stilwell and the American Experience in China, 1911–1945*. This was a prime example of the convergence of history, biography, and journalism. For in that year the History Jury reported that Mrs. Tuchman's work was "outstanding but we believe it should be a more serious candidate for a prize in biography." The Biography Jury ranked it second to *Eleanor and Franklin*, called it the "work of a brilliant pro" and "fascinating historical journalism," but ruled: "More impressive however as history than biography. Perhaps ought to be considered in the history category." What the Board did was to give *Stilwell* first place in non-fiction, thus setting aside that jury's recommendation for Gay Talese's story of a Mafia chieftain, *Honor Thy Father*. The Non-Fiction Jurors, Robert Cromie, Lon Tinkle, and Robert Kirsch of the Los Angeles *Times*, pointed out privately that they had never had a chance to judge the Tuchman book but they made no public protest.

Mrs. Tuchman was away at the time of the prize announcement, working on a new book at her cabin in Connecticut, which has no phone, and didn't know about her second Pulitzer award until she came home that evening. She was also unaware for a long time of all the difficulties *Stilwell* had to overcome to emerge, finally, as a well-deserved winner.[39]

The same classification problem bedeviled the Non-Fiction Jury and the Advisory Board in 1973. The rivals were Robert Coles's second and third volumes of his *Children of Crisis*, a Harvard psychoanalyst's view of America's social problems, and Frances FitzGerald's classic study of the Vietnamese and the Americans in Vietnam, *Fire in the Lake*. Roderick Nordell, Maurice Dolbier, and William McPherson, book critic of the Washington *Post*, praised both works so highly in their jury report that the Advisory Board once again decided to vote two coequal prizes.[40]

In 1974, there was another unanimous selection, Ernest Becker's *The Denial of Death*, chosen by Messrs. McPherson, Duhamel, and Robert Sorensen of the Minneapolis *Tribune*. It became a posthumous award, for the author died on March 6, 1974, of cancer. The jury had picked his work out of more than 180 volumes that had been nominated.

The central problem of how to separate the wheat from the chaff in non-fiction remained unresolved, however. As Teddy White stated it: "Although I have not counted, I believe that perhaps more than one hundred and fifty books were sent to me in the last three months of the year (1970). It would have required eight hours a day in that period had I read all of them from cover to cover. This is manifestly unfair to many writers whose work and pages I only swiftly skimmed. I believe that no more than twenty-five such books should be passed on to the jury each year; if any judge wishes, he should be allowed to add books of his own acquaintance to the list, and the Advisory Board can always send copies on to the other two members." [41]

It sounded very sensible. But who was to select the twenty-five books for the jury to judge? It was on this question that efforts to simplify the judging process, for the time being at least, broke down.

6
Poetry and Music: No Time for Tradition

Sooner than any member of the Advisory Board had expected, the musical revolution that Aaron Copland had predicted came to pass. Four years after he had spoken of computerized music before the fiftieth anniversary celebration of the Pulitzer Prizes, the first electronic composer received the music award. He was Charles Wuorinen, a controversial, 32-year-old member of the Columbia Music Department, and the composition for which he was honored was *Time's Encomium*, a two-movement work that was composed on the RCA Mark II Synthesizer and performed at the 1969 Berkshire Festival. Vincent Persichetti of the Juilliard School, the chairman, and his associates on the Music Jury, Gunther Schuller, president of the New England Conservatory of Music, and Otto C. Luening, an emeritus Professor of Music at Columbia, reported to the Advisory Board:

"The Jury considered it to be a major statement in the purely electronic field in that it combines a perfect technical mastery of the medium with the imagination, inventiveness, and musicality always associated with the highest standards of musical expression."

In the following year, Copland himself took a hand in the furtherance of the musical revolution as chairman of the Music Jury, which also included Virgil Thomson and Robert Craft. They selected another electronic composer from Columbia, 37-year-old Mario Davidovsky, for the 1971 award for a piece called *Synchronisms No. 6 for Piano and Electronic Sound,* which also had been performed at the Berkshire Festival. The report said it "shows mastery of a new medium and its imaginative use in combination with the solo pianoforte."

The two electronic awards scarcely constituted a trend, however. A year after winning the prize, Wuorinen failed to receive tenure by vote of the Columbia Music Faculty and resigned in a flurry of published recriminations, to which an emeritus Professor of Music, Paul Henry Lang, replied in kind.[42] Clearly, the time had not yet come when orchestras were about to go out of style and crowds would storm Philharmonic Hall to hear music by computer.

What the interest in the electronic field did indicate was that American composers were turning away from traditional methods and most of the Pulitzer Prize juries were encouraging them. In the great universities of the land that had become the strongholds of American musical instruction, the message came through loud and clear even before the first electronic music awards. Illustrative of newer concepts were such compositions as *Variations for Orchestra* by Professor Leslie Bassett of the University of Michigan, the 1966 winner; Quartet No. 3, by Professor Leon Kirchner of Harvard, for 1967; *Echoes of Time and the River* by Professor George Crumb of the University of Pennsylvania for 1968; and String Quartet No. 3, by Professor Karel Husa of Cornell, for 1969.

The recommendation for Crumb's work showed what Pulitzer Music Juries were seeking. A jury consisting of Norman Dello Joio, Vincent Persichetti, and Robert W. Ward, chairman, wrote: "George Crumb's *Echoes of Time and the River* was the heavy favorite in that it speaks in a musical language which has emerged only in the past decade, and yet reflects a great sense of the classical traditions. The choice will, we believe, be applauded by those more sympathetic to avant-garde developments. At the same time, George Crumb commands the highest respect among the most demanding conservatives."

After the two electronic awards of 1970 and 1971, a jury headed by Aaron Copland, with Vincent Persichetti and Irving Lowens of the Washington *Evening Star* as members, picked another of the newer composers, 44-year-old Jacob Druckman of the Juilliard School, for an orchestral work, *Windows.* The 1972 winner was described as a "freshly conceived work of a daring nature, uniquely combining the various materials and techniques of our time." [43]

But for 1973, the pendulum swung back to one of the great names in American music, Elliott Carter, who received his second Pulitzer for his String Quarter No. 3. The jury of William Bergsma of the University of Washington, the chairman, and two Pulitzer Prize winners, George Crumb and Hugo Weisgall hailed the work as "impressive and—to some extent enigmatic." The report said, "In this work, Carter is proceeding logically and powerfully along the path he has pursued for more than twenty years, which combines the rigorous intellectual control of musical materials with an intuitive exploration of opposing textures in the tradition of Charles Ives." [44]

In the 1974 awards, the Music Prize went to Donald Martino for a novel chamber music piece, *Notturno,* and one of the surviving masters of American music, Roger Sessions, was honored at 77 years of age with a special award.

Assuredly, looking beyond Copland, Carter, and the other major American composers of this era, there would be many more experiments with the new music. But the question posed so neatly by Virgil Thomson still remained to be answered: "Is it music or is it noise?" Both as composer and critic, Thomson himself wasn't sure. But he wrote, with a splendid show of confidence:

> Myself I see no hindrance to the survival of both noise-art and music. Photography did not kill oil painting; on the contrary, it set off in landscape painting a development known as impressionism which invigorated all painting. Similarly, the gramophone and the radio, far from killing off music, have contributed to their distribution, changed their sociology, and corrected their aesthetics.
>
> So I am not worried. Let the boys have fun. Let us all have fun. Let Europe survive. Let America exist. Indeed, I am convinced in music it already does exist. At least that. [45]

The Advisory Board had always been reluctant to interfere in the deliberations of the Music and Poetry Juries. To most journalists who became members of the Board, these were fields that were admittedly outside their competence. On several occasions, primarily because of a lack of general interest in the Music Prize, there were suggestions that it should be dropped but Chairman Pulitzer would never hear of it. As for the Poetry Prize, most of the Board's membership had the feeling that juries were sometimes too restrictive in selecting poets to be honored. However, for much of their history, very little was done about either the music or poetry awards at Board meetings except for an annual reading from the winning volume of verse by W. D. Maxwell of the Chicago *Tribune* and, on one memorable occasion, an imitation of a far-out musical composition performed by Vermont Royster of the *Wall Street Journal*.

For the most part, there was little room for argument about a Poetry Jury report. In 1966, for example, a jury consisting of Robert Penn Warren and Stanley Kunitz urged a long-deferred Pulitzer Prize for one of the most eminent of American poets, Richard Eberhart, for his *Selected Poems*. No one could quarrel with that—and no one attempted it. But in the following year, the Board came face to face with a crisis in poetry because two of the jurors, Phyllis McGinley and Louis Simpson, wished to give a posthumous award to Theodore Roethke and the chairman, Eberhart, was sternly opposed to all posthumous prizes as a matter of principle. One of the Board's few students of American poetry, Barry Bingham Sr., undertook to try to resolve the impasse with the jury and, with patience and persuasion, produced unanimous agreement among the jurors on Anne Sexton's admirable volume of verse, *Live or Die*. She became the 1967 winner without further argument, but the Board did not attempt any further interventions.[46]

Another widely respected American poet was honored in 1968 when Anthony Hecht's *The Hard Hours* was chosen by a jury of Louis Simpson, W. D. Snodgrass, and Lawrance Thompson. As the report explained the overdue honor: "Anthony Hecht writes, for the most part, in traditional forms, and for this reason his work has been somewhat neglected in recent years when free verse has been so widely practiced. . . . In honoring Hecht, we are honoring poetry itself."

But that marked an end, for the time being at least, to the respectful recognition of traditional forms. While the jurors did not throw caution aside and plump for the recognition of young, untried poets, they spread their honors among those whose careers had been distinguished by innovative verse. One of the oldest, 61-year-old George Oppen, won the prize in 1969 for his volume, *Of Being Numerous*, which reflected his career as an "objectivist" of the school of William Carlos Williams and Ezra Pound. In the next two years, the award went to poets who also were prolific translators of foreign poetry, Richard Howard for *Untitled Sub-*

jects in 1970 and William S. Merwin for *The Carrier of Ladders* in 1971. Howard was 41 and Merwin was 44 at the time the prize was bestowed on each of them. Professor James Wright of Hunter College won in 1972 for his *Collected Poems* when he was 44, and in 1973 the award was given to Maxine Winokur Kumin, a 48-year-old mother of four children, for *Up Country*. Robert Lowell, one of the dominant poetic voices of his time, won his second award in 1974 with *The Dolphin*.

Louis Simpson, the chairman of the Poetry Jury from 1968 through 1973 with the exception of 1970, always stressed that he sought to give the prize for "original work" whenever possible.[47] With Howard Nemerov and Francis Fergusson of Rutgers as fellow-jurors, Simpson recommended the 1972 award for Wright because of his steady development away from tradition toward "new forms and new uses of imagery." Similarly, a jury of Anne Sexton, Professor William Alfred of Harvard, and Simpson proposed the 1973 prize for Mrs. Kumin, so heavily influenced by Robert Frost, because her pastoral poetry was "shaped with great skill" and her New England scenes were "newly and sharply observed."

Thus, while the poets of an older tradition were passing from the scene, the poets of middle age were struggling for new modes of expression. There was, no doubt, stronger stuff yet to come from the young poets, impatiently clamoring for recognition, and the radical innovators of new times. For them, the agonies of a turbulent and changing land were desperately real, far more so than for their well-established and greatly honored elders. There were cries of passion and anger from the ghetto areas of the big cities, where the poetry of politics and protest was rising out of the more familiar work of Langston Hughes and Melvin Tolson.

If tradition was moldering away, great poetry was not. Many a Pulitzer Prize jury would still take off on a rough but occasionally ecstatic voyage of discovery in the years yet to come.

7
Facing the Future

The Pulitzer Prizes, like all living things, must grow or die but there are many kinds of growth and most of them are superior to the mere expansion of numbers. Character, quality, responsibility—all these are matters of continual concern to those who administer, recommend, judge, and award the Pulitzer Prizes.

"We're dealing with something very powerful here," Arthur Krock used to tell his associates on the Advisory Board during their annual discussions of the prizes. "Let's proceed with care."

Krock's assumption remains fundamental for the Advisory Board today and his advice on procedure is still heeded. Nor is there any prospect of a basic change in the philosophy of the Board during the forseeable future. For new members and old, there is a lively awareness that a prize bestowed at the right moment can encourage a genius like Eugene O'Neill, thrust an unknown such as James Michener into instant fame and fortune, or grace the illustrious careers of leading writers like Ernest Hemingway, Ellen Glasgow, and William Faulkner.

Such an award can signify recognition at the highest professional level for an editor struggling in a revolutionary social cause, an editor of the quality of Ralph McGill, or for embattled newspapers like the New York *Times* in the Pentagon Papers case and the Washington *Post* in the Watergate inquiry. It can also reward magnificent personal efforts such as the coverage of the Kennedy assassination by Merriman Smith, the exposure of the My Lai tragedy by Seymour Hersh, and the self-sacrifice of combat correspondents and photographers, from Ernie Pyle to Kyoichi Sawada, both of whom were killed in action. These monuments in the Pulitzer record can scarcely be defaced by the mistakes of the past.

The twin standards of quality of achievement and excellence of performance, therefore, will continue to be the guides for the Advisory Board in selecting the prize winners. The Board's right to exercise its supremacy over juries and to recommend a final decision over each prize to the university's Trustees remains firmly imbedded in the will of the first Joseph Pulitzer. Since the Trustees have sparingly and even reluctantly exercised their authority to accept or reject the Board's recommendations, overturning only one since 1917 and disassociating themselves from two others, it is unlikely that their role in the awards will increase.

On the contrary, some Trustees have even questioned whether they should continue to have a role in the prize structure, notably with the 1974 announcements, in which President McGill said some of them were disturbed by the awarding of prizes for what they called "illegal acts," such as the disclosure of the Pentagon Papers and President Nixon's income tax returns. However, the uneasy relationship between Board and Trustees has continued.

Specifically, the Trustees have in effect taken the position of the first Joseph Pulitzer, who tried to appoint distinguished non-journalists to the Advisory Board and failed because of President Butler's opposition. What many of the Trustees want is a larger Board which would be more representative of the arts and professions other than journalism, which is fully represented. This is not merely a matter of opposition to what President McGill called "Xerox journalism"—the awarding of prizes for publishing the Pentagon Papers and President Nixon's income tax returns. There is a fundamental principle involved that goes back to the earliest days of the Butler-Pulitzer negotiations over the Pulitzer Prizes.

Except for the changes in its own membership, however, the Board historically has resisted major shifts in the structure governing the Pulitzer Prizes. The Board also has other problems, one of the most vexing being the constant growth of the number of entries in all categories. Ever since Oxie Reichler of the Yonkers *Herald-Statesman* came stumbling out of a jury room, crying out in protest that it was impossible for anybody to read 10,000 editorials, there has been a disposition among most Pulitzer judges to regard an extraordinarily large number of entries with both distaste and suspicion. And now, in the sixth decade of the Pulitzer Prizes, the total for all categories is approaching 1,500 exhibits annually and conceivably could go to 2,000 in a fruitful and controversial year.

What would happen if the prizes were publicized, promoted, and advertised beyond the annual announcement of winners, the current procedure, is too horrendous to contemplate. Even with the continued unpublicized growth in the number of entries, the issue of maintaining an entirely open competition will have to be faced, no matter how little enthusiasm there is within the Board or the university for any limitation on quantity.

The prospect of more than 150 novels each year, plus as many histories and biographies and perhaps 200 non-fiction entries, is enough to dismay the most devoted book juror. And in journalism, it will not be long before juries will have to tackle in excess of 100 public service entries and as many as 200 bulky and intricate investigative reporting submissions. Not even the champion of all fast-reading and fast-acting editors and jurors, Norman E. Isaacs, could remain unmoved before such a mountain of print.

It is always possible, of course, that the computer and the use of modern duplicating devices could be used to help resolve this dilemma, given sufficient funds and technical help in the Pulitzer Prize office. But it is hopeless to look for the day when a computer will pick the Pecos *Independent and Enterprise* in Texas out of a pile of entries as a local reporting winner, or point unhesitatingly to a struggling new play like Thornton Wilder's *Our Town* as the most deserving on Broadway. Nor will it help very much if investigative reporting entries, which even today regularly exceed 1,000 individual articles, are transmitted quickly by microfilm to the office of a dismayed editor for assessment. If no way is found to check the quantity of entries, in order to safeguard the judgment of quality, then the appointment of a full-time Pulitzer Prize administrator with an enlarged staff will become a necessity. With such a bumper increase in costs, the Pulitzer Prizes might very well become frozen into their current commitments or even slimmed down.

Another problem—the clamor for admitting television, radio, films, and magazines to the Pulitzer Prizes—is not as severe as it once was, primarily because suitable awards now exist in each of these branches of journalism. But in any event, neither the personnel nor the funds would be available now for any venture by the Board into areas with which it has little familiarity. The more likely prospect, as has already been suggested, is a limitation of its operations, at least for a few years. Despite the growth of the initial $500,000 Pulitzer Prize Fund and its increased yield, the income is not inexhaustible and only about $100,000 has been added to principal from outside sources since the bequest was made.

Curiously, despite the effect of a galloping inflation on almost everything else in the United States, the relatively modest $1,000 check that comes with each Pulitzer Prize except public service and the $250 fee for the non-journalism jurors have aroused no protest whatever. Nor has any journalism juror ever bowed out because neither he nor his organization was willing to underwrite the expenses of his trip to New York. In effect, the Pulitzer Prizes have been maintained in part because of the willingness of newspapers and newspaper people to make a special and entirely voluntary contribution to the operation. Equally valuable has been the continued agreement of writers, critics, and composers of national and international importance to serve as jurors in the non-journalism categories for what amounts to only a token fee.

Another jury problem that causes little concern today is the old bugaboo of secrecy. Except for the years of the Ackerman regime when Columbia journalism faculty members alone judged the journalism entries, those who have served on journalism juries have always been publicly identified. In Letters, Drama, and Music, the issuance of the forty-year listing of juries in 1957 broke the seal of secrecy. Only the objections of a handful of jurors delayed the release of subsequent jury memberships, as had been pledged by the Advisory Board with the initial announcement. But even the objectors, for the most part, conceded that their identities were known in the field they were judging. With the approval of the board, therefore, juries generally have been identified in this historical record.

Somewhat more troublesome is the continual all-America emphasis of the Pulitzer Prizes. The question has cropped up at Board meetings now and then when a non-American novel or a non-American play has been deemed superior to anything produced in this country during a competitive year. Like President Butler in the case of John Drinkwater's *Abraham Lincoln*, the tendency has been to try to find some way to honor a great work regardless of nationality. Once, in recent years, a Board member asked Joseph Pulitzer Jr., "Why are we so chauvinistic?" The response from the Board's chairman was, "That was old J. P. His main notion was to improve things in this country and he put it in his will."

It is within the realm of possibility, of course, that the Board at some future date could decree a whole set of international prizes if it ever had the funds and the will to do so. But if that happened, it would be violating one of its own cherished principles by invading an area where a major prize already exists. If the Pulitzers are not about to challenge the Oscars or the Emmys, it isn't likely that they will try to rival the Nobel Prizes.

There have been notable exceptions to the all-American design. Through action of the Biography Jury, Jean Jules Jusserand, French ambassador to the United States in World War I, became the first biography winner. And because the Music Prize permitted non-Americans resident in the United States to win a Pulitzer, Gian-Carlo Menotti, an Italian, carried off two of them; however, beginning in 1974, the Music Prize became as American as the rest.

It is also an agreeable feature of the Pulitzer Prizes in Journalism that foreign contributors to the American press are eligible. The list includes General Carlos P. Romulo of the Philippines (for a prize won while he was an American), Frederick T. Birchall of Britain, Sanche de Gramont * of France, and the following photographers: Hector Rondon, a Venezuelan; Horst Faas and Michel Laurent, a German-French team; Kyoichi Sawada, Toshio Sakai, and Yasushi Nagao of Japan; and Huynh Cong Ut of South Vietnam. There is little doubt, with the inclusion of so many foreign nationals in the staffs of American news organizations abroad, that the number of foreign prize winners will grow.

Under the glorious old golden dome of the Pulitzer Building on Park Row in the early days of the Pulitzer Prizes, Herbert Bayard Swope would roar with indignation over the annual announcements of the awards. Grasping any first page of the New York opposition that was handy, he would shake it furiously under the nose of a hapless bystander who ventured into his office at the *World* and hoarsely demand, "Why are these fellows so ashamed of their own business? Why don't they feature the journalism prizes?"

Swope was not alone in his resentment over the tendency of the editors of the time to play the fiction and drama awards for all they were worth, particularly during a controversy, and pay as little attention as possible to the journalism prizes. Unfortunately for the partisans of journalism awards at that period, they really didn't have much of a case. The dramatists, the novelists, the historians, the biographers—yes, even the poets—were the leaders in the post-World War I renaissance in America and most of the journalists bore up in the rear. For despite the notable feats of both newspapers and newspaper people, they did not then have the impact on American public opinion of the writers who dealt with ideas. It was an era when even the printers, in their dark and smelly composing rooms, looked down with amused contempt at the out-at-the-seat reporters who posed as ersatz intellectuals and whose eyes were on the stars when they weren't reading H. L. Mencken's *Smart Set* or *American Mercury*.

Public recognition of the newspaper as a responsible leader of national or even local opinion came slowly, for the journalist had never been a personage of high repute in American life. Benjamin Franklin, ink-

---

* Since applying for American citizenship in 1973, Sanche deGramont has written under the name of Ted Morgan, an anagram of deGramont.

stained though he was from his earliest years, became known in history as almost anything except a journalist. And it was merely a curiosity that Alexander Hamilton happened to be influential in the founding of the New York *Evening Post* in 1801. Nor did their successors of modern times find any more satisfaction in the practice of their occasionally noble profession. What happened after World War II was that the leading newspapers of the land found public leadership thrust upon them through the insensible decline in moral responsibility among politicians and the preoccupation of many intellectuals with almost anything except public life.

Beginning with the contest between press and government over the reporting from Vietnam, and continuing into the civil rights struggle, the case of the Pentagon Papers, and the Watergate inquiry, many newspapers throughout the land featured the journalism prizes over the rest because it was the journalists who usually made the news for the post-World War II era. It would have gratified the restless, demanding Swope, but now it was the turn of the people of the world of books, the stage, and the concert hall to be unhappy. The change, no doubt, was temporary. In due course, the pendulum would swing back. Such, at least, was the impression that was given by the Pulitzer Prize record.

In the 58 Pulitzer Prize announcements since 1917, there have been a total of 714 awards. They have been won by 657 individuals, 591 men and 66 women, plus 57 newspapers, one book publishing firm, one newspaper chain, and two group awards that went respectively to World War II correspondents and cartographers. There have been 58 multiple winners, including nine newspapers, 19 newspaper people, and 30 from the literary awards, the stage, and music. Both prizes and special citations are included in these summary statistics. In addition, 46 prizes have been skipped, 19 in journalism and 27 in non-journalism.

The breakdown between journalism and the other categories does not show much of a gap between the total number of prizes under each heading. For journalism, 398 prizes have been awarded to 324 individuals, 312 men and 12 women, plus the previously mentioned 57 newspapers, one newspaper chain, and two group awards. For letters, drama and music, 316 awards have gone to 333 individuals, 279 men and 54 women, plus one book publishing firm. As a rough estimate, some 350 of the individual winners are living.

The multiple winners in letters, drama, and music are Robert Frost, Eugene O'Neill, and Robert E. Sherwood, four prizes each; Archibald

MacLeish, Edwin Arlington Robinson, and Thornton Wilder, three each; and the following with two each: Samuel Barber, Samuel Flagg Bemis, Stephen Vincent Benet, Elliott Carter, William Faulkner, Burton J. Hendrick, Richard Hofstadter, Marquis James, George S. Kaufman, George F. Kennan, Margaret Leech, Robert Lowell, Gian-Carlo Menotti, Samuel Eliot Morison, Allan Nevins, Walter Piston, Richard Rodgers and Oscar Hammerstein II (a prize and citation), Carl Sandburg, Arthur Meier Schlesinger Jr., Booth Tarkington, Barbara W. Tuchman, Robert Penn Warren, and Tennessee Williams.

In journalism, the news organizations and their staff members who have won five or more prizes are the New York *Times*, 40; Associated Press, 29; St. Louis *Post-Dispatch*, 16; New York *Herald Tribune*, Chicago *Daily News* and Knight Newspapers, 15 each; Baltimore *Sun*, Washington *Post*, New York *World* and *Evening World*, and the Des Moines *Register* and *Tribune*, 9 each; * Los Angeles *Times* and United Press International, 8 each; *Wall Street Journal* and Washington *Star-News*, 7 each; Scripps-Howard News Service, New York *World Telegram*, and Hearst Newspapers, 6 each; Chicago *Tribune*, Louisville *Times* and *Courier-Journal*, and Kansas City *Star*, 5 each.

Of the individual multiple winners in journalism, Arthur Krock took two prizes and a citation and the following received two prizes each: Homer Bigart, Horst Faas, Anthony Lewis, William L. Laurence, Walter Lippmann (a prize and a citation), Relman Morin, James Reston, William Allen White, and Don Whitehead; for the editorial cartoonists, Edmund Duffy and Rollin Kirby won three prizes each and the following received two each: Herblock, Paul Conrad, J. N. Darling, Daniel R. Fitzpatrick, Nelson Harding, W. H. Mauldin, and Vaughn Shoemaker.

There have been seven sets of family winners: Albert Hackett and his wife, Frances Goodrich, in Drama; Will Durant and his wife, Ariel, in Non-Fiction; Andrew C. McLaughlin and his daughter, Constance McLaughlin Green, both in History; Malcolm Johnson of the New York *Sun* and his son, Haynes Johnson of the Washington *Star;* two Washington *Star* cartoonists, Clifford K. Berryman and his son, James T.; two Columbia faculty members, Carl Van Doren in Biography and his brother, Mark, in Poetry; and Stephen Vincent Benet and William Rose Benet, brothers, both of them poetry winners.

* The Des Moines papers also claimed two awards for J. N. Darling of the New York *Herald Tribune*, whose work they published, for a total of 11.

The oldest prize winners have been Will Durant and Lawrence H. Gipson, both historians and both 82 when they received their awards. The youngest, all 21 when they won their prizes, were John Paul Filo of the *Valley Daily News* in Pennsylvania, Alvin H. Goldstein of the Chicago *Daily News*, and William Burke Miller of the Louisville *Courier-Journal*.

Women have been the most numerous among the prize winners in fiction, 17, against 28 for men, and in poetry, 14, against 33 for men. They have to date been entirely shut out of prizes in music, editorial writing, and cartooning. There have been three black prize winners, Gwendolyn Brooks, Charles Gordone, and the photographer, Moneta Sleet Jr. And 12 laureates, all newspaper people, have come from Joseph Pulitzer's school.

While the winners in Letters, Drama, and Music have ranged widely over the whole of American life, the issues that have occupied the attention of the journalists are more sharply reflected in the Pulitzer Prizes. In a previous compilation of subject matter for the Pulitzer Prizes in Journalism from 1917 to 1958, the following basic headings were developed [48] and are now brought up to date, with new headings being shown in italics:

	1917–1958	1959–1974	Total
Exposing graft and corruption at all levels of government	33	28	61
War reporting	22	26 *	48
U.S. racial conflict	16	14	30
Crime reporting	12	15	27
Civil liberties	12	12	24
Reporting from Russia (except war)	9	5	14
Human interest	6	6	12
General Washington coverage	6	4	10
General international coverage	8	2	10
Science (including the atom)	8	0	8
Storms, accidents, etc.	6	2	8
Community affairs, improvements, etc.	0	5	5
Reporting on the ecology	1	4	5
Cold war (domestic results)	4	0	4

* 16 prizes were for Vietnam reporting & related domestic affairs.

The rest of the awards were scattered over a broad area including criticism, labor, economics, international conferences, sports, health, education, medicine, and other subjects. It is an oddity that no prizes were won in reporting American moon travel, but the fact is that TV really told this story at first hand and the still pictures submitted on behalf of the astronauts in the Pulitzer Prizes were ruled out of consideration. There was, the jurors pointed out, no possibility for free journalistic competition on the moon.

The Pulitzer Prizes have survived two World Wars, a great Depression, the bitterness of racial conflict, a tragic national schism over the Vietnam War, and the natural tensions between press and government. Many an award has created rejoicing but others have caused both controversy and criticism—all perfectly understandable reactions that are bound to continue. Barring some monstrous catastrophe, therefore, the thousandth winner of a Pulitzer Prize is likely to be selected shortly before the end of this century if the current rate of award-giving continues.

It is tempting to speculate on the manner in which that symbolic winner will be chosen, and the nature and character of the work that will be rewarded. But, as experience has demonstrated, it is difficult enough to deal with the awards of a current year without trying to peer into the murky dawn of a new century. Juries are unpredictable. And when the Advisory Board meets, none can say what will happen. The one basic certainty is that the strong-minded people who take part in the prize-giving process will maintain their independence, come what may.

As long as there is genius in America, with workable guarantees of freedom of speech and freedom of the press, there will be prizes to encourage and reward it. Given continued strong direction and support, the Pulitzer Prizes assuredly will remain among them.

An Acknowledgment

This book was made possible through the cooperation of Columbia University, the Advisory Board on the Pulitzer Prizes, more than a hundred Pulitzer Prize winners, and numerous jurors, past and present, who have served with distinction. I am grateful, too, for the support of my associates and my predecessors at Columbia University and its Graduate School of Journalism, without whom I could not have functioned in preparing this social and cultural history for the sixtieth anniversary of the awards.

In particular, my thanks go to President William J. McGill of Columbia University, Chairman Joseph Pulitzer Jr. of the Advisory Board on the Pulitzer Prizes, and their associates on the 1973 Board: Benjamin C. Bradlee, Wallace Carroll, John Cowles Jr., Price Day, William B. Dickinson, Robert J. Donovan, Lee Hills, Sylvan Meyer, Newbold Noyes Jr., James Reston, and Vermont Royster. In addition to their decision to open the private files of the awards to me, they gave me both encouragement and invaluable insights into some of the problems as well as the satisfaction of prize-giving.

When I began my research, one of the most surprising and gratifying developments was the enormous response I received from Pulitzer Prize winners to a general appeal for help. The letters, interviews, and telephone calls, if put together, would have provided sufficient material for still another book. In extracting some letters, and paraphrasing others, I have tried to reproduce the widely varied reactions of the winners, both pleasant and unpleasant, and hereby gratefully acknowledge the assistance of the following laureates who wrote so vividly of their experiences:

Individual Pulitzer Prize Winners

George Abbott
Brooks Atkinson
Hanson W. Baldwin
C. D. Batchelor
Walter Jackson Bate
Keyes Beech
George Bliss
Jerry Bock
Gwendolyn Brooks
Malcolm W. Browne
William A. Caldwell
Bruce Catton
Paul Conrad
Ed Cony
Aaron Copland
Virginius Dabney
George Dangerfield
David Brion Davis
Horance G. Davis Jr.
Sanche de Gramont
Norman Dello Joio
David Herbert Donald
John Fetterman
Edward T. Folliard
Alfred Friendly
Frank D. Gilroy
Gene S. Graham
Shirley Ann Grau
Constance McL. Green
Sheldon Harnick
John R. Harrison
W. R. Hearst Jr.
Lynn Heinzerling
John M. Hightower
Lee Hills
John Hughes
Peter R. Kann
George Kennan
John S. Knight
Arthur Krock
Joseph P. Lash
Timothy Leland
Leonard W. Levy
Anthony Lewis
Charles A. Lindbergh
Archibald MacLeish
Norman Mailer
Bernard Malamud

Reuben Maury
Edgar May
Arthur Miller
Norman C. Miller
William B. Miller
Samuel Eliot Morison
Edgar Ansel Mowrer
Jack Nelson
Roy F. Nichols
George Oppen
Miriam Ottenberg
Eugene C. Patterson
Walter Piston
Thomas Powers
Merlo J. Pusey
Richard Rodgers
Carlos P. Romulo
A. M. Rosenthal
Joe Rosenthal
Vermont C. Royster
Morrie Ryskind
Harrison E. Salisbury
Ernest Samuels
Louis Simpson
Moneta Sleet Jr.
Lauren Soth
Jean Stafford
Wallace Stegner
John Strohmeyer
W. A. Swanberg
Virgil Thomson
John Toland
R. Kenneth Towery
Vance Trimble
Barbara Tuchman
Wallace Turner
Mark Van Doren
Paul Vathis
Arthur Walworth
Paul W. Ward
Robert Penn Warren
George Weller
Theodore H. White
Thornton Wilder
T. Harry Williams
Tennessee Williams
Herman Wouk

Representing Newspaper Gold Medal Winners

Eric W. Allen, for the Medford (Oregon) *Mail-Tribune*
Barry Bingham Sr., for the Louisville *Courier-Journal*
Wallace Carroll, for the Winston-Salem (N.C.) *Journal and Sentinel*
Howard H. Hays Jr., for the Riverside (Calif.) *Press-Enterprise*
David Laventhol, for *Newsday*, Garden City, N.Y.
Dick Leonard, for the Milwaukee *Journal*
Frank Orr, for the Watsonville (Calif.) *Register-Pajaronian*
Nelson Poynter, for the St. Petersburg (Fla.) *Times*
A. M. Rosenthal, for the New York *Times*
Howard Simons, for the Washington *Post*
Thomas Winship, for the Boston *Globe*

I owe a great deal to the following for their expert appraisals of their special fields or for providing me with particular information, and sometimes both: John Barkham, Carlos Baker, Aaron Copland, David Herbert Donald, Maxwell Geismar, Samuel Eliot Morison, Archibald Mac-Leish, Orville Prescott, and Louis Simpson. To Dean Elie Abel and Associate Dean Norman E. Isaacs of the Columbia Graduate School of Journalism, I have a special debt of gratitude for their suggestions, their patience, and their forbearance. And for help in various ways, I thank Henry Graff, Daryle Feldmeir, James Hoge, and Mark Schorer.

In the Pulitzer Prize Office, my reliance for administration and research was on the invaluable Rose Valenstein, to whom I express my deepest thanks. I am grateful also to Marilyn Skwire for putting together, with such infinite skill and patience, the long lists of jurors who have served over six decades and for her help in other matters. In Columbia's Journalism Library, Wade Doares once again assisted in many ways, as did the thoughtful and expert Jonathan Beard. And at Columbia University Press, I took the greatest of pleasure in renewing my partnership with Robert J. Tilley, the editor in chief.

I absolve all these of responsibility for whatever is written herein.

I gratefully acknowledge permission from Archibald MacLeish to quote from his definition of "the poet's labor" and to reprint his quotation from Lu Chi's *Wen-fu*, both published in his *Poetry and Experience* (Boston: Riverside Press, 1961). The original version of the lines from the *Wen-fu* was in a translation by Achilles Fang, published in the *New Mexico Quarterly*, Vol. XXII, No. 3.

I also express my gratitude for permission to quote from "This Amber Sunstream" in Mark Van Doren's *Collected and New Poems* (New York: Hill & Wang, 1963).

I cannot conclude without expressing my gratitude to Grayson Kirk, with whom I worked so closely for fifteen years while he was president of Columbia University, and to his successor, Andrew W. Cordier, my old friend of United Nations days, even though neither had anything to do with the preparation of this volume. Both helped me over many a rough spot in my years in the Pulitzer Prize Office. And finally, let me say thanks once again to my adored life-long companion, my wife, Dorothy Lannuier Hohenberg.

John Hohenberg

Appendixes

1
Members of the Advisory Board on the Pulitzer Prizes Revised, April, 1974

Barry Bingham Sr.	*Louisville Times & Courier-Journal*	1956–1968
Samuel Bowles	*Springfield* (Mass.) *Republican*	1912–1915
Benjamin Bradlee	*The Washington Post*	1969–1977
Sevellon Brown	*The Providence Journal-Bulletin*	1938–1956
Sevellon Brown 3rd	*The Providence Journal-Bulletin*	1961–1965
John Stewart Bryan	*Richmond News Leader*	1923–1924
Nicholas Murray Butler	Columbia University	1912–1945
Erwin D. Canham	*Christian Science Monitor*	1958–1970
Wallace Carroll	*Winston-Salem* (N.C.) *Journal-Sentinel*	1969–1973
Hodding Carter *	*Delta Democrat-Times*, Greenville, Miss.	1949–1961
Turner Catledge	*The New York Times*	1955–1967
Norman Chandler	*Los Angeles Times*	1957–1969
Robert Choate	*The Boston Herald*	1943–1958
Kent Cooper	*The Associated Press*	1931–1956
Andrew W. Cordier	Columbia University	1969–1970
Gardner Cowles Jr.	*The Des Moines Register & Tribune*	1947–1958
John Cowles Jr.	*The Minneapolis Star & Tribune*	1971–1975
Price Day *	*The Baltimore Sun*	1971–1975
William B. Dickinson	*The Philadelphia Bulletin*	1969–1973
Robert J. Donovan	*Los Angeles Times*	1971–1975
Dwight D. Eisenhower	Columbia University	1949–1950
Frank D. Fackenthal	Columbia University	1946–1948
J. D. Ferguson	*Milwaukee Journal*	1952–1961
Solomon B. Griffin	*Springfield* (Mass.) *Republican*	1916–1925
Julian Harris	*Columbus* (Ga.) *Enquirer Sun*, *Atlanta Constitution, Chattanooga Times*	1927–1942

* Denotes individual Pulitzer Prize winner.

Walter M. Harrison	*The Daily Oklahoman*, Oklahoma City	1938–1946
John L. Heaton	*The New York World*	1912–1934
Lee Hills *	Knight Newspapers Inc.	1970–1978
Alfred Holman	*The Argonaut*, San Francisco	1924–1931
Arthur M. Howe	*Brooklyn Daily Eagle*	1920–1946
Palmer Hoyt	*The Denver Post*	1947–1949
Norman E. Isaacs	*Louisville Times & Courier-Journal*	1969–1970
George S. Johns	*St. Louis Post-Dispatch*	1912–1920
Frank R. Kent	*The Baltimore Sun*	1928–1953
Grayson Kirk	Columbia University	1950–1968
Clayton Kirkpatrick	*Chicago Tribune*	1975–1979
John S. Knight *	Knight Newspapers Inc.	1944–1958
Arthur Krock *	*The New York Times*	1940–1954
Robert Lathan	*Asheville* (N.C.) *Citizen & Times*	1932–1937
Victor F. Lawson	*Chicago Daily News*	1912–1925
Kenneth MacDonald	*The Des Moines Register & Tribune*	1958–1970
William J. McGill	Columbia University	1971–
Benjamin McKelway	*The Evening Star*, Washington, D.C.	1951–1963
St. Clair McKelway	*Brooklyn Daily Eagle*	1912–1922
William R. Mathews	*The Arizona Daily Star*, Tucson	1943–1956
W. D. Maxwell	*Chicago Tribune*	1958–1970
Sylvan Meyer	*Miami News*	1969–1974
Charles R. Miller	*The New York Times*	1912–1922
Paul Miller	Gannett Newspapers Inc.	1956–1968
Edward P. Mitchell	*The New York Sun*	1912–1927
Newbold Noyes Jr.	*Washington Star-News*	1963–1975
Robert L. O'Brien	*The Boston Herald*	1920–1941
Rollo Ogden	*The New York Times*	1924–1936
Eugene C. Patterson *	*The St. Petersburg* (Fla.) *Times*	1974–1978
Stuart H. Perry	*The Adrian* (Mich.) *Telegram*	1928–1956
Marlen E. Pew	*Editor & Publisher* magazine	1933–1936
Harold S. Pollard	*New York World-Telegram*	1937–1951
Joseph Pulitzer	*St. Louis Post-Dispatch*	1921–1955
Joseph Pulitzer Jr.	*St. Louis Post-Dispatch*	1955–
Ralph Pulitzer	*The New York World*	1912–1939
Whitelaw Reid	*The New York Tribune*	1912
James Reston *	*The New York Times*	1968–1976
Roy A. Roberts	*Kansas City Star*	1943–1946
Vermont C. Royster *	*Wall Street Journal*	1967–1976
Louis B. Seltzer	*Cleveland Press*	1956–1968
Melville E. Stone	The Associated Press	1912–1930
Charles H. Taylor	*Boston Globe*	1912–1921
Samuel C. Wells	*Philadelphia Press*	1912–1922
William Allen White *	*Emporia Gazette*, Emporia, Kansas	1937–1943
Walter Williams	University of Missouri	1931–1932
Thomas Winship	*Boston Globe*	1974–1978
Casper S. Yost	*St. Louis Globe-Democrat*	1927–1930

Administrators and Secretaries of the Board

Jerome Landfield   1925–1929
R. A. Parker   1930–1931
Carl W. Ackerman   1933–1953
John Hohenberg   1954–

2
Pulitzer Prize Awards

A. PULITZER PRIZES IN JOURNALISM

Meritorious Public Service
1917 No award.
1918 *New York Times*
1919 *Milwaukee Journal*
1920 No award.
1921 *Boston Post*
1922 *New York World*
1923 *Memphis Commercial Appeal*
1924 *New York World*
1925 No award.
1926 *Columbus* (Ga.) *Enquirer Sun*
1927 *Canton* (Ohio) *Daily News*
1928 *Indianapolis Times*
1929 *New York Evening World*
1930 No award.
1931 *Atlanta Constitution*
1932 *Indianapolis News*
1933 *New York World-Telegram*
1934 *Medford* (Oregon) *Mail Tribune*
1935 *Sacramento Bee*
1936 *Cedar Rapids* (Iowa) *Gazette*
1937 *St. Louis Post-Dispatch*
1938 *Bismarck* (N.D.) *Tribune*
1939 *Miami News*
1940 *Waterbury* (Conn.) *Republican-American*
1941 *St. Louis Post-Dispatch*
1942 *Los Angeles Times*
1943 *Omaha World-Herald*
1944 *New York Times*
1945 *Detroit Free Press*
1946 *Scranton* (Pa.) *Times*
1947 *Baltimore Sun*
1948 *St. Louis Post-Dispatch*
1949 *Nebraska State Journal*
1950 *Chicago Daily News* and *St. Louis Post-Dispatch*

1951 *Miami Herald* and *Brooklyn Eagle*
1952 *St. Louis Post-Dispatch*
1953 *Whiteville* (N.C.) *News Reporter* and *Tabor City* (N.C.) *Tribune*
1954 *Newsday*, Garden City, N.Y.
1955 *Columbus* (Ga.) *Ledger* and *Sunday Ledger-Enquirer*
1956 *Watsonville* (Calif.) *Register-Pajaronian*
1957 *Chicago Daily News*
1958 *Arkansas Gazette*, Little Rock
1959 *Utica* (N.Y.) *Observer-Dispatch* and *Utica Daily Press*
1960 *Los Angeles Times*
1961 *Amarillo* (Texas) *Globe-Times*
1962 *Panama City* (Fla.) *News-Herald*
1963 *Chicago Daily News*
1964 *St. Petersburg* (Fla.) *Times*
1965 *Hutchinson* (Kansas) *News*
1966 *Boston Globe*
1967 *Louisville Courier-Journal* and *Milwaukee Journal*
1968 *Riverside* (Calif.) *Press-Enterprise*
1969 *Los Angeles Times*
1970 *Newsday*, Garden City, N.Y.
1971 *Winston-Salem* (N.C.) *Journal & Sentinel*
1972 *New York Times*
1973 *Washington Post*
1974 *Newsday*, Garden City, N.Y.

Reporting
(NOTE: The Reporting category originally embraced local, national, and international but developed into separate categories as indicated in the following listing:)
1917 Herbert Bayard Swope, *New York World*
1918 Harold A. Littledale, *New York Evening Post*
1919 No award.
1920 John J. Leary Jr., *New York World*
1921 Louis Seibold, *New York World*
1922 Kirke L. Simpson, Associated Press
1923 Alva Johnston, *New York Times*
1924 Magner White, *San Diego Sun*
1925 James W. Mulroy and Alvin H. Goldstein, *Chicago Daily News*
1926 William Burke Miller, *Louisville Courier-Journal*
1927 John T. Rogers, *St. Louis Post-Dispatch*
1928 No award.
1929 Paul Y. Anderson, *St. Louis Post-Dispatch*
1930 Russell D. Owen, *New York Times*
1931 A. B. MacDonald, *Kansas City Star*
1932 W. C. Richards, D. D. Martin, J. S. Pooler, F. D. Webb, and J. N. W. Sloan, *Detroit Free Press*
1933 Francis A. Jamieson, Associated Press
1934 Royce Brier, *San Francisco Chronicle*
1935 William H. Taylor, *New York Herald Tribune*
1936 Lauren D. Lyman, *New York Times*

1937 John J. O'Neill, *New York Herald Tribune;* William L. Laurence, *New York Times;* Howard W. Blakeslee, Associated Press; Gobind Behari Lal, Universal Service; and David Dietz, Scripps-Howard Newspapers

1938 Raymond Sprigle, *Pittsburgh Post-Gazette*

1939 Thomas L. Stokes, Scripps-Howard Newspapers

1940 S. Burton Heath, *New York World-Telegram*

1941 Westbrook Pegler, *New York World-Telegram*

1942 Stanton Delaplane, *San Francisco Chronicle*

1943 George Weller, *Chicago Daily News*

1944 Paul Schoenstein and Associates, *New York Journal-American*

1945 Jack S. McDowell, *San Francisco Call-Bulletin*

1946 William L. Laurence, *New York Times*

1947 Frederick Woltman, *New York World-Telegram*

1948 George E. Goodwin, *Altanta Journal*

1949 Malcolm Johnson, *New York Sun*

1950 Meyer Berger, *New York Times*

1951 Edward S. Montgomery, *San Francisco Examiner*

1952 George de Carvalho, *San Francisco Chronicle*

Local General Reporting

1953 *Providence Journal-Bulletin*

1954 *Vicksburg* (Miss.) *Sunday Post-Herald*

1955 Mrs. Caro Brown, *Alice* (Texas) *Daily Echo*

1956 Lee Hills, *Detroit Free Press*

1957 *Salt Lake Tribune*

1958 *Fargo* (N.D.) *Forum*

1959 Mary Lou Werner, *Washington Star*

1960 Jack Nelson, *Atlanta Constitution*

1961 Sanche de Gramont, *New York Herald Tribune*

1962 Robert D. Mullins, *Deseret News*, Salt Lake City

1963 Sylvan Fox, Anthony Shannon, and William Longgood, *New York World-Telegram and Sun*

1964 Norman C. Miller, *Wall Street Journal*

1965 Melvin H. Ruder, *Hungry Horse News*, Columbia Falls, Mont.

1966 *Los Angeles Times*

1967 Robert V. Cox, *Chambersburg* (Pa.) *Public Opinion*

1968 *Detroit Free Press*

1969 John Fetterman, *Louisville Times & Courier-Journal*

1970 Thomas Fitzpatrick, *Chicago Sun-Times*

1971 *Akron Beacon Journal*

1972 Richard Cooper and John Machacek, *Rochester* (N.Y.) *Times-Union*

1973 *Chicago Tribune*

1974 Arthur M. Petacque and Hugh F. Hough, *Chicago Sun-Times*

Local Specialized and Investigative Reporting

1953 Edward J. Mowery, *New York World-Telegram*

1954 Alvin Scott McCoy, *Kansas City Star*

1955 Roland Kenneth Towery, *Cuero* (Texas) *Record*

1956 Arthur Daley, *New York Times*

1957 Wallace Turner and William Lambert, *Portland Oregonian*

1958 George Beveridge, *Washington Evening Star*
1959 John Harold Brislin, *Scranton* (Pa.) *Tribune*
1960 Miriam Ottenberg, *Washington Evening Star*
1961 Edgar May, *Buffalo* (N.Y.) *Evening News*
1962 George Bliss, *Chicago Tribune*
1963 Oscar Griffin Jr., *Pecos* (Texas) *Independent and Enterprise*
1964 James V. Magee, Albert V. Gaudiosi, and Frederick A. Meyer, *Philadelphia Bulletin*
1965 Gene Goltz, *Houston Post*
1966 John A. Frasca, *Tampa Tribune*
1967 Gene Miller, *Miami Herald*
1968 J. Anthony Lukas, *New York Times*
1969 Albert L. Delugach and Denny Walsh, *St. Louis Globe-Democrat*
1970 Harold E. Martin, *Montgomery Advertiser & Alabama Journal*
1971 William Jones, *Chicago Tribune*
1972 Timothy Leland, Gerard M. O'Neill, Stephen A. Kurkjian, and Ann DeSantis, *Boston Globe*
1973 Sun Newspapers of Omaha
1974 William Sherman, *New York Daily News*

Correspondence
1929 Paul Scott Mowrer, *Chicago Daily News*
1930 Leland Stowe, *New York Herald Tribune*
1931 H. R. Knickerbocker, *Philadelphia Public Ledger* and *New York Evening Post*
1932 Walter Duranty, *New York Times*, and Charles G. Ross, *St. Louis Post-Dispatch*
1933 Edgar Ansel Mowrer, *Chicago Daily News*
1934 Frederick T. Birchall, *New York Times*
1935 Arthur Krock, *New York Times*
1936 Wilfred C. Barber, *Chicago Tribune*
1937 Anne O'Hare McCormick, *New York Times*
1938 Arthur Krock, *New York Times*
1939 Louis P. Lochner, Associated Press
1940 Otto D. Tolischus, *New York Times*
1941 Group award to American war correspondents
1942 Carlos P. Romulo, *Philippines Herald*
1943 Hanson W. Baldwin, *New York Times*
1944 Ernest Taylor Pyle, Scripps-Howard Newspapers
1945 Harold V. Boyle, Associated Press
1946 Arnaldo Cortesi, *New York Times*
1947 Brooks Atkinson, *New York Times*

Telegraphic Reporting (*National*)
1942 Louis Stark, *New York Times*
1943 No award.
1944 Dewey L. Fleming, *Baltimore Sun*
1945 James Reston, *New York Times*
1946 Edward A. Harris, *St. Louis Post-Dispatch*
1947 Edward T. Folliard, *Washington Post*

National Reporting
1948 Bert Andrews, *New York Herald Tribune*, and Nat S. Finney, *Minneapolis Tribune*
1949 C. P. Trussell, *New York Times*

1950 Edwin O. Guthman, *Seattle Times*
1951 No award.
1952 Anthony Leviero, *New York Times*
1953 Don Whitehead, Associated Press
1954 Richard Wilson, Cowles Newspapers
1955 Anthony Lewis, *Washington Daily News*
1956 Charles L. Bartlett, *Chattanooga Times*
1957 James Reston, *New York Times*
1958 Relman Morin, Associated Press, and Clark Mollenhoff, *Des Moines Register & Tribune*
1959 Howard Van Smith, *Miami News*
1960 Vance Trimble, Scripps Howard Newspapers
1961 Edward R. Cony, *Wall Street Journal*
1962 Nathan G. Caldwell and Gene S. Graham, *Nashville Tennessean*
1963 Anthony Lewis, *New York Times*
1964 Merriman Smith, United Press International
1965 Louis M. Kohlmeier, *Wall Street Journal*
1966 Haynes Johnson, *Washington Evening Star*
1967 Stanley Penn and Monroe Karmin, *Wall Street Journal*
1968 Howard James, *Christian Science Monitor*, and Nathan K. (Nick) Kotz, *Des Moines Register* and *Minneapolis Tribune*
1969 Robert Cahn, *Christian Science Monitor*
1970 William J. Eaton, *Chicago Daily News*
1971 Lucinda Franks and Thomas Powers, UPI
1972 Jack Anderson, syndicated columnist
1973 Robert Boyd and Clark Hoyt, Knight Newspapers
1974 James R. Polk, *Washington Star-News*, and Jack White, *Providence* (R.I.) *Journal-Bulletin*

Telegraphic Reporting (International)
1942 Laurence Edmund Allen, Associated Press
1943 Ira Wolfert, North American Newspaper Alliance
1944 Daniel de Luce, Associated Press
1945 Mark S. Watson, *Baltimore Sun*
1946 Homer William Bigart, *New York Herald Tribune*
1947 Eddy Gilmore, Associated Press

International Reporting
1948 Paul W. Ward, *Baltimore Sun*
1949 Price Day, *Baltimore Sun*
1950 Edmund Stevens, *Christian Science Monitor*
1951 Keyes Beech and Fred Sparks, *Chicago Daily News;* Marguerite Higgins and Homer William Bigart, *New York Herald Tribune;* Relman Morin and Don Whitehead, Associated Press
1952 John M. Hightower, Associated Press
1953 Austin Wehrwein, *Milwaukee Journal*
1954 Jim G. Lucas, Scripps Howard Newspapers
1955 Harrison E. Salisbury, *New York Times*
1956 William Randolph Hearst Jr., Kingsbury Smith, and Frank Conniff, International News Service
1957 Russell Jones, United Press

1958 *New York Times*
1959 Joseph Martin and Philip Santora, *New York Daily News*
1960 A. M. Rosenthal, *New York Times*
1961 Lynn Heinzerling, Associated Press
1962 Walter Lippmann, *New York Herald Tribune*
1963 Hal Hendrix, *Miami News*
1964 Malcolm W. Browne, Associated Press, and David Halberstam, *New York Times*
1965 J. A. Livingston, *Philadelphia Bulletin*
1966 Peter Arnett, Associated Press
1967 R. John Hughes, *Christian Science Monitor*
1968 Alfred Friendly, *Washington Post*
1969 William Tuohy, *Los Angeles Times*
1970 Seymour M. Hersh, Dispatch News Service
1971 Jimmie Lee Hoagland, *Washington Post*
1972 Peter R. Kann, *Wall Street Journal*
1973 Max Frankel, *New York Times*
1974 Hedrick Smith, *New York Times*

Editorials
1917 *New York Tribune*
1918 *Louisville Courier-Journal*, by Henry Watterson
1919 No award.
1920 Harvey E. Newbranch, *Omaha Evening World Herald*
1921 No award.
1922 Frank M. O'Brien, *New York Herald*
1923 William Allen White, *Emporia* (Kansas) *Gazette*
1924 *Boston Herald* and Frank I. Cobb, *New York World*
1925 *Charleston* (S.C.) *News and Courier*
1926 *New York Times*, by Edward M. Kingsbury
1927 *Boston Herald*, by F. Lauriston Bullard
1928 Grover C. Hall, *Montgomery* (Ala.) *Advertiser*
1929 Louis Isaac Jaffe, *Norfolk Virginian-Pilot*
1930 No award.
1931 Charles S. Ryckman, *Fremont* (Neb.) *Tribune*
1932 No award.
1933 *Kansas City Star*
1934 E. P. Chase, *Atlantic* (Iowa) *News-Telegraph*
1935 No award.
1936 Felix Morley, *Washington Post*, and George B. Parker, Scripps Howard Newspapers
1937 John W. Owens, *Baltimore Sun*
1938 William Wesley Waymack, *Des Moines Register & Tribune*
1939 Ronald G. Callvert, *The Oregonian*, Portland
1940 Bart Howard, *St. Louis Post-Dispatch*
1941 Reuben Maury, *New York Daily News*
1942 Geoffrey Parsons, *New York Herald Tribune*
1943 Forrest W. Seymour, *Des Moines Register & Tribune*
1944 *Kansas City Star*, by Henry J. Haskell
1945 George W. Potter, *Providence Journal-Bulletin*
1946 Hodding Carter, *Delta Democrat-Times*, Greenville, Miss.

1947 William H. Grimes, *Wall Street Journal*
1948 Virginius Dabney, *Richmond Times Dispatch*
1949 John H. Crider, *Boston Herald,* and Herbert Elliston, *Washington Post*
1950 Carl M. Saunders, *Jackson* (Mich.) *Citizen Patriot*
1951 William H. Fitzpatrick, *New Orleans States*
1952 Louis LaCoss, *St. Louis Globe Democrat*
1953 Vermont Connecticut Royster, *Wall Street Journal*
1954 *Boston Herald,* by Don Murray
1955 *Detroit Free Press,* by Royce Howes
1956 Lauren K. Soth, *Des Moines Register & Tribune*
1957 Buford Boone, *Tuscaloosa* (Ala.) *News*
1958 Harry S. Ashmore, *Arkansas Gazette,* Little Rock
1959 Ralph McGill, *Atlanta Constitution*
1960 Lenoir Chambers, *Norfolk Virginian-Pilot*
1961 William J. Dorvillier, *San Juan* (Puerto Rico) *Star*
1962 Thomas M. Storke, *Santa Barbara* (Calif.) *News-Press*
1963 Ira B. Harkey Jr., *Pascagoula* (Miss.) *Chronicle*
1964 Hazel Brannon Smith, *Lexington* (Miss.) *Advertiser*
1965 John R. Harrison, *Gainesville* (Fla.) *Daily Sun*
1966 Robert Lasch, *St. Louis Post-Dispatch*
1967 Eugene Patterson, *Atlanta Constitution*
1968 John S. Knight, Knight Newspapers
1969 Paul Greenberg, *Pine Bluff* (Ark.) *Commercial*
1970 Philip L. Geyelin, *Washington Post*
1971 Horance G. Davis Jr., *Gainesville* (Fla.) *Sun*
1972 John Strohmeyer, *Bethlehem* (Pa.) *Globe-Times*
1973 Roger B. Linscott, *Berkshire Eagle,* Pittsfield, Mass.
1974 F. Gilman Spencer, *The Trentonian,* Trenton, N.J.

Editorial Cartoons
1922 Rollin Kirby
1923 No award.
1924 Jay N. Darling, *New York Tribune*
1925 Rollin Kirby, *New York World*
1926 D. R. Fitzpatrick, *St. Louis Post-Dispatch*
1927 Nelson Harding, *Brooklyn Eagle*
1928 Nelson Harding, *Brooklyn Eagle*
1929 Rollin Kirby, *New York World*
1930 Charles R. Macauley, *Brooklyn Eagle*
1931 Edmund Duffy, *Baltimore Sun*
1932 John T. McCutcheon, *Chicago Tribune*
1933 H. M. Talburt, *Washington Daily News*
1934 Edmund Duffy, *Baltimore Sun*
1935 Ross A. Lewis, *Milwaukee Journal*
1936 No award.
1937 C. D. Batchelor, *New York Daily News*
1938 Vaughn Shoemaker, *Chicago Daily News*
1939 Charles G. Werner, *Oklahoma City Daily Oklahoman*
1940 Edmund Duffy, *Baltimore Sun*

1941 Jacob Burck, *Chicago Times*
1942 Herbert Lawrence Block (Herblock) NEA Service
1943 Jay N. Darling, *New York Herald Tribune*
1944 Clifford K. Berryman, *Washington Evening Star*
1945 Sgt. Bill Mauldin, United Feature Syndicate
1946 Bruce A. Russell, *Los Angeles Times*
1947 Vaughn Shoemaker, *Chicago Daily News*
1948 Reuben L. Goldberg, *New York Sun*
1949 Lute Pease, *Newark Evening News*
1950 James T. Berryman, *Washington Evening Star*
1951 Reginald W. Manning, *Arizona Republic*
1952 Fred L. Packer, *New York Mirror*
1953 Edward D. Kuekes, *Cleveland Plain Dealer*
1954 Herbert L. Block (Herblock), *Washington Post & Times-Herald*
1955 D. R. Fitzpatrick, *St. Louis Post-Dispatch*
1956 Robert York, *Louisville Times*
1957 Tom Little, *Nashville Tennessean*
1958 Bruce M. Shanks, *Buffalo* (N.Y.) *Evening News*
1959 William H. (Bill) Mauldin, *St. Louis Post-Dispatch*
1960 No award.
1961 Carey Orr, *Chicago Tribune*
1962 Edmund S. Valtman, *Hartford Times*
1963 Frank Miller, *Des Moines Register*
1964 Paul Conrad, *Denver Post*
1965 No award.
1966 Don Wright, *Miami News*
1967 Patrick B. Oliphant, *Denver Post*
1968 Eugene Gray Payne, *Charlotte Observer*
1969 John Fischetti, *Chicago Daily News*
1970 Thomas F. Darcy, *Newsday*, Garden City, N.Y.
1971 Paul Conrad, *Los Angeles Times*
1972 Jeffrey K. MacNelly, *Richmond News-Leader*
1973 No award.
1974 Paul Szep, *Boston Globe*

Photography
1942 Milton Brooks, *Detroit News*
1943 Frank Noel, Associated Press
1944 Frank Filan, Associated Press, and Earle L. Bunker, *Omaha World-Herald*
1945 Joe Rosenthal, Associated Press
1946 No award.
1947 Arnold Hardy, Atlanta, Ga.
1948 Frank Cushing, *Boston Traveler*
1949 Nathaniel Fein, *New York Herald Tribune*
1950 Bill Crouch, *Oakland Tribune*
1951 Max Desfor, Associated Press
1952 John Robinson and Don Ultang, *Des Moines Register & Tribune*
1953 William M. Gallagher, *Flint* (Mich.) *Journal*
1954 Mrs. Walter M. Schau, San Anselmo, Calif.
1955 John L. Gaunt, Jr., *Los Angeles Times*

1956 *New York Daily News*
1957 Harry A. Trask, *Boston Traveler*
1958 William C. Beall, *Washington Daily News*
1959 William Seaman, *Minneapolis Star*
1960 Andrew Lopez, United Press International
1961 Yasushi Nagao, Mainichi Shimbun, Tokyo, for UPI
1962 Paul Vathis, Associated Press
1963 Hector Rondon, La Republica of Caracas, for AP
1964 Robert H. Jackson, *Dallas Times-Herald*
1965 Horst Faas, Associated Press
1966 Kyoichi Sawada, UPI
1967 Jack R. Thornell, AP

Spot News Photography
1968 Rocco Morabito, *Jacksonville Journal*
1969 Edward T. Adams, AP
1970 Steve Starr, AP
1971 John Paul Filo, *Valley Daily News*, New Kensington, Pa.
1972 Horst Faas and Michel Laurent, AP
1973 Huynh Cong Ut, AP
1974 Anthony K. Roberts, Beverly Hills, Calif.

Feature Photography
1968 Toshio Sakai, UPI
1969 Moneta Sleet Jr., *Ebony*
1970 Dallas Kinney, *Palm Beach Post*
1971 Jack Dykinga, *Chicago Sun-Times*
1972 Dave Kennerly, UPI
1973 Brian Lanker, *Topeka Capital-Journal*
1974 Slava Veder, AP

Commentary
1970 Marquis W. Childs, *St. Louis Post-Dispatch*
1971 William A. Caldwell, *The Record*, Hackensack, N.J.
1972 Mike Royko, *Chicago Daily News*
1973 David S. Broder, *Washington Post*
1974 Edwin A. Roberts Jr., *National Observer*

Criticism
1970 Ada Louise Huxtable, *New York Times*
1971 Harold C. Schonberg, *New York Times*
1972 Frank Peters Jr., *St. Louis Post-Dispatch*
1973 Ronald Powers, *Chicago Sun-Times*
1974 Emily Genauer, Newsday Syndicate

Newspaper History Award
1918 Minna Lewinson and Henry Beetle Hough

Special Citations—Journalism
1938 *Edmonton* (Alberta) *Journal*
1941 *New York Times* foreign news report
1944 Byron Price, director of Office of Censorship, and William Allen White
1945 American press cartographers

1947 Columbia University, its Graduate School of Journalism and the *St. Louis Post-Dispatch*, marking the centennial of Joseph Pulitzer's birth
1948 Dr. Frank Diehl Fackenthal
1951 C. L. Sulzberger, *New York Times*, and Arthur Krock, *New York Times*
1952 Max Kase, *New York Journal-American*
1952 *Kansas City Star*
1953 *New York Times* Review of the Week
1958 Walter Lippmann, *New York Herald Tribune*
1964 Gannett Newspapers

B. PULITZER PRIZES IN LETTERS

Novel
1917 No award.
1918 *His Family*. By Ernest Poole
1919 *The Magnificent Ambersons*. By Booth Tarkington
1920 No award.
1921 *The Age of Innocence*. By Edith Wharton
1922 *Alice Adams*. By Booth Tarkington
1923 *One of Ours*. By Willa Cather
1924 *The Able McLaughlins*. By Margaret Wilson
1925 *So Big*. By Edna Ferber
1926 *Arrowsmith*. By Sinclair Lewis
1927 *Early Autumn*. By Louis Bromfield
1928 *The Bridge of San Luis Rey*. By Thornton Wilder
1929 *Scarlet Sister Mary*. By Julia Peterkin
1930 *Laughing Boy*. By Oliver LaFarge
1931 *Years of Grace*. By Margaret Ayer Barnes
1932 *The Good Earth*. By Pearl S. Buck
1933 *The Store*. By T. S. Stribling
1934 *Lamb in His Bosom*. By Caroline Miller
1935 *Now in November*. By Josephine Winslow Johnson
1936 *Honey in the Horn*. By Harold L. Davis
1937 *Gone with the Wind*. By Margaret Mitchell
1938 *The Late George Apley*. By John Phillips Marquand
1939 *The Yearling*. By Marjorie Kinnan Rawlings
1940 *The Grapes of Wrath*. By John Steinbeck
1941 No award.
1942 *In This Our Life*. By Ellen Glasgow
1943 *Dragon's Teeth*. By Upton Sinclair
1944 *Journey in the Dark*. By Martin Flavin
1945 *A Bell for Adano*. By John Hersey
1946 No award.
1947 *All the King's Men*. By Robert Penn Warren
[Note: *The name of this category was changed to Fiction for 1948 and thereafter.*]

Fiction
1948 *Tales of the South Pacific*. By James A. Michener
1949 *Guard of Honor*. By James Gould Cozzens
1950 *The Way West*. By A. B. Guthrie, Jr.

1951 *The Town.* By Conrad Richter
1952 *The Caine Mutiny.* By Herman Wouk
1953 *The Old Man and the Sea.* By Ernest Hemingway
1954 No award.
1955 *A Fable.* By William Faulkner
1956 *Andersonville.* By MacKinlay Kantor
1957 No award.
1958 *A Death In The Family.* By James Agee
1959 *The Travels of Jaimie McPheeters.* By Robert Lewis Taylor
1960 *Advise and Consent.* By Allen Drury
1961 *To Kill A Mockingbird.* By Harper Lee
1962 *The Edge of Sadness.* By Edwin O'Connor
1963 *The Reivers.* By William Faulkner
1964 No award.
1965 *The Keepers Of The House.* By Shirley Ann Grau
1966 *Collected Stories.* By Katherine Anne Porter
1967 *The Fixer.* By Bernard Malamud
1968 *The Confessions of Nat Turner.* By William Styron
1969 *House Made of Dawn.* By N. Scott Momaday
1970 *Collected Stories.* By Jean Stafford
1971 No award.
1972 *Angle of Repose.* By Wallace Stegner
1973 *The Optimist's Daughter.* By Eudora Welty
1974 No award.

Drama
1917 No award.
1918 *Why Marry?* By Jesse Lynch Williams
1919 No award.
1920 *Beyond the Horizon.* By Eugene O'Neill
1921 *Miss Lulu Bett.* By Zona Gale
1922 *Anna Christie.* By Eugene O'Neill
1923 *Icebound.* By Owen Davis
1924 *Hell-Bent Fer Heaven.* By Hatcher Hughes
1925 *They Knew What They Wanted.* By Sidney Howard
1926 *Craig's Wife.* By George Kelly
1927 *In Abraham's Bosom.* By Paul Green
1928 *Strange Interlude.* By Eugene O'Neill
1929 *Street Scene.* By Elmer L. Rice
1930 *The Green Pastures.* By Marc Connelly
1931 *Alison's House.* By Susan Glaspell
1932 *Of Thee I Sing.* By George S. Kaufman, Morrie Ryskind, and Ira Gershwin
1933 *Both Your Houses.* By Maxwell Anderson
1934 *Men in White.* By Sidney Kingsley
1935 *The Old Maid.* By Zoë Akins
1936 *Idiot's Delight.* By Robert E. Sherwood
1937 *You Can't Take It With You.* By Moss Hart and George S. Kaufman
1938 *Our Town.* By Thornton Wilder
1939 *Abe Lincoln in Illinois.* By Robert E. Sherwood

1940 *The Time of Your Life.* By William Saroyan
1941 *There Shall Be No Night.* By Robert E. Sherwood
1942 No award.
1943 *The Skin of Our Teeth.* By Thornton Wilder
1944 No award.
1945 *Harvey.* By Mary Chase
1946 *State of the Union.* By Russel Crouse and Howard Lindsay
1947 No award.
1948 *A Streetcar Named Desire.* By Tennessee Williams
1949 *Death of a Salesman.* By Arthur Miller
1950 *South Pacific.* By Richard Rodgers, Oscar Hammerstein, 2nd, and Joshua Logan
1951 No award.
1952 *The Shrike.* By Joseph Kramm
1953 *Picnic.* By William Inge
1954 *The Teahouse of the August Moon.* By John Patrick
1955 *Cat on A Hot Tin Roof.* By Tennessee Williams
1956 *Diary of Anne Frank.* By Albert Hackett and Frances Goodrich
1957 *Long Day's Journey Into Night.* By Eugene O'Neill
1958 *Look Homeward, Angel.* By Ketti Frings
1959 *J.B.* By Archibald MacLeish
1960 *Fiorello!* Book by Jerome Weidman and George Abbott, music by Jerry Bock, and
       lyrics by Sheldon Harnick
1961 *All The Way Home.* By Tad Mosel
1962 *How To Succeed In Business Without Really Trying.* By Frank Loesser and Abe Burrows
1963 No award.
1964 No award.
1965 *The Subject Was Roses.* By Frank D. Gilroy
1966 No award.
1967 *A Delicate Balance.* By Edward Albee
1968 No award.
1969 *The Great White Hope.* By Howard Sackler
1970 *No Place To Be Somebody.* By Charles Gordone
1971 *The Effect of Gamma Rays on Man-in-the-Moon Marigolds.* By Paul Zindel
1972 No award.
1973 *That Championship Season.* By Jason Miller
1974 No award.

History

1917 *With Americans of Past and Present Days.* By His Excellency J. J. Jusserand, Ambas-
       sador of France to the United States
1918 *A History of the Civil War, 1861–1865.* By James Ford Rhodes
1919 No award.
1920 *The War with Mexico,* 2 vols. By Justin H. Smith
1921 *The Victory at Sea.* By William Sowden Sims in collaboration with Burton J. Hendrick
1922 *The Founding of New England.* By James Truslow Adams
1923 *The Supreme Court in United States History.* By Charles Warren
1924 *The American Revolution—A Constitutional Interpretation.* By Charles Howard McIl-
       wain
1925 *A History of the American Frontier.* By Frederic L. Paxson

1926 *The History of the United States.* By Edward Channing
1927 *Pickney's Treaty.* By Samuel Flagg Bemis
1928 *Main Currents in American Thought,* 2 vols. By Vernon Louis Parrington
1929 *The Organization and Administration of the Union Army, 1861–1865.* By Fred Albert Shannon
1930 *The War of Independence.* By Claude H. Van Tyne
1931 *The Coming of the War: 1914.* By Bernadotte E. Schmitt
1932 *My Experiences in the World War.* By John J. Pershing
1933 *The Significance of Sections in American History.* By Frederick J. Turner
1934 *The People's Choice.* By Herbert Agar
1935 *The Colonial Period of American History.* By Charles McLean Andrews
1936 *The Constitutional History of the United States.* By Andrew C. McLaughlin
1937 *The Flowering of New England.* By Van Wyck Brooks
1938 *The Road to Reunion, 1865–1900.* By Paul Herman Buck
1939 *A History of American Magazines.* By Frank Luther Mott
1940 *Abraham Lincoln: The War Years.* By Carl Sandburg
1941 *The Atlantic Migration, 1607–1860.* By Marcus Lee Hansen
1942 *Reveille in Washington.* By Margaret Leech
1943 *Paul Revere and the World He Lived In.* By Esther Forbes
1944 *The Growth of American Thought.* By Merle Curti
1945 *Unfinished Business.* By Stephen Bonsal
1946 *The Age of Jackson.* By Arthur Meier Schlesinger, Jr.
1947 *Scientists Against Time.* By James Phinney Baxter 3rd
1948 *Across the Wide Missouri.* By Bernard DeVoto
1949 *The Disruption of American Democracy.* By Roy Franklin Nichols
1950 *Art and Life in America.* By Oliver W. Larkin
1951 *The Old Northwest, Pioneer Period 1815–1840.* By R. Carlyle Buley
1952 *The Uprooted.* By Oscar Handlin
1953 *The Era of Good Feelings.* By George Dangerfield
1954 *A Stillness at Appomattox.* By Bruce Catton
1955 *Great River: The Rio Grande in North American History.* By Paul Horgan
1956 *Age of Reform.* By Richard Hofstadter
1957 *Russia Leaves the War: Soviet-American Relations, 1917–1920.* By George F. Kennan
1958 *Banks and Politics in America.* By Bray Hammond
1959 *The Republican Era: 1869–1901.* By Leonard D. White, with the assistance of Miss Jean Schneider
1960 *In The Days of McKinley.* By Margaret Leech
1961 *Between War and Peace: The Potsdam Conference.* By Herbert Feis
1962 *The Triumphant Empire, Thunder-Clouds in the West.* By Lawrence H. Gipson
1963 *Washington, Village and Capital, 1800–1878.* By Constance McLaughlin Green
1964 *Puritan Village: The Formation of a New England Town.* By Sumner Chilton Powell
1965 *The Greenback Era.* By Irwin Unger
1966 *Life of the Mind in America.* By Perry Miller.
1967 *Exploration and Empire: The Explorer and the Scientist in the Winning of the American West.* By William H. Goetzmann
1968 *The Ideological Origins of the American Revolution.* By Bernard Bailyn
1969 *Origins of the Fifth Amendment.* By Leonard W. Levy
1970 *Present at the Creation: My Years in The State Department.* By Dean Acheson
1971 *Roosevelt, The Soldier of Freedom.* By James MacGregor Burns

1972 *Neither Black Nor White.* By Carl N. Degler
1973 *People of Paradox: An Inquiry Concerning the Origins of American Civilization.* By Michael Kammen
1974 *The Americans: The Democratic Experience.* By Daniel J. Boorstin

Biography or Autobiography
1917 *Julia Ward Howe.* By Laura E. Richards and Maude Howe Elliott assisted by Florence Howe Hall
1918 *Benjamin Franklin, Self-Revealed.* By William Cabell Bruce
1919 *The Education of Henry Adams.* By Henry Adams
1920 *The Life of John Marshall,* 4 vols. By Albert J. Beveridge
1921 *The Americanization of Edward Bok.* By Edward Bok
1922 *A Daughter of the Middle Border.* By Hamlin Garland
1923 *The Life and Letters of Walter H. Page.* By Burton J. Hendrick
1924 *From Immigrant to Inventor.* By Michael Idvorsky Pupin
1925 *Barrett Wendell and His Letters.* By M. A. DeWolfe Howe
1926 *The Life of Sir William Osler,* 2 vols. By Harvey Cushing
1927 *Whitman.* By Emory Holloway
1928 *The American Orchestra and Theodore Thomas.* By Charles Edward Russell
1929 *The Training of an American. The Earlier Life and Letters of Walter H. Page.* By Burton J. Hendrick
1930 *The Raven.* By Marquis James
1931 *Charles W. Eliot.* By Henry James
1932 *Theodore Roosevelt.* By Henry F. Pringle
1933 *Grover Cleveland.* By Allan Nevins
1934 *John Hay.* By Tyler Dennett
1935 *R. E. Lee.* By Douglas S. Freeman
1936 *The Thought and Character of William James.* By Ralph Barton Perry
1937 *Hamilton Fish.* By Allan Nevins
1938 *Pedlar's Progress.* By Odell Shepard
   Andrew Jackson, 2 vols. By Marquis James
1939 *Benjamin Franklin.* By Carl Van Doren
1940 *Woodrow Wilson, Life and Letters. Vol. VII and VIII.* By Ray Stannard Baker
1941 *Jonathan Edwards.* By Ola Elizabeth Winslow
1942 *Crusader in Crinoline.* By Forrest Wilson
1943 *Admiral of the Ocean Sea.* By Samuel Eliot Morison
1944 *The American Leonardo: The Life of Samuel F. B. Morse.* By Carleton Mabee
1945 *George Bancroft: Brahmin Rebel.* By Russel Blaine Nye
1946 *Son of the Wilderness.* By Linnie Marsh Wolfe
1947 *The Autobiography of William Allen White.*
1948 *Forgotten First Citizen: John Bigelow.* By Margaret Clapp
1949 *Roosevelt and Hopkins.* By Robert E. Sherwood
1950 *John Quincy Adams and the Foundations of American Foreign Policy.* By Samuel Flagg Bemis
1951 *John C. Calhoun: American Portrait.* By Margaret Louise Coit
1952 *Charles Evans Hughes.* By Merlo J. Pusey
1953 *Edmund Pendleton 1721–1803.* By David J. Mays
1954 *The Spirit of St. Louis.* By Charles A. Lindbergh
1955 *The Taft Story.* By William S. White

1956 *Benjamin Henry Latrobe*. By Talbot Faulkner Hamlin
1957 *Profiles in Courage*. By John F. Kennedy
1958 *George Washington*, Volumes I–VI, by Douglas Southall Freeman, and Volume VII, written by John Alexander Carroll and Mary Wells Ashworth after Dr. Freeman's death in 1953.
1959 *Woodrow Wilson, American Prophet*. By Arthur Walworth
1960 *John Paul Jones*. By Samuel Eliot Morison
1961 *Charles Sumner and the Coming of the Civil War*. By David Donald
1962 No award.
1963 *Henry James*. By Leon Edel
1964 *John Keats*. By Walter Jackson Bate
1965 *Henry Adams*, three volumes. By Ernest Samuels
1966 *A Thousand Days*. By Arthur M. Schlesinger Jr.
1967 *Mr. Clemens and Mark Twain*. By Justin Kaplan
1968 *Memoirs*. By George F. Kennan
1969 *The Man from New York: John Quinn and His Friends*. By Benjamin Lawrence Reid
1970 *Huey Long*. By T. Harry Williams
1971 *Robert Frost: The Years of Triumph, 1915–1938*. By Lawrance Thompson
1972 *Eleanor and Franklin*. By Joseph P. Lash
1973 *Luce and His Empire*. By W. A. Swanberg
1974 *O'Neill, Son and Artist*. By Louis Sheaffer

Poetry
Previous to the establishment of this prize in 1922, the following awards had been made from gifts provided by the Poetry Society:
1918 *Love Songs*. By Sara Teasdale
1919 *Old Road to Paradise*. By Margaret Widdemer
 Corn Huskers. By Carl Sandburg
THE PULITZER POETRY PRIZES FOLLOW:
1922 *Collected Poems*. By Edwin Arlington Robinson
1923 *The Ballad of the Harp-Weaver; A Few Figs from Thistles;* Eight Sonnets in *American Poetry, 1922, A Miscellany*. By Edna St. Vincent Millay
1924 *New Hampshire: A Poem with Notes and Grace Notes*. By Robert Frost
1925 *The Man Who Died Twice*. By Edwin Arlington Robinson
1926 *What's O'Clock*. By Amy Lowell
1927 *Fiddler's Farewell*. By Leonora Speyer
1928 *Tristram*. By Edwin Arlington Robinson
1929 *John Brown's Body*. By Stephen Vincent Benét
1930 *Selected Poems*. By Conrad Aiken
1931 *Collected Poems*. By Robert Frost
1932 *The Flowering Stone*. By George Dillon
1933 *Conquistador*. By Archibald MacLeish
1934 *Collected Verse*. By Robert Hillyer
1935 *Bright Ambush*. By Audrey Wurdemann
1936 *Strange Holiness*. By Robert P. Tristram Coffin
1937 *A Further Range*. By Robert Frost
1938 *Cold Morning Sky*. By Marya Zaturenska
1939 *Selected Poems*. By John Gould Fletcher
1940 *Collected Poems*. By Mark Van Doren

1941 *Sunderland Capture*. By Leonard Bacon
1942 *The Dust Which Is God*. By William Rose Benet
1943 *A Witness Tree*. By Robert Frost
1944 *Western Star*. By Stephen Vincent Benét
1945 *V-Letter and Other Poems*. By Karl Shapiro
1946 No award.
1947 *Lord Weary's Castle*. By Robert Lowell
1948 *The Age of Anxiety*. By W. H. Auden
1949 *Terror and Decorum*. By Peter Viereck
1950 *Annie Allen*. By Gwendolyn Brooks
1951 *Complete Poems*. By Carl Sandburg
1952 *Collected Poems*. By Marianne Moore
1953 *Collected Poems 1917–1952*. By Archibald MacLeish
1954 *The Waking*. By Theodore Roethke
1955 *Collected Poems*. By Wallace Stevens
1956 *Poems—North & South*. By Elizabeth Bishop
1957 *Things of This World*. By Richard Wilbur
1958 *Promises: Poems 1954–1956*. By Robert Penn Warren
1959 *Selected Poems 1928–1958*. By Stanley Kunitz
1960 *Heart's Needle*. By W. D. Snodgrass
1961 *Times Three: Selected Verse From Three Decades*. By Phyllis McGinley
1962 *Poems*. By Alan Dugan
1963 *Pictures from Breughel*. By William Carlos Williams
1964 *At The End Of The Open Road*. By Louis Simpson
1965 *77 Dream Songs*. By John Berryman
1966 *Selected Poems*. By Richard Eberhart
1967 *Live or Die*. By Anne Sexton
1968 *The Hard Hours*. By Anthony Hecht
1969 *Of Being Numerous*. By George Oppen
1970 *Untitled Subjects*. By Richard Howard
1971 *The Carrier of Ladders*. By William S. Merwin
1972 *Collected Poems*. By James Wright
1973 *Up Country*. By Maxine Kumin
1974 *The Dolphin*. By Robert Lowell

General Non-Fiction
1962 *The Making of the President 1960*. By Theodore H. White
1963 *The Guns of August*. By Barbara W. Tuchman
1964 *Anti-Intellectualism in American Life*. By Richard Hofstadter
1965 *O Strange New World*. By Howard Mumford Jones
1966 *Wandering Through Winter*. By Edwin Way Teale
1967 *The Problem of Slavery in Western Culture*. By David Brion Davis
1968 *Rousseau and Revolution*. By Will and Ariel Durant
1969 *So Human an Animal*. By René Jules Dubos
     The Armies of the Night. By Norman Mailer
1970 *Gandhi's Truth*. By Erik H. Erikson
1971 *The Rising Sun*. By John Toland
1972 *Stilwell and the American Experience in China, 1911–1945*. By Barbara W. Tuchman

1973 *Children of Crisis*, Vols. II and III. By Robert Coles
  Fire in the Lake: The Vietnamese and the Americans in Vietnam. By Frances FitzGerald
1974 *The Denial of Death.* By Ernest Becker

Special Citations—Letters

1944 *Oklahoma!* By Richard Rodgers and Oscar Hammerstein, 2nd
1957 A special citation is awarded to Kenneth Roberts for his historical novels which have long contributed to the creation of greater interest in our early American history.
1960 A special citation is awarded to *The Armada* by Garrett Mattingly, published by Houghton, Mifflin. It is a first class history and a literary work of high order.
1961 A special citation is given to *The American Heritage Picture History of the Civil War* as a distinguished example of American book publishing.
1973 A special citation is awarded to *George Washington*, Vols. I–IV, by James Thomas Flexner.
1974 A special citation is awarded to Roger Sessions for his life's work as a distinguished American composer.

C. PULITZER PRIZES IN MUSIC

1943 William Schuman for his *Secular Cantata No. 2, A Free Song*, performed by the Boston Symphony Orchestra and published by G. Schirmer, Inc., New York.
1944 Howard Hanson for his *Symphony No. 4, Opus 34*, performed by the Boston Symphony Orchestra on December 3, 1943.
1945 Aaron Copland for his *Appalachian Spring*, a ballet written for and presented by Martha Graham and group, commissioned by Mrs. E. S. Coolidge, first presented at the Library of Congress, Washington, D.C., October, 1944.
1946 Leo Sowerby for *The Canticle of the Sun*, commissioned by the Alice M. Ditson Fund, first performed by the Schola Cantorum in New York, April, 1945.
1947 Charles Ives for his *Symphony No. 3*, first performed by Lou Harrison and Chamber Orchestra in New York, April, 1946.
1948 Walter Piston for his *Symphony No. 3*, first performed by the Boston Symphony Orchestra in Boston, January, 1948.
1949 Virgil Thomson for his music for the film *Louisiana Story*, released in 1948 by Robert Flaherty Productions.
1950 Gian-Carlo Menotti for his music in *The Consul*, produced at the Barrymore Theatre, New York.
1951 Douglas S. Moore for his music in *Giants in the Earth*, produed by the Columbia Opera Workshop, March 28, 1951.
1952 Gail Kubik for his *Symphony Concertante*, performed at Town Hall, January 7, 1952.
1953 No award.
1954 Quincy Porter for *Concerto For Two Pianos and Orchestra*, first performed by the Louisville Symphony Orchestra, March 17, 1954. This was one of the works commissioned under a grant of the Rockefeller Foundation for new American compositions for orchestra, or soloists and orchestra.
1955 Gian-Carlo Menotti for *The Saint of Bleecker Street*, an opera first performed at the Broadway Theatre, New York, December 27, 1954.
1956 Ernst Toch for *Symphony No. 3*, first performed by the Pittsburgh Symphony Orchestra, December 2, 1955.
1957 Norman Dello Joio for his *Meditations on Ecclesiastes*, first performed at the Juilliard School of Music on April 20, 1956.

1958 Samuel Barber for *Vanessa*, an opera in four acts. Libretto by Gian Carlo Menotti. First presented January 15, 1958, at the Metropolitan Opera House.

1959 John LaMontaine for his *Concerto for Piano and Orchestra*, first performed in Washington, D.C. by the National Symphony Orchestra on November 25, 1958.

1960 Elliott Carter, for *Second String Quartet*, first performed at the Juilliard School of Music, March 25, 1960.

1961 Walter Piston, for his *Symphony No. 7*, first performed by the Philadelphia Orchestra on February 10, 1961, and commissioned by the Philadelphia Orchestra Association.

1962 Robert Ward, for *The Crucible*, an opera in three acts. Libretto by Bernard Stambler, based on the play by Arthur Miller. First performed at New York City Center, on October 26, 1961, by the New York City Opera Company.

1963 Samuel Barber for *Piano Concerto No. 1*, which had its world premier with the Boston Symphony at Philharmonic Hall on September 24, 1962.

1964 No award.

1965 No award.

1966 Leslie Bassett for his *Variations for Orchestra*.

1967 Leon Kirchner for his *Quartet No. 3*.

1968 George Crumb for *Echoes of Time and the River*.

1969 Karel Husa for his *String Quartet*.

1970 Charles Wuorinen for *Time's Encomium*.

1971 Mario Davidovsky for his *Synchronisms No. 6 for Piano and Electronic Sound*.

1972 Jacob Druckman for *Windows*.

1973 Elliott Carter for his *String Quartet No. 3*.

1974 Donald Martino for *Notturno*.

3
A Note on the Pulitzer Scholarships

A total of 236 persons received scholarships and fellowships between 1917 and 1974 under the bequest of Joseph Pulitzer, as administered by the Advisory Board on the Pulitzer Prizes.

The largest number, 168, came from Columbia's journalism school which from 1920 on awarded traveling fellowships each year to three of its outstanding graduates. From 1917 to 1919, one graduate of each class was so honored.

There were also 22 music scholarships, granted between 1917 and 1942; 38 art scholarships, awarded between 1917 and 1959; and 8 critical writing fellowships, given between 1962 and 1969.

Among those who received these grants were Samuel Barber, Lukas Foss, and Douglas Moore in music, Messrs. Barber and Moore going on to win Pulitzer Prizes in Music. Among the journalism winners were Dean Elie Abel, of the Columbia Graduate School of Journalism; Herbert Brucker, who became president of the American Society of Newspaper Editors; Emanuel R. Freedman, who was for many years the foreign editor of *The New York Times;* and Larry Jinks, the executive editor of the *Miami Herald*.

There have been, in addition, more than 700 persons who have received the Pulitzer Free Scholarships, administered by Columbia College. These were established in 1889 by Joseph Pulitzer to aid deserving graduates of the New York City school system and are not connected with the Pulitzer Prizes and Fellowships.

The scholarship holders receive $250 annually for the four years they are enrolled in a college; in addition, if they attend Columbia College or Columbia's School of Engineering and Applied Science or the School of Architecture, they receive free tuition. In consequence, most recipients attend Columbia. Among them have been three distinguished members of Columbia University Faculties—Meyer Schapiro, University Professor; Edwin B. Matzke, Professor of Botany; and Andrew J. Chiappe, Professor of English.

Joseph Pulitzer wrote of his scholarships:

> I believe in self-made men. But it is not the aim of this [scholarship] plan to help people for ordinary money-making purposes. . . . There are nobler objectives in life. And my hope is not that these scholarships will make better butchers, bakers, brokers, and bank cashiers, but that they will help to make teachers, scholars, physicians, authors, journalists, judges, lawyers, and statesmen. They certainly ought to increase, not diminish, the number of those who, under our free institutions, rise from the humblest to the highest positions.

Pulitzer's faith in scholarships has been amply fulfilled.

4
Prizes Withheld: A Summary

Drama: 1917, 1919, 1942, 1944, 1947, 1951, 1963, 1964, 1966, 1968, 1972, 1974.
Fiction: 1917, 1920, 1941, 1946, 1954, 1957, 1964, 1971, 1974.
Music: (first awarded in 1943) 1953, 1964, 1965.
History: 1919.
Biography: 1962.
Editorial Writing: 1919, 1921, 1930, 1932, 1935.
Public Service: 1917, 1920, 1925, 1930.
Reporting: 1919, 1928; telegraphic reporting, 1943; national reporting, 1951.
Cartoons: (first awarded in 1922) 1923, 1936, 1965, 1973.
Photography: (first awarded in 1942) 1946.

Notes and Comment

This history of the Pulitzer Prizes has been based in large part on the following primary sources, some of which are given a symbol because of frequent reference in the notes:

a. Joseph Pulitzer Papers (JPP), Special Collections, Columbia University.

b. Pulitzer Prize Collection, Journalism Library, Columbia University. Available in microfilm.

c. Jury reports, Secretary's reports, internal memos, and associated Pulitzer Prize Papers (PPP). Mainly in the Pulitzer Prize Office, Journalism Building, Columbia University. *Restricted.*

d. Advisory Board Minutes (ABM). *Restricted.*

e. My correspondence with Pulitzer Prize winners and losers, jurors, Advisory Board members, and others connected with the Prizes.

f. Speeches, interviews, personal recollections, and my diary, which I have kept for more than twenty-five years.

g. The complete record of the Pulitzer Prizes, a Columbia University booklet entitled, "The Pulitzer Prizes, 1917–1966," with one-page inserts for each additional annual announcement.

h. Extracts from the Will of Joseph Pulitzer, dated April 16, 1904, as well as copies of the original Plan of Award and its many revisions.

Biographical sources other than those indicated elsewhere include the *Dictionary of American Biography*, *Who's Who in America*, *Who Was Who* and other standard reference works.

A particular effort has been made to reduce the notes by omitting most general references to primary sources listed above where the origin is clearly indicated in the text. Where there are specific papers or reports that are not described in the text, however, the source is given in the notes. I have also consolidated notes wherever possible. In citing jury reports, I have given relevant dates when they were available; where no date is mentioned, the original report has been undated. Dates of theater reviews, which usually follow the opening of plays, have for the most part been omitted.

Notes

AN INTRODUCTION: PRIZES AND CONSEQUENCES

1. MacLeish address May 10, 1966. The quotation is W. B. Yeats's epitaph to himself. See Yeats, *Collected Poems* (New York, 1951), p. 344.

2. Each prize winner mentioned here expressed reactions in letters to me in late 1972 or early 1973 except Albee, whose position was stated in the New York *Times* May 3, 1967, and Senator Kennedy, whose relevant correspondence with me was in 1957–58.

3. From my diary.

1. THE GRAND SCHEME, 1902–1916

1. JPP.   2. Andrew Carnegie, *The Gospel of Wealth* (New York, 1900).

3. JPP.   4. R. T. Baker, pp. 18–19.

5. From Seitz and Swanberg biographies.   6. Pringle, pp. 59, 303, 337–338.

7. Seitz, p. 435.

8. JPP. Butler to Hosmer, April 13, 1903; Hosmer to Butler, April 15 and 27, 1903; Hosmer memo, "The Making of a Journalist"; text of agreement of April 10, 1903.

9. R. T. Baker, p. 37.   10. Ibid., p. 38.   11. JPP.

12. Swanberg, p. 410. Pulitzer's defense of journalism education was in *North American Review*, May, 1904.

13. ABM, May 24, 1915.

14. ABM Plan of Award, May 24, 1915, revised June 10, 1915; jury system described, Butler to Fackenthal, May 10, 1915.

15. John Hay died in 1905 and never acted as a Board member. Walter Williams of the University of Missouri was a Board member 1930–32 but there is no record that he ever attended a meeting.

16. ABM, Butler letter, April 19, 1916.   17. ABM, April 23, 1948.

2. PRIZES FOR A BRAVE NEW WORLD, 1917–1923

1. Hofstadter & Metzger, pp. 501–502. Beard later resigned. Ibid., p. 499, for Butler speech. See also Carol Signer Gruber, "The Case of James McKeen Cattell," *AAUP Bulletin*, 58, No. 3 (Autumn, 1972), pp. 297–305, and Charles A. Beard, "A Statement," *New Republic* XIII (Dec. 29, 1917), p. 250.

2. Henry Beetle Hough letter to me, Dec. 27, 1972.   3. ABM, May 24, 1917.

4. Sloan to Fackenthal, Feb. 26, 1917, and unsigned draft invitation to jurors, March 5, 1917.

5. ABM, May 24, 1917.   6. ABM, May 16, 1918; May 20, 1919.

7. ABM, May 20, 1920.

8. For the background of this period, I am indebted to the histories of May, Allen and Friedel. It helped, too, to have lived through the era.

9. Ralph McGill, "Pulitzer Editorial Awards." *Columbia Library Columns* VI, No. 3 (May, 1957), pp. 23–24.

10. Editorial Jury Report, April 19, 1918; ABM, May 16, 1918. Biographical sources are Watterson, *Marse Henry*, and Wall, *Henry Watterson*. Letter, Watterson to Arthur Krock, Oct. 18, 1921, in Arthur Krock Papers, Princeton.

11. Cunliffe's appointment recorded in ABM, May 20, 1919. Among his faculty members who served on journalism juries were Professors Cooper, Brown, Will, and Robert Emmet MacAlarney, ex-city editor, New York *Evening Mail*. Text of Simpson piece in Hohenberg, *The Pulitzer Prize Story*.

12. Kahn, *The World of Swope*, for Walker quotation, which is in introduction; other comments, pp. 221, 232, 238–45 passim. Remarks about Swope's character are from my own recollection and diaries. Record of World prizes in ABM, 1922–1923. Lippmann's letter in Ackerman Papers, Library of Congress, dated March 5, 1943.

13. O'Brien letter dated May 17, 1921 in ABM, May 21, 1921.

14. White, *Autobiography*, pp. 610–614.   15. Atkinson, *Broadway*, p. 79.

16. Garland to Fackenthal, March 22, 1919. ABM, May 20, 1919. *Why Marry?* ran for *120* performances at the Astor, New York.

17. Biographical sources are Sheaffer's two-volume study, the Gelbs' book, and Toohey. PPP contain 1920 correspondence as follows: Garland to Fackenthal, April 19, 21, 26, 30, and May 6; Hamilton to Garland, April 25; Garland to Butler, May 11; Fackenthal to O'Neill, June 15; O'Neill to Fackenthal, June 20. Drinkwater resolution in ABM, May 20. See also Gelb, pp. 426–427, for O'Neill and Eaton comments. More's views in letter to Fackenthal, April 26, 1918.

18. ABM, May 20, 1920. Garland to Fackenthal, May 22, 1921. See also Toohey, pp. 16–21.

19. PPP for 1922: Garland to Matthews, May 7; Phelps to Fackenthal, May 1; O'Neill to Fackenthal, May 25; Fackenthal to O'Neill, July 11. See also Gelb, pp. 478–482, 496, 500 and 508; Atkinson, *Broadway*, pp. 160–161, 198, 205. For Shaw's classic excuse, see *Androcles and the Lion* (New York, 1914), p. 209.

20. Grant to Butler, April 29, 1920; Fackenthal to Butler, Feb. 6, 1931. Original wording of Fiction award in ABM, May 24, 1915. Sherman to Grant in Zeitlin & Woodbridge, V. 2, pp. 399–400.

21. Letters of Grant and Phelps to Fackenthal; Butler telegram to Board, May 21, 1919.

22. PPP for 1921: Garland to Fackenthal May 22; Fackenthal to Mrs. Wharton, June 3; Mrs. Wharton to Fackenthal, June 10. ABM, May 24, 1921, but the Fiction Jury report is missing. See also Schorer, pp. 230, 248, 269; Garland, pp. 337–338, 347; Lovett in *New Republic*, June 22, 1921, p. 114; Lovett, *All Our Years*, pp. 198–199; Zeitlin & Woodbridge, pp. 401–402; Coolidge, pp. 183–185, 192.

23. Carlos Baker in *Princeton University Library Chronicle*, p. 61; Mizener article in *Atlantic Monthly*, p. 42.

24. Fletcher to Fackenthal, April 3, 1923; Schorer, pp. 334, 374.

25. Samuels, p. 364; Higham, p. 70.

26. Quoted in Howard K. Beale, "The Professional Historian: His Theory and Practice," *Pacific Historical Review* XXII (1953), p. 228.

27. James Truslow Adams Papers, Columbia University.

28. Henry Steele Commager, "The Literature of American History, 1935," *Social Studies* XXVII (1936), p. 252.

29. Samuels, pp. 360–362, 452, 559–571 passim.   30. Adams, *Education*, p. 502.

31. Cross to Fackenthal, Feb. 13, 1922; March 26, 1923.

32. Robinson, *Collected Poems*.   33. Millay, *A Few Figs From Thistles*.

34. Robinson's life sketch from Smith biography.

35. Millay biographical material from Gould, Churchill, and Waggoner. Miss Atkins quoted in Waggoner, pp. 464, 465; Waggoner's own estimate, p. 466.

3. CHANGING TIMES, CHANGING AWARDS, 1924–1933

1. Reporting Jury report, March 8, 1929. For Teapot Dome case and Anderson's role, see Russell, pp. 488–532, 559–560, 604–649 passim; Markham, 90–106; Allen, 136–158 passim.

2. Boston *Herald* editorial, Oct. 26, 1926. Details of Mellett and Loeb-Leopold reporting in Hohenberg, *The Pulitzer Prize Story*. Reporting Jury report, March 7, 1924.

3. From Miller's letter to me, Dec. 26, 1972.

4. Correspondence Jury report, March 14, 1933. Further details in E. A. Mowrer's letter to me Jan. 25, 1973. See also Hohenberg, *Foreign Correspondence*, pp. 291–293.

5. Fiction Jury reports for April 1, 1924; April 3, 1925 (with W. A. White minority report); March 15, 1926; also, the following 1926 letters: Fackenthal to Lewis, April 23, May 6, May 7, May 10, May 13; Lewis to Pulitzer committee, May 6; Lewis to Fackenthal, May 14. Fackenthal's announcement on May 14. Also, Schorer, pp. 445–454.

6. Quoted in Lovett, *All Our Years*, p. 199.

7. Fiction Jury report March 6, 1928, with R. M. Lovett letter of March 7; also, Wilder to Fackenthal, April 2, 1928, and Fackenthal to Wilder, May 4 and 10, 1928.

8. Fiction Jury report, March 13, 1929, with 1929 correspondence as follows: Burton to Fackenthal, April 18; Oliver to Fackenthal, May 22; Fackenthal to Oliver, May 24; Fackenthal to Butler, Sept. 26. ABM, April 25, 1929.

9. Fiction Jury report, March 10, 1930; ABM, April 24, 1930; Fackenthal to Butler, Feb. 6, 1931.

10. Butler to Fackenthal, May 25, 1931. Fiction Jury reports of March 26, 1931, March 14, 1932, and March 19, 1933. ABM, April 28, 1933.

11. Barkham's letter to me Feb. 24, 1973; Carlos Baker's letter to me March 3, 1973.

12. Drama Jury report, April 3, 1924; ABM, April 18, 1924. See also Toohey, p. 37.

13. Drama Jury report, March 15, 1925; also, the following correspondence: Garland to Fackenthal, Nov. 11, 1924; Fackenthal to Garland, Nov. 12, 1924; Garland to Fackenthal, March 9, 1925; Fackenthal to Garland, March 11, 1925; Garland to Fackenthal, March 14, 1925. See also Eaton *in Theatre Annual* (1944), p. 25.

14. Drama Jury reports March 25, 1926, March 15, 1927, March 17, 1928. As inveterate theater-goers and occasional critics, my wife and I saw nearly all of the leading plays that

were presented during the era; the evaluations of them, other than those attributed to critics or jurors, are my own. Atkinson's *Broadway* was helpful, as was his re-evaluation, *The Lively Years, 1920–1973*.

15. Drama Jury reports April 1, 1929 with separate letter from Hamilton April 3, 1930. Pulitzer anecdote from Eaton, *Theatre Annual* (1944), p. 37.

16. Drama Jury reports March 23, 1931, with dissent by Strong dated March 21, 1931. Eaton defense in *Theatre Annual* (1944), pp. 26–27.

17. Drama Jury reports of March 16, 1932, including note by Strong dated March 15, 1932, and March 23, 1933. Rodgers' comment in letter to me Oct. 31, 1972. Eaton comment in *Theater Annual* (1944), p. 27. See also Teichmann, p. 100.

18. Hofstadter, *The Progressive Historians*, and Higham give the best evaluation of the work of Parrington and Turner.

19. History Jury report on Parrington March 10, 1928, on Channing and Fay March 11, 1926, on Van Tyne March 25, 1930.

20. Hofstadter, *The Progressive Historians*, p. 350. Other quotations from Hofstadter, pp. 349–351.

21. Parrington, I, i; Hofstadter, *The Progressive Historians*, p. 350, 352.

22. Beard quoted in Hofstadter, *The Progressive Historians*, p. 48; Donald, in letter to me, Jan. 8, 1973.

23. The essay, "The Frontier in American History," is included in Ray Billington, ed., *Frontier and Section* (New York, 1961).

24. Quoted in Hofstadter, *The Progressive Historians:* Roosevelt, p. 56; Wilson, pp. 60–61; Turner, p. 110.

25. History Jury report, March 17, 1933.

26. Hofstadter, *The Progressive Historians*, pp. 163–164.

27. Quoted in Higham, p. 206.

28. Ibid., p. 81. History Jury report on Nevins' *Grover Cleveland*, March 11, 1933.

29. Monroe in *Poetry*, pp. 210–216.

30. Poetry Jury reports, March 9, 1925, and Feb. 25, 1933. ABM, April 20, 1925, and April 28, 1933.

31. MacLeish, *Poetry and Experience*, p. 101. On Frost, I have consulted the Thompson and Sergeant biographies. The discussion in Waggoner, *American Poets*, pp. 293–327, was also helpful.

32. Quoted in Sergeant, p. 380.   33. Frost, *In The Clearing*, p. 31.

34. Sergeant, p. 353.   35. Ibid., p. 419.

36. MacLeish, *Poetry and Experience*, pp. 8–9.

37. Poetry Jury reports Feb. 28, 1927; March 7, 1931; Feb. 25, 1933.

38. Letter from MacLeish to me Nov. 14, 1972.

39. "You, Andrew Marvell" and "Einstein" as published in Untermeyer, pp. 1170–1176; "Voyage to the Moon" on p. 1 of New York *Times*, July 21, 1969.

4. *THE LAUREATES FACE THE STORM, 1934–1942*

1. Hachten, pp. 90–93.

2. Berger, pp. 505, 535, 545–547, 549–550; Kahn, pp. 232, 234, 236, 473; Hohenberg, *The Pulitzer Prize Story*, pp. 22–28. Krock's citation in ABM, April 27, 1951.

3. Berger, pp. 326–7, 419, 424, 505, 535.

4. Johnson, *The Lines Are Drawn*, reproduces prize-winning cartoons 1917–1958 with sketches of the cartoonists.

5. General Romulo wrote about the incident in a letter to me Jan. 17, 1973. See also Philippines *Herald*, Oct. 29, 1963, p. 1. Romulo was recommended in undated report on Correspondence Prize in 1942 prize folder.

6. Cowley in *New Republic*, May 22, 1935, p. 51.

7. Fackenthal to Butler, May 1, 1934.

8. Undated report of Fiction Jury for 1934; Butler to Fackenthal, May 8, 1934; Fackenthal to Butler, May 9, 1934; ABM, April 26, 1934.

9. Fiction Jury report March 18, 1935; ABM, May 3, 1935.

10. ABM, May 1, 1936.

11. Fiction Jury report, March 15, 1936; ABM, May 1, 1936. Lewis was quoted as having said he served on jury in New York *Times*, May 5, 1936, p. 18, col. 1, at bottom of article about H. L. Davis; Schorer, in a letter to me June 28, 1973, offered a refutation.

12. Undated 1937 Fiction Jury report. ABM, April 30, 1937.

13. Fiction Jury reports March 11, 1938, and March 13, 1939.

14. John Steinbeck, *New York Times Magazine*, Feb. 1, 1953.

15. Undated report of 1940 Fiction Jury; Harrison letter, April 2, 1940; O'Brien letter, April 3, 1940. Cowley in *New Republic*, May 3, 1939, pp. 382–383.

16. ABM, May 2, 1941. PPP, Fiction Jury report for 1941; Butler to Ackerman and Ackerman to Butler, July 7 and 8, 1941, respectively; Butler to Fackenthal and Fackenthal to Butler, July 11 and 12, 1941, respectively. Fourth annual *Saturday Review* poll was appended to jury report. Krock column, "In the Nation," New York *Times*, May 11, 1962, p. 30, was first published indication of the rejection of *For Whom the Bell Tolls*. Krock in 1972–73 gave me further details.

17. Fiction Jury 1942 report; Woodward to Joseph Pulitzer, April 15, 1942; Harris to Butler, April 14, 1942. ABM, May 1, 1942.

18. ABM, April 26, 1934. Drama Jury report for 1934. See also Eaton in *Theatre Annual* (1944); Gaver, 9–13; Toohey, 112–120; Atkinson, *Broadway*, p. 293.

19. Drama Jury report, March 14, 1935; also, the following 1935 correspondence: Phelps to Fackenthal, March 20; Fackenthal to Butler, March 28, enclosing New York *Times* "form chart" of March 24; Phelps to Fackenthal, March 27, April 16; Phelps's column, July 12; Fackenthal to Phelps, July 15; Hamilton to Fackenthal, Sept. 19, 28, Oct. 5; Fackenthal to Hamilton, Sept. 23, Oct. 2; Fackenthal to Butler, Sept. 11, Feb. 6, 1935. See also Atkinson, pp. 258–259; Gaver, pp. 12–14; Toohey, pp. 122–128. Burns Mantle's forecast in New York *Daily News* for April 21, 1935. Hamilton's public attack in New York *Times* May

7, 1935. For Phelps's extra-curricular cultural activities see Hutchens and Oppenheimer, pp. 444–450.

20. Atkinson, *Broadway*, pp. 258–265; Gaver, pp. 13–22. See also Eaton in *Theatre Annual* (1944); Hamilton in *American Mercury*, May, 1935, and New York *Times* interview with Atkinson, Oct. 31, 1973, p. 36.

21. ABM, May 1, 1936, April 28, 1939, May 2, 1941. Drama Jury reports for 1936, 1939, and 1941, the latter in two sections, April 3 and April 23. See also Brown, pp. 342–343, 361, 382, 385–386.

22. Drama Jury report April 7, 1937; ABM, April 30, 1937. See also Teichmann, pp. 16–51 passim, 116–129 passim, and Atkinson, *Broadway*, pp. 230–237.

23. Drama Jury report March 15, 1938; ABM, April 29, 1938. See also Atkinson, *Broadway*, pp. 309–311, and Toohey, pp. 148–155.

24. Drama Jury 1940 report favoring Saroyan play touched off voluminous correspondence in that year including Fackenthal to Saroyan telegram May 6; Saroyan to Fackenthal telegram May 6; Fackenthal to Saroyan telegram May 7 and letters May 9 and 18; Saroyan to Fackenthal, May 15. When Saroyan telegraphed Fackenthal May 2, 1941, asking to have his new play considered for a prize, there was no response to this obvious bid for more publicity.

25. Drama Jury report, April 12, 1942.

26. Gaver, 15; Atkinson, p. 263; Eaton in *Theatre Annual* (1944), p. 29.

27. History Jury 1934 report: ABM, April 26, 1934; criticism quoted in Stanley Frank *Saturday Evening Post* article May 3, 1947, and Cowley in *New Republic* May 22, 1935.

28. History Jury reports March 19, 1935, March 14, 1938, and undated documents for 1940 and 1942. See also James C. Y. Chu, "Carl Sandburg, His Association with Henry Justin Smith." *Journalism Quarterly* (Spring, 1973), p. 43 et. seq.

29. Biography Jury report, Feb. 23, 1935. See also R. T. Baker, p. 107.

30. Biography Jury reports for 1937 and 1942.

31. Poetry Jury reports for 1934 and March 11, 1939.

32. Mizener's *Atlantic* article, p. 42; Cowley in the *New Republic*, May 22, 1935, p. 51.

33. Poetry Jury reports for 1937, 1940–41–42.

34. Poetry Jury report for 1940. Mark Van Doren's letter to me Dec. 4, 1972. Biography from New York *Times* obit, Dec. 12, 1972. For "This Amber Sunstream," see *Collected and New Poems*, by Mark Van Doren (New York, 1963).

35. Ackerman sketch from my own recollection and diaries. William R. Mathews, "Recollections of the Pulitzer Committee," *Arizona Daily Star*, May 22, 1966, supplied other details.

36. ABM, May 1, 1942.

37. Letter dated Dec. 17, 1941, from departmental chairman, Professor Douglas Moore.

38. According to a memo from Fackenthal to Butler, full responsibility for the journalism awards was transferred to Ackerman on May 20, 1932, the date of the document.

39. Correspondence Jury reports for 1936; ABM, April 23, 1948. Carroll Binder's article

was in April, 1948, issue of *American Mercury*. Krock's views in statement of March 18, 1971, sent to Copley Newspapers and to me.

40. Henry Pringle wrote the 1941 Reporting Prize report recommending Laurence and ignoring Pegler.

41. Butler to Fackenthal, March 20, 1944. This is the last of Butler's memos on the prizes in the Pulitzer Prize Papers. The report of Butler's reading the awards to the press and assailing photographers was in New York *Times*, May 5, 1936, p. 18.

5. THE PRIZES IN WAR AND PEACE, 1943–1954

1. ABM, May 1, 1942; April 28, 1944.

2. Correspondence Jury 1944 report. In addition to the Pyle exhibit in the Pulitzer Prize Collection, some of his best material is in *Brave Men* (New York, 1943–44). Biographical detail is from Lee G. Miller, *The Story of Ernie Pyle* (New York, 1950).

3. Correspondence Jury report for 1943. Hanson W. Baldwin described his experience in a letter to me Jan. 6, 1973.

4. George Weller's experience is described in a letter to me Feb. 1, 1973.

5. Fackenthal to Ackerman, May 18, 1943. The information about the deduction is from Wolfert himself.

6. Walter Cronkite, UP file Feb. 27, 1943.

7. Reporting Prize 1946 report. See also Groves, pp. 35–36, 325–327, 347; Laurence, pp. 42–43, 95–97, 112–114, 153–160; Berger, pp. 510–515, 524; Kahn, pp. 297–298, 308.

8. Johnson, 145–149.

9. Photography Prize 1945 report; ABM, April 27, 1945. Rosenthal in AP file, March 7, 1945; also, in letter to me Dec. 31, 1972.

10. National Reporting report for 1945. See also Berger, pp. 498–500.

11. ABM, April 24, 1953.

12. Atkinson describes his experience in a letter to me Jan. 5, 1973.

13. Folliard's experience is given in a letter to me Jan. 12, 1973.

14. International Reporting Jury report, March 21, 1951, with appended Ackerman comment. ABM, April 27, 1951. This is enlarged upon in Keyes Beech's letter to me March 23, 1973.

15. ABM, April 25, 1952. John Hightower elaborates in letter to me Jan. 8, 1973.

16. Pulitzer's views on *Wall Street Journal* are given in Krock paper for the Copley Newspapers, March 18, 1971. ABM, April 28, 1933, for the Board's action on Nevins' *Grover Cleveland*. Relevant material in 16th printing of *Grover Cleveland* (New York, 1964), on pp. 242–243. Royster's views are in his letter to me Jan. 2, 1973.

17. Mathews (see Ch. 4, Note 35).   18. Fiction Jury report for 1943.

19. Fiction Jury report, March 14, 1944. ABM, April 28, 1944.

20. Fiction Jury report, March 14, 1945. ABM, April 27, 1945. Krock's paper for Copley Newspapers, March 18, 1971, is source for Patton incident.

21. ABM, April 25, 1947. Details in letter from Robert Penn Warren to me, Oct. 22, 1972; Fiction Report for 1947 is missing.

22. Orville Prescott, in a letter to me June 27, 1973, and Arthur Krock, in a letter to me March 19, 1969, are the two main sources of the Michener story. Michener himself made no response to a request for comment. The decision is in ABM April 23, 1948. As for the addition of Logan's name in the *South Pacific* listing, Ackerman told me he had done it and was pleased by his action.

23. Norman Mailer's letter to me Dec. 28, 1972. PPP, Fiction Jury report March 24, 1949.

24. Fiction Jury reports April 5, 1950, and March 23, 1951, with supplementary report April 17, 1951. ABM for April 27, 1951.

25. Fiction Jury report March 10, 1952. ABM April 25, 1952. Wouk's letter to me Nov. 1, 1972.

26. Fiction Jury report March 24, 1953. ABM April 24, 1953. See also "Hemingway Letters Reproach Critics," New York *Times*, March 9, 1972, p. 36. And Carlos Baker, p. 363, 510.

27. Fiction Jury report, March 8 and 16, 1954. ABM, April 23, 1954.

28. Drama Jury reports for 1943 and 1944. ABM, April 30, 1943, and April 28, 1944. See also Atkinson, *Broadway*, pp. 334–341. Characterization of Hammerstein from my knowledge of him and his work. Rodgers' letter to me about Gershwin dated Oct. 31, 1972.

29. Drama Jury report April 3, 1945.

30. ABM, April 26, 1946, April 25, 1947 and April 23, 1948. Walter Kerr in New York *Times*, May 6, 1973, II, 1; Williams' letter to me Oct. 21, 1972. See also Atkinson, *Broadway*, pp. 394–397.

31. Drama Jury report April 6, 1949. ABM, April 29, 1949. See also Atkinson, *Broadway*, pp. 397–400. For Atkinson's later comment, see New York *Times*, Oct. 31, 1973, p. 36. Miller's letter to me Dec. 10, 1972.

32. Drama Jury reports April 3, 1950, April 2, 1951, April 2, 1952. ABM, April 18, 1950, April 27, 1951, April 25, 1952.

33. Drama Jury report March 31, 1953. Inge's background from New York *Times* obit, June 11, 1973, p. 1.

34. Drama Jury report March 31, 1954.

35. Schlesinger's thesis developed in *The Age of Jackson* (New York, 1945), p. 307. See also Higham, pp. 217–218. PPP, History Jury report Feb. 27, 1946.

36. History Jury reports for 1943, March 16, 1944, and March 10, 1945. ABM, April 27, 1945.

37. History Jury report March 24, 1949. For Nichols' career, see Higham, pp. 134–136. Also, letter from Nichols to me Nov. 9, 1972.

38. History Jury report March 11, 1954. ABM, April 23, 1954. Details in Krock's letter to me March 19, 1969, and Catton's letter to me Dec. 20, 1972.

39. Biography Jury report for 1943. Morison's letter to me Dec. 4, 1972.

40. Biography Jury reports for March 8, 1946, and March 24, 1954; ABM, April 26, 1946, and April 23, 1954. For evaluation of Bemis, see New York *Times* obit Sept. 28, 1973, p. 36.

41. History Jury report for March 24, 1949; Biography Jury report March 8, 1946. Memo, Ackerman to Advisory Board Oct. 12, 1950, describes Eisenhower remarks at Faculty Club dinner the previous evening.

42. Poetry Jury reports for March 12, 1945, 1947, and March 23, 1954. See also Waggoner, pp. 585–586.

43. Fackenthal, in a memo, commented on the 1945 report which recommended Auden, saying that the poet's citizenship problem would make it desirable to give the award to Shapiro and "leave Auden for later." Governor Cross agreed. Auden was also recommended in the 1946 report, dated March 5, but the Board passed the Poetry Prize that year. For evaluation of Auden, see New York *Times* obit Sept. 3, 1973, pp. 1 and 64.

44. Poetry Jury report Feb. 20, 1950. Letter from Gwendolyn Brooks to me, undated, in January, 1973, gives her comments on the prize. Other quotations are from her autobiography, *Report From Part One* (New York, 1971). See also critique of this book in *New York Times Book Review*, Jan. 7, 1972, p. 1.

45. Poetry Jury report March 4, 1952. See also Waggoner, pp. 364–368. Miss Moore's quotations are from her obituary in the New York *Times*, Feb. 6, 1972, p. 1.

46. Thomson, xvi, 1–39 passim.

47. Music Jury report April 6, 1945. This is elaborated on in Copland's letter to me Dec. 26, 1972. See also Thomson, 49–58.

48. Music Jury report April 14, 1949, elaborated on in Thomson's letter to me Dec. 2, 1972, and Piston's letter to me Jan. 2, 1973. See also Thomson, pp. 91–109.

49. Music Jury report April 9, 1951. Biographical material through the courtesy of Professor Moore's family and Professor Paul Henry Lang's sketch of him in the Century Club's *Memorial*.

50. Music Jury report April 5, 1950. Menotti had the rare distinction of being placed first in 1950 in both music and drama.

51. Music Jury report April 2, 1953.

52. ABM April 18, 1950. Plan of Award revisions April 25, 1947, and April 24, 1953.

53. ABM April 23, 1954.   54. ABM April 29, 1955.

6. A CHANGE IN DIRECTION FOR THE PRIZES, 1955–1965

1. Columbia press release Dec. 20, 1959.

2. *Editor & Publisher*, Dec. 5, 1959, p. 14. This summarizes a Policy Statement on the Journalism Prizes drafted by the Advisory Board. The 24-page statement itself is a part of the Advisory Board Minutes for April 28, 1960.

3. McGill, pp. 24–25, 170–171. Martin, pp. 152–153.   4. ABM, April 25, 1958.

5. Martin, pp. 157–159. Characterization of McGill is from my own knowledge.

6. "Portrait of a Fighting Lady," by Hodding Carter; St. Louis *Post-Dispatch*, Nov. 26, 1961.

7. Anthony Lewis' letter to me Jan. 16, 1973.

8. Background of Hills's reporting from articles by Dale Nouse and Frank Angelo in Detroit *Free Press* May 8, 1956.

9. Soth's letter to me Jan. 2, 1973.

10. The 1956 International Reporting Jury report by Ralph McGill and John R. Herbert recommended the Hearst articles, particularly four by Kingsbury Smith. The ABM for May 21, 1956, give the decision in favor of the Hearst team. Argument before the Board is from my diary. Subsequent material is from an interview with William Randolph Hearst Jr.

11. ABM, April 26, 1957, and April 28, 1960. Rosenthal's background from *Times Talk* XIII, No. 3, November, 1959; also a remarkable Rosenthal letter to me April 4, 1973.

12. Johnson, pp. 200–204.   13. *Times Talk*, April, 1962, pp. 1–8.

14. ABM, April 23, 1964. New York *Times*, May 5, 1964, p. 1. Letter from Browne to me Jan. 18, 1973. Details of jury remarks and Board meeting from my diary.

15. UPI file.

16. Pulitzer Prize Secretary's report, 1961.   17. Fiction Jury report for 1965.

18. Fiction Jury report for 1961.   19. Fiction Jury 1958 report; ABM, April 25, 1958.

20. Fiction Jury report for 1959; ABM, April 23, 1959.

21. Fiction Jury 1960 report; ABM, April 28, 1960.

22. Fiction Jury reports for 1956, 1957, 1962, 1964.

23. Fiction Jury reports for 1955 and 1963. ABM, April 29, 1955, and April 25, 1963.

24. Drama Jury report for 1955. ABM, April 29, 1955. Details of Board meeting from my diary.

25. Drama Jury report for 1957.   26. Drama Jury reports for 1956, 1958, and 1959.

27. Drama Jury 1960 report. ABM, April 28, 1960. Details of Board meeting from my diary. Brown's letter to me June 1, 1960, included in Secretary's report for 1961. Bock's letter to me Nov. 13, 1972; Harnick's Nov. 8, 1972.

28. Drama Jury 1963 report. ABM, April 25, 1963 (details from my diary), plus Brown letter of May 7, 1963, in Secretary's report for 1964. See also New York *Times*, May 7, 1963, p. 1.

29. Drama Jury reports for 1964 and 1965. Gilroy letter to me Nov. 2, 1972.

30. Biography Jury 1957 report. ABM April 26, 1957; details of Board meeting from my diary, also from my letter to President Kirk, April 21, 1966. My correspondence on the Pearson-Kennedy incident included the letter from Senator Kennedy to me of Jan. 10, 1958, following my letter to him of Jan. 7. See Burns biography on Pulitzer Prize, pp. 162–163, 212.

31. Biography Jury 1962 report. ABM April 26, 1962, details of Board meeting from my diary. Several Trustees told me informally what had happened at their meeting of May 7, 1962. Comments are from Peter Kihss's articles about the Pulitzer Prizes in New York *Times*, May 8, 1962, p. 1. Report of change in biography award is in Secretary's report for 1963.

32. Biography Jury reports for 1955 and 1960. ABM record action on White book April 29, 1955. ABM for April 28, 1960, record decisions on Leech and Morison books.

33. Letters to me from Bate, Dec. 11, 1972; Donald, Dec. 18, 1972; Samuels, Feb. 25, 1973.

34. History Jury report for 1956. Hofstadter quotations from Higham, pp. 212–214; Hofstadter, *The Paranoid Style in American Politics*, ix–x, and Christopher Lasch, "On Richard Hofstadter," *New York Review of Books*, March 8, 1972, pp. 7–13.

35. Non-Fiction Jury reports for 1962–1965. Letters to me from White, Dec. 11, 1972, and Mrs. Tuchman, Dec. 11, 1972.

36. Copland letter to me Dec. 26, 1972.   37. Music Jury report, 1964.

38. Music Jury report, 1965. ABM April 22, 1965. The following publications in 1965: New York *Times*, May 4, p. 1; May 5, p. 49; May 13, p. 39; *Time*, May 14; *Newsweek*, May 17, p. 93; New York *Times*, June 14, p. 44. Quotation from Copland letter, Dec. 26, 1972.

39. Simpson's letter to me Dec. 28, 1972.   40. Ibid.

7. THE PRIZES: PRESENT AND FUTURE, 1966–1974

1. Texts of addresses by Messrs. Kirk, Copland, MacLeish, Schlesinger, Reston, and Warren. Details in Columbia booklet, "Fiftieth Anniversary Dinner." News report in New York *Times*, May 11, 1966, p. 33.

2. From my diary.

3. International Jury 1967 report. ABM April 14–15, 1967. Details of Board meeting from St. Louis *Post-Dispatch*, May 1, 1967, and New York *Times*, May 2, 1967. See also Salisbury *Hanoi*. Catledge's views in *My Life and the Times*. Hughes's reaction in letter to me Feb. 26, 1973. National Reporting disagreement in New York *Post*, May 8, 1967, p. 5, and New York *Times*, May 8, 1967, p. 48. My diary was helpful in recalling details.

4. International Jury 1970 report. ABM April 9, 1970.

5. ABM April 10, 1968. Details in Knight's "Editor's Notebook" column in Detroit *Free Press*, May 12, 1968, and letter to me Feb. 7, 1973.

6. Cartooning Jury report for 1973.

7. Public Service and National Jury reports for 1972. Details of the Board meeting of April 13, 1972, and subsequent events are from my diary.

8. New York *Times*, May 2, 1972.   9. Rosenthal's letter to me April 4, 1973.

10. Fritchey in Washington *Star* April 24, 1970.

11. Public Service Jury report for 1973.

12. ABM, April 12, 1973. Details from my diary.

13. Washington *Post*, May 2, 1973; *Time*, May 7, 1973, p. 82.

14. Washington *Post* and New York *Times*, May 8, 1973. Additional details from my diary.

15. Swanberg, *Pulitzer*, p. 374.

16. Fiction Jury reports for 1966–1967, 1968. Malamud letter to me Dec. 12, 1972.

17. Fiction Jury report for 1969. ABM April 10, 1969. New York *Times*, May 6, 1969, p. 35, for Momaday comment and publishers' reaction. John Leonard in *New York Times Book Review*, May 14, 1972, p. 47.

18. Fiction Jury report for 1970. ABM April 9, 1970.

19. Fiction Jury reports for 1971 and 1972. Leonard criticism, see Note 17. Stegner's letter to me Dec. 19, 1972. The New York *Times* was much kinder to Stegner in his new book, a biography of Bernard DeVoto, giving it a front page review in the *Book Review*, Feb. 10, 1974.

20. Fiction Jury report for 1973.   21. Drama Report for 1970.

22. Drama Jury report for 1966.

23. Drama Jury report for 1967. ABM April 14–15, 1967. See also New York *Times*, May 2–3, 1967.

24. Drama Jury reports for 1968 and 1969. New York *Times*, May 6, 1969.

25. Drama Jury report for 1970. ABM April 9, 1970. Details from my diary.

26. Drama Jury reports for 1971 and 1972.   27. Drama Jury report for 1973.

28. Reston speech May 10, 1966.

29. Biography Jury report for 1966.

30. Biography Jury report for 1973. ABM April 12, 1973. Swanberg letter May 12, 1972. Letters to me from Kennan, Dec. 17, 1972; Lash, Jan. 10, 1973; and Williams, Dec. 12, 1972.

31. History Jury report for 1966.

32. History Jury report for 1969. Levy's letter to me Dec. 4, 1972.

33. History Jury report for 1970.

34. History Jury report for 1971. ABM April 8, 1971.

35. History Jury reports for 1972 and 1973.

36. White letter in Secretary's report for 1971.

37. Non-Fiction Jury report for 1971. Letter from Toland to me Jan. 7, 1973.

38. Non-Fiction Jury report for 1969. ABM April 10, 1969. Mailer's letter to me Dec. 28, 1972.

39. Non-Fiction, History, and Biography Jury reports for 1972. Other information from my diary.

40. Non-Fiction Jury report for 1973. ABM April 12, 1973.

41. White letter (see Note 36).

42. Music Jury reports for 1970, 1971. Wuorinen and Lang articles were in New York *Times* on Aug. 8 and Aug. 29, 1971, respectively.

43. Music Jury reports for 1968 and 1972.   44. Music Jury report for 1973.

45. Thomson, p. 90.

46. Poetry Jury reports for 1966 and 1967. Report of Bingham intervention and its outcome in Secretary's report for 1967.

47. Letter from Simpson to me Dec. 28, 1972.

48. Hohenberg, *The Pulitzer Prize Story*, pp. viii–ix.

Bibliography

(Author's Note: In compiling the following list of sources, I have selected those in the main that bear directly on the Pulitzer Prizes and their supporting organization, the people who won and lost the awards, and the changing nature of the age in which the prizes were bestowed. It has seemed to me to be neither necessary nor desirable to set down here a lifetime's reading, theater-going and concert attendance that have gone into the preparation of this work. For a list of primary sources see Notes and Comment.)

Unpublished Material

Ackerman, Carl W. "Eisenhower in Wonderland." Unpublished ms. about the General at Columbia in the Ackerman Papers, Library of Congress.
—— "Pulitzer Prizes vs. Ivy League Colleges." Partial ms. in Ackerman Collection, Library of Congress.
Krock, Arthur. Unpublished 7-page ms. for Copley Newspapers which was included in letter to me March 19, 1971.
Robinson, William Reynolds. "Joseph Pulitzer." An unpublished dissertation. Columbia University Libraries.

Books

Acheson, Dean. *Present at the Creation: My Years in the State Department.* New York, 1969.
Adams, Henry. *The Education of Henry Adams.* Boston, 1918.
Allen, Frederick Lewis. *Only Yesterday: An Informal History of the 1920s.* New York, 1931.
Atkinson, Brooks. *Broadway.* New York, 1970.
—— *The Lively Years, 1920–1973.* New York, 1973.
Baker, Carlos. *Ernest Hemingway: A Life Story.* New York, 1969.
Baker, Richard T. *A History of the Graduate School of Journalism, Columbia University.* New York, 1954.
Barrett, James W. *Joseph Pulitzer and His World.* New York, 1941.
Beard, Charles A. and Mary. *The Rise of American Civilization,* 2 vols. New York, 1941.
Beech, Keyes. *Tokyo and Points East.* New York, 1954.
Berger, Meyer. *The Story of The New York Times, 1851–1951.* New York, 1951.
Bonsal, Stephen. *Heydey in a Vanished World.* New York, 1937.
Brown, John Mason. *The Worlds of Robert E. Sherwood: Mirror to His Times.* New York, 1965.

Browne, Malcolm W. *The New Face of War*. Indianapolis, 1965.

Brustein, Robert. *The Theatre of Revolt*. Boston, 1962.

Burns, James McGregor. *John Kennedy: A Political Profile*. New York, 1959.

Butler, Nicholas Murray. *Across the Busy Years*. 2 vols. New York, 1935–1939.

Canham, Erwin D. *Commitment to Freedom: The Story of the Christian Science Monitor*. Boston, 1958.

Carter, Hodding. *Where Main Street Meets the River*. New York, 1952.

Catledge, Turner. *My Life and "The Times."* New York, 1971.

Childs, Marquis, and James Reston, eds. *Walter Lippmann and His Times*. New York, 1959.

Churchill, Allen. *The Improper Bohemians*. New York, 1959.

Coolidge, Olivia. *Edith Wharton, 1862–1937*. New York, 1964.

Cox Commission Report: *Crisis at Columbia*. New York, 1968.

Curti, Merle. *The Growth of American Thought*, 2nd ed. New York, 1951.

Donovan, Robert J. *Eisenhower: The Inside Story*. New York, 1956.

Emery, Edwin. *The Press and America*. Englewood Cliffs, N.J., 1962.

Essary, J. Fred. *Covering Washington*. Boston, 1927.

Fenton, Charles A. *The Apprenticeship of Ernest Hemingway*. New York, 1954.

Ferber, Edna. *A Peculiar Treasure*. New York, 1940.

Friedel, Frank. *America in the Twentieth Century*. New York, 1960.

Frost, Robert. *In the Clearing*. New York, 1962.

Garland, Hamlin. *My Friendly Contemporaries*. New York, 1932.

Gassner, John. *Theatre at the Crossroads*. New York, 1960.

Gaver, Jack, ed. *Critics' Choice: New York Drama Critics' Circle Prize Plays, 1935–1955*. New York, 1955.

Gelb, Arthur and Barbara. *O'Neill*. New York, 1960.

Gould, Jean. *The Poet and Her Book: A Biography of Edna St. Vincent Millay*. New York, 1969.

Gramling, Oliver. *AP: The Story of News*. New York, 1940.

—— *Free Men Are Fighting*. New York, 1942.

Grant, Robert. *Fourscore, An Autobiography*. New York, 1934.

Groves, Leslie R. *Now It Can Be Told: The Story of the Manhattan Project*. New York, 1962.

Hachten, William A. *The Supreme Court on Freedom of the Press*. Ames, Iowa, 1968.

Halberstam, David. *The Making of a Quagmire*. New York, 1964.

Hendrick, Burton J. *The Training of an American*. Boston, 1928.

Herblock (Herbert A. Block). *Special for Today*. New York, 1958.

Higham, John. *History*. Englewood Cliffs, N.J., 1965.

Hofstadter, Richard. *The Age of Reform*. New York, 1955.

—— *The Paranoid Style in American Politics*. New York, 1965.

—— *The Progressive Historians: Turner, Beard, Parrington*. New York, 1970.

Hofstadter, Richard, and Walter P. Metzger. *The Development of Academic Freedom in the United States*. New York, 1955.

Hohenberg, John. *Free Press/Free People: The Best Cause*. New York, 1971.

—— *Foreign Correspondence: The Great Reporters and Their Times*. New York, 1964.

—— *The Pulitzer Prize Story*. New York, 1959.

Hotchner, A. E. *Papa Hemingway*. New York, 1966.

Hughes, Glenn. *A History of the American Theatre*. New York, 1951.

Hutchens, John K., and George Oppenheimer, eds. *The Best in the World*. New York, 1973.

Ireland, Alleyne. *An Adventure With a Genius*. New York, 1920.

Johnson, Gerald W. *The Lines Are Drawn*. Philadelphia, 1958.

Juergens, George. *Joseph Pulitzer and the New York "World."* Princeton, 1966.
Kahn, E. J., Jr. *The World of Swope.* New York, 1965.
Kennedy, John F. *Profiles in Courage.* New York, 1956.
King, Homer W. *Pulitzer's Prize Editor.* Durham, N.C., 1965.
Krock, Arthur, ed. *The Editorials of Henry Watterson.* New York, 1923.
Lash, Joseph P. *Eleanor and Franklin.* New York, 1971.
Laurence, William L. *Men and Atoms.* New York, 1959.
Leckie, Robert. *Conflict: The History of the Korean War.* New York, 1962.
Levy, Leonard W. *Legacy of Suppression.* New York, 1960.
Lovett, Robert Morss. *All Our Years.* New York, 1948.
Mailer, Norman. *The Armies of the Night.* New York, 1968.
MacLeish, Archibald. *Poetry and Experience.* Boston, 1961.
Kazin, Alfred. *Starting Out in the Thirties.* Boston, 1962.
——— *Bright Book of Life.* Boston, 1973.
McGill, Ralph. *The South and the Southerner.* Boston, 1959.
Markham, James W. *Bovard of the "Post-Dispatch."* Baton Rouge, 1954.
Martin, Harold H. *Ralph McGill, Reporter.* Boston, 1973.
May, Henry F. *The End of American Innocence.* New York, 1959.
Miller, Webb. *I Found No Peace.* New York, 1936.
Morison, Samuel Eliot. *The Oxford History of the American People.* New York, 1965.
Morris, Joe Alex. *Deadline Every Minute: The Story of the United Press.* New York, 1957.
Mott, Frank Luther. *American Journalism,* 3rd ed. New York, 1962.
Nevins, Allan. *Grover Cleveland: A Study in Courage.* New York, 1962.
Nowell, Elizabeth. *Thomas Wolfe.* New York, 1960.
Parrington, V. L. *Main Currents in American Thought.* 3 vols. New York, 1927–1930.
Pollard, James E. *The Presidents and the Press.* New York, 1947.
Pringle, Henry F. *Theodore Roosevelt.* New York, 1931.
Pulitzer, Joseph, Jr. *A Tradition of Conscience.* St. Louis, 1965.
Rammelkamp, Julian S. *Pulitzer's "Post-Dispatch."* Princeton, 1967.
Reston, James. *The Artillery of the Press.* New York, 1966.
Russell, Francis. *The Shadow of Blooming Grove: Warren G. Harding in His Times.* New York, 1968.
Salisbury, Harrison E. *Behind the Lines—Hanoi.* New York, 1967.
Samuels, Ernest. *Henry Adams: The Major Phase.* Cambridge, Mass., 1964.
Schlesinger, Arthur M., Jr. *The Age of Jackson.* Boston, 1945.
——— *A Thousand Days.* Boston, 1965.
Schorer, Mark. *Sinclair Lewis: An American Life.* New York, 1961.
Seitz, Don C. *Joseph Pulitzer, His Life and Letters.* New York, 1924.
Sergeant, Elizabeth Shepley. *Robert Frost: The Trial by Existence.* New York, 1960.
Sheaffer, Louis. *O'Neill, Son and Playwright.* Boston, 1968.
——— *O'Neill, Son and Artist.* Boston, 1973.
Sherwood, Robert E. *Roosevelt and Hopkins: An Intimate History.* New York, 1948.
Smith, Chard Powers. *Where the Light Falls: A Portrait of Edwin Arlington Robinson.* New York, 1965.
Stevenson, Elizabeth. *Babbits and Bohemians: The American 1920s.* New York, 1967.
Stuckey, W. J. *The Pulitzer Prize Novels.* Norman, Okla., 1966.
Sullivan, Mark. *Our Times.* New York, 1926 ff.
Swanberg, W. A. *Citizen Hearst,* New York, 1961.
——— *Luce and His Empire.* New York, 1972.

Swanberg, W. A. *Pulitzer.* New York, 1967.

Teichmann, Howard. *George S. Kaufman: An Intimate Portrait.* New York, 1972.

Thomas, Augustus. *The Print of My Remembrance.* New York, 1922.

Thompson, Lawrance. *Robert Frost: The Years of Triumph, 1915–1938.* New York, 1970.

Thomson, Virgil. *American Music Since 1910: 20th Century Composers.* New York, 1970.

Toohey, John L. *A History of the Pulitzer Prize Plays.* New York, 1967.

Truman, Harry S. *Memoirs,* 2 vols. New York, 1956.

Tuchman, Barbara. *Stilwell and the American Experience in China, 1911–1945.* New York, 1971.

Turner, Frederick J. *The Significance of Sections in American History.* New York, 1932.

Untermeyer, Louis. *A Treasury of Great Poems.* New York, 1942.

Wagenknecht, Edward. *Cavalcade of the American Novel.* New York, 1952.

Waggoner, Hyatt H. *American Poets: From the Puritans to the Present.* New York, 1968.

White, Theodore H. *The Making of the President 1960, 1964, 1968, 1972.* New York, 1961, 1965, 1969, 1973.

White, William Allen. *Autobiography.* New York, 1946.

Wilder, Thornton. *Three Plays,* Preface. New York, 1957.

Zeitlin, Jacob, and Homer Woodbridge. *Life and Letters of Stuart P. Sherman.* New York, 1929.

Periodicals

Ackerman, Carl W. "Handbook of the Advisory Board of the Graduate School of Journalism." Columbia University. New York, 1946.

———— "Pulitzer Secrecy." Letter to editor, *Saturday Review,* 14 July 1951.

Anderson, John. "The Circle." *Theatre Annual,* 1942.

Baker, Carlos. "Forty Years of Pulitzer Prizes." *Princeton University Library Chronicle* XVIII (Winter, 1957), pp. 42–45.

Bendiner, Robert. "The Truth About the Pulitzer Awards." *McCall's,* May 1966, p. 82 et seq.

Clemons, Walter. "The Pulitzer Non-Prize for Fiction." *New York Times Book Review,* 6 June 1971, p. 55.

Cowley, Malcolm. "The Mid-Victorian Cross." *New Republic,* 22 May 1935, p. 51.

DeVoto, Bernard. "The Pulitzer Prize in History." *Saturday Review,* 13 March 1937, pp. 12–14.

Eaton, Walter Pritchard. "The Pulitzer Prize." *Theatre Annual,* 1944.

Hamilton, Charles V. " 'Nat Turner' Reconsidered: The Fiction and the Reality." *Saturday Review,* 22 June 1968, p. 22.

Hamilton, Clayton. "The Poor Old Pulitzer Prize." *American Mercury,* May 1935, pp. 25–32.

Hohenberg, John, ed. Pulitzer Prize issue of *Columbia Library Columns* VI, No. 3 (May, 1957).

Hutchens, John K. "Time: 4:24 P.M. Prizes: Pulitzer." *New York Herald Tribune Book Review,* 8 May 1955, p. 2.

———— "One Thing and Another." *Saturday Review,* 20 April 1968, p. 33.

Krock, Arthur. In The Nation. *The New York Times,* 11 May 1962, p. 30.

Leonard, John. "The Pulitzer Prizes: Fail-Safe Again." *New York Times Book Review,* 14 May 1972, p. 47.

Loveman, Amy. "Pulitzer Awards." *Saturday Review,* 19 May 1951, pp. 100 –101.

Lovett, Robert Morss. "The Pulitzer Prize." *New Republic,* 11 Sept. 1929, pp. 100–101.

Lukas, J. Anthony. "The Story So Far." *New York Times Magazine,* 22 July 1973.

Mathews, William R. "Recollections of the Pulitzer Committee." *Arizona Daily Star,* 22 May 1966.

Maydeck, Robin, and others. "What's Behind the Pulitzer Prizes?" *Seminar* (quarterly). Copley Press. September 1971, p. 34 et seq.

Mizener, Arthur. "The Pulitzer Prizes." *Atlantic Monthly* CC (July, 1957), pp. 42–44.

Monroe, Harriet. "Pulitzer Award System." *Poetry* Magazine XXX (July, 1927), pp. 210–216.

Time. "The Watergate Three." 7 May 1972, p. 82.

Index